Elf Queens and Holy Friars

THE MIDDLE AGES SERIES

Ruth Mazo Karras, Series Editor
Edward Peters, Founding Editor

ELF QUEENS AND HOLY FRIARS

Fairy Beliefs and the Medieval Church

Richard Firth Green

PENN

UNIVERSITY OF PENNSYLVANIA PRESS

PHILADELPHIA

Copyright © 2016 University of Pennsylvania Press

All rights reserved. Except for brief quotations used for purposes of review or scholarly citation, none of this book may be reproduced in any form by any means without written permission from the publisher.

Published by
University of Pennsylvania Press
Philadelphia, Pennsylvania 19104-4112
www.upenn.edu/pennpress

Printed in the United States of America on acid-free paper
1 3 5 7 9 10 8 6 4 2

A Cataloging-in-Publication record is available from
the Library of Congress
ISBN 978-0-8122-4843-2

For Sharon, still my fairy queen

> The elf-queene, with hir joly compaignye,
> Daunced ful ofte in many a grene mede.
> This was the olde opinion, as I rede;
> I speke of manye hundred yeres ago.
> But now kan no man se none elves mo,
> For now the grete charitee and prayeres
> Of lymytours and othere hooly freres,
> . . . .
> This maketh that ther ben no fayeryes.
> —Chaucer, *The Wife of Bath's Tale*

CONTENTS

Introduction	1
Chapter 1. Believing in Fairies	11
Chapter 2. Policing Vernacular Belief	42
Chapter 3. Incubi Fairies	76
Chapter 4. Christ the Changeling	110
Chapter 5. Living in Fairyland	147
Postscript	194
Notes	207
Bibliography	253
Index	277
Acknowledgments	287

Elf Queens and Holy Friars

Introduction

> For many pious Christians, as for the inquisitors of Joan of Arc, this was a distinction without a difference. Fairies were demons, plain and simple.
> —Carl Sagan, *The Demon-Haunted World*

On Trinity Sunday sometime around the year 1400 a sermon was preached in England containing an extended denunciation of popular superstition.[1] Palmists, dream readers, pythoners, nigromancers, astrologers, and the makers of wax effigies were all quickly dismissed, and then the preacher turned to those who believed in fairies:

> There are also others who say that they see women and girls dancing by night whom they call *elvish folk* and they believe that these can transform both men and women or, leaving others in their place, carry them with them to *elfland*; all of these are mere fantasies bequeathed to them by an evil spirit. For when the devil has won over the soul of such a person to believing such things, he transforms himself otherwise, now into the form of an angel, now a man, now a woman, now other creatures, now in dances and other games, and thus by the weak faith of their souls such wretches are deceived. But those who believe in the aforesaid things, or stubbornly defend them, or propagate them, especially when they shall have learned the truth, are faithless and worse than pagans, and four times a year they are cursed by the Lord and his holy church.... They should know that they have forsaken the faith of Christ, betrayed their baptism, and incurred the anger and enmity of God.[2]

This attack is not entirely original, for it draws heavily on an early fourteenth-century preachers' manual, the *Fasciculus Morum* (which had also included tournaments and jousts in its list of fairy activities),[3] but it will serve as a useful introduction to the subject of this book: fairyland as a contested site in the struggle between the official and unofficial cultures of the Middle Ages.

As this quotation implies, the default position of the clerical elite when it came to fairyland was one of unrelieved antagonism (though in practice, as we shall see, not all churchmen were as implacably hostile as our preacher), and the official record is the story of an ever-increasing demonization of fairies and infernalization of fairyland throughout the course of the Middle Ages. Vernacular culture on the other hand might make remarkable efforts to adjust its beliefs to the orthodoxies of the church, either consciously engaging in what Carlo Ginzburg has termed "cultural compromise formation"[4] or unconsciously echoing what Antonio Gramsci would have regarded as the church's dominant hegemonic discourse. Thus we should not be surprised to encounter fairies who swear by the Virgin Mary, who are eager to attend mass, or who anticipate salvation on Doomsday. The history of this aspect of medieval popular culture and its systematic suppression is accordingly far from straightforward, and it is made all the more difficult by the nature of the evidence, which overwhelmingly reflects the views of the clerical elite. An analysis of the kinds of evidence available to us and suggestions for ways we might read them will occupy the first two chapters of this study. Fundamental to my approach is the assumption that the beliefs of those for whom fairies were a living presence were sincerely held and that we should do them the courtesy of taking their beliefs seriously. I will argue that this makes a great difference to the way we approach the medieval literary genre that has most to tell us about fairies—that of the popular romance.

The last three chapters will offer readings of various aspects of fairy belief, but from the outset it is important that I establish what the reader should *not* expect to find there. First, I will have nothing to say on the vexed question of fairy taxonomy.[5] Are fairies different from elves? or goblins? or dwarves? or pucks? or brownies? and how do they relate to French *netons* or *luitons*? or German *Nixen* or *Kobolde*? Moreover, are they of human stature or smaller? Are they ruled by a king, or a queen, or even a trio of queens? And what color are they? In my view all such questions are unanswerable, and any attempt at a totalizing definition will prove illusory. For instance, while some fairies were small (such as the pygmies in Walter Map's story of King Herla), others must have been human sized or they could hardly have had love affairs with mortals. It is not a matter on which we can properly legislate. Simon Young has shown convincingly how little agreement there is about the meanings of terms for fairies collected by folklorists in nineteenth-century Cornwall, concluding that "there is enormous blurring in lore and very often taxonomic categories misrepresented the beliefs of a given area"; if this is true of a single well-documented English county in a recent century, what hope can there be of our reconstructing a coherent fairy taxonomy for the whole of the European Middle Ages with the far scantier evidence that is available to us? As Young writes, "anyone who studies history has to constantly remind themselves that those people living hundreds of years ago did not structure their experience as we do."[6]

Even in the Middle Ages fairy taxonomy seems to have been problematic. Thomas of Cantimpré, for instance, tries to categorize fairies in the final section of his mid-thirteenth-century book of moral instruction, *De bonum universale de apibus* [On the Universal Good of Bees], but the enterprise quickly falls apart.[7] Turning from his admirable bees, he sets out, under the headings of 'wasps,' 'cockroaches,' 'hornets,' and 'beetles' [*vespae, blattae, crabrones,* and *buprestes*], to describe the depredations of various kinds of demon. Wasp demons, he says, cause tempests, and cockroach demons cause bad dreams, but when he turns to what we might call 'fairies' (under the heading of 'hornets'), we discover that these too can cause tempests and bad dreams. Hornet demons, he says, can be divided into four classes: *neptuni*, who swim in water; *incubi*, who roam the earth; *dusii*, who live under the earth; and *spiritualia nequitie in celestibus*, who inhabit the air. This is already an eccentric classification since for Saint Augustine (as for most of the medieval commentators who followed him), *incubi* and *dusii* were clearly one and the same thing.[8] Moreover, none of these terms is likely to have been used at the level of popular speech, nor is his classification likely to have represented any kind of popular taxonomy. *Neptuni* is evidently a commonization from the Roman god, and it is just possible that some such term was in popular usage, if only as a folk etymology for the French *neton*.[9] On the other hand, there does not seem to have been anything particularly aquatic about *netons*,[10] and whatever *wassergeister* Thomas of Cantimpré may have had in mind were probably called something quite different in common speech. The word *dusius* may well be the Latin form of a Gaulish word current in Augustine's day, but it seems to have died out in European vernaculars by the thirteenth century.[11] *Incubus*, probably the most widely used general scholastic term for 'fairy' in the Middle Ages, derives etymologically from the sense of being weighed down (*incubitus*) or smothered in sleep.

The closest equivalent in English for this specialized sense would have been 'nightmare' (in French *cauchemar* and in German *nachtmahr*), but *incubus* underwent semantic generalization early—though not, as Thomas of Cantimpré would have it, to 'earthbound spirit' but rather (as we shall see in Chapter 3) to 'fairy lover.' Finally, when he comes to 'the wicked spirits of the air' (evidently Thomas has no specific name for them and must resort to *Ephesians* 6:12), he starts out by describing demonic tempests (not obviously different from those caused by the *vespae*) and then falls back on the general category of illusions (which turn out to include *blattae*-like dreams and *incubi*-like seductions!). After all this we should not be surprised to find that Thomas seems to have completely forgotten about the beetles (*buprestes*) with which he started out. In the end he simply gives up and launches into a recital of miscellaneous marvels, some of which he claims to have experienced personally. At least the taxonomy supplied by John Walsh, a Devonshire cunning man, in 1566 has the virtue of simplicity: "[he] saith that ther be .iii. kindes of Feries, white, greene, and blacke ... Wherof (he sayth) the blacke Feries be the worst."[12] Incidentally, the question of fairy coloring is its own mare's nest. In addition to white, black, and green (green is sometimes mentioned—as with the green children of Woolpit—but it is by no means universal), we also have gray (in *The Merry Wives of Windsor*), red (in an account from Thomas Walsingham),[13] and polychrome (as with Tristram's fairy dog Petitcriu). Perhaps the key to all this is the innate volatility of fairies: they can be any size (or shape) they wish, and, as in Petitcriu's case, their color is inherently unstable.

No attempt, whether medieval or modern, to impose a logical order on spontaneous local traditions can ever be totally satisfactory (though those who still feel themselves in need of such answers can always turn for help to Katharine Briggs or Claude Lecouteux).[14] My own solution to this problem, however, is functional: for the purposes of this study I am concerned primarily with that class of numinous, social, humanoid creatures who were widely believed to live at the fringes of the human lifeworld and interact intermittently with human beings.[15] In this they differed from those solitary creatures who inhabited the wilderness (giants and the like) or the social creatures who lived among humans (the various kinds of household spirit). Of the multitude of potential terms for these creatures in both Latin and the vernacular, few, if any, seem to have had a generally agreed and fixed meaning, but they were most commonly referred to as 'elves' in English (at least down to the middle of the fifteenth century)[16] and in French as *fées*. The equivalence of these two terms in learned usage is nicely illustrated by a spell "Pur *faies*" from a thirteenth-century Anglo-Norman medical treatise that begins, "Conjuro vos, elves."[17] From the middle of the fifteenth century they were increasingly referred to as *fairies* in England,[18] but other terms for them (*wodwose*s, *pouk*s, *goblin*s, or *hob*s, for example) were sometimes used. Whatever the name, I shall treat as fairies all creatures who behave in the way I have just described.

A second issue that will not detain me in this study is the Celtic origins of fairy lore. As far as I can see just about every region in medieval Europe had its fairy traditions. Fairies are to be found from Iceland to Sicily and from the Pyrenees to the Ruhr, but the notion that Wales, Scotland, and Ireland have a particular claim on them is deeply ingrained in the consciousness of the English-speaking world. Two main factors seem to be responsible for this view. In the first place, stories concerning King Arthur, many of which are filled with fairy lore, have proved to be among the most enduring of all medieval legends; since they clearly arose among Celtic speakers, particularly the Welsh, we tend instinctively to locate the source of all medieval fairy beliefs in Wales. On the other hand, had the legend cycles of Huon of Bordeaux or Godfrey of Bouillon, both of which contain prominent fairy elements, attained a postmedieval reputation comparable to King Arthur's, we might now have a very different notion of the epicenter of European fairy beliefs. Second, fairy traditions have survived more tenaciously in Celtic-speaking countries, perhaps most notably Ireland, than anywhere else in the English-speaking world; since Irish fairies have a firm place in modern popular culture, we tend to assume that they somehow preempt similar beliefs elsewhere. The fairy beliefs of the Nordic world, particularly Iceland, have proved to be just as long-lived, however, and only their far greater cultural distance from English speakers has made them appear more tangential. No doubt other factors—the relative prominence of Celtic scholars among English folklorists, for instance,[19] or the literary prestige of writers such as W. B. Yeats and J. R. R. Tolkien (whose elves are unmistakably Celtic)—have reinforced the impression that fairies are primarily a Celtic phenomenon.[20]

It is not even necessarily true that texts in Welsh and Irish contain the earliest medieval literary references to fairies, at least not if we go by manuscript date rather than the hypothetical dating of the material itself. At one point in the Latin epic *Waltharius*, for example, when Walter of Aquitaine is defending himself in a pass in the Vosges against the Burgundian King Gunther and his men, one of his enemies, a man named Ekivrid, taunts him with the implication that he is a fairy: "You seem just like a woodland sprite [*saltibus assuetus faunus*] to me" (line 763).[21] This is evidently a clever Latin pun on Walter's name (*woud heer* or *woudt-her*='faunus agrestis'), and he "is saying in effect 'So you're called Walthere, are you? Well you really (*quippe*) do seem to be Waltheer, the wood-sprite, by the incorporeal way you've been avoiding arrows and lances."[22] There could hardly be anything less ostensibly Celtic than this poem about Germanic heroes, set in the Vosges mountains and quite possibly written in Switzerland,[23] and yet the *Waltharius* can hardly be later than the tenth century and may well have been composed in the ninth; moreover, at least one of its manuscripts can be dated to the mid-eleventh century—earlier than the Irish *Book of the Dun Cow* and considerably earlier than the oldest manuscript of the Welsh *Mabinogion*.[24] One might of course argue that such Celtic legendary material predates the manuscripts that record them, but this is an argument that can be applied to the Germanic materials as well.

As an illustration of the distortion that the Celtic fallacy can cause, we might consider Dorena Allen's otherwise excellent article "Orpheus and Orfeo: The Dead and the Taken." Having noted in postmedieval Celtic folklore examples of those 'taken' by the fairies (something we shall explore more fully in Chapter 5), she expresses surprise at coming across this motif in a thirteenth-century Belgian writer, Thomas of Cantimpré, and concludes, quite unnecessarily, that "we must have tales of Celtic origin with which, in ways too fortuitous to be discovered, [a Flemish narrator has] become acquainted, and to which [he has] given a local coloring."[25] Thomas spent much of his early life near Cambrai, some fifty miles northwest of the Ardennes forest, an area with a strong fairy tradition: *Partonopeu de Blois* is set in the Ardennes, and so too is the episode in *Reinbrun* in which the hero rescues his father's friend Amis from fairy captivity. Judging by his name, Jean d'Arras, the author of the fairy romance *Mélusine*, came from a town near Cambrai, and this Jean seems also to have been one of the collectors of old wives' tales that make up *Les Évangiles des quenouilles*. There is no reason to suppose that the fairy lore appearing in the *Évangiles*, or in any of these romances, is anything other than homegrown or that when Thomas of Cantimpré reports stories of neighbors taken by the fairies he is merely giving "local coloring" to imported Celtic material. The single most informative source for medieval fairy beliefs, cited many times in this book, is William of Auvergne's *De Universo*, and it is quite clear that this Parisian scholar draws heavily on the traditions of south-central France, where he was brought up. One danger of an overconcentration on the Celtic connection is that fairy allusions from other areas tend to be missed; for instance, the Cambridge lyric "Heriger, Bishop of Mainz," from early thirteenth-century Germany, is about a fortune-teller who attends a mysterious feast deep in the woods, and yet scholars have rarely noted its obvious fairy associations.[26] My point is not, of course, that Celtic traditions were unimportant in this respect (we shall be using the Breton forest of Brocéliande as a test case in Chapter 1) but simply that they were not the *fons et origo* of all medieval fairy lore.[27] The fairies with whom I am concerned in this book are pan-European, and the questions they raise should not be quarantined to the margins, either geographical or cultural, of medieval society.

A further disclaimer concerns the role of folklore. I have not been professionally trained as a folklorist, nor can I lay claim to any special proficiency in this area. In one regard, like, I suspect, many of my medievalist colleagues, I am wary of the use of customs and beliefs recorded in more recent times to throw light on medieval practices. Folklore, as Antonio Gramsci was quick to point out, is far from static, and the notion of a popular culture so deeply conservative that it is possible to treat any given nineteenth-century custom not only as a potential medieval relic but also as evidence for actual medieval practice seems to me highly dubious. On the other hand, the modern folklorist does have one enormous advantage over any medievalist who sets out to construe earlier popular culture: she can question her informants and attempt to expose what it is they think they are doing and why they are doing it. While projecting back the results of such investigations to the Middle Ages can never constitute proof, it does offer us a valuable analogical tool. Valdimar Hafstein, for instance, compares a thousand-year-old vision in the *Þáttr Þiðranda ok Þórhalls* of "many a hill . . . opening, and every living thing, both small and large, . . . packing its bags and moving" in the face of impending Christianization to stories of elves being displaced by new roads and housing developments in late twentieth-century Iceland, and concludes that "urbanization is as anathema to modern day elves as Christianity was to their pagan forebears."[28] Looking at the present through the lens of the past, Hafstein sees elf belief as deeply conservative—rooted in nostalgia for an imagined authentic Iceland threatened by modernization. However, if we reverse the polarities, if we consider medieval beliefs in the light of the modern experience, a further dynamic emerges—one that has more the look of spontaneous resistance than of nostalgic resignation; after all, even in present-day Iceland fear of offending the elves can cause roads to be diverted and housing developments to be relocated.

This view of the political significance of folkloric beliefs is one propounded by the Marxist Antonio Gramsci,[29] whose views have admittedly not always been welcomed by folklorists.[30] Writing in Mussolini's Italy, Gramsci evidently regarded whatever challenge contemporary folklore was able to offer fascism as fragmented and incoherent compared with "the philosophy of praxis" (that is, the version of Marxism that he himself espoused), but at the same time he remained an astute observer of popular resistance to the dominant culture particularly as a historical phenomenon, as his account of the nineteenth-century Tuscan preacher Davide Lazzaretti demonstrates.[31] As Kate Crehan writes, "while Gramsci could be harsh on the blinkered parochialism of subaltern culture, at the same time he was fascinated by it and believed that much could be learnt from it" (p. 119). My reading of the subversive role of fairy beliefs in the medieval polity owes much to his insights.

Concentration on the political significance of fairyland means that this book makes no claim to provide a comprehensive survey of all fairy phenomena in the Middle Ages. It treats here only in passing, if at all, many of the activities that were commonly associated with fairies: their modification of the weather; their association with great wealth; the trouble they might cause benighted travelers; their ability to induce or ward off sickness; their influence for good or ill on harvests; their skill at prognostication—to name but a few. Diane Purkiss has stressed the way fairies preside at and govern "the big crises of mortal life: birth, childhood and its transitions, adolescence, sexual awakening, pregnancy and childbirth, old age, death . . . the borders of our lives, the seams between one phase of life and another."[32] Of course in the Middle Ages a very different kind of institution, the Christian church, claimed to have jurisdiction over these areas too, and the last three chapters will examine the consequences of its attempts to discipline rival folkloric beliefs. Not that all ideas about fairyland were heterodox—the church had no argument with those prepared to accept that fairies were demons—but wherever it felt obliged to exercise authority it exposed a further aspect of the operation of what R. I. Moore has characterized as a persecuting society.[33] Of course clerical regulation of those who believed that fairies were non-demons was of a different order from its attempts to discipline Cathars, Jews, lepers, and homosexuals. Not only were fairy beliefs so ubiquitous that they could not be quarantined in ghettos and leprosaria or made the targets of self-serving crusades, but they also touched (as we shall see) the higher levels of secular society (and even penetrated the church itself), so that focused persecution was infeasible. However, as Foucault has taught us, social regulation can take different forms, and there are clear signs that many of those who participated in the discourse of fairyland in the Middle Ages felt themselves under surveillance. Moreover, from the fifteenth century onward, as education began to close the cultural gap between clerical and secular authorities, the control of vernacular belief became more and more exacting, culminating in the terrible witch hunts of the early modern period.

Accordingly the last three chapters of this book will examine the church's attempts to regulate fairyland in three critical domains. Chapter 3 follows its campaign to marginalize popular attitudes to copulation, pregnancy, and childbirth and in particular its demonization of one especially prominent fairy lover, Merlin's father. In Chapter 4 we see how a motif popularly associated with child rearing, that of the fairy changeling, disturbed the sensibilities of both churchmen and *patresfamilias*, and how it resisted their attempts to suppress it; here we focus particularly on the representation of the changeling in the mystery plays. In Chapter 5 we consider fairyland as the resort of old heroes such as King Arthur and some of the ways in which the church responded to the scandalous notion of a deathless survival in Avalon; an exploration of the role played by Avalon in the twelfth-century 'birth of purgatory' concludes this study. In a brief Postscript I discuss fairy lore as an important target for sixteenth-century witch-hunters and associate the comparative leniency of English witch-hunting with a discourse of skepticism that can be traced in part to the prestige of Geoffrey Chaucer, a celebrated fairy unbeliever.

CHAPTER I

Believing in Fairies

> One asking what hee thought of Fayries: hee answered, he thought they were spirits; but hee distinguished betweene them and other spirites, as commonly men distinguish betweene good witches and bad witches.
> —Richard Greenham, Pastor of Drayton (1597)

Let us begin with some thoughts on the marvelous from what was intended to be the first chapter of a book that C. S. Lewis never lived to complete:

> The reader who sees in all the (let us call them) "ferlies" [*marvels*] of medieval romance mere "sports of fancy" . . . utterly misunderstands the best specimens of the *genre* he is reading. . . . A satisfactory theory of ferlies and their effect is, I believe, still to seek. I suspect that it will not succeed unless it fulfils two conditions. In the first place, it will have to be sure that it has exhausted the possibilities of purely literary diagnosis before it looks further afield. . . . The second condition . . . is that *the theory should deeply study the ferlies as things (in a sense) in the real world* [my italics]. Probably such things did not occur. But if no one in real life had either seen, or thought he saw, or accepted on hearsay, or dreaded, or hoped for, any such things, the poet and romancer could do nothing with them. As anthropologists we may want to know how belief in them originated. But it will illuminate the literary problem more if we can imagine what it would feel like to

witness, or think we had witnessed, or merely to believe in, the things. What it would feel like, and why.[1]

Perhaps the innate elusiveness of all such *ferlies* must render any theory of them finally inadequate ("the medieval fantastic," writes Francis Dubost, "is just as evanescent as its modern counterpart"),[2] but for whatever reason, more than fifty years later Lewis's challenge is still to be met.

Progress, however, has been made on both fronts. In fulfillment of Lewis's first condition, that of purely literary analysis, we can point to a number of fine studies. In England, Helen Cooper, Corinne Saunders, and James Wade have recently made important contributions,[3] and in France literary study of *le merveilleux* is now regarded as mainstream.[4] In the United States literary scholars such as Jeffrey Jerome Cohen and Geraldine Heng have concerned themselves with the more extreme manifestations of the marvelous, in particular associating the grotesque and the monstrous with issues of race, identity, and gender.[5] Fulfillment of Lewis's second condition, the study of *ferlies* as things, has been made much easier by the work of historians of medieval *mentalité*s, particularly that of the *annalistes* Jacques Le Goff and Jean-Claude Schmitt in France[6] and in the English-speaking world by a number of premodernists following in the footsteps of Keith Thomas.[7] Though it should now be much simpler than it would have been in 1966 to illuminate the *ferlies* of romance by imagining "what it would feel like ... to believe in the things," the dominant mode of critical analysis has remained stubbornly functionalist ("magic used as a literary tool"),[8] at least in the Anglophone world.[9] Even Fredric Jameson, for all that his recognition that magical narratives (that is, romances) belong to a world where nature remains "a mysterious and alien border around the still precarious and minute human activities of village and field,"[10] treats magic as a literary device, a solution to the problem of apprehending unstable chivalric loyalties in a period of emergent class solidarity (p. 161). My own conviction is that we will make real progress only when we learn to treat magic, or at least its manifestations in medieval literature (those things that Lewis called *ferlies*), less as tenor and more as vehicle, to adapt I. A. Richards's terminology; the first task is not to establish what such *ferlies* represent or exemplify or epitomize, but rather to ask what they *are* and what cultural work they are doing. From this perspective Lewis was putting the cart before the horse: literary diagnosis, I believe, should properly follow, not precede, the study of *ferlies* as things. Even with this proviso, however, I cannot pretend to be responding to Lewis's general call to arms here; my aim in what follows is rather more modest: to elucidate not the whole territory of the medieval marvelous but merely one of its most prominent fiefdoms—that of fairyland.

For sixteenth-century England, it is a comparatively simple matter, in M. W. Latham's words, "to reproduce the everyday belief of the Elizabethans concerning the fairies, to treat the fairies not as mythical personages or as fanciful creations of the literary imagination or of popular superstition, but to regard them, as did their human contemporaries of the 16th century, as credible entities and as actual and existing beings."[11] For the Middle Ages, however, the problem of trying to imagine what it would feel like to believe in fairies is compounded by the fact that much of what little evidence there is comes from texts written by members of a clerical elite who officially did *not* believe in them, at least not "as credible entities and as actual and existing beings," and who felt obliged for the most part to show open hostility to all such beliefs. Nevertheless the attempts of such people to rationalize, negate, or dismiss fairy beliefs can tell us a great deal about both their vigor and their ubiquity.

One of the most concise and thorough descriptions of the kind of creature I am concerned with in this book appears in a treatise on the geography of Iceland written in the late sixteenth century probably by Oddur Einarsson, the Lutheran bishop of Skálholt; it will provide us with a useful point of departure:

> But some [beings], who live in the hills close to men, are more amicable and not so dangerous unless they chance to have been harmed by some kind of injury and provoked to wickedness. They seem, indeed, to be endowed with bodies of incredible subtlety, since they are even thought to enter into mountains and hills. They are invisible to us unless they wish to appear of their own volition, yet the properties of certain men's eyes are such that the presence of no spirit can ever escape their sight (as was Lynceus's unhappy situation). They know a thousand devices and an infinite number of tricks with which they harass men in wretched ways, but their young people are said to have a similar stature, clothing, and even way of life to that of their human neighbors, and to take excessive pleasure in coupling with humans. Examples are not lacking of a number of the rogues who are said to have impregnated women beneath the earth and had access to them at fixed times or as many times as they wished. And from time to time the women

of our land have been oppressed by these earth-dwellers and
innocent boys and girls and the young people and adolescents of
both sexes have very often been taken away, though quite a few are
restored safe and sound after a number of days, or sometimes a
number of weeks, but some are never seen again, and certain ones are
found half-alive, etc. But it would be tedious to waste more of this
study on them; for whether these things are brought about by the
frauds, impostures, and illusions of the devil, which seems to be
the view of almost all the more reasonable people, or whether they are
some kind of mixed species created between spirits and animals, as
some conjecture, yet it is certain that the appearance of these spirits
has been common in many other regions, not only in Iceland, so that
it is pointless to take this [their ubiquity in Iceland] as evidence that
these curious creatures were fashioned in the underworld.[12]

Some European traditions locate fairies in castles deep in the woods or even in realms beneath the surface of lakes, rather than in underground kingdoms, but otherwise Oddur Einarsson's description conforms closely to the common understanding of the vast majority of medieval people. Though several other kinds of interaction are certainly possible, fairies most often impinge on the human life world in two ways: by copulating with mortals or by abducting them. What is more interesting about Oddur's account for our immediate purposes, however, is the attempt he makes to explain these creatures in terms of a standard Christian cosmology. The two possibilities he suggests—that they are either a trick of the devil (*fraus Sathanae*) or some kind of mixed species (*genus mixtum*) halfway between spirit and animal—are found elsewhere,[13] though his apparent reluctance to concede that fairies may actually be devils (a third explanation that was widely entertained by other authorities) seems due to an understandable reluctance to endorse the common belief that the mouth of hell was situated in Iceland.[14]

Citing James I's statement that the "spirites that are called vulgarlie called the Fayrie" are one of the four kinds of devil "conversing in the earth," C. S. Lewis suggested that the idea that fairies were really devils became the "official view" only around the beginning of the seventeenth century.[15] In actuality, however, it had been the orthodox position of the church for more than three hundred years. While traces of it can be detected much earlier,[16] it was first set out systematically in William of Auvergne's *De Universo* (written in the 1230s) and was frequently reiterated throughout the later Middle Ages.

The popular late eleventh-century theological handbook the *Elucidarium*,[17] composed in England by Honorius of Autun (or Augsberg),[18] though it deals at length with good and bad angels, has nothing whatsoever to say about fairies. This silence is unsurprising since the earliest position taken by the church on the question of fairies seems to have been to deny their reality altogether: "Credidisti quod quidam credere solent," asks Bishop Burchard of Worms in a penitential from around the year 1000, "quod sint agrestes feminae, quas sylvaticas vocant?" [Have you believed what some are accustomed to believe that there are rural women whom they call sylvans?] The bishop then makes quite clear the fatuity of such a belief: "Si credidisti, decem dies in pane et aqua poeniteas" [If you have believed it, do penance on bread and water for ten days].[19] Things were very different, however, by the thirteenth century, when, in an adaptation of another of Burchard's warnings against superstitious practices (this one against making gifts to "satyri vel pilosi" to obtain their goodwill), these creatures were changed to "diaboli . . . quos faunos vocant" [devils whom they call fauns], and the penance increased from ten days to fifteen.[20]

By the time of an early fourteenth-century French Dominican redaction and translation of the *Elucidarium* known as the *Second Lucidaire*,[21] the faithful are left in no doubt not only that fairies exist, but also that they are quite simply devils: "*And* vnto the regarde of þe feyryes the which man sayth were wonte to be in tymes past, they were not men ne women naturalles but were deuylles þe whiche shewed themselfe vnto þe people of þat tyme, for they were paynyms, ydolatres *and with*out fayth."[22] Things are a little more complicated than this, however, for the *Lucydarye* has a second explanation of fairy phenomena; they can also be devilish illusions (what Oddur Einarsson calls *fraudes Sathanae*), rather than actual devils: "And theyr vysyons ben semblables vnto theym of a man the whiche is dronke, vnto whome it semeth that the house turneth vnder his fete, by þe whiche he falleth, and al the house ne the erthe remeueth not. In lyke wyse the deuyl them sheweth these vysyons in theyr entendemente" (p. 51). This distinction, which goes back at least to William of Auvergne, may seem like hairsplitting, but it was evidently important to medieval churchmen as a way of accounting for different kinds of fairy phenomena, particularly the ability of fairies to impersonate humans. Thus Étienne de Bourbon retells the old story of how Saint Germain, "recognizing that it was the trickery of demons" [cognoscens autem esse demonum ludificationem], exposed the true nature of what appeared to be a group of local people attending a feast set out for the fairies ("*bone res*") by proving that their human counterparts were actually still sleeping soundly in their beds.²³

The recognition that in the discourse of the late medieval church fairies are demons (or demonic illusions) has important consequences for the study of vernacular belief. If fairies are demons, it follows that demons, or at least some demons, are fairies, and this insight opens up a world of still largely unexplored ecclesiastical material for investigation. Understandably, writers on medieval fairy beliefs have hitherto concentrated mainly on vernacular writing, chiefly romances, where fairyland is generally treated with something like transparency, though they have often supplemented these sources with the commentary of learned writers such as Gerald of Wales, Walter Map, Gervase of Tilbury, and William of Newburgh. However, when we turn to pastoral manuals, saints' lives, sermons, exempla, and miracle tales, we encounter a host of fairies masquerading as devils. Admittedly they are generally more shadowy figures than their counterparts in vernacular romance, but they offer the great advantage of highlighting the attitudes of the representatives of official culture toward them. It is this interplay of learned and vernacular culture in the Middle Ages that constitutes the main theme of this book.

Strictly speaking, if fairies are devils, then it must also follow that any belief in fairies as non-devils is potentially heretical. Surprisingly, such an uncompromising line is rarely openly expressed in medieval ecclesiastical discourse, at least before the fifteenth century, but it is certainly implicit in a remarkable story told by the thirteenth-century Belgian Dominican Thomas of Cantimpré in his *Bonum Universale de Apibus*. Augustine in his *City of God* briefly discusses creatures he calls *dusii*, which he represents as the Gaulish equivalents of those "Silvans and Pans, commonly called *incubi*" [silvanos et panes, quos vulgo incubos vocant] who were said to seduce women—in other words, creatures that a later age would call 'fairies.'²⁴ Thomas gives this dramatic account of how such "*dusii*-demons inhabit the mountains and corrupt and derange their dupes":

> In 1231 when Master Conrad was preaching against the heretics in Germany and died a blessed death at their hands,²⁵ a certain heretic who had been corrupted by demons solicited a Dominican friar to join his heresy (as I heard many years ago from Brother Conrad, the Dominican Provincial in Germany).²⁶ When he saw

the friar immediately recoil, he said to him: "You are very firm in your faith yet you have seen no more credible evidence of it than what is found in certain books. But if you should wish to believe my words I might show you Christ and his mother and the saints in plain sight." The friar at once suspected a demonic illusion, but wishing to put it to the test, said, "Not without cause would I then believe, were you to put your promises into effect." The joyful heretic set a date for the friar. The friar however secretly took along a pix containing Christ's holy body concealed under his cloak. The heretic then led the friar into a very spacious palace in a cave in a mountain, which shone with a wonderful brightness. They came directly to the lower part of the palace, where they saw thrones placed, as if made of the purest gold, and on them a king, surrounded with glittering splendor, and next to him a most beautiful queen with a radiant face, and on either side benches on which were older men like patriarchs or prophets with a great multitude of angels sitting around, and they were all glittering with starlight (though they might be judged to be nothing less than demons). As soon as he saw them, the heretic adored them lying down before them. But the friar stood motionless, deeply stunned by such a spectacle, and the heretic turned to him at once and said, "Why do you not adore the son of God when you see him? Go and prostrate yourself; worship him whom you see and you will receive the secrets of our faith from his mouth."[27]

At this point Brother Conrad finally displays his concealed host, the illusion vanishes, and the crestfallen heretic is returned to the true faith.

I give this story at such length because there can be little doubt that Conrad's heresy has been built up from a number of elements of traditional fairy lore. We have only to ask ourselves why demons should be portrayed as living in a palace (and this is not the only place where a Dominican preacher describes demons in this way)[28] to recognize that Thomas's demonology has been infiltrated by vernacular conceptions of fairyland. The "very spacious palace in a cave in a mountain, which shone with a wonderful brightness" is an extremely common fairy locale; in English romance, for instance, it occurs in *Sir Orfeo*, *Thomas of Erceldoune*, and *Reinbrun*.[29] The king, surrounded with glittering splendor, and his beautiful queen with her radiant face are as likely to remind us of a fairy king and queen as of Christ and his mother. Once again, *Sir Orfeo* offers an example:

> Þer-in her maister king sete,
> & her quen, fair & swete:
> Her crounes, her cloþes schine so briȝt
> Þat vnneþe bihold he hem miȝt. (lines 413–16)

In the popular mind fairy lore might have been reconciled with Christian teaching in ways that would have scandalized the more educated members of the clergy. Finally, the shape-shifting ability of these 'demons' (evident in *Thomas of Erceldoune*, among others) is also a fairy commonplace. What is particularly striking about this story, however, is Thomas of Cantimpré's translation of such fairy lore into an actual heresy (in fact, a potential target for the notorious inquisitor Conrad of Marburg), with the suggestion that it constitutes an organized doctrinal system: "you will receive the secrets of our faith from his mouth." Fairy beliefs hover at the edge of consciousness for some medieval inquisitors,[30] but (except where the imagery of fairyland becomes entwined with the discourse of witchcraft, as was certainly to happen in the early-modern period) it is unusual to find them cast as a full-fledged heresy in this way.

No doubt Margaret Murray, had she known of this account, would have regarded it as conclusive evidence for her imaginative theories about the survival of the 'old religion,'[31] but as with the later Scottish witchcraft trials on which she drew so heavily, whatever coherent structure these beliefs appear to possess seems largely a projection of their adversaries' own fantastic obsessions rather than a reflection of their holders' esoteric knowledge.[32] As important as the substance of such charges, however, is their tone. From our perspective Thomas of Cantimpré's response seems out of all proportion to the seriousness of the threat, but there is no mistaking its antagonism. By linking it with Conrad of Marburg's German crusade, indeed, he is setting it on a par with the far better documented heresy of the Cathars.[33] (Conrad was not alone in making such an association, however (as we shall see with Huon de Méri's poem the *Tornoiement de l'antichrist*).

Not all medieval churchmen shared Thomas's paranoia, for a curious Middle English poem called the *Disputation Between a Christian and a Jew*, presents a similar set of motifs in a rather more even tone.[34] It is found in a famous anthology of religious verse, the Vernon Manuscript, compiled in the west of England in the late fourteenth century. Despite its title, the *Disputation Between a Christian and a Jew* has little to do with any kind of genuine intellectual exchange between the representatives of Christianity and those of Judaism. The author's grasp of even the most basic tenets of the Jewish faith is clearly shaky, but in his eagerness to demonstrate the superiority of Christianity to other religions, he appears to have constructed an entirely factitious old law out of such scraps of fairy belief as he was able to gather. The central episode closely resembles Thomas of Cantimpré's anecdote in that the true believer is taken by the Jew to a wonderful land where he is shown a simulacrum of Christ on the cross surrounded by Mary and the disciples, but when he exhibits a mass wafer, the whole illusion vanishes.[35] The machinery of fairyland, however, is even more precisely elaborated. The two men, described rather surprisingly as clerks of divinity in Paris, enter a cleft in the earth and follow a paved road leading to a handsome manor adorned with purple and gold; there, in a natural landscape of luxuriant richness, time is felt to pass more swiftly than in the human world ("Hose lenge wolde long, / fful luitel him þouht" [lines 163–64]),[36] and it is particularly striking that they should encounter King Arthur and "al þe rounde table good" (line 185) among the residents. The visitors pass on to a nunnery, where "a ladi so fre," who seems to be a cross between an abbess and a fairy queen, welcomes them "wiþ rial rehet" (line 224);[37] it is in her splendid hall that the Christian unmasks the illusory crucifixion scene, the building 'bursts,' the lights go out, and the two men find themselves standing "o þe hulle / Þer þey furst were" (lines 271–72).

Accounts such as these might seem to reflect the delusions of clerics out of touch with vernacular culture, but (as we shall see in the next chapter) it would be a mistake to overstate the gulf between clergy and laity in such matters or underestimate the complexity of vernacular beliefs. The testimony of a Suffolk woman named Marion Clerk, examined in the course of an archiepiscopal visitation in 1499, suggests that these accounts may well have had some basis in reality. It is worth quoting at length:

> Marion Clerk, daughter of John and Agnes Clerk, was noted for the use of superstitious art . . . in that, it was asserted, she had the art of healing people of various diseases, of prophesying future events and declaring what misfortunes would befall those who came to her, and revealing the whereabouts of certain hidden treasures. To this charge she replied that she did have this ability. The judge asked her where and from whom she had learnt this art,

and she replied that she had it from God and the Blessed Virgin and the gracious fairies. The judge asked her what they might be, and Marion replied that they were little people who gave her information whenever she wanted it. The judge asked her whether these little people believed in the Father, the Son, and the Holy Spirit, and she replied that they believed only in the Father Almighty. He asked her if she had ever been in heaven, and she said that she had. He asked her if she had seen God in heaven, and she said that she had, and He was wearing a golden mantle. She also said that by the power of the gracious fairies she had talked with the Archangel Gabriel and St Stephen.[38]

Evidently the judge was sufficiently intrigued by this account of fairy transportation to set a trap for her: he "asked if she had been to Canterbury through the power of the fairies and she said yes, and asked where was the tomb of the blessed martyr Thomas, she said [wrongly, of course] it was in the churchyard" (p. 215). Unsurprisingly, a later court in Norwich Cathedral declared "all such arts to be superstitious and to lead to suspicion of heretical pravity" (p. 216), and Marion was forced to recant. As with Thomas of Cantimpré's story, what is so striking about Marion's testimony is less her belief that she had visited some kind of fairy *locus amoenus* (John Bromyard had written of certain deluded women who believed themselves taken off by a certain race and led to certain beautiful and unknown places [quae dicunt se rapi a quodam populo, & duci ad loca quaedam pulchra, & ignota])[39] than the way in which (like a later cunning man from Sussex who claimed to be aided by the archangel Uriel, "a great prince of the Fayries")[40] her account has become entangled with Christian machinery. The celebrated Cambridge song "Heriger, urbis Maguntiacensis," which tells of an otherworld deep in the woods visited by a 'prophet' who says he saw Christ, John the Baptist, and Saint Peter sitting at a feast, offers a much earlier instance of this phenomenon.[41]

We are accustomed to thinking of popular superstitions as falling well outside the boundaries of heresy because they can have posed no coherent intellectual challenge to orthodox dogma, but by the fifteenth century the English church's attitude to them was clearly hardening, and there is evidence that in pastoral, if not in scholastic, circles such beliefs may have regularly been felt to be heretical. A remarkable passage in John Capgrave's *Life of Saint Katherine*, for instance, speaks of witches and elves in the same breath as Lollards; the Virgin Mary is here instructing the hermit who is to convert the saint:

> So sayd my Sone to His aposteles twelve,
> "Whan ye stand," He seyd, "befor the dome
> Of many tyrauntys, and ye alone youreselve,
> Thow thei yow calle Lollard, whych, or elve,
> Beth not dysmayd—I schall gyve yow answere." (3:324–28)[42]

This is evidently based on an apocalyptic passage that appears in three of the four gospels,[43] but none of them alludes to anything that remotely suggests fairies. Peter Idley in the mid-fifteenth century insisted that even white magic was heretical:

> And thoughe by thi Pater noster þou coniure
> And by hooly wordis doo mervelous werkis,
> It is playn Eresye—I referre me to clerkis.[44]

In a similar vein, the articles of excommunication recorded in the register of Godstow Abbey at about the same time condemn "Alle þat knoweth heresy, wicchecrafte, enchauntement, Nigromancy, coniurisones, or any fals beleve aȝens the feyth of holichurch, but ȝif þei distroye hit be þer power."[45] Interestingly, not everyone seems to have been quite so obdurate, for the article also includes, "And al þat ben ordened to enquere þer-on, ȝif þei leue the sute þer-of"; some, apparently, were reluctant to inquire too closely into the unorthodox beliefs of their flock. No matter where on the spectrum their opinions lay, however, all medieval clerics seem to have been prepared to accept that fairy belief was a potentially serious issue.

All this raises questions that are not often asked in such a context. Can we learn anything significant about the actual nature of such beliefs, and is it possible to discover how seriously they were taken by those who held them? After all, it might plausibly be claimed that we are witnessing nothing more than the paranoid projections of a dominant class seeking to impose its own values on an indifferent and inarticulate subject class. Even if some laypeople might actually have been prepared to rationalize and defend their traditional beliefs, where might we look for evidence of this recalcitrance? Latin sources, whether openly hostile or rather more accommodating, have little interest in contextualizing such radically unorthodox views, and even vernacular materials can be frustratingly circumspect.

However rarely, we may still sometimes glimpse signs of actual resistance to the ecclesiastical proscription of vernacular belief. In the mid-fourteenth century John Bromyard reported that attempts to prohibit rituals for recovering stolen property (a standard activity for cunning men and women) might be met with defiance: "they say it is not the work of the devil but of the fair folk [that is, the fairies], for we haven't learnt it from the devil, nor do we believe in him, but from the fair folk" [sed dicunt non per diabolum, sed pulchrum populum, nec a diabolo didicimus nec ei credimus sed pulchro populo].[46] Occasionally, indeed, acts of civil disobedience might invoke fairy protection, apparently reflecting an instinctive association of fairies with other targets of oppressive regulation. In January 1450 Thomas Cheyne led a rebellion in Kent (a harbinger of the much more serious uprising of Jack Cade later in the same year), and among the pseudonyms adopted by its leaders were those of the King of Fairyland and the Queen of Fairyland (*Regem de ffeyre* and *Reginam de ffeyre*).[47] Popular sentiment was clearly in favor of the rebels, but the "oon calling hym self Queen of the feyre" seems to have been particularly charismatic—a contemporary London chronicler remarking that he "did noon oppression nor hurt to any persone."[48] Though the full significance of this impersonation is now impossible to recover, evidently the discourse of fairyland offered the rebels a shared language that they felt they could use against their oppressors: a slightly later indictment accuses a group of poachers of disguising themselves with long beards and blackened faces and proclaiming themselves "the servants of the Queen of Fairyland, intending that they should identify [themselves] by the name" [nuncupantes se esse servientes Regine del Faire ea intencione ut ipsi a nomine cognoscerent].[49] A similar rising, "popular in origin . . . and plebeian in character,"[50] occurred in the north of England in 1489; William Paston III recounts the rebels' call to arms and then adds sarcastically, "And thys is in the name of Mayster Hobbe Hyrste, Robyn God-felaws brodyr he is, as I trow."[51] Robin Goodfellow is of course a well-known fairy name, but Hob Hurst is much more obscure, surviving only in a Derbyshire place-name for a prehistoric tumulus, Hob Hurst's House.[52] Like Cheyne's Queen of Fairyland, Robin Goodfellow's brother here looks very much like an early instance of the common people turning to fairy impersonation in defense of their traditional rights. Hobbe was to have many descendants, however, his line reaching down to the nineteenth century.[53]

We may infer that the crude characterization of fairies as simply devils, or devilish illusions, did not go unchallenged, for pastoral (as opposed to scholastic) theology seems early to have evolved a rather more palatable variation (more palatable, that is, to those who were apparently ready to regard fairies as potentially benevolent creatures). By this account, fairies, while still devils, were only minor devils, less culpable than those who had been thrown into the pit of hell with Satan. Gervase of Tilbury in his *Otia Imperialia* (ca. 1215) suggests that fairies who roam the earth can hardly be equated with the fallen angels who were thrust down to the dungeons of nether darkness to remain there till Doomsday (2 Pet. 2:4): "it must be, then, that those who sided with the devil but whose pride was less grievous were reserved to provide phantoms of this nature to punish humankind."[54] In Caesarius of Heisterbach's *Dialogus Miraculorum*, when the novice observes that some devils are better than others [non omnes daemones aequaliter mali sunt], his master replies that "certain ones, it is said, while others were raising themselves up against God with Lucifer, merely consented, and these indeed fell with the others, but are less evil and harm men less than the others" [quidam, ut dicitur, aliis cum Lucifero contra Deum se extollentibus simpliciter consenserunt, et hi quidem cum ceteris ruerunt, sed ceteris minus mali sunt, hominesque minus laedunt].[55] He then goes on to illustrate this point with the example of a handsome young servant who helped his knightly master escape from his enemies and healed his mistress from a serious disease and then revealed himself to have been a demon (and even after this offered to pay for a bell in the local church!); it seems likely that Caesarius is here recalling some popular tale about a figure such as Gyfre, the fairy servant in the Middle English version of Marie de France's *Lanval*, who accompanies the hero on his adventures and gives him money and martial assistance.[56]

The idea that there were two classes of devil (the hardcore supporters of Lucifer and some less-committed fellow travelers) is an old one, at least as old as Origen in the third century,[57] and it was employed to solve a number of theological difficulties. We will probably never know at what point these 'neutral' or 'craven' angels came to be associated with the fairies of vernacular belief,[58] but clearly the idea was generally current from at least the beginning of the thirteenth century. In England we find it in the late fourteenth-century Vernon Manuscript's *Life of Adam and Eve*: "And after that while [the Fall of Lucifer] heo beon pynet, summe more and summe lasse . . . heo fullen out as thikke as the drift of the snough; summe astunte in the eyr and summe in the eorthe. Yf eny mon is elve-inome other elf-iblowe, he hit hath of the angelus that fellen out of hevene" [and after that time they were tortured, some more, some less. . . . They fell down as thick as snow drifts. Some stopped in the air, some on the ground. If any man is elf-taken or elf-blown (that is, falls sick) he receives it from the angels that fell from heaven].[59] A hundred years earlier *The South English Legendary* had provided an even more radical account,[60] not only pairing these lesser devils with fairies but even suggesting that they might merit pardon at Doomsday:

> Oþer were þat for hom somdel . in misþo3t were
> Ac naþeles hi hulde bet mid God . ac vnneþe hi forbere
> Þulke wende out of heuene ek . and aboue þe oþere beoþ
> Anhei vnder þe firmament . and Godes wille iseoþ
> And so ssolleþ be[o] somdel in pine . forte þe worles ende
> Ac hi ssolleþ a Domesday . a3en to heuene wende (lines 201–6)

[There were others who, because their thoughts strayed somewhat (even though they were more inclined to God, they barely held themselves back) also departed from heaven, and they are above the others, raised up below the heavens, and recognize God's will; and so they must be punished somewhat until the end of the world, but they shall return again to heaven at Doomsday]

and again, "Þat beoþ of þe wrecche gostes . þat of heuene were inome / And mony of hom a Domesday . ssolleþ 3ute to reste come" (lines 257–58) [They are the wretched spirits who were taken from heaven, and many of them shall yet find peace at Doomsday]. This idea turns up elsewhere and may even be responsible for Dante locating his neutral angels in the vestibule of hell (*Inferno* 3:37–39). The fairy Melusine, for example, tells her husband that her natural lot is to remain in "greuouse and obscure penytence . . . vnto the day of domme,"[61] and that this view had penetrated vernacular consciousness is proved by the testimony of a suspected Cathar dragged before the inquisition in the early fourteenth century: "but all the spirits who did not expressly consent or believe in the devil, but were only swept up in the disturbance created by the devil and sinned, as it were, unknowingly, spirits of this kind are human [?mortal] and all shall at length be saved on the Day of Judgment" [set omnes spiritus qui non expresse consenserunt vel crediderunt dyabolo, set solum accesserunt ad turbationem quam dyabolys fecit, et quasi inscii peccaverunt, cuiusmodi sunt spiritus humani, omnes finaliter in die iudicii salvarentur].[62]

This attempt to offer an acceptably anodyne version of the demon/fairy conjunction ultimately satisfied no one. Scholastic theology could not accept the idea that there were degrees of guilt among the followers of Satan,[63] while the notion that some devils were actually redeemable lay even further beyond the pale. Walter Map tells two Faust-like tales of men who put themselves in the power of demons, and both are lulled into a sense of false security when their Mephistopheles figures (in one case a female called, significantly, Meridiana) claim to be harmless fairies. "You fear perhaps an illusion," says Meridiana, "and are meaning to evade the subtlety of a succubus in my person. You are mistaken";[64] and the other tells his victim, a young knight called Eudo, "We can do anything that makes for laughter and nothing that makes for tears. Now I am one of those exiles from heaven who, without abetting or consenting to the crime of Lucifer, were foolishly and unthinkingly carried away in the train of his accomplices" (p. 321). "Deceived by these and similar stories," says Map, "Eudo cheerfully assented to the pact" (p. 329). Clearly some clerics felt that the fable of the neutral angels was fraught with spiritual danger, while the notion of redeemable demons was, if anything, even worse. "That some demons are good, others well-intentioned, others omniscient, others neither saved nor damned. Error!" [quod aliqui demones boni sint, alii benigni, alii omniscientes, alii nec salvi nec damnati. Error] was the unequivocal pronouncement of the Paris theological faculty in 1398.[65]

Vernacular tradition too seems to have balked at the idea of fairies as neutral angels. For instance, the French romance of *Esclarmonde* (a continuation of *Huon of Bourdeaux*) is careful to distinguish neutral angels from genuine fairies. Having narrowly escaped from a shipwreck as he is hastening to arrive at the deathbed of his fairy mentor, Oberon, Huon comes upon a monastery, where he attends a strangely truncated form of the mass; by producing a holy object (a stole) he forces one of the monks to reveal his true nature to him, and he and his fellows turn out to be neutral angels.[66] The whole point of this episode seems to be to differentiate these neutral angels from the actual fairies (whose chief is Oberon). Though the Middle English translation draws no clear distinction between neutral and fallen angels ("al we that be here were chasyd out of paradyse with lucyfer"),[67] it portrays these spirits as holding out a hope of salvation: "but we that be here yet we hope to come to saluacyon" (p. 593). The French original, though, makes it quite plain that they do in fact belong to the third party of angels, those who sided with neither God nor Lucifer: "La tierce pars ne se sot v tenir / Ou a celui [Lucifer] ou au vrai Jesuscrist" (lines 2717–18). The Middle English translation does distinguish these beings from both humans and fairies—"[we] be conuersant amonge the people, & as well as they of the fayery" (p. 593)—but implies that they exercise some power over the fairies: "we be tho that hathe the conducte of al the fayery of the world" (p. 594). The French original by contrast makes the storm in which Huon is almost drowned the work of these demon monks but attributes his delivery to fairy power:

> "Sire," dist il, "jou t'ai dit verité:
> De faerie oïs onques parler."
> "Oïl," dist Hües, "j'en ai oï assés;
> Si m'a ëu grant mestier en la mer
> Il m'ont aidié ma vie a respiter."
> "Hües," dist il, "vous dites verité." (lines 2740–45)

["Sir," he said, "I have told you the truth: have you never heard tell of fairy magic." "Yes," said Huon, "I have heard enough about it: when I was in great need in the sea, they helped me to save my life." "Huon," he said, "you speak the truth."]

Harf-Lancner suggests that we are dealing here with an amalgam of two conceptions of fairyland, one learned and the other folkloric,[68] but I think rather that the author is drawing a deliberate distinction between the real world of the fairies (that represented by Oberon and his followers) and a demonic substitute (the monkish neutral angels), devised by learned culture as a way of rendering vernacular beliefs less dangerous. This point is illustrated even more clearly in the Scottish romance of *Thomas of Erceldoune*. When Thomas first encounters the fairy queen, he mistakes her for the Virgin Mary,[69] but he is quickly disabused:

> Qwene of heuen ne am I noghte,
> ffor I tuke neuer so heghe degre.
> But I ame of ane oþer countree (lines 91–93).[70]

It is made equally clear, however, that this country is not the devil's, for as she rides with Thomas to fairyland, she warns him against picking the fruit that borders their path: "Thomas, þou late þame stande, / Or ells þe fende the will atteynt" (lines 197–98). Even more significant is the reason she gives a reluctant Thomas, after his seven-year sojourn in fairyland, for his return to the world:

> Bot langere here þou may noghte duelle,
> The skylle I sall þe telle whare fore:

> To Morne, of helle þe foulle fende
> Amange this folke will feche his fee;
> And þou art mekill mane and hende,—
> I trowe full wele he wole chese the. (lines 287–92)

If the fiend of hell regularly takes an inhabitant of fairyland as his "fee," clearly the fairies are to be distinguished from devils, even lesser devils. This point is reiterated in two unique passages in one of the five manuscripts of the poem, B.L., MS Lansdowne 762. In the first section of the poem Thomas sexually assaults the fairy queen and then watches her beauty fade before his eyes:[71]

> Thomas stode vpe in þat stede,
> and he by helde þat lady gaye;
> Hir hare it hange all ouer hir hede,
> Hir eghe semede owte, þat are were graye,
> and alle þe riche clothynge was a waye. (lines 129–33)

At this point the Lansdowne manuscript adds a passage that balances the earlier one in which Thomas had mistaken her for the Virgin:

> Sche woxe so grym and so stowte
> The dewyll he wende she had be,
> In the Name of the trynite,
> he coniuryde here anon ryght
> That she shulde not come hym nere,
> But wende away of his sight.
> She said, "thomas, this is no nede,
> ffor fende of hell am I none." (lines 143–50)

In a later passage, when Thomas asks her about her transformation, she explains that it had been a ruse to deceive her jealous husband and that otherwise, "Me had been as good to goo / To the brynnyng fyre of hell" (lines 247–48). If all this were not enough, four of the manuscripts (the fifth, B.L., MS Sloane 2578, is defective at this point) preserve a remarkable passage (lines 201–20) in which the path to fairyland is contrasted with four other paths: those leading to heaven, to the earthly paradise, to purgatory, and to hell. In the traditional ballad derived from this medieval romance these five paths have been reduced to three:

> O see not ye yon narrow road,
> So thick beset wi thorns and briers?
> That is the path of righteousness,
> Tho after it but few enquires.
>
> And see not ye that braid braid road,
> That lies across yon lillie leven?
> That is the path of wickedness,
> Tho some call it the road to heaven.
>
> And see not ye that bonny road,
> Which winds about the fernie brae?
> That is the road to fair Elfland,
> Whe[re] you and I this night maun gae.[72]

These passages provide clear evidence that some people felt that fairyland lay beyond the boundaries of a conventional Christian cosmology, and a curious aside in the popular vade mecum *Sidrak and Bokkus* seems to imply that such an attitude was widespread; in response to the question "Wheþer in thatt oþer world may be Any hous, toun, or citee?" Sidrak describes the three paths to be taken by the soul after death (to heaven, hell, and purgatory) and then adds (in the English version) the otherwise otiose remark, "Wonyng stedes be there no moo / That man or woman shall goo to."[73] (We shall return in Chapter 5 to the difficult question of fairyland as an abode of departed souls.)

Clearly fairy beliefs occupied an anomalous status in the official culture of the later Middle Ages. While scholastic theology may have regarded them as demonic, at the pastoral level they were far too deeply entrenched in the vernacular consciousness to be easily extirpated, and an uneasy truce was maintained. Is it, then, possible to delve further into this vernacular consciousness, to discover any direct evidence for the nature and extent of these beliefs?

Jacques Le Goff has written of "the near impossibility of transporting to the past the methods of observation, investigation, and enumeration, applied by sociologists to contemporary societies,"[74] and while there is no reason to suppose that popular belief was any more homogeneous in the Middle Ages than it is now ("ther ben many folk that beleeven because it happeneth so often tyme to fallen after here fantasyes," writes Sir John Mandeville, "and also there ben men ynowe that han no beleve in hem"),[75] its nuances are far more difficult to penetrate. Certainly the nearest thing to a statistical sample we possess—the thirty-four people from Domrémy and the surrounding area who were questioned about a fairy tree ("*arbor Fatalium, gallice* des fees") in 1452 as part of the process to nullify Joan of Arc's condemnation twenty years earlier—yields very modest results, at least statistically.[76] In 1431 Joan herself had informed her inquisitors that she had never seen fairies at the tree "as far as she knew" [dixit quod nunquam vidit predictas Fatales apud arborem, quod ipsa sciat]—though she did concede that one of her godmothers claimed to have seen them—and she stoutly denied that the gatherings at the fairy tree that she had attended as a young girl were anything other than innocent springtime picnics.[77] Of the thirty-four later witnesses questioned about the *arbre des dames*, ten knew, or affected to know, nothing at all about it (though hardly any of these were from the immediate area of Domrémy) and only nine admitted to having heard that in the old days fairies were to be seen there; no one admitted to believing in fairies personally, though a forty-four-year-old laborer named Michel Buin did say that he did not know where they had gone, because they no longer visited the tree. The Domrémy villagers were under no particular threat from the commission (indeed the commissioners were eager for reassurance that Joan's youthful activities were entirely innocent), yet even so their responses were warily noncommittal. In view of the fact that Bernard Gui's famous inquisitors' manual requires further investigation of anyone who believes in "fairy women, whom they call *the good things*" [de fatis mulieribus quas vocant bonas res],[78] perhaps we can hardly blame them.

In default of statistics we must resort to anecdotal evidence to see what inferences can be drawn about the extent of fairy beliefs in the Middle Ages. One of the most fascinating test cases is provided by Jean d'Arras's romance *Mélusine* (ca. 1393), which traces the origins of the great crusading family of the Lusignans back to its founder's ill-fated marriage to a fairy bride. *Mélusine* was one of the most popular stories in fifteenth-century Europe: alongside Jean d'Arras's prose version, there is another in verse (ca. 1401) by a man called Coudrette, and altogether thirty manuscripts survive of these two renderings. In one or other form it was translated into almost every major European language (with English translations of both texts). Coudrette may well have been a cleric, and he seems to have been somewhat wary about raising the question of his story's factual status (indeed one might detect a certain defensiveness in his insistence that he was writing only at the behest of Guillaume Larchevêque, Lord of Parthenay, and in the elaborate prayers for the soul of his patron with which he concludes). Jean d'Arras, in contrast, was fully prepared to tackle the problems of factual corroboration head on, and with a patron as powerful as Jean de France, Duc de Berri, he need hardly have worried about any consequences. He begins by telling us that "in many partes of the sayd lande of Poytow haue ben shewed vnto many oon right famylerly many manyeres of thinges the whiche somme called Gobelyns [Fr. *luitons*] the other ffayrees, and the other "bonnes dames" or good ladyes,"[79] and then he invokes the authority of Gervase of Tilbury, "a man worshipfull & of credence," for the belief that their activities "be permytted & doon for som mysdedes that were doon ayenst the playsure of god wherfore he punysshed them so secretly & so wounderly wherof none hath parfytte knowlege but alonely he and they may be therefore called the secrets of god, abysmes without ryuage and without bottom."[80] Two French vernacular translations of Gervase of Tilbury's *Otia Imperialia* survive from the Middle Ages,[81] and though there is no record of the Duc de Berri's owning a copy, his brother Charles V certainly did.[82] D'Arras concludes his history of *Melusine* with another extended discussion of the existence of fairies and (at least in the French original) another reference to Gervase:

> Therfore yf I haue wryton or shewed ony thing that to som semeth neyther possible to be nor credible, I beseche them to pardonne me. For as I fele & vnderstand by the Auctours of gramaire & phylosophye [Fr. *des anciens autteurs tant de Gervaise comme d'autres anciens autteurs et philosophes*] they repute and hold this present hystorye for a true Cronykle & thinges of the fayry. And who that saith the contrary / I say the secret jugements of god and his punysshments are inuysible & impossible to be vnderstand or knowe by the humanyte of man. / For the vnderstanding of humayne Creature is to rude to vnderstande the spyce espirytuel, & may not wel comprehend what it is / but as ferre as the wylle of god wyl suffre hym [Fr. *et la puissance de Dieu y puet adjouster qu'il lui plaist*]. For there is found in many hystoryes Fayries that haue be maryed & had many children / but how this may be the humayn creature may not conceyue.[83]

But it is not just written authority that Jean d'Arras invokes. When, at a critical point in the story, Melusine, learning that her husband has disregarded a solemn prohibition, flies off in the shape of a dragon from an upper window, Jean offers us marmoreal proof of this marvel: "And wete it wel that on the basse stone of the wyndowe apereth at this day themprynte of her foote serpentous [Fr. *Et sachiéz que la pierre sur quoy elle passa a la fenestre y est encores, et y est la fourme du pié toute escripte*]."[84] Predictably, Coudrette omits this detail, but even he felt the need to reassure his audience at this point: "Which I writte is trouth, therof ly no thyng [Fr. *Il est voir tout que je escry; / Je m'en daigneroye mentir*]."[85]

This is not quite all there is to it, however, for Jean d'Arras, or at least his patron, might well be thought to have had a political motive for publicly endorsing the legend of Melusine. Among the many stories connected with Melusine was one that she would appear on the ramparts of Lusignan whenever control of the fortress was about to change hands. In the summer and fall of 1376, with Lusignan, the last remaining major English stronghold in Poitou, under siege by the forces of Jean, Duc de Berri, what better way might have been found of encouraging the attackers than to report that Melusine had put in an appearance? Predictably, then, Jean d'Arras says that he had learned from the duke himself that John Cresswell, the English castellan who was defending the castle, had been visited by Melusine three days before its surrender—at the time he was in bed with a woman named Alexandrine, and "he was neuer in his dayes so aferd."[86] Cresswell, a grizzled old *routier*,[87] was certainly not a man to be easily frightened—a fact not lost on his sarcastic bedfellow: "Ha, valyaunt Sersuel how ofte haue I sene your mortal enemyes tofore your presence that neuer ye were aferd, and now for a serpent of femenyne nature ye shake for fere." It is easy, then, to dismiss this story as mere propaganda, especially since some of its details can be shown to be inaccurate: for instance, d'Arras says that the apparition occurred three days before Cresswell surrendered the castle, but in fact when Lusignan finally fell into French hands, on 1 October, Cresswell had actually been languishing in a French dungeon for over three months;[88] moreover Lusignan did not exactly 'fall' to the besiegers; the English handed it over to the duke by way of discharging the ransom of Sir Thomas Percy.[89] To be fair, the Duc de Berri was probably embroidering the details of a story, retold for Jean d'Arras's benefit, after an interval of perhaps fifteen years, but this passage of time raises further problems. By, say, 1390 Lusignan was firmly in French hands and the story had lost whatever propaganda value it might once have had; could it be that the duke, Lusignan's new castellan, was now wondering whether he might not be next on Melusine's visiting list? Certainly the cultural work being done by the prose *Mélusine* at this point seems to have changed radically. Cresswell's story is being invoked here not to dishearten an English garrison but to establish the actual existence of a fairy apparition.

As told in the French original, the story contains a number of circumstantial details left out of the English translation. We learn, for instance, that all the doors to the bedroom Cresswell was sharing with Alexandrine were locked and that there was a good fire burning in the grate (so that Melusine could not have come down the chimney): "Et ne sçot oncques par ou elle entra, et estoient tous les huiz fermèz et barréz et le feu ardoit grant en la cheminee."[90] Moreover, others are said to have seen her. The English translation does mention a man named Godard who swore on the Evangelists that he had often encountered her without ever coming to harm (pp. 369–70), but it leaves out the vivid detail that it was near an old chicken coop next to the castle well ("il a un lieu a Lusegnen empréz le puis ou on a du temps passé nourry pollaille") as well as the important fact that the man himself was still alive ("un homme qui encores demeure en la forteresse") (p. 814). Similarly, a Welshman called Evan is mentioned as a further witness,[91] but not the fact that he saw Melusine twice. Finally, the English translation makes no mention whatsoever of a Poitevin called Perceval de Couloigne, the chamberlain of Peter I of Cyprus (a descendant of the Lusignans), who swore that his master claimed to have seen Melusine three days before he was murdered on 7 January 1369 (p. 814)—a notorious crime, recorded in Chaucer's *Monk's Tale*. All this wealth of circumstantial detail makes it hard to accept that, whatever its origins, Jean d'Arras is telling the story of John Cresswell for any other reason than to prove the factual basis of the apparition, and that the Duc de Berri had related it to him out of a genuine concern with establishing the facts.

Jean d'Arras may be unusual in the lengths he goes to to authenticate his remarkable tale, but there is nothing surprising about finding the issue of fairy belief raised by a writer of romance. Fairies, it seems, like ghosts, have their favorite haunts, and of all the European locations where one might hope to encounter a fairy, perhaps the most auspicious was the forest of Brocéliande near Rennes in Brittany. A description of Brocéliande in the mid-thirteenth-century romance of *Claris and Laris* (1268) makes it sound rather like a fairy theme park (complete with a golden arch):

> Dusqu'a midi ont chevauchie
> Lors ont .i. grant bois aprouchie,
> Qu'on apele Broceliande;
> Trop est la forest fiere et grande
> Et plaine de trop grant merveille;
> . . . .

Les fees ont lor estage,
En .i.des biaus leis du boscage
Est lor maison et lor repaire
Si riches, con le porroit faire
Cil, qui le sorent compasser.
. . . .
A l'entrer de la riche lande,
Qu'on apele Broceliande,
Sont li baron arresteu;
Atant ont .i. arvout veu,
Haut et bien fet de grant richece;
Bien avoit .x. piez de largece;
Dedenz avoit letres escrites
D'or, qui n'estoient pas petites;
Toutes les choses devisoient,
Qui dedenz la forest estoient. (lines 3289–334)[92]

[They [Claris and Laris] rode until midday, when they arrived at a great wood which is called Brocéliande. It is a very large and noble forest, full of many great wonders. . . . The fairies have set up residence there; their dwelling and their resort is in one of the fair clearings in the forest. It is as rich as the builders, who knew their business, could make it. . . . At the entrance to this rich woodland they call Brocéliande the knights halted. Then they saw a high arch, well made at great expense, at least ten feet tall. Within were sizable gold letters written; they listed all the things that were to be seen in the forest.]

Most modern readers will take this passage as pure fantasy and will regard its fairy paraphernalia as a mere plot device—the function of Brocéliande is simply to provide an elaborate chivalric proving ground for the two young heroes. As Jeff Rider puts it, medieval otherworlds "serve as narrative engines whose representatives, messages, or gifts intervene to set a story going, keep it going, or change its direction."[93] In Helen Cooper's words, "magic is above all a narrative issue, a way of telling a story."[94] To take the fairy machinery of medieval romance as nothing more than a convenient narrative device, however, is to ignore the fact that people in the Middle Ages were themselves far from indifferent to truth claims about fairies. As Arthur Brown showed long ago, the torrent of disparaging epithets—*nugae, fallaces, fabulae, figmenta*—hurled against Arthurian romances by twelfth-century clerics arose from their very real indignation that such things as "disappearing castles, magic fountains, and enchanted forests" should have been represented as credible.[95] If the question mattered to them, perhaps it should also matter to us.

Let us then return to the Forest of Brocéliande. In the *Roman de Rou*, written at least a hundred years before *Claris and Laris*, the Norman poet Wace inserts the following amusing aside into an account of the forces gathered by William for his invasion of England:

> e cil devers Brecheliant
> donc Breton vont sovent fablant,
> une forest mult longue e lee
> qui en Bretaigne est mult loee.
> La fontaine de Berenton
> sort d'une part lez le perron;
> aler i solent veneor
> a Berenton par grant chalor,
> et a lor cors l'eve espuisier
> e le perron desus moillier;
> por ço soleient pluie aveir.
> Issi soleit jadis ploveir
> en la forest e environ,
> *mais jo ne sai par quel raison.*
> *La seut l'en des fees veeir*
> *se li Breton nos dient veir*
> *e altres mereveilles plusors;*
> . . . .
> La alai jo merveilles querre,
> vi la forest e vi la terre,
> merveilles quis, mais nes trouvai,
> fol m'en revinc, fol i alai;
> fol i alai, fol m'en revinc,
> folie quis, por fol me tinc. (3:6374–98)[96]

[and some [came] from near Brocéliande which the Bretons often tell stories about, a forest, long and broad, which is greatly prized in Brittany. The spring of Barenton flows on one side, beside the great stone. Huntsmen were accustomed to go to Barenton when it was very hot and pour water from their horns and splash it over the great stone; this way they would make it rain. This is the way it rained in the old days in the forest and the surrounding area, *but I don't know what the reason was. People were accustomed to seeing fairies and many other wonders there, if the Bretons are telling us the truth.* . . . I went there to see wonders, I saw the forest and I saw the region; I searched for wonders but I didn't find any; I came back a fool—I went there a fool; I went there a fool—I came back a fool; I looked for folly—I found myself the fool [my emphasis].]

Wace, then, was a skeptic; he had sought empirical evidence and found it lacking, but the real point is that he *did* seek it (or represents himself as having done so).

What of his successor Chrétien de Troyes? Chrétien had evidently read this passage in Wace, for Calogrenant is clearly echoing it in the opening scene of *Yvain*. Reporting his unsuccessful adventures in Brocéliande to King Arthur, Calogrenant concludes:

> Ensi alai, ensi reving,
> Au revenir por fol me ting;
> Si vos ai conté come fos
> Ce qu'onques mes conter ne vos. (lines 577–80)[97]

[Thus I went, thus I returned; on my return I found myself a fool; if I have told my story like a fool I wish that I may never tell it again.]

Calogrenant's folly, however, is quite different from Wace's; it is not the folly of a man who has been naive and gullible—pouring water over the stone has, after all, produced the promised effect—but of one who has overreached himself and been shamed in battle with the knight whom his actions conjured up. At the end of the romance, Yvain, desperate to get his indignant lady, Laudine, to see him, threatens to flood her out by exploiting the magical properties of the spring at Barenton:

> Puis errerent tant que il virent
> La fontainne et plovoir i firent.

> *Ne cuidiez pas, que je vos mante,*
> Que si fu fiere la tormante,
> Que nus n'an conteroit le disme. (lines 6533–37)

[Then they [Yvain and his lion] traveled until they saw the spring and made it rain there. *Don't imagine that I'm lying to you:* the tempest was so severe that no one could tell the tenth of it [my emphasis].]

What are we to make of Chrétien's disclaimer, "Ne cuidiez pas, que je vos mante"? Is it an ironic joke? Is it a genuine appeal for credence? Is it merely a conventional tic designed to carry his audience along with him at an improbable moment? Whatever we make of it, however, it shows that Chrétien was no less aware than Wace of the contested nature of fairy belief.

There is one other early literary text whose setting is the Forest of Brocéliande, Huon de Méri's *Torneiment Anticrist* (1235–40). This is not a true romance but rather an odd mixture of allegorical psychomachia and social satire: Anticrist's followers, for instance, include not only a character called Pub Crawl [*Guersois*], whose gang consists of Scotsmen, English, and Normans, but also the gods Pluto and Proserpina, who bear a clear resemblance to Chaucer's fairy king and queen in *The Merchant's Tale*.[98] Proserpina is Anticrist's lover and supplies him with a pennon made from her chemise (lines 570–74), while Pluto bullies Anticrist into fighting the archangel Michael (lines 2918–19). Interestingly, among the butts of Huon de Méri's satire are the Albigensians (lines 878–96 and 22767–95)—a further sign that fairy beliefs hovered at the edge of heresy. The *Torneiment*'s opening lines are clearly inspired by Chrétien de Troyes's account of the visits of Calogrenant and Yvain to Brocéliande; the poet, seeking to discover the truth about the spring of Barenton and its properties ("Kar la verté volei e aprendre / De la perilluse fontaine" [lines 62–63]), finds it just as Chrétien had described ("cum l'a descrit Crestiens" [line 103]). But instead of suppressing its fairy elements like Chrétien, de Méri demonizes them. By pouring water over the stone (not once but twice), he summons both a tremendous storm and the terrifying figure of Bras de Fer, the chamberlain of Anticrist, who then conducts him to the tournament that occupies the remainder of the poem. But even here, in an allegorical poem that makes no claims to verisimilitude, the poet feels obliged to authenticate his account of the spring with its storm-raising properties. Not only does he give a circumstantial account of how he came to be in the area (an account so detailed, in fact, that it allows us to date the poem), but he even remarks in the course of his description of the violence of the tempest that he has no wish to lie about it: "ne talent n'en ai de mentir" (line 117).

We have seen that Chrétien was influenced by Wace and Huon de Méri was influenced by Chrétien, so there is a natural enough temptation to take this to mean that we are dealing not with actual beliefs at all but with a succession of writers who are using the Forest of Brocéliande as a literary shorthand, a stock location with as little connection to the real world as Shakespeare's Illyria. The final three pieces of evidence I wish to adduce, however, are non-literary and should make it quite clear that if Wace, Chrétien, and de Méri were worried that describing a fairy spring made them look like fools or liars, there were others who seem to have had few doubts that they were dealing with a genuine meteorological event.

Jacques de Vitry, for instance, in his *Historia Orientalis seu Hierosolymitana* (begun in 1219) includes the Spring of Barenton among a group of marvels he judges it safe to believe in since they are contrary to neither faith nor good morals ("ea tamen credere que contra fidem non sunt vel bonos mores, nullum periculum aestimamus"): "in Brittany there is said to be a certain spring and if its waters are sprinkled over a nearby rock they are said to produce rain and thunder" [in minori Britannia fons quidam esse refertur, cuius aque supra propinquum lapidem proiecte pluvias & tonitrua provocare dicuntur].[99] A generation later the Dominican Thomas of Cantimpré in his *Bonum Universale de Apibus* went to great lengths to make this phenomenon seem credible:

> I have heard Friar Henry the German, at one time a Dominican Reader in Cologne,[100] a man of conspicuous learning and piety of whom I have written above, tell, with friars as witnesses, what I will now relate. When a certain well-born and wealthy friar from the region of Brittany entered the Dominican order he lived with the French friars in Lyon. As the time of his vows approached he sought permission from his prior to return to his own land in order that he might dispose of his possessions; the prior agreed and undertook the journey with him. When they had arrived in the wastes of Brittany, the novice said to his prior, "Would you like to see the ancient wonder of Brittany?" The prior asked what it was, and the friar, leading him to a sparkling clear spring above which was placed a stone on marble columns in the manner of an altar, immediately poured water over [it]. At once the skies darkened, the

clouds began to gather, thunder to rumble, rain to pelt down, lightning to flash, and it instantly caused so great a flood that the surrounding land seemed to be covered to the distance of a league. The prior was amazed by the sight and talked about it in the hearing of brother Henry, Bishop John of blessed memory, master of the order,[101] and many other friars. Forty years ago I heard this same thing from my father, who had campaigned in those parts with King Richard of England. When brother Henry told me, and many others, these things, I asked how they could have come about. He replied, by a magic art, now unknown to humans, and by the working of demons, who are able to stir and whip up the air into storms and rain-showers when they wish, though only by permission of the hidden decree of God.[102]

At this point it is probably worth pointing out something that underlies the traditions surrounding the Spring of Barenton and that may not be immediately obvious to the modern reader: the popular understanding that there was a connection between fairies and bad weather. Chaucer seems to be alluding to such a connection when he mentions the "ayerissh bestes" that engender "Cloudes, mystes, and tempestes, / Snowes, hayles, reynes, wyndes" in *The House of Fame* (lines 964–69),[103] but even clearer evidence is found in, of all places, an early fifteenth-century Wycliffite sermon: "And summe dremen of þes feendis [of the loweste rank] þat summe ben elues and summe gobelynes, and haue not but litil power to tempte men in harme of soule; but siþ we kunne not proue þis ne disproue þis spedili, holde we vs in þe boundis þat God telliþ vs in his lawe. But it is licli þat þes feendis haue power to make boþe wynd and reyn, þundir and lyʒttyng and oþir wedrus; for whan þei moeuen partis of þis e[y]re and bryngyn hem nyyʒ togidere, þes partis moten nedeli bi kynde make siche wedir as clerkis knowen."[104] Another, hardly less surprising, source is a set of Latin exercises composed for use in Exeter Grammar School around 1450, one of which reads, "A general rumour is spreading among the people that the spirits of the air, invoked by necromantic art . . . have appeared in bodily form, stirring up great tempests in the air which are not yet calmed, it is believed, nor allayed."[105] When Wace, Chrétien, and Huon de Méri wrote of a magic stone with the power to summon up storms, then, they would have expected their readers to assume a fairy agency. It is quite clear that *daemones* in the passage from Thomas of Cantimpré is a Dominican code word for the vernacular term *fées* and that Thomas is thus echoing a popular association of the spring with fairies. What is far more striking, however, is the absolute credence that Thomas, a pupil of Albertus Magnus, places in this story of the spring; he gives circumstantial evidence, cites reliable witnesses, and even tries to offer a credible explanation for it. As with the anonymous Wycliffite preacher (and Jean d'Arras), the question is not whether fairies (or *daemones/feendis*) exist but how they work their magic and what the limits of their powers are.

One final piece of evidence is the most surprising of all. It comes from a sober legal text, the *Coutumier* of the forest of Brocéliande, written down in the fifteenth century but probably based on a thirteenth-century original. At the end of a lengthy exposition of the assorted hunting, logging, and pasturage rights of the various secular and ecclesiastical lords having domain in the forest, we find the following: "Item, next to the said spring there is a great rock, called the rock of Bellenton, and every time the Lord of Montfort comes to the said spring and sprinkles its water and moistens the said rock, however hot it may be, [with] the weather clear of rain, and in whatever direction the wind might lie, and however much people might say that the weather is not looking at all like rain, very soon (sometimes shortly before the said lord is able to return to his castle of Comper and sometimes shortly after) and in any case before the end of that same day, it rains in the region so plentifully that the land and its crops are watered by it much to their benefit."[106] It is unclear whether this entry is intended to confirm the Lord of Montfort's exclusive right to sprinkle water on the rock or merely to prove that he has jurisdiction over this particular area, but in either case the passage confirms the existence of a local belief and one that, to judge by its presence in the *Coutumier*, must have been shared by the landholding class. Moreover the author of the *Coutumier* clearly recognizes that some will find the phenomenon incredible and goes to some lengths to assert its actuality. After reading such a passage we might understand why Roger Loomis should have asked so indignantly, "Can anyone seriously believe that it was Chrétien's poem which gave rise to this popular custom of seeking relief from drought at the fountain?"[107]

Not only in Brocéliande was the question of the credibility of fairy beliefs an issue. The Yorkshireman William of Newburgh tells the story of a local peasant ("ex hoc vico rusticus") who, having stumbled upon a fairy feast taking place inside a hillock that lay on his way home, rashly steals a cup from the fairies. William notes that he was personally familiar with the hillock in question ("tumulo quem saepius vidi") and goes to some lengths to detail the subsequent history of the cup: "Eventually this cup of unknown material, unusual colour, and strange shape was offered as a splendid gift to the elder Henry, king of England. Subsequently it was passed on to the queen's brother, David king of Scots, and kept for many years among the treasures of Scotland. Some years ago, as I learned from a reliable account, Henry II wished to see it, and it was surrendered to him by William king of Scots."[108] No doubt William of Newburgh names these royal witnesses for the same reason that Walter Map had stressed that the fairy bride of a man named Eadric the Wild was examined in person by William the Conqueror,[109] as a way of lending unimpeachable authority to his strange tale. Yet William of Newburgh was far from being a credulous reporter;[110] his skepticism about the reliability of Geoffrey of Monmouth's account of Arthur, for instance, is well known.[111] Nor for that matter was Walter Map, who dryly remarks of the story that Triunein, reputedly the son of a Welsh fairy, survived defeat in battle to live with his mother at the bottom of a lake, "a delusion like this might have been invented about a man whose body was never found" [de non inuento fingi potuit error huiusmodi].[112]

The quasi-objective stance of men such as William of Newburgh and Walter Map closely resembles that of a modern ghost-story teller seeking to exploit the frisson that comes with an audience's readiness to entertain the possibility that it is listening to a true account. The fifteenth-century French courtier Antoine de la Sale professed himself a skeptic on the fairy question, and at the end of his account of the paradise of Queen Sibyl (which he describes as a fairy realm of magical gardens and palaces, populated by elegant knights and beautiful ladies, and ruled over by a gracious sovereign), he wrote, "I pray God to guard every good Christian from such false belief, and from exposing himself to such danger."[113] But when he describes how he himself had sought to visit this magic realm (entered through a cave high in the Apennines) in 1420, he recounts an unnerving experience that proves that even such a sophisticated outsider was not wholly impervious to the queen's power. He claims that the local authorities prevented him from passing beyond the cave's first chamber, and yet even there, "[my companions] and I heard from within a sharp voice, like the sound of a peacock crying out, as if from a long way off. They said that it was an utterance from the Sibyl's Paradise, but for my part I don't believe it; I rather think that it was my horses who were at the foot of the mountain, although they were a long way below me" [Iceulx et moy oysmes leans une haulte voix criant ainsi que ce feust le cry du paon, qui sembloit estre moult loings. Si dirent les gens que c'estoit une voix de paradis de la Sibille. Mais, quant a moy, je n'en croy riens; ainsi croy que feussent mes chevaulx qui au pié du mont estoient, combien que'ilz feussent moult bas et loings de moy (p. 15)]. For all his bravado, la Sale's "although" here betrays an underlying uneasiness; he sounds rather like the hotel guest who, while disclaiming any belief in ghosts, would still rather not sleep in a room reputed to be haunted. But there is a significant difference. Ghost stories in the modern world carry with them only limited ideological baggage; the proselytizing atheist might regard them as dangerous nonsense, but most people would treat them as harmless entertainment. This was not true of fairies in the Middle Ages.

It is a relatively simple matter to show that some people during the Middle Ages believed in fairies, but we have still not gone very far in understanding the general attitude toward such beliefs. While there may be a strong temptation to explain them in terms of modern phenomena, like a belief in ghosts, such analogies have only limited value. This is true even in the case of a more commonly invoked parallel, the modern belief in alien abductions—a belief that actually bears a strong formal resemblance to some medieval tales of people stolen by the fairies;[114] Diane Purkiss has even gone so far as to claim that "aliens are our fairies, and they behave just like the fairies of our ancestors."[115] In one sense this is quite true—both might be argued to fill a similar, even identical, social or psychological niche—but ideologically their roles are very different, and the cultural work performed by each is quite distinct.

For one thing, modern belief in alien abduction, however widespread (in 2012 about a third of Americans were reported to believe in UFOs), remains a minority cult, indulged in by a fringe population. Its adherents may relish the support of the Harvard psychiatrist John Edward Mack (just as medieval fairy believers were glad to have the learned Gervase of Tilbury on their side), but by and large they have made few inroads into civil society. However, fairy beliefs were very far from being a fringe phenomenon in the Middle Ages (as we shall see). A second way in which medieval fairy beliefs differed from modern theories of alien abduction is yet more significant. Champions of alien abduction, for all their love of conspiracy theories, pose little threat to established society; no one in power apparently feels any great need to censor, silence, or persecute them. As our opening discussion of the church's representation of fairies as devils and of fairy beliefs as potentially heretical demonstrates, however, medieval stories of fairyland were far from ideologically neutral. It is to the ideological significance of medieval fairy stories that we will now turn.

CHAPTER 2

Policing Vernacular Belief

> Adde we to these, the parts and representations of Satyres, Silvanes, Muses, Nymphes, Furies, Hobgoblins, Fairies, Fates, with such other heathen vanities, which Christians should not name, much lesse resemble.
> —William Prynne, *Histrio-mastix* (1633)

While most scholars would have little difficulty treating a belief in fairies as an aspect of medieval 'popular culture,' many would find it harder to agree on what precisely they mean by this term. The European Middle Ages, as is well known, conceived of society as a static threefold structure—its estates divided among churchmen, knights, and peasants—but modern historiography is more likely to apply a binary, and dynamic, model to medieval culture: either high/low (churchmen and knights vs. peasants) or learned/lay (churchmen vs. knights and peasants).[1] Thus, as Aron Gurevich puts it, "the very concept of 'popular culture' as applied to the high Middle Ages remains to a great extent undefined. Was it only the culture of the lower, oppressed classes of society? Or was it the culture of all *illiterati*, as opposed to that of educated people?"[2] In what follows, I take vernacular culture to represent the culture of the laity as a whole, knights as well as peasants, while conceding that *la culture savante* must always be understood to have included some educated members of the laity, and *la culture populaire*, some of the less literate members of the clergy. More specifically, I adopt here the model proposed by Peter Burke for early modern Europe when he speaks of the "'great tradition' of the educated few and the 'little tradition' of the rest,"[3] always remembering his important proviso that the term 'little tradition' must take account of "upper class participation in popular culture" (p. 24). Though Burke is an early modernist, his model can arguably be applied to the late Middle Ages and perhaps even earlier.[4] Such a model must always be heuristic, of course: the existence of a credulous bishop or a skeptical peasant no more invalidates it than the existence of a reactionary member of a socialist party or a progressive member of a conservative one invalidates the standard ideological model of modern Western democracy.

For many, the notion that *la culture populaire* should be understood to include members of the secular elite will be counterintuitive, particularly since there is a common perception that the primary thrust of the French *annalistes* has been, in John Van Engen's words, "to dredge up from the bottom, as it were, the residues of peasant religious 'folklore.'"[5] Whether or not such an assessment is altogether just,[6] and whether indeed the very term 'folklore' can properly be used in such a reductive sense,[7] my adoption of Peter Burke's model in this context obviously requires justification. To be clear, I do not claim merely that medieval aristocrats occasionally drew upon aspects of peasant belief, which appears to be Le Goff's position: "this whole world of the marvelous came to enrich the cultural armory of the knights."[8] Still less do I claim that they were merely playing at being peasants: to read an event such as Charles VI's *bal des sauvages*, for instance, as if it were the medieval equivalent of Marie Antoinette's playing at shepherdesses in the *Hameau de la reine* would, in my view, be gravely anachronistic; to a near contemporary, after all, it had very much the appearance of "a dance for conjuring a demon" [*una corea procurante demone*].[9] Charges of sorcery were rife in the late medieval courts of England and France, and while it is all too easy to dismiss them as merely a cynical political ploy,[10] they could hardly have been leveled at all if the substance of such charges had been widely discredited among the courtiers themselves. Moreover, the claim that while folk beliefs may have circulated among the nobility they must have originated much further down the social scale seems to me a quite unprovable projection back from nineteenth- and twentieth-century experience; the fact that a brutal and ignorant Irish laborer named Michael Cleary murdered his wife in 1895 in the apparently sincere belief that she was really a fairy changeling[11] tells us nothing at all about the propagators of such beliefs five hundred years earlier.

When the Limbourg brothers painted the castle of Lusignan in the March scene of the Duc de Berri's luxurious *Trés Riche Heures*, they assumed that the duke would wish them to include an image of Melusine. The main focus of their page, however, is a plowman, who "turns away quite leisurely" from the apparition of Melusine flying above the castle's turrets, with all the studied indifference of his counterpart in Breughel's *Fall of Icarus*. While it would certainly be wrong to take his pose as emblematic of the limited scope of such so-called popular beliefs, I believe it would be equally wrong to confine these beliefs, as has often been done, to some hypothetical primitive folk culture. In my view, medieval aristocrats were perfectly capable of entering into the belief system of the little tradition as fully participating members. As we have already seen, Jean d'Arras may well have drawn upon a memorate from the Duc de Berri when, around 1393, he came to describe John Cresswell's terrifying encounter with Melusine in his bedroom, but such clear examples of direct aristocratic engagement with folkloric beliefs are relatively rare. On the other hand, had we come across this story in a preacher's exemplum collection or even an anonymous popular romance, we would probably have been tempted to dismiss it as an obvious example of peasant superstition. In the *Otia Imperialia* at a point where Gervase of Tilbury is paraphrasing an account of "Silvans and Pans" from the well-known passage in Augustine's *City of God* on *incubi*,[12] a recent edition's facing-page translation renders the phrase *creberrima fama* (literally, 'a very frequent rumor') as "a widespread *folk-belief*."[13] This may seem a small point, but such mistranslation typifies the unreflective assumption that such beliefs must always have originated at the lower levels of society. The two medieval translations, by contrast, make no such assumption: one reads, *aucuns racontent et dient* [some say], and the other, *maintes gens ont oÿ* [many have heard].[14] Gervase after all was writing not for peasants but for a German emperor (Otto IV), and a copy of one of the translations of his book found its way into the French royal library. Furthermore many of the stories Gervase tells (including a precursor of the Melusine story) concern the nobility.

One of these stories in particular is worth singling out for the glimpse it offers us into a possible social context for such storytelling. Gervase tells us about a mysterious knight who occupied a deserted earthwork on Wandlebury Hill near Cambridge and would fight anyone prepared to ride up there on a moonlit night and challenge him "to come out knight against knight [*miles contra militem veniat*]."[15] By way of authenticating this story he reports that a knight named Osbert Fitz Hugh was staying in Cambridge, "and in the evening after dinner the household of his wealthy host gathered round the hearth and, as is the custom among the nobility [*ut potentibus moris est*], turned their attention to recounting the deeds of people of old."[16] One of the stories that Osbert hears that evening is the tale of the Wandlebury knight, and he immediately rides off to challenge, fight, and even, at least in the short term, triumph over him: "[He] emerged from the field victorious, while his adversary disappeared." It hardly matters for present purposes whether what Osbert heard that night was a fairy legend or a ghost story; the fact remains that we can class it as a folk belief only as long as we are prepared to include these Anglo-Norman *potentes* among the 'folk.'

As we have seen, Jean d'Arras implies that Jean de France—whose honors included the duchy of Berri and Auvergne and the county of Poitiers, who was the third son of King John II and brother to Charles V, Louis I of Anjou (King of Naples), and Philip the Bold (Duke of Burgundy)—was intrigued by fairy beliefs, but interestingly, the appearance of Melusine in John Cresswell's bedroom in 1376 was not the first time the fairy world had given his opponent trouble. During the early 1370s Cresswell had been hounded throughout Poitou by Bertrand du Guesclin, constable of France,[17] and du Guesclin, as was well known, was married to a fairy. The trouvère Cuvelier tells us that the young du Guesclin had married a handsome and well-educated young woman named Tiffany de Raguenel, whom he had met while he was defending Dinan against the English in 1359. Cuvelier does his best to make this marriage seem unexceptional, but others apparently felt there was something odd about it:

> Encore disoit on que c'estoit une fee
> Et que le sens de quoy elle estoit si fondee
> Lui venoit proprement par parole de fee. (lines 2699–701)[18]

> [Yet it was said that she was a fairy and that the sagacity with which she was so well supplied really came to her from a fairy spell.]

Du Guesclin had been born only a few miles north of Brocéliande, so perhaps such an association was inevitable. In any event, the fact that in the 1370s a prince of the French royal blood and the constable of France were both thought to have had close encounters with fairies makes it difficult to argue that fairy beliefs should be relegated to the peasant fringes of medieval society.

To give one final illustration: we have seen that in the spring of 1420 the French courtier Antoine de la Sale traveled to Montemonaco in the central Apennines to see for himself the famous paradise of Queen Sibyl, a magic realm that medieval popular imagination had clearly modeled on descriptions of fairyland. Almost as interesting as his report of the visit itself, however, is la Sale's account of its early readership. It was written in the first instance, he tells us, as an ironic travel guide for his former pupil John of Calabria (the son of Duke René d'Anjou) and his new wife, Marie de Bourbon, but a second copy was promised to John's mother-in-law, Agnès de Bourgogne, and her husband, the Duke de Bourbon, "si le plaisir de mondit seigneur et le vostre feust d'y aler, ainsi que souventffois après disner ou soupper avez acoustumé de vous esbatre" [in case my lord and you should be pleased to go there, an idea you have often amused yourselves with after dinner or supper].[19] Such people were among the grandest magnates in France, and coupled with the Duke de Berri's interest in Melusine, their evident fascination with Queen Sybil's paradise confirms that the discourse of fairyland was far from being the exclusive preserve of the laboring classes.

When the higher nobility could evince such an interest in the existence of fairyland, we should not be surprised to discover that the lower aristocracy shared their concerns. We have already seen that the lords of Montfort were thought to invoke fairy aid to make it rain in Comper, and that some people believed that Bertrand du Guesclin, who despite his rise to the constableship came from the minor nobility, had married a fairy. Joan of Arc's nullification proceedings offer two further examples of the 'folklore' of such *petite aristocratie*. Sir Albert d'Ourches, who met Joan in Vaucouleurs, was not a local (Ourches-sur-Meuse is some twenty miles to the north of Domrémy), and yet he was prepared to testify to having heard that in the old days fairies used to be seen beneath the Fairy Tree ("subtus illam arborem antiquitus fées solebant ire"), and then adds, by way of exonerating Joan, that this was twenty or thirty years before she was even heard of (or, in other words, fifty years earlier, when he was a young boy).[20] Perhaps he had learned of the fairy tree on a visit to the de Bourlémont family (the lords of Domrémy), a family that with the death of Pierre de Bourlémont in 1412 had become extinct. Another deponent, the widow Jeanette de Veau, however, recalled hearing stories about the de Bourlémonts: the tree was called the Ladies Tree, she said, "because in the old days a certain lord, called Sir Peter Gravier, knight, lord of Bourlémont, and a lady who was called *Fée* would meet each other under that tree and speak together. And she said she heard these things read in a romance ('hec in uno romano legi audivit')" (pp. 264–65). Unless Jeanette was simply confused,[21] we may possibly be dealing here with some local counterpart of the Melusine legend,[22] but in any case four other witnesses specifically attested to an association between the de Bourlémont family and the Fairy Tree,[23] and several more mentioned *domini et domine temporales* in connection with it. Taken as a whole, these testimonies convey a clear impression that fairy 'folklore' was far from being restricted to the laboring classes. There is no reason to suppose that things were any different in England nor that such attitudes were restricted to the late Middle Ages.[24] Perhaps then, with Ferlampin-Acher, we should speak "rather of *lore* than *folklore,* or at least give to the term *people* a very wide interpretation."[25]

A second important issue raised by the notion of popular culture concerns periodization. Obviously, vernacular culture did not remain static and unchanging across a thousand years of medieval history, and yet the best-known attempt to supply a chronology for it, that of Jacques Le Goff, remains problematic. In an introductory sketch to the study of the marvelous in his *Imaginaire médiéval* Le Goff offers us a three-stage process:

1. The Dark Ages and the repression of the marvelous.
2. The explosion of the marvelous: twelfth and thirteenth centuries.
3. The aestheticization of the marvelous: fourteenth and fifteenth centuries.[26]

A few pages later he fills in this bare schema with a little more detail:

> The very rough periodization which I have proposed applies essentially to learned marvels. In the first period, it seems to me that learned culture succeeded for the most part in occluding the marvelous element in popular culture, which certainly existed and which can be detected between the lines and in other texts. By contrast, in the twelfth and thirteenth centuries learned culture is much more receptive to the popular marvelous [*le merveilleux populaire*], with the clear object of either reclaiming or distorting it. Finally, it seems to me that there is a kind of turn to aestheticization, where the dialogue (or the struggle) between the learned and the popular versions of the marvelous is no longer of the first importance. (p. 38)

While acknowledging the significance of Le Goff's ground-clearing work here and recognizing the essential open-endedness of such terms as *le merveilleux savant* and *le merveilleux populaire,* I still have difficulty with this chronology. In fact it seems to me to suffer from precisely the weaknesses that Le Goff himself detects in the kind of study of popular culture that privileges cultural objects over cultural participants;[27] when viewed from below, insofar as such a thing is possible, a somewhat different pattern emerges.

In the Dark Ages the church certainly repressed, in the sense of sought to eradicate, such aspects of popular culture as a belief in fairies, but in the British Isles, at least, good evidence for such beliefs, much of it in the vernacular, survives nonetheless.[28] It is worth pointing out that this evidence derives almost entirely from the *culture savante*, since written material of clear lay provenance is virtually nonexistent.[29] A survey of the pastoral literature of the period, however, leaves a strong impression that church discipline seems to have been relatively light-handed: local superstitions were as likely to be mocked for their folly as castigated for their wickedness. Furthermore, in Bernadette Filotas's words, "Pastoral literature does not support the view that popular culture was a matter of class. References to social standing are rare, but when they appear, they reinforce the idea of a common culture."[30]

This observation calls into question Le Goff's contention that the explosion (*irruption*) of the marvelous in the twelfth and thirteenth centuries reflects the "growth of lay popular culture, rushing into the breach opened during the eleventh and twelfth centuries by a lay aristocratic culture thoroughly imbued with the one available culture-system distinct from the clergy's, namely the tradition of folklore."[31] Rather, I believe that the twelfth century witnessed the emergence of a bicultural system arising from a laity increasingly comfortable with the medium of letters and a clerisy "increasingly dependent on, and concerned with, the goodwill and co-operation of the whole population."[32] While it is tempting to locate the actual tipping point a little later, in the years immediately following the Fourth Lateran Council (1215) and the founding of the Dominican order (1216)—the period of Caesarius of Heisterbach, William of Auvergne, and Étienne of Bourbon—this can be done only by excluding such important figures as Gervase of Tilbury (whose writing is contemporary with the Fourth Lateran Council), and both Gerald of Wales and Walter Map (who were at work a generation earlier). Certainly writers such as William of Auvergne and Étienne of Bourbon convey the strong impression that fairy beliefs circulated primarily among the poor and ignorant: William, for instance, speaks of the old women who call demons of this kind 'ladies' ("huiusmodi demones, quas dominas vocant vetulae"), of the witlessness of old women who, amazingly enough, spread the belief that fairies steal children ("vetularum autem nostrarum desipientia opinionem istam mirabiliter disseminavit"), and of the debased language of the old crones who speak of 'changelings' ("quos vulgus cambiones nominant, de quibus vulgarissimi sunt sermones aniles").[33] The same is true of Étienne de Bourbon, who tells of a *pauper vetula* who tricked people into believing she was a prophetess; of a *quidam rusticus*, possibly a thief,[34] who encountered Arthur's household while prowling about at night; and of the group of *homines rusticani* who originated the cult of Saint Guinefort.[35] On the other hand, both Walter Map and Gervase of Tilbury were writing for aristocratic audiences, and many of their stories concern noblemen and noblewomen; and even Caesarius of Heisterbach's fairies/demons move primarily in knightly circles. No doubt the third estate offered some churchmen an easier target than the second, and what Filotas observes of the Dark Ages ("the authorities were quicker to detect paganism and superstition in the customs of subordinate groups than in those of their betters"[36]) remained true of this later period.

Of Le Goff's three stages in the development of the medieval marvelous, I have most difficulty in accepting the third: his characterization of *le merveilleux* in the fourteenth and fifteenth centuries—he is probably thinking here of *Mélusine*—as having become somehow 'aestheticized.'[37] What he means by this term is made clearer in a later essay, where he employs an essentially high/low version of the bicultural model: "The approach of opposing the two cultures tends to make of 'popular' culture, a culture essentially dominated, manipulated, and exploited by the 'superior' culture. Learned culture [*la culture savante*], from this perspective, either destroys, perverts, or occludes popular culture, forcing upon it an acculturation from above drawn from ecclesiastical, aristocratic—later bourgeois—models, or it rehabilitates it aesthetically, when it has lost its power to resist and retains only 'the beauty of a corpse.' "[38] In my view, vernacular culture (that is to say, the culture of the little tradition) was far from having lost its power to resist in the late Middle Ages despite the church's having stepped up its campaign against it.[39] Writers such as Jean Gerson, Johannes Nider, and Heinrich Kramer give no sign of believing that the battle against popular beliefs had been won; indeed by shifting their *casus belli* from mere superstition to actual heresy they put the conduct of the war on a dangerous new footing.[40]

If anything, the official attitude seems to have hardened throughout the Middle Ages, and on the eve of the early modern period things were very much darker than they had been earlier. By the end of the fifteenth century Burchard of Worms's penance of ten days on bread and water for those who believed that corporeal "sylvans" took pleasure with their lovers[41] would have seemed remarkably mild. The authors of the *Malleus Maleficarum*, themselves perfectly ready to believe in such sylvans (or rather in their own demonic reimagination of them as *succubi*), no longer regarded penance alone as sufficient to counter the danger of heterodox beliefs; they were quite prepared to condemn to death those who held such views: "the only possible way for these and similar practices to be remedied is for the judges who are responsible for the sorceresses to get rid of them or at least punish them as an example for all posterity."[42]

The state of hostility, or at least deep suspicion, existing between representatives of the great tradition and those espousing such aspects of the little tradition as a belief in fairies is one of the major themes of this book. For me, its presence permeates medieval romance and helps us to disambiguate what James Wade has termed "the ambiguous supernatural" of medieval fairyland.[43] While Le Goff's characterization might possibly apply to later works such as Spenser's *Faerie Queene*, most fourteenth- and fifteenth-century romances, still energized by this contested ideology, offer us something quite different from "the beauty of a corpse."

Such a contest can be detected even in a writer as thoroughly imbued with the ideology of the great tradition as Geoffrey Chaucer.[44] When Chaucer turns to the discourse of fairyland to explore gender relations in *The Wife of Bath's Tale*, for instance, it is not merely because fairies, as the Countess d'Aulnoy or Angela Carter might have said, are good to think with. It is because issues of female sovereignty are deeply rooted in this aspect of the little tradition: as Partonopeu de Blois says of his fairy mistress, "Cele est mes cuers, cele est ma vie; / Cele a de moi la segnorie" (or, as the English translation in Oxford, MS Rawlinson Poet. 14, puts it, "And as she lyste she may gyde me, / She hathe of me þe soueraynete").[45] For all that his clerical contemporaries would doubtless have found Chaucer's views on fairies unexceptionable, and despite the fact that he prefaces his Loathly Lady's actual transformation with a sermon steeped in the discourse of learned culture, Chaucer's *Wife of Bath's Tale* derives much of its real power from this traditional discourse and its long-standing resistance to the crooked-rib propaganda of the great tradition. Beneath its androcentric quest for what women really want, then, lies a much older ideological level where masculine violation of natural harmony is subject to the discipline and correction of a magical universe—a pattern that may be sensed in Walter Map's tale of Eadric the Wild, in the romance of *Thomas of Erceldoune*, and in the strange proto-grail romance *L'Élucidation*, where a rapist's abuse of fairy hospitality is what brings about the scourge of the Wasteland:

> Des puceles une esforcha,
> Sor son pois le despucela,
> . . . .
> Li roiaumes si agasti
> K'ains puis n'i ot arbre fuelli;
> Li pre et les flor[s] essecierent
> Et les aiges apeticierent. (lines 69–70, 95–98)

> [He forced one of the maidens and took her virginity against her will. . . . The realm was so wasted that its trees never again flourished, meadow and flowers withered, and waters dwindled.]⁴⁶

Whether or not we choose to read Chaucer's Loathly Lady as the metaphorical equivalent of this Wasteland (and the hideous transformation of the violated fairy queen in *Thomas of Erceldoune* might offer support for such a reading), the presence of two conflicting levels of signification in the tale seems undeniable.⁴⁷ As Alice of Bath implies, the expiation that Chaucer's knight must suffer for his rape is diametrically opposed to the ideological discipline of the lubricious "lymytours and othere hooly freres" who lurk "in every busshe or under every tree"—though by putting his fairy romance in the mouth of a provincial *vetula* worthy of William of Auvergne, Chaucer the poet might appear to be disclaiming responsibility for the implications of this aspect of his own creation.

In such a context it is important to recognize that Alice's amusing account of the friars' banishment of elves from the English countryside at the beginning of *The Wife of Bath's Tale* reflects a very real situation:

> In th'olde dayes of the Kyng Arthour,
> Of which that Britons speken greet honour,
> All was this land fulfild of fayerye.
> The elf-queene, with hir joly compaignye,
> Daunced ful ofte in many a grene mede.
> This was the olde opinion, as I rede;
> I speke of manye hundred yeres ago.
> But now kan no man se none elves mo,
> For now the grete charitee and prayeres
> Of lymytours and othere hooly freres,

> That serchen every lond and every streem,
> As thikke as motes in the sonne-beem,
> Blessynge halles, chambres, kichenes, boures,
> Citees, burghes, castels, hye toures,
> Thropes, bernes, shipnes, dayeryes,
> This maketh that ther been no fayeryes. (lines 863–78)[48]

Chaucer illustrates the typical mendicant understanding of fairy encounters when he has a summoner "under a forest syde" chance upon "a gay yeman" wearing "a courtepy of grene" in *The Friar's Tale* (lines 1380–82); we might expect this shape-shifting yeoman (lines 1462–72) to be a fairy, but as the friar explains, he is really a fiend who dwells in hell (lines 1447–48).[49] An anecdote in a mid-thirteenth-century Dominican exemplum collection has sometimes been cited to illustrate the mendicant war on fairy belief:[50] two friars, sent to preach in the Scottish Isles, find fairies ("spiritus incubi") abusing the young women there, but after being instructed in the faith, the women find themselves able to resist these demons ("quo facto, venerunt demones comminantes mulieribus et eis invadere more solito attemptantes, licet non poterant prevalere"), which are last heard of howling through the ether ("auditus est ululatus et eiulatus magnus in aere"). Medieval people would generally have understood the term 'incubi demons' to refer to fairies, at least down to the fifteenth century (as we shall see in the next chapter), but in fact wherever we encounter accounts of friars triumphing over *demones* who inhabit woods and groves or ride about in mounted bands, it is reasonable to suppose that we are witnessing a skirmish in their campaign against traditional fairy beliefs.

A story in the early fourteenth-century *Scala Coeli*, for instance, shows Dominicans wrestling with a different aspect of fairy possession: two friars, lost in the mountains of Ireland, encounter a small man, who, they discover, had been in the service of demons for thirty years and who bore their mark on his hands; these demons visit him in various forms, and he is forced to do whatever they command ("triginta annis demonibus hic servivi, homagium eis feci, et sigillum in meis manibus porto, visitant mei in diversis figuris, et quicquid precipiunt facio semper"); as soon as he has been confessed by the friars, however, the mark disappears, and he can be left alone in a grove to survive unscathed an encounter with a mounted fairy host ("cum magnis equitaturis . . . venisset demon").[51] Even more interesting is the Franciscan Thomas O'Quinn's account of a plague in mid-thirteenth-century Clonfert, Ireland:[52] carters and men working the fields or walking in the woods, he says, were accustomed to seeing armies of demons passing by and sometimes fighting among themselves ("videre solebant . . . exercitus demoniorum transeuncium et alioquociens inter se compugnancium"), a sight that caused many of them to fall sick and die. This seems to be a rare expression of a popular belief, reflected in Titania's speech at the beginning of *A Midsummer Night's Dream*, that human misfortunes may be caused by disruptions in the fairy world: "And this same progeny of evils comes / From our debate, from our dissension" (2. i). Similar fairy hosts are encountered elsewhere: William of Auvergne devotes part of a chapter to the topic;[53] Gerald of Wales's *Expugnatio Hibernica* describes "Speris and sparris rutlynge to-giddyr, wyth cryynge so grymly, that none ende was Of elf fare";[54] and John Capgrave reports that in 1402 in Bedford and Biggleswade there "appered certeyn men of dyuers colouris, renninge oute of wodes and fytyng horibily. This was seyne on morownyngis and at mydday, and whan men folowid to loke what it was, thei coude se rite nawt."[55] However, I know of none that is claimed to have the same direct human repercussions. In this case O'Quinn's remedy is to preach a sermon in which he construes the plague as God's punishment for the villagers' imperfect Christian faith and challenges the demons to come out and take him on ("Veniant, inquit, demones si audent, et omnes veniant! Quare non veniunt? Quid faciunt? Ubi sunt?"). Their inevitable failure to appear wins the friars yet another victory in their ongoing campaign against the fairy world: "Et ecce ab illa hora evanuerunt demones, ita quod nunquam postea in terra illa apparuerunt" [and, lo, from that moment the demons vanished, so that never again did they appear in that region].[56]

Unsurprisingly, in the eyes of the mendicants the church's main weapon against the fairies was preaching, but there can be no doubt that routine work proceeded less dramatically at a parochial level. The pastoral manuals that proliferated throughout Europe after the Fourth Lateran Council generally include such popular superstitions as witchcraft, sorcery, nigromancy, and *sortilegium* in their treatment of the First Commandment, and though explicit fairy beliefs are only occasionally listed in such a context, it is clear that "Thou shalt have no other gods before me" provided the justification for the church's routine offensive against them.[57] Jean d'Outremeuse, in his fanciful *Myreur des histors* (written toward the end of the fourteenth century), describes the fairy castle of Plaisant, built by Morgan, and concludes, "Asseis regnoit, jusqu'à tant que li pape defendit, sour paine de excommunication, que nuls n'estudiast [ni]gremanche; fut faite et chantee adont I ympne à complie pour gardeir des fantasiez, c'on appelle *Te lucis ante terminum*, car les feez regnoient adont mult publement" [she ruled for a long time, until the pope forbade, on pain of excommunication, anyone to study nigromancy; at that time the hymn called *Te lucis ante terminum* was written and sung at Compline to guard us against phantoms, for at that time fairies ruled quite openly].[58] To judge from John the Carpenter's attempt to *crouch* Nicholas "from elves and fro wightes" in Chaucer's *Miller's Tale*, this well-known Latin hymn, or at least its substance, had been thoroughly assimilated into popular culture by the end of the fourteenth century:

> Therwith the nyght-spel seyde he anon-rightes
> On foure halves of the hous aboute,
> And on the thresshfold of the dore withoute:
> "Jhesu Crist and Seinte Benedight,
> Blesse this hous from every wikked wight,
> For nyghtes verye, the white *pater-noster*!" (lines 3480–85)[59]

Whatever precisely *nyghtes verye* means, the phrase is evidently, pace Donaldson,[60] a homespun counterpart to the great Latin hymn's *noctium phantasmata*.

Once again Joan of Arc's nullification proceedings offer us a glimpse of the work of this Kulturkampf at ground level. Jean Morel, a laborer, recalls hearing that women and fairies ("persone fatales, que vocabantur *fées*") used to dance beneath the tree in the old days but says that after St. John's Gospel was read aloud they do not go there anymore ("postquam evangelium beati Johannis legitur et dicitur, amplius not vadunt").[61] Beatrice Estellin, a laborer's widow, says that she well remembers the time (on the eve of the Ascension) when the priest carried crosses through the fields, went beneath the tree, and read the Gospel (pp. 258–59). This lesson was not lost on another laborer, Simonin Musnier: he has heard that fairies used to go there in the old days, he says, not that he himself has ever seen any sign of any 'evil spirits' ("quamvis nunquam vidit aliqua signa de aliquibus malignis spiritibus") (p. 281). Interestingly, the local priest, Jean Colin, is the only inhabitant of Domrémy and the nearby village of Greux who claims to know nothing whatsoever about any Fairy Tree ("dixit se nichil scire").[62]

No doubt the church found the obduracy of peasant belief frustrating, but the extent to which aristocratic romance was pervaded by the marvelous in the later Middle Ages must have provided the great tradition with a rather different kind of challenge. In the next chapter we will be exploring in greater detail its systematic demonization of fairy beliefs, but for now I wish to examine the way the romances themselves reflect this hostile campaign and express their resistance to it. I do not mean to suggest, of course, that all demons in the Middle Ages should be reread from the viewpoint of vernacular culture as fairies (though such a transposition can account for a surprisingly large corner of the field of medieval demonology),[63] but we should notice that wherever there was an obvious semantic overlap it generated a fascinating kind of cultural schizophrenia in the romances.

Consider descriptions of the physical appearance of these creatures, for instance. Imagined as demons (so long as they are not out to deceive us with specious beauty), they naturally appear hideous. Caesarius of Heisterbach tells us of a knight who did not believe in demons ("daemones esse dubitaret") until shown one by a nigromancer: "Finally, he observed in a nearby grove, a foul human form, like a shadow, towering over the top of the trees.... He was like a huge man, the hugest and blackest imaginable, dressed in a smoky garment, and so misshapen that the knight couldn't bear to look at him" [Novissime vero contemplabatur in nemore vicino quasi umbram humanum tetram, summitatem arborum excedentem.... Erat autem quasi magnus vir, imo maximus et nigerrimus, vesteque subnigra indutus, et tantae deformitatis, ut in eum miles respicere non posset].[64] By contrast, when the little tradition reports encounters with fairies, they are invariably beautiful. Here is how Sir Launfal's fairy mistress Triamour is described, for instance:

> Sche was as whyt as lylye yn May,
> Or snow that sneweþ yn wynterys day—
>   He seygh neuer non so pert.
> Þe rede rose, whan sche ys newe,
> Aȝens her rode nes nauȝt of hewe,
>   J dar well say, yn sert.
> Her here schon as gold wyre;
> May no man rede here atyre,
>   Ne nauȝt wel þenke yn hert. (lines 289–300)[65]

In the same spirit, Aucassin searching for Nicolette in the forest hears of her from some shepherds: "une pucele vint ci, li plus bele riens du monde, si que nos quidames que ce fust une fee, et que tot cis bos en enclarci" [a maid was here, the most beautiful thing in the world, so that we thought she was a fairy, and she illuminated the whole wood].[66] When the emperor of Rome encounters the foundling William of Palerne in the woods, his first thought is that he must be from fairyland because he is so handsome: "þemperour wend witerly, for wonder of þat child, / þat fei3þely it were of feyrye for fairenes þat it welt."⁶⁷ The beauty of fairies seems to have been proverbial: in the Anglo-Norman *Lai du Cor*, for instance, Caradoc's wife is described as "resembling a fairy" because of her beauty;⁶⁸ *The Wars of Alexander* describes Candace as being "so faire & so fresche as . . . an elfe oute of an-othire erde";⁶⁹ and even John Gower describes his lady as possessing "la bealté plus qe faie."⁷⁰ Interestingly, when Guillaume de Lorris describes Venus as being so elegant that she resembled a fairy, the Chaucerian translation alters this to

> Bi hir atyr so bright and shen
> Men myght perceyve . . .
> She was not of religioun [that is, she was no nun!].⁷¹

Of course fairies are shape-shifters by nature (Yonec's father in Marie de France's *lai* turns himself into a hawk in order to visit his human lover),⁷² so it was a simple matter for the great tradition to represent their beauty as mere outward show. Not that we should necessarily assume that whenever a fairy in romance takes on a frightening new form (Melusine's transformation into a dragon, for instance, or the dramatic moment when Thomas of Erceldoune's fairy mistress "fadyde þus in þe face, / Þat schane by fore als þe sonne so bryght")⁷³ there has necessarily been interference from the great tradition. Gerald of Wales tells of a man called Meilerius whose experience is reminiscent of Thomas's; after he had sexually assaulted a fairy, "in place of a beautiful girl, he found a vile, rough, hairy, and grotesquely deformed shape" [loco puellae formosae, formam quandam villosam, hispidam, et hirsutam, adeoque enormiter deformem invenit].⁷⁴ Fairies may be beautiful, but they can also be dangerous, particularly when their prohibitions are ignored or (as is the case with both Thomas and Meilerius) when their persons are violated, so the little tradition was quite capable of imagining such violent metamorphoses without any outside help.⁷⁵ Be that as it may, the fact remains that despite the insistence of the great tradition that fairies were in reality hideous demons, the little tradition stubbornly maintained the default position that they were creatures of surpassing beauty.⁷⁶

While many other elements in the popular conception of fairy nature (such as youthfulness, courtliness, and conspicuous wealth) must have galled representatives of the great tradition, four things caused them particular difficulties: the overt sexuality of fairies; their fecundity; their mortality; and their prescience. None of these qualities is easy to reconcile with the notion that fairies were really demons, and as a result medieval demonologists spilled a great deal of ink trying to find ways to rationalize them.

Fairies are evidently highly sexed, and their relations with humans are often frankly voluptuous. The English translator of *Partonope of Blois*, for example, lingers sensuously over his hero's first physical encounter with his fairy mistress.[77] It takes him four hundred lines to get Melior from the bedroom door to the moment of her final surrender, and the description of the climax (which, despite the fact that the whole encounter has been stage managed by Melior herself, comes uncomfortably close to rape) is as graphic as anything in the fabliau:

> Hys arme ffreshely he ouer her caste,
> And she hyt suffered pasyentlye.
> Than sayde sho to hym full mekely:
> "For þe loue of Gode, I praye yowe lette be."
> And wyth þat worde a-none ganne he
> In hys armes her faste to hym brase.
> And fulle softely þen sho sayde: "Allas!"
> And her legges sho gan to knytte,
> And wyth hys knees he gan hem on-shote.
> And þer-wyth-all she sayde: "Syr, mercy!"
> He wolde not lefe ne be þer-by;
> For of her wordes toke he no hede;
> But þys a-way her maydenhede
> Haþe he þen rafte, and geffe her hys. (lines 1558–71)[78]

This particular scene evidently expresses a brand of male wish-fulfillment, but there are others in which masculine fairy lovers are embraced by human women with equal ardor:

> La dame l'a molt esgardé,
> e son semblant e sa biauté,
> angoisseusement l'aama
>
> [The lady gazed at him intently, at his bearing and his beauty, and she loved him cruelly].[79]

The author of the non-cyclic prose *Lancelot*, though keen to rationalize fairies as demons, apparently has no difficulty imagining them as hot and lustful ("il sont chaut et luxurieus"),[80] but clerics such as William of Auvergne are more circumspect. William is happy to explain the corporeal presence of demon lovers, and even their mechanical ability to simulate sexual organs, but such evident self-serving sensuality in creatures who have been consigned to eternal torment is clearly a different matter. William feels it incumbent upon him to insist "that undoubtedly they do those things which they do with men and women not from a love of copulating nor from a desire for that kind of pleasure, but rather they pollute them and seduce them to the foulness of lechery out of a zeal for malice" [indubitanter, quia non amore concubitus, neque desiderio voluptatis huiusmodi faciunt quae faciunt viris et muleribus, sed potius studio malignitatis polluunt eos et eas et ad spurcitiam inducunt luxuriae].[81]

The fecundity of fairies and their ability to interbreed with human beings (a feature that will be explored more fully in the next chapter) is another commonplace of the little tradition that worried the clerics. As the *South English Legendary* puts it:

>Þe ssrewen wolleþ ek oþerwile mankunne to bitraie
>Aliȝte adoun in monnes forme biniȝte & bidaie
>And liggeþ ofte bi wymmen as hi were of fleiss & blode
>Ac þe engendrure þat hi makeþ ne comþ neuere to gode
>   (lines 239–42)[82]

>[The devils wish to betray mankind at other times and light down in man's shape by night and by day and often lie with women as if they were made of flesh and blood, but the offspring that they beget never come to good].

Walter Map too tells us that the products of unions between humans and fairies are rarely successful but records one notable exception: a man called Alnoth, who lived an exemplary life and survived to an advanced age.[83] Melusine is said to have borne her husband Raymondin ten sons, and though the sixth, Geoffrey of the Big Tooth, was notably cruel, and the tenth, Horrible, was as unprepossessing as his name, the rest, despite minor physical blemishes, seem to have turned out well enough; indeed one, Fromond, became a monk. Fairy parentage is common enough in romance (*Yonec*, for instance, has a fairy father and *Le bel inconnu*, a fairy mother), while in *Tydorel* the hero's ability to go without sleep is specifically said to be a mark of his fairy paternity.⁸⁴ The existence of Middle English surnames such as Elfeg, Fayrey, and Wudewuse implies that this belief was not restricted to the pages of romance, however, and one remarkable document, a deposition in the trial of Bishop Guichard of Troyes in 1308, confirms this; among other things it was claimed that Guichard was the son of a fairy (a *neton*), because his mother was famous for her beautiful tresses and fairies were known to consort with women with fine hair ("quod netoni libenter frequentare consueverunt cum mulieribus que habent pulcras trecias capillorum").⁸⁵ This is all the more remarkable because by the fourteenth century the church (as we shall see in the next chapter) had already fully confronted the obvious difficulty of attributing generative powers to demons; Thomas Aquinas, for one, saved appearances by articulating the ingenious theory that devils are able to make use of collected human semen for the purposes of demonic artificial insemination, a theory that was to undergo bizarre refinements in the early modern period.⁸⁶ That Guichard's accusers were able to ignore this theological caveat suggests the power of its popular appeal, though of course even a Thomist construction would still have made the poor bishop illegitimate and therefore in theory unfit for holy office.

Devils, of course, cannot die, so another difficulty faced by those who wished to demonize fairies was the fact that although popular tradition certainly regarded them as long lived, it did not regard them as immortal.⁸⁷ Martianus Capella calls pans, fauns, satyrs, silvans, and nymphs the '*longaevi*' and reports that after long ages they die just like men ("hi omnes post prolixum aeuum moriuntur ut homines"); and Bernardus Silvestris writes of such creatures that "sero tamen obeunt in tempore dissolvendi" [at length they pass away when the time comes for their dissolution].⁸⁸ Matthew Paris reports that in 1249 a Welsh *incuba* died giving birth to a son,⁸⁹ and romance presents us with a number of mortal fairies. Thus the father of Yonec in Marie de France's *lai* dies at the hands of a jealous husband, and in an early version of the *Naissance du Chevalier au Cygne*, the hero's mother, the *fée* Elioxe, dies in childbed: "Morte est bele Elioxe, l'espris s'en est alés" (line 1272).⁹⁰ In *Huon of Bordeaux*, Oberon (to English ears, the archetypal fairy king) foretells his own death: "'Huon,' quod Oberon, 'know for trouth I shal not abyde longe in this worlde, for so is the pleasure of god. it behoueth me to go in to paradyce, wher as my place is apparelled; in yᵉ fayrye I shal byde no lenger."⁹¹ The contrary position is taken by William of Auvergne, who disputes a report "that in the time of the Emperor Anastasius a certain faun was killed by arrows in a certain battle, since he might not be conquered otherwise" [quia tempore Anastasii Imperatoris faunus quidam in proelio quodam interfectus fuit sagittis, cum aliter non possit vinci]; this creature cannot really have been a faun, says William, since all spirits of this kind are indubitably immortal ("cum omnes huiusmodi spiritus indubitanter immortales sint"). Interestingly, one of his alternative explanations is that the faun might have been "one of those warriors who are commonly said to be 'fairied'" [unus ex militibus qui vulgo fatati dicuntur],[92] though what precisely he means by this is unclear.[93] In a later discussion he argues that any fairy who appears to engage in human activities such as warfare, jousting, or feasting can only be a demonic illusion since immortal spirits cannot be harmed by weapons and have no need of food.[94] In the same vein, John Trevisa uses Merlin's mortality as proof that he could not have had a fairy (demonic) father:

> There myȝte childe non suche deye.
> Clergie makeþ mynde
> Deeþ sleeþ nouȝt fendes kynde;
> But deth slowe Merlyn,
> Merlyn was ergo no gobelyn.[95]

Oberon (like Merlin and indeed Melusine), a fairy half caste, is particularly interesting from this viewpoint, for the English translation of *Huon of Bordeaux*, based on a fifteenth-century prose version, feels compelled to have him explain that his mortality derives from his human father (Julius Caesar) even though other fairies (his own mother for example) are immortal: "ye knowe that euery mortall thynge cannot always endure / I speke it for my owne selfe who am sone to a mortall man, and was engendered on the ladye of the preuye Ile who can neuer dye, bycause she is one of the fairy engendered of a man of the fayrey and doughter to a woman of the fayrey."[96] There is nothing of this in the thirteenth-century verse original, however,[97] and though Harf-Lancner takes such romance references to fairy immortality at face value,[98] I suspect they are really concessions to the theological objections of men such as William of Auvergne.

A final popular attribute of fairies that caused difficulties for theologians was their association with arcane knowledge, particularly the knowledge of future events. The little tradition seems often to have associated exceptional psychic powers with fairies and those who consorted with them: the non-cyclic prose *Lancelot* explains that Niniene was said to be a fairy because "in those days anyone who knew about magic and charms was called a fairy" [a celui tens estoient apelees fees totes iceles qui savioent d'anchantement et de chaies].[99] We have seen that Du Guesclin's wife was rumored to be a fairy because of her cleverness, and even John of Salisbury reports that some people thought that Aristotle was the son of an incubus demon because of "the clarity of his mind."[100] From here it is only a short step to associating fairies with prescience.

Merlin, the most celebrated of medieval seers, was the son of a fairy/incubus, and Geoffrey of Monmouth's attribution of prophetic powers to him was a particular source of irritation for William of Newburgh: "They [demonic incubi] are often deceived and deceive by their guesses, though they are quite sophisticated, but by means of trickery in their predictions they lay claim amongst naive people to a foreknowledge of the future which they do not at all possess."[101] Merlin's Scottish counterpart, Thomas of Erceldoune, acquired the gift of prophesy on his return from a visit to fairyland: "Thomas, þou sall neuer lesynges lye, / Whare euer þou fare by frythe or felle."[102] It is sometimes forgotten that the narrative portion of *Thomas of Erceldoune* (the visit to fairyland) is merely a prologue to an extended set of actual prophesies. Similarly, the account of a strange fairy encounter ("ay litel man y mette withalle") that is appended to an early fourteenth-century manuscript of Langtoft's *Chronicle* serves to introduce a rival set of political prophesies.[103] We have seen that when the French courtier Antoine de la Sale visited the reputed cave of the prophetic Sybil in the Italian province of Marche in 1420, he naturally conceived of it in terms of a visit to fairyland.[104] A fifteenth-century recension of the *Second Lucidaire* (itself an early fourteenth-century version of the popular theological handbook the *Elucidarium*) proves that the association between fairies and fortune-telling was commonplace:

> Þe sayd feyryes sayd þat þe people were destenyed þe one vnto good þat other to yll after þe course of heuen and of nature, as a chylde borne in suche an houre & at suche a course he was destenyed to be hanged or drowned, or þat he sholde be ryche or poore, or þat he sholde wedde suche a woman, þe whiche thynges ben false. For the man hath in hymselfe lyberall arbytre and fre wyll to do good or ylle in suche wyse þat yf he wyll, he shall do nothynge wherfore he sholde be hanged, ne yet put hym in þe daunger to be drowned; nor also he shall not marye a woman, but yf he wyll, and so [hir] destynacyons shall be false. By these reasons a man sholde put to no fayth.[105]

One might have thought that such official condemnation would have been universal, but in an age that took astrology particularly seriously, an appetite for prophesy must have been difficult to stamp out, and even a pious churchman like John of Bridlington might be credited with prophetic powers.[106] If we add to this the fact that no less an authority than Augustine allowed that demons might enjoy a certain limited degree of foresight,[107] we may come to understand how even William of Auvergne could attribute prescience to "someone from Great Britain [evidently Merlin] who was reputed to be the son of an incubus demon" [qui in majori Britannia filius dæmonis incubi fuisse dicitur]: "Now this man was held to be a seer in that land, in that he seemed to have prophetically foretold many future things; not without merit might it be believed that he received this from his upbringing or paternal instruction, for it is certain that demons know many things about the future and other hidden matters, and sometimes reveal them to others, especially their sons" [autem propheta in eadem regione habitus est, eo quod multa de futuris vaticinatus fuisse visus est prophetice; ex instructione, vel doctrina paterna hoc accepisse non immerito credi potest, multa enim de futuris, et aliis absconditis, certum est nosse dæmones, et interdum aliis, nedum filiis, revelare].[108]

Such points of tension between the clerical and the popular views of fairies had some important consequences for the way fairies came to be portrayed in romance. A few authors take the bull by the horns and assert unflinchingly that the fairy realm is fully compatible with Christianity. For instance, in a description of the death of Oberon (based on an early continuation of *Huon of Bordeaux*) we might almost imagine that we are reading the apotheosis of a Christian martyr rather than the last moments of a fairy king: "king Oberon drewe faste to his laste end, who lay in a ryche cowche in the myddes of his palayes makyng his prayers to our lorde Iesu cryste, and holdynge Huon by the hande, and at laste sayde, 'my dere frende Huon, pray for me' / & then he made the synge of ye cros recommendyng his sowle to god, the which incontynent was borne in to paradyce by a greate multytude of angelles sent fro our lord Iesu cryst, who at ther depertynge made such shynynge and clerenes in ye palays that ther was neuer none suche sene before / and there with there was so swete a smell that euery man thought they had bene rauysshed in to paradyse, wherby they knewe suerly that kynge Oberons sowle was saued."[109] Though Melusine's spirit, by contrast, must suffer "greuouse and obscure penytence" until Doomsday, this is due less to her fairy nature than to her husband's bad faith; had he not broken his word, she suggests, she too might have made a good end: "[I] shuld haue had al my ryghtes, & hadd lyued the cours natural as another woman; & shuld haue be buryed, aftir my lyf naturel expired, within the chirche of our lady of Lusynen, where myn obsequye & afterward my annyuersary shuld haue be honourably & deuoutely don."[110]

Jean d'Arras had a powerful patron and evidently felt comfortable discussing fairy phenomena quite openly, but some writers and copiers of popular romances display rather more circumspection. I recall once teaching *Sir Degarré* and remarking on the hero's fairy paternity, only to have my students complain that there was nothing in the text to support this. The source of our disagreement became clear as soon as I realized that I had been citing the poem from an edition based on the early fourteenth-century Auchinleck Manuscript (Advocates Library of Scotland, MS 19.2.1),[111] while the text the students had been reading was based on the much later Bodley, MS Rawlinson Poet. 34.[112] When Degarré's father encounters his mother-to-be deep in the woods, his first speech to her, according to the Auchinleck Manuscript, is,

> Damaisele, welcome mote þou be!
> Be þou afered of none wih3te;
> Iich am comen here a fairi kny3te.
> Mi kynde is armes for to were,
> On horse to ride wiþ scheld and spere;
> Forþi afered be þou nowt[.] (lines 98–103)

However, the same passage in the Rawlinson manuscript reads,

> Madame, God the see;
> Be noughtt adrad, thou swete wyght,
> Y am come to the as a knyght;
> My kynd ys armys for to bere,
> On horss to ryde wyth scheld and spere,
> Be dradd of me ryght noughtt[.] (lines 88–93)

A similar suppression occurs in another fifteen-century manuscript of the poem (Cambridge University, MS Ff. II. 38).[113] There can be little doubt that the Rawlinson scribe (or an intermediate scribe in the textual tradition) has deliberately bowdlerized this passage: not only is the reference to fairyland suppressed, but in addition the knight now greets the lady in God's name. Lest we should be tempted to ascribe this to a simple scribal slip, a few lines later, when the lady abandons her newborn child, she furnishes him with a suitable identification token; in the Auchinleck MS it is "a paire of gloues / Þat here lemman here sent of fairi londe" (lines 191–92),[114] but in Rawlinson this becomes simply "a peyr of glovys / Hur lemman to hur for to sonde" (lines 178–79).

Degarré belongs to a group of romances that employ the 'fair unknown' motif.[115] That the hero's noble pedigree should be obscured by his fairy parentage—either a father (as in *Degarré*) or a mother (as in *Le Bel Inconnu*)—conforms closely to Jameson's hypothesis about the role of magic in romance, since this meme (to use Cooper's term) functions primarily to reinforce class solidarity (despite his obscure upbringing, and sometimes deliberate countermeasures on the part of his mother, the hero always adapts 'naturally' to the demands of the chivalric life). Pressure from the great tradition meant that such connections were always liable to be suppressed. *Lybeaus Desconus*,[116] the English adaptation of Renaut de Beaujeu's early thirteenth-century *Le Bel Inconnu*, offers a particularly good example. In the French original the hero, Guinglain, the product of a liaison between Gawain and the fairy Blancemal (line 3237), is torn between his attraction for two women: a fairy seductress, the Pucele as Blances Mains; and a human queen (whom Guinglain rescues from enchantment), the Blonde Esmeree.[117] In this battle between the competing sides of his nature, Li Biaus Descouneüs finally submits to the dynastic imperative and, with Arthur's encouragement, marries Esmeree. In contrast, the fifteenth-century Middle English adaptation of this romance removes all the fairy allusions: there is no hint that the mother who begets Gyngelayne "vnder a forest syde" is anything other than Gawain's human mistress.[118] Similarly, the Pucele as Blances Mains (here called the Dame d'Amour) offers Gyngelayne nothing more than a brief distraction on his quest to rescue the Blonde Esmeree (here called the Lady of Synadowne); the only suggestion that she has any otherworldly associations is the remark that she

> Cowthe more of sorcerye
> Than other suche fyve;
> . . . .
> Whan he sawe hir face
> Hym thought that he was
> Jn paradice on lyve;
> With false lies and fayre
> Th[u]s she blered his eye:
> Evill mote she thryue![119]

The accusation of sorcery (as we shall see later with *Partonope of Blois*) was a way of rationalizing and repressing fairy discourse, and that this passage has undergone bowdlerization is suggested by the fact that the line "With false lies and fayre" appears in another manuscript (B.L., MS Cotton Caligula A. II) as "Wyth fantasme and feyrye."[120]

The disenchantment of the fairy world we encounter in *Lybeaus Desconus* may be seen as part of a larger pattern,[121] for while the deliberate suppression of fairy elements is not often exposed to view as clearly as in the Rawlinson manuscript of *Degarré*,[122] a similar process may be suspected in several romances that lack a definite source. The couplet version of *Generides* offers an especially clear example.[123] In the opening scene King Aufreus, following a mysterious hart while out hunting, is led to a palace deep in the woods, where he meets a beautiful lady. In early romances women encountered in such mysterious silvan settings (Melusine, for example) are often explicitly identified as fairies, and here the fairy atmosphere is enhanced by the absence of a visible household in the palace (as happens in *Guingamor, Tydorel, Partonopeu of Blois*, and others):[124] the lady is accompanied by only a single maid and an old man, "and elles he saw no moo meigney" (214). Even more telling is the pillow Aufreus finds when he is led to a bedchamber:

> In noo lond marchaunt ther nys
> That devise it couth I-wis.
> An hundreth sith in day and night
> Chaunge it wil his colour bright;
> Oft it was white, and oft grene.
> Oft reid, and oft blew, I wene,
> To all coloures it would chaunge;
> That was to the king ful straun[ge]. (lines 292–99)

The general association of rich cloth with fairy work was a romance commonplace,[125] but this particular type of chromatic instability was specifically associated with fairies. When the narrator encounters the protean figure of "Prevy Thought" in the late fifteenth-century allegory *The Court of Love*, he is immediately reminded of fairyland:

> "Yon is," thought [I], "som spirit or som elf,
> His sotill image is so curious:
> How is," quod I "that he is shaded thus
> With yonder cloth, I not of what colour?" (lines 1270–73)[126]

Petitcriu, the dog from Elfland that Tristram sends as a present to Ysolt, is similarly elusively polychrome: no one "could relate or record its shape or appearance, for however one looked at the dog it displayed so many colors that no one could discern or fix them."[127] In Malory the ring that Lyones lends to Sir Gareth for the tournament at the Castel Peryllous magically endows him with a similar quality: "at one tyme he semed grene, and another tyme at his gayne-commyng hym semed blewe. And thus at every course that he rode too and fro he chonged whyght to rede and blak, that there myght neyther kynge nother knyghte have no redy cognysshauns of hym."[128] Predictably, King Aufreus is joined in the bed by the lady of the castle, who with fairy prescience predicts that the issue of their union will be the great knight Generides. Everything in this opening scene, in other words, suggests that we are dealing with a fairy encounter, yet pointedly the words 'fairy' and 'elf' are never used.

The fashion, associated in English scholarship particularly with Roger Sherman Loomis, for uncovering hidden Celtic motifs in medieval romance has long passed,[129] and while I have no desire to resurrect it here, the fact remains that earlier scholars often made a plausible case for suppressed fairy elements, not only in fair-unknown romances (the English *Sir Percyvell of Gales*, for example)[130] but also in the world of medieval romance in general. When Lancelot in the *Chevalier de la charete* crosses the sword bridge into Melegeance's kingdom of Gorre, is he not really passing into a fairy realm, and when Yvain marries Laudine, the Lady of the Fountain, in the *Chevalier au lion*, is he not marrying into a fairy lineage? Admittedly such readings are unprovable, particularly with a writer whose "uneasiness with folkloric beings" is as patent as Chrétien's,[131] but the campaign of cultural repression I have been trying to sketch offers at the very least a plausible context for them. Similarly, one need not accept Jessie Weston's far-fetched theories of displaced pre-Christian rituals in order to recognize that medieval grail romances sometimes reveal clear evidence of a substratum of fairy lore: the black knights with flaming lances who appear in the *Perlesvaus*, for instance,[132] look very like the *arzei* (feu-follets?) described by Étienne de Bourbon;[133] and at least one text, the enigmatic *Elucidation*, attributes the scourge of the Wasteland to human violation of fairy hospitality.[134]

Suppression is only one of the ways in which medieval writers display their "uneasiness with folkloric beings." Another is displacement, both temporal and geographical. Keith Thomas, discussing the views of early modern writers such as Reginald Scot, Sir William Temple, and John Aubrey, remarks that "it seems that commentators have always attributed [fairies] to the past," a move he traces back as far as the opening lines of *The Wife of Bath's Tale*.[135] The villagers of Domrémy used just such a tactic for deflecting the curiosity of inquisitors away from issues of current belief, and at an early date it had clearly hardened into a widely deployed defense mechanism. Similarly, the way its magical domain is always displaced to a distant past appears symptomatic of the pressure exerted on popular romance by clerical disapproval: "In Bretayne bi hold time / Þis layes were wrouȝt so seiþ þis rime."[136] Thus fairy romances generally employ a once-upon-a-time (*jadis*) setting that helps insulate them from contemporary censure: "En Bretaigne ot .I. roi jadis" (*Guingamor*, line 5); "Un vavasur i out jadis" (*Désiré*, line 13); "Jadis au tens qu'Artur regna" (*Tyolet*, line 1).[137] The far-off time of King Arthur, of course, serves this purpose particularly well, but in *Sir Orfeo* the classical world provides a similarly safe haven for fairy encounters (a tactic parodied by Chaucer at the end of *The Merchant's Tale*). In much the same vein, Oberon in the *Huon of Bordeaux* cycle is said to be the son of Julius Caesar, though he lives long enough to encounter both Arthur and Charlemagne. So too fairies are often displaced in space as well as time: Huon of Bordeaux first encounters Oberon in Arabia; Melior, the fairy mistress of *Partonopeu de Blois*, comes from Byzantium and abducts her lover while he is hunting in Ardern (the Ardennes); and the Ardennes is the site of another fairy abduction in *Reinbrun*, a continuation of *Guy of Warwick*. Interestingly, other genres do not exhibit a similar tendency to displacement: the fabliau *Le Chevalier qui fist parler les cons* and Adam de la Halle's farce *Jeu de la feuillée*, both of which employ fairy agency, show no such aversion to a contemporary setting or a recognizable location. No doubt humor, as in the case of Chaucer's *Sir Thopas*, served to defuse difficult questions of orthodoxy and belief.

A final way in which romance writers might respond to clerical disapproval was to collude with it. The most dramatic example is to be found in the works of Robert de Boron, but since Merlin's fairy/demon paternity is discussed at length in the next chapter, I illustrate this point here by reference to *Sir Gowther*.[138] In the Breton lai of *Tydorel* a queen of Brittany, after ten years of childless marriage, is seduced by a handsome knight who lives in secret deep in the forest. It is made quite clear that this knight is a fairy, and their child, Tydorel, betrays his fairy paternity by his inability to sleep at night.[139] (Interestingly, the non-cyclic prose *Lancelot* applies this characteristic to devils: "car deiables ne puet dormir.")[140] The popular romance of *Robert the Devil*, found throughout Europe and appearing in England as *Sir Gowther*, is clearly a sanitized retelling, if not of this specific romance, then of one very like it.

Gowther, described at one point as "eyvon Marlyon halfe brodur" (line 95), is fathered by the devil upon a childless Duchess of Austria (interestingly, like Uther Pendragon, he assumes the appearance of her husband to accomplish this), but where Tydorel's father is described as "the most handsome man in the world" [*li plus biaus hon du mont*] (line 43), Gowther's soon reveals his true colors: "When he had is wylle all don, / A feltured fende he start up son" (lines 70–71). The offspring of these two unions lead very different lives. Tydorel grows up to be an ideal king of Brittany:

> De Tydorel firent seignor.
> Onques n'orent eü meillor,
> tant preu, tant cortois, tant vaillant,
> tant large, ne tant despendant,
> ne miex tenist em pes la terre
> nus ne li osa fere guerre.
> De puceles ert molt amez
> e de dames molt desirrez,
> li sien l'amoient et servoient,
> e li estrangé le cremoient. (lines 221–30)

[They made Tydorel their lord. They had never had a better, nor one so gallant, courteous, brave, generous, and open-handed, nor one who better kept the peace of the land so that no one dared make war upon him. Much loved by maidens and desired by ladies, his people loved and served him, and outsiders feared him.]

Gowther, in contrast, when he becomes Duke of Austria, immediately institutes a reign of terror; in addition to indiscriminate rape and murder, he takes particular pleasure in pushing friars off cliffs and setting fire to hermits:

> All that ever on Cryst con lefe,
> Yong and old, he con hem greve
> In all that he myght doo.
> Meydyns' maryage wolde he spyll
> And take wyffus ageyn hor wyll,
> And sley hor husbandus too.
> And make frerus to leype at kraggus
> And persons forto heng on knaggus,

And odur presys sloo.
To bren armettys was is dyssyre:
A powre wedow to seyt on fyre,
And werke hom mykyll woo. (lines 190–201)

Both Tydorel and Gowther confront their mothers with the question of their paternity. When Tydorel learns who his father is, he sets off to join him in the forest. After Gowther discovers that he is the son of a fiend, he sets off for Rome to confess his sins to the pope. Only after a lengthy period of penance can Gowther return to his homeland, where he rules wisely and where after his death he receives a Christian burial.

Few fairy romances provide such a thoroughgoing illustration of cultural compromise formation as *Sir Gowther* (though, as we shall see, the French *Robert le diable* has been even more thoroughly sanitized), but it is not uncommon to encounter specific details that betray the author's desire to demonstrate his orthodoxy. At times this is clearly a perfectly conscious strategy, but at others it looks more like the involuntary deference of the little tradition to hegemonic clerical models. Thus vernacular culture has no problem imagining Christian fairies: Partonope is reassured to hear his invisible lady, whose bed he happens to be sharing at the time, swear by the Virgin Mary, and in much the same vein, Oberon presents Huon of Bordeaux with a magic cup whose powers are activated by making the sign of the cross over it.[141] Yonec's father in Marie de France's *lai*, despite living in an underground kingdom and being able to turn himself at will into a hawk, feels the need to protest to his lady that he is a true Christian, and *Désiré*'s fairy mistress is similarly insistent on her own religious orthodoxy; indeed both are prepared to display the soundness of their faith by receiving mass.[142] By contrast, in Walter Map's account of *Henno cum dentibus* (an analogue to the *Melusine* story) we encounter a fairy bride who whenever she attends church always finds an excuse to leave before the consecration of the host.[143] Similarly, when Richard I's bride in the romance of *Richard the Lionheart* faints at the elevation of the host in their nuptial mass,[144] we are immediately ready to suspect her fairy origins, and our suspicions are confirmed when fifteen years later "an erl off gret pouste" who has noticed her avoiding the mass tries to force her to remain, with alarming consequences:

Sche took here douȝtyr in here hond,
And Johan her sone she wolde not wonde;

> Out of the rofe she gan her dyght,
> Openly before all theyr syght.
> Johan fell frome her in that stounde,
> And brak his thygh on the grounde.
> And with her doughter she fled her waye,
> That never after she was isey. (lines 227–34)

If the Plantagenets had once had a foundation myth similar to that of the Lusignans, their fairy ancestor has been worked over far more thoroughly than Melusine;[145] the author of this dramatic scene, at least, displays open collusion with the assumptions of the great tradition.

I have suggested a number of ways in which the great tradition's *Kulturkampf* against fairy beliefs are reflected in vernacular romance, but the question of belief goes deeper than this. Most literary critics will share Helen Cooper's relative lack of interest in whether romance audiences actually believed in fairies: "even in the pre- or early-modern period, the fairies of romance did not require belief, but they probably needed rather less suspension of disbelief. What they do require is a recognition on the part of readers and audiences that the real world cannot be reduced to the rational."[146] But, we might counter, when belief in fairies could offer a reasonable explanation for many things that would otherwise have seemed inexplicable, rationality, in this sense, must be viewed as every bit as historically contingent as belief.[147] Setting aside the question of whether rationality/irrationality might not be a misleading binary to evoke in such contexts, implying as it does some version of Lévy-Bruhl's prelogical society,[148] we would do well to remember that all metaphysical beliefs, our own included, must be in some sense non-empiricist and thus open to a charge of irrationality. When we apply this term to medieval beliefs, then, we are not necessarily imputing a general failure of reason to medieval people; we are simply expressing our disagreement with a set of principles upon which they sometimes put reason to work. No one who has followed Albertus Magnus wrestling with the problems of demonic insemination would dream of challenging his logic; it is not the deductive process but the acceptability of his premises that disturbs us. In this sense, then, medieval people were no more irrational than we are. As R. G. Collingwood puts it, "the common characteristic of [fairy] tales is their magical character. To understand them means understanding magic: understanding why people behaved in the ways for which we use magic as a general term. Now if magical behavior is irrational behavior, this cannot be done."[149] Neither of the usual literary explanations—the poetic (magic as a play of the imagination) nor the narratological (magic as a way of telling a story)—gets to grips with this problem, for both assume an irrationality that needs to be justified or explained away. The consequences for literary analysis, once we accept that the question of fairy belief might have been a perfectly serious matter in the Middle Ages, are threefold.

First, there is the question of genre. For Helen Cooper, folktale and romance belong to quite separate discursive realms: "the folklore history of fairies has been the subject of much scholarship and more speculation, but lies beyond the scope of this book. The question here is what kind of generic niche was occupied by the fairy, and the fairy lady in particular, after her arrival on the romance scene."[150] In this context, however, we should perhaps think less of immutable literary genres provoking predictable responses in their readers and more of genres that are to some degree controlled or defined by reader response. As Hans-Robert Jauss puts it, "the history of genres in this perspective also presupposes reflection on that which can become visible only to the retrospective observer: ... the historical as well as the aesthetic significance of masterworks, which itself may change with the history of their effects and later interpretations, and thereby may also differently illuminate the coherence of the history of their genre."[151] It is important to recognize that our perception of medieval romance itself, and not just its constitutive memes, is historically contingent and has been deeply affected by the changing history of fairies. Specifically, our generic horizon of expectation, as the *rezeptionsästhetiker* would say, has been profoundly distorted by eighteenth-century attitudes to fairy stories: the very coinage 'fairy tale' (a calque on the French *conte de fées*) includes among its senses "an unreal or incredible story; a falsehood" (*Oxford English Dictionary* [OED]). In other words, we have been conditioned by the age of enlightenment to construe any story containing fairies as a literary fantasy, and we tend unreflectively to project such conditioning back upon our medieval ancestors. As I have been at some pains to show, such an attitude would have found far fewer supporters in the Middle Ages than it does now. It is not that medieval fairy stories (in the sense of improbable *Märchen*) did not exist, but as with their modern descendants (in which, as Derek Brewer points out, "few actual fairies, of whatever kind, appear"),[152] their narrative impulse seems generally to lie elsewhere.[153]

The older, less contextualized, folkloric approach to narrative genre, typified by Jacob Grimm's famous dictum "das Märchen ist poetischer, die Sage, historischer,"[154] might help us to bridge this gap. From the folklorist's perspective the Lusignan family's foundation narrative looks like prime legend material, so that a romance such as *Melusine* will resemble a legend (*eine Sage*)—or, perhaps better, a combination and elaboration of several legends—far more closely than a fairy tale (*ein Märchen*).[155] Not only is *Melusine* clearly based on earlier short narratives that must once have circulated orally, but there is every reason to suppose that they would have represented themselves as *historischer* (Gervase of Tilbury calls his version a true account, a *veredicta narratione*).[156] Interestingly, one of the *Melusine* authors was arguably himself a proto-folklorist (Jean d'Arras may well have collaborated with two others on a collection of old-wives tales called *Les Évangiles des quenouilles*),[157] and we have seen that he tries to buttress his romance's plausibility with personal anecdotes that look very like what we would now term 'memorates.' For the modern reader to treat the fairy elements of a work such as *Melusine* as primarily *poetische* (in other words, to read a figure like Raymondin as if he were a character from an Angela Carter story) is in my view to commit a generic solecism.

Second—and here I move from Le Goff's first method of studying vernacular culture, which "privileges cultural objects by searching in the corpus itself . . . for the nature and sense of this culture," to the second, which privileges the participants, "seeking a definition of the popular in their attitudes towards the cultural objects, in the way they consume cultural products"—one might argue that it was precisely the contested nature of fairy belief that guaranteed its narrative potency for medieval people.[158] I believe that far from being a convenient, if picturesque, plot device, magic constitutes the narrative mainspring of a great many romances—very much their 'substance' rather than a mere 'decoration.'[159] As creatures of the book, we naturally tend to construe issues of belief in terms of an internal literary economy ("it is the work which makes sense of the wonder, not the other way about," writes Francis Dubost),[160] but there is an important sense in which the wonder itself may indeed generate the work. One aspect of recent folklore research seems particularly relevant here. Unlike the medievalist, the folklorist can ask her informants about their beliefs and expect to find in her field notes evidence of their attitudes and motives far more transparent than anything preserved in a six-hundred-year-old text. When the folklorist Gillian Bennett talked to women in Manchester in the 1980s about ghosts, she discovered that they "customarily respond[ed] to questions of belief with narrative answers,"[161] and it seems probable that medieval people too often used stories about fairies to explore difficult questions of belief. Such a claim receives support from the prominent legend scholar Linda Dégh, who contends that contested belief is a fundamental characteristic of all legends: "a story becomes a legend," she writes, citing Helge Gerndt, "only if it is presented in the twilight zone of credence and doubt."[162] As Elliott Oring, another folklorist, puts it, "the narration of a legend is, in a sense, the negotiation of the truth of [its central episode]. . . . It might be that a particular narrative is regarded as false, or true, or false by some and true by others. The diversity of opinion does not negate the status of the narrative as legend because, whatever the opinion, the truth status of the narrative is what is being negotiated."[163]

Third (and most important), then, there is the ideological issue. When Linda Dégh writes of belief as "the given, underlying ideological foundation of legends,"[164] she imagines the modern legend as a medium for political engagement (however loosely defined). Medieval fairy legends, given the far greater gulf between the great and little traditions, were, I suggest, still more ideologically loaded. The Marxist Antonio Gramsci fully recognized the potential of folklore to resist the hegemonic constrictions of civil society, and this insight is brilliantly exploited for the eighteenth century in E. P. Thompson's *Customs in Common*.[165] Unfortunately, the historian of the Middle Ages is denied the wealth of material that was available to Thompson, but let me offer here a single medieval illustration of what Gramsci termed "the conditions of cultural life of the people."[166] Jacques de Vitry (d. ca. 1240) tells us that he had encountered people in some areas who crossed themselves when they first met a priest in the morning, "saying that it was bad luck to cross paths with a priest" [*dicentes quod malum omen est obviare sacerdoti*];[167] the Dominican John Bromyard proves that the custom was still alive in mid-fourteenth-century England (he tells of a priest, angered by catching a woman crossing herself at the sight of him, who tosses her into a ditch to prove her premonitions true),[168] and the Benedictine Robert Rypon recounts a similar story involving a monk early in the fifteenth century.[169] This monastic variant is equally old (it is discussed by Peter of Blois)[170] and equally widespread (it was still alive in fifteenth-century France).[171] We even find such unlucky encounters given a name in a late fourteenth-century version of the *Manuel de Péchés*: "Evel fote he me browhte."[172] There can be no question that the wonderfully parodic custom of 'evil-footing' stands, as Gramsci puts it, "in opposition . . . to 'official' conceptions of the world,"[173] nor could there be better illustration of the workings of Gramscian hegemony than this glimpse of peasants employing the sign of the cross to protect themselves from ecclesiastical officiousness;[174] clearly folklore from this perspective is not "to be considered an eccentricity, an oddity or a picturesque element, but as something which is very serious and is to be taken seriously."[175]

Evidently some medieval authors (such as Geoffrey Chaucer) were deeply skeptical about the existence of fairies, but even Chaucer, when he ventriloquizes a fairy legend (in *The Wife of Bath's Tale*) or parodies it (in *The Tale of Sir Thopas*), was writing at a time when many of his contemporaries still took fairies seriously, and this fact ought to make a difference to the way we, as informed readers, approach his poetry now. In practice, of course, this is far from easy to do. It is all very well for me to claim that *Sir Thopas* is much more than simply a stylistic parody, that its hero's bizarre quest to find an elf queen throws important light on the poet's own ideological stance, though for a modern reader to recover this dimension of the tale will require a considerable imaginative investment on her part. But it is surely not impossible, and perhaps early modernists, better schooled in the new historicism than medievalists, may be able to point us the way. Marjorie Swann's discussion of fairy lore in the poetry of Stuart England, for instance, offers an excellent illustration of why we "need to recognize that this literary mode was self-consciously topical and politicized";[176] by contrast, the medievalist Aisling Byrne, having made the suggestive, and ideologically loaded, observation that romances "make no attempt to articulate a framework that explains or excuses the sexual morality of otherworldly beings,"[177] simply turns her attention to taboo as a narratological device.

The acknowledgment that fairies were serious business, an integral part, as Gramsci might have said, of the folkloric common sense of medieval people,[178] does more than simply modify the generic or narratological assumptions we bring to medieval romance, then; it also carries important ideological implications that have been barely recognized hitherto.[179] The fifteenth-century Parisian theologian Jean Gerson, for one, had no doubt that the literary discourse of fairyland was ideologically loaded. Demonic deceptions ("ex daemonum suggestione et illusione") lay at the heart of what Gerson regarded as an alarming increase in superstition at the beginning of the fifteenth century, so it is particularly significant that he took "the concoctions of the poets" [*ex Poetarum confictione*] to be one of the chief conduits of such deception: "the reading of certain romances, that is books of so-called poetry composed in French about knightly deeds, of which the greatest part is fabrication, more for the sake of purveying novelty and wonder than the apprehension of the truth" [ex lectione quorumdam Romanciorum id est librorum compositorum in Gallico, quasi poeticorum, de gestis militaribus, in quibus maxima pars fabulosa est, magis ad ingerendum quamdam novitatem & admirationem quam veritatis cognitionem].[180] With hindsight we will imagine that Gerson was overestimating the degree to which medieval folklore could mount a coherent challenge to the dominant ideology (most of those who listened to stories about fairies would have been horrified to learn that they were not good Christians), but even if its resistance was spontaneous rather than considered, it remained, as Gerson understood, something to be taken seriously. We ourselves might do well to bear this in mind whenever we are tempted to think of medieval fairy romances as nothing more than poetic escapism or magic as simply a convenient plot device.

CHAPTER 3

Incubi Fairies

> Many old women, that then had more wit than those that are now living and have lesse, sayd that a fayry had gotten her with childe; and they bid her be of good comfort, for the childe must needes be fortunate that had so noble a father as a fayry was.
> —*Robin Good-Fellow, his mad prankes, and merry iests* (1628)

Sometime around the middle of the eleventh century, Guibert of Nogent's mother had a terrifying experience. Just before going to bed she had learned that her husband had been captured by the Normans and was unlikely to be ransomed: "That same night a storm arose. Overwhelmed with anxious dread, she was lying secure in her bed, when suddenly the Enemy, who has a habit of plunging into souls lacerated by sorrow, crawled in with her as she lay awake and nearly crushed her to death under his enormous weight. Her breath grew tight, suffocating her; all freedom of movement left her limbs, and she could not utter any sound. Her power to reason was mute but free, so she called upon God, the only help she had." Guibert's description of the response to this cry for help is a little confused: a good spirit manifests itself and, after calling upon Mary for aid, is able to drive the evil one from her bed—"Its strength from God, the spirit threw down the devil with a tremendous crash."[1] Whatever we make of her rescuer(s), however, the nature of the experience itself and the way she chooses to frame it are matters of some interest.

Terrifying as it must have been, Guibert's mother's experience was far from unique. Many people, men as well as women and from a wide variety of cultures, have reported the horrific feeling of awaking from sleep to find themselves paralyzed by an alien presence. Early in our present century, 'Shawna,' a twenty-eight-year-old Boston graduate student and bartender, had an experience similar to that of Guibert's mother: "one night I woke up in the middle of the night and couldn't move. I was filled with terror and thought there was an intruder in the house. I wanted to scream, but couldn't get any sound to come out"; *her* explanation, however, involved an encounter not with the enemy but with an alien from outer space.² On the other hand, Susan Clancy, the Harvard psychologist to whom she reported this experience, accounted for it rather differently; Shawna, she believed, had been a victim of sleep paralysis, "a condition that occurs when our sleep cycles become temporarily desynchronized. Instead of moving seamlessly between sleeping and being awake, we find ourselves in a limbo where the two states briefly overlap."³ As we shall see, the competition between such popular and learned explanations for this phenomenon has a very long history.

In the Middle Ages too such experiences prompted two kinds of interpretation. An attempt to elucidate the popular account will occupy most of what follows, but we might begin by noting that medieval academic explanations fell into two distinct camps, the theological and the medical. As a churchman, Guibert predictably believed that his mother had been visited by a demonic incubus, but a member of the medical profession might have offered a quite different account: "Skilled physicians call the nocturnal demon 'hot ague' [*epialtam*], saying that it comes from the squeezing of the heart when a man sleeps on his back. At that time, the stomach extends to the area of the heart which, if [the stomach] is filled, the heart is compressed because the vital spirit cannot be drawn off to the limbs."⁴ In his *Daemonologie*, James the Sixth argues that these two kinds of explanation, the theological and the physiological, refer to two quite distinct kinds of experience and that the latter only "makes us *think* that there were some unnatural . . . spirit lying upon us":

> *Phi[lomathes]*. It is not the thing which we cal the *Mare*, which takes folkes sleeping in their beddes, a kinde of these spirites, whereof ye are speaking?
>
> *Epi[stemon]*. No, that is but a naturall sicknes, which the Mediciners hath giuen that name of *Incubus* vnto *ab incubando*, because it being a thicke fleume, falling into our breast vpon the harte, while we are sleeping, intercludes so our vitall spirites, and takes all power from vs, as maks vs think that there were some vnnaturall burden or spirite, lying vpon vs and holding vs downe.⁵

My concern in this chapter is not with experiential explanations such as these but with their cultural ramifications,[6] which for the Middle Ages are particularly complex.[7]

Evidently not all nocturnal visits were as unwelcome as the one experienced by Guibert's mother; had they been so, indeed, the church would have had little difficulty in convincing its flock of their demonic origins. Some people seem to have had rather more pleasurable encounters, and it was because of this that the church had its work cut out for it. Experientially these two kinds of dreams (hair-raising and erotic) are easily distinguished, but chiefly because one word, 'incubus,' was employed to describe the source of both, the discursive line between them was blurred in the Middle Ages.[8] Gervase of Tilbury's *Otia Imperialia*, for instance, speaks of "unclean spirits which are called incubi, from their oppression (*incubatio*) of the mind; for they afflict people's minds in their sleep, making them believe they are falling from a height or suffocating. . . . We have actually observed that some demons love women with such passion that they break out into unheard-of acts of lewdness, and when they come to bed with them they bear down upon them with extraordinary pressure, and yet are seen by no one else."[9] Gervase cites Apuleius's *De deo Socratis* in support of his views, but their ultimate source is doubtless Augustine's polemic against Apuleius in *The City of God* (a passage Le Goff has justly called the birth certificate of the medieval incubus): "Moreover there is a very widespread report, corroborated by many people, either through their own experience or through accounts of others of indubitably good faith who have had the experience, that Silvans and Pans [var. fauns], who are commonly called *incubi*, often misbehaved towards women and succeeded in accomplishing their lustful desires to have intercourse [*concubitum*] with them."[10] So heavily did Augustine's authority weigh upon later tradition that it became almost impossible for medieval commentators to distinguish between these two kinds of incubi simply in terms of their functions.

Behind the academic incubus it is possible to discern a popular tradition analogous to Shawna's alien abductor. Augustine himself hints at such a folkloric dimension with his "Silvans and Pans," and signs of this association can be detected in scholastic discourse throughout the Middle Ages and beyond. It is no accident, for instance, that James the Sixth's discussion of incubi occurs in that section of his *Daemonologie* given over to "these kinde of spirites that are called vulgarlie the Fayrie" (p. 57). Gervase's interpretation of Augustine's "Silvans and Pans" is even more explicit: "For, indeed, we know that this has been daily proved by men of unimpeachable reputation, because we have heard of certain lovers of these kinds of spirit (which are called fairies [*quas fadas nominant*]), and how, when they committed themselves in marriage to other women, they died before they intermingled themselves in carnal coupling with their consorts. And we have observed that most enjoyed the highest state of worldly fortune, but when they extricated themselves from the embraces of this kind of fairy [*hiuiscemodi fadarum*], or spoke of them in public, they lost not only worldly prosperity but even the paltry comfort of life itself."[11] At the time he was writing the *Otia,* Gervase was living in Arles in southern France,[12] and the words *fadas/fadarum* here are clearly Latinized forms of Provençal *fada*, 'fairy'—itself a reflex of Latin *fata,* the etymon of Middle French *feie* > Modern French *fée*. In much the same way, Walter Map renders the fairy nature of Eadric the Wild's bride, whom he later describes as a succubus, by the word *fatalitas*.[13]

In fact, it would not be an exaggeration to say that for much of the Middle Ages the word 'incubus,' whatever its connotations in clerical discourse, meant simply 'fairy' in such contexts. If we imagine a series running *demon* > *demon-fairy* > *fairy-demon* > *fairy,* then, for most of those who were familiar with the word at all, 'incubus' would have to be placed toward the right-hand end of such a spectrum (we should remember, moreover, that 'demon' itself began life as a somewhat less harsh term than 'devil' [*diabolus*]). Thus when an early fourteenth-century scribe, who was copying Wace's *Roman de Brut,* came upon the line "incubi demones unt nun" [they are called incubi-demons] in his exemplar, he altered the word *incubi* to *luiton* 'fairy,' presumably in the interest of clarity.[14] Later in the century Raoul de Presles, commenting on Augustine's silvans and pans, recommended that his reader consult William of Auvergne's *De Universo* on 'incubi' and 'succubi': "and also he speaks in that place of Hellekin's court and of Lady Abundance and of the spirits that they call fairies, which appear in stables and woods" [et aussi parle il en celle partie de la maisnie de hellequin et de dame habonde et des esperis quilz appellent faes qui aperent es estables et es arbres].[15]

There is clear evidence that as late as the fifteenth century the word 'incubus' might still have been imagined as a fancy word for 'fairy': thus, "L'om folez e satereaus" [the wild men and satyrs], whom Benoit de Saint-Maure says inhabit Pannonia[16] and who become the "multos satiros faunosque bicornes" [many satyrs and two-horned fauns] of Guido della Colonna,[17] are supplemented by incubi in Lydgate's *Troy Book*:

> For diuerse goddis of þe wodis grene
> Appere þere, called Satiry,
> Bycornys eke, fawny and incuby,
> Þat causen ofte men to falle in rage.¹⁸

Even clearer is a definition in the early fifteenth-century tract *Dives and Pauper* (ca. 1405): "Þe fendis þat temptyn folc to lecherie ben mest besy for to aperyn in mannys lycnesse & womannys to don lecherye with folc & so bryngyn hem to lecherie, & in speche of þe peple it arn clepyd eluys. But in Latyn whan þei aperyn in þo lycnesse of man it arn clepyd *incubi*, and whan þei aperyn in þo lycnesse of woman it arn clepyd *succuby*."¹⁹ In the same vein an early fifteenth-century German demonologist introduces a discussion of 'incubi' and 'succubi' by stating that "the demon which is termed incubus is also called a fairy" [demon ille, qui incubus nominatur, eciam silvanus dicitur].²⁰ As late as the early sixteenth century, a cunning man named William Stapleton could refer to two spirits by the proper names of Oberion and Inchubus.²¹

Perhaps the most striking example of all is the lengthy description of an incubus we find in an early fifteenth-century German chronicle by Dietrich Engelhus (though the events he describes seem to date from the late 1380s):

> There was a certain incubus, calling himself King Goldemar, who attached himself to a certain knight called Neveling de Hardenburg, from the County of Mark, near the River Ruhr. The incubus spoke with men, played a musical instrument, joined in games of dice, spent money, drank wine, and was seen giving answers to many, both religious and secular, but he frequently dismayed the religious by exposing their hidden vices. He often warned his aforementioned host of the approach of his enemies and gave him advice about dealing with them. He offered only his hands to be touched, and his hands were graceful and soft, as if one were touching a mouse or a frog. . . . I heard all these things from many people, and understood them more fully from Neveling himself twenty-six years later. Neveling was also instructed by him, as can be seen from this verse: "The Father is uncreated; the Son is uncreated; the Holy Spirit is uncreated." And after he had lived with him for three years he departed without doing any kind of harm.²²

Goldemar is quite clearly a fairy—a fairy king in fact—and any whiff of the demonic is dispelled by Engelhus's anecdote of his conversing about the Trinity. All the more remarkable, then, that Goldemar should be described as an incubus, for there is no evidence that he has sexual relations with anyone at all.

Clearly, even in Engelhus's day the extended campaign of the church to demonize this aspect of popular belief was still not totally successful, though the fact that we should have such difficulty thinking of an incubus as simply a fairy shows how effective it would prove to be in the long run. Nevertheless, if we are to respond fully to this facet of the medieval popular imaginary, it is vital that we try to shed the associations that the word 'incubus' inevitably conjures up for us and seek to recover something of its earlier significance. One useful exercise is to try to read as coded fairy stories the tales of women heroically resisting, or sinfully submitting to, the advances of seductive incubi with which the homiletic and pastoral literature of the medieval church abounds. Let us briefly consider three of them here—all English, though there is no dearth of such stories from the Continent.[23]

The first comes from the canonization proceedings (1291–92) of Thomas of Cantilupe, Bishop of Hereford:

> A certain girl, the daughter of Nicholas Nevenon, of Inglethorp in Norfolk, in the diocese of Norwich, had for five years been solicited and greatly wearied by a certain incubus-demon, as was believed. He promised her many and varied gifts if she would allow him to sleep with her, but she, utterly refusing and recoiling from him and defending her body with the sign of the cross, remained still unharmed, despite many vexations. Also on one occasion the same wicked spirit led her into a certain beautiful place [*in quemdam locum amœnum*] where she saw many wonderful things, among them an ornate table supplied with many varieties of delicious dishes, which he invited her to eat. She was terrified, however, and invoked God's aid by crossing herself in her usual way, by which she remained free of these illusions.[24]

Elsewhere such journeys to mysterious and beautiful places are associated with the fairies (as in John Bromyard's description of deluded women who believe themselves "carried off by a certain race and led to certain beautiful and unknown places" [quae dicunt se rapti a quodam populo, & duci ad loca quaedam pulchra, & ignota]),²⁵ and the invitation to partake in a sumptuous, but dangerous, feast is another fairy commonplace: William of Newburgh, for instance, tells of a fellow Yorkshireman returning home, a little drunk, late one night, "when suddenly from a hillock close by . . . he heard voices singing, as though people were feasting in celebration. . . . In the side of the hill he saw an open door; he approached and looked inside. Before his eyes was a large well-lit dwelling crowded with men and women reclining at table as if at a formal feast. One of the servants . . . offered him a cup."²⁶

My second example comes from Adam of Eynsham's late twelfth-century life of Hugh of Lincoln.²⁷ Here a woman who has struggled with a demon for a long time is approached by "another spirit in the shape of a young man," who offers to rid her of her oppressor on condition that she enter a love pact (*"amoris fedus"*) with him: "he then leads her to a place near her dwelling and shows her a plant growing near by, saying, 'Take this plant and hide it in your bosom and scatter it round your house. You will see for yourself when you have done so that my promise has come true.'" The first would-be seducer is indeed effectively repelled by this herb, but the sensible young woman manages to avoid the blandishments of the second by leaving his herb in position: "you can come if you wish and if you can, for I ought not to break my promise, but, as long as I live, never will I cast away from me this plant, which is my only defence against my lascivious seducer." Predictably the second would-be lover is as effectively repelled as the first. We are told that the herb is St. John's Wort, though the reason for connecting this story with Saint Hugh of Lincoln is never really made clear to us.²⁸ It is, in fact, far easier to believe that what we are really being presented with here is a standard folk remedy against fairy seduction.²⁹

In my third example, Thomas of Monmouth, the twelfth-century biographer of William of Norwich, states unequivocally what was only implicit in our other two stories, that the seducing incubus is a fairy. He tells of a pious virgin from the Suffolk town of Dunwich who was assaulted by "one of those beings whom they call fairies and incubi [*faunos dicunt et incubos*]—who are prone to lust and are often the seducers of women—changing himself into the form of a very beautiful young man." Not only beautiful but elegant in his manners and aristocratic in his bearing, he is also, like the fairies of romance, endowed with vast wealth. On one occasion he says, "'I am better supplied than all others in the abundance of my riches; and that I may prove my words, if only you give your assent, straight way I will endow you with such immense gifts as your parents never yet possessed.' Thereupon he produced rings, necklaces, collars, brooches, earrings, and many things of the kind." On another occasion, "silken robes all glistening with gems, silver and gold, and whatever can be imagined most precious and fair in the glory of this world he heaped up before her and offered them all."[30] He passes at will in and out of her bedchamber (like other fairy lovers), and until the saint intervenes no one is able to prevent him.[31]

It is important to note that none of these stories is told about a distant time and place; all three assume that experiences such as these are part of the common fabric of life in medieval England. British Library MS Royal 7. D. I, a collection of exempla made, probably in the 1250s, by a Cambridge Dominican, contains a number of these fairy/incubus stories, including one about a sixteen-year-old girl to whom "a certain man frequently appeared, dressed in noble attire, sometimes in silk, at other times in cloth of gold, soliciting her to consent to carnal intercourse with him, and on occasion when she was sitting in the hall with others, he approached her and kissed her, though no one could see him but her" [apparuit ei quidam in habitu nobili frquenter, quandoque in serico, quandoque in vestibus deauratis indutus, sollicitans illam ut ei consentiret ad carnalem copulam, et quandoque, dum sederet in aula cum aliis, accessit ille et osculabatur eam, nemine tamen percipiente preter ipsam].[32] This story, the narrator says, was told him by "a certain man of religion, who was worthy of credence [*quidam vir religiosus, fidedignus*]," and he ends with the information that his informant had asked him to withhold the place, the time, and the name of the woman concerned, all of which implies that she was still alive. In the same vein, the Dominican Thomas of Cantimpré introduces the topic of "incubi-demons [that] have oppressed certain women and enticed others to have sex by lascivious discourse" by saying that he had often heard about them in confession ("in confessione pluries audivimus"), and he claims that several of the stories he gives are based on personal reminiscence;[33] Thomas's old master, Albertus Magnus, also claims to have seen the victims of incubi at firsthand: "vidimus personas cognitas ab eis."[34] Finally, Hector Boece, who finished his *Scotorum Historia* in 1526, offers his readers three instances of modern-day incubi, "so that [they] might discern that what is commonly said of the dealings of wicked demons with men is not completely fictitious" [ut legentes dignoscerent haud prorsus esse fictitia que de malorum demonum cum hominibus consuetudine feruntur].[35]

The church, committed as it was to disciplining the sexual impulses of its flock, was inevitably concerned about reports of couplings between its members and incubi/fairies, but as long as these could be rationalized as the overheated imaginings of sheltered young women (even when the women were sheltered by the walls of a nunnery), the threat must always have seemed manageable. Reports of women made pregnant by incubi, however, were quite another matter. On the face of it such pregnancies might seem absurd—"sed sic proprie generare incubum non dicemus" [let us not say that an incubus can reproduce of its own accord], writes Thomas of Cantimpré, or as *Dives and Pauper* succinctly puts it, "fend with fend may nout gendryn."[36] However, the fact that the church took such enormous trouble to combat the idea (and the fact that earlier commentators like William of Auvergne were not entirely sure how they should refute it) suggests that it enjoyed considerable popular currency, that whatever the church taught them about the sterility of demons, the people continued to believe that fairies were not only sexy but also fertile. After all, fairy insemination offered medieval women a convenient way to account for any pregnancy that, for whatever social reasons, could not safely be attributed to a specific human father.

The story of Saint Marina, as it is told in the Vernon Manuscript, offers us a charming illustration of this. Saint Marina, having joined a monastery disguised as a monk, is sent on an errand outside the walls of the abbey. This gives a brewer's daughter who finds herself pregnant a chance to try to foist her child's paternity on the supposed Brother Marin who had stayed at her mother's inn. The abbot takes his/her guilt for granted, and the saint bears the ensuing opprobrium with patient humility until her true gender is revealed some years later. At this point the brewer's daughter, deprived of her first explanation, is forced to come up with an alternative one:

> þis Breuesteres douhtur wox wood,
> And com criȝinde wiþ grisly mood
> And tolde þe folk as wodewose wilde
> who gat on hire þis forseyde childe. (lines 207–10)[37]

> [This brewer's daughter grew angry and, crying pitifully, told the people that it was a wild woodwose that had fathered the foresaid child on her.][38]

Evidently it was fair game for people to ascribe an unexplained pregnancy (like other deviations from the social norm—sudden wealth, an unconventional marriage, a conspicuously beautiful or erudite woman, or a mysterious disappearance) to the intervention of fairy agency.

Despite the fact that in vernacular romance, where fairy lovers abound, fairy paternity (not to mention fairy maternity) is commonplace, the great tradition had little reason to pay much attention to it before the appearance of Geoffrey of Monmouth's *Historia Regum Britannie*. However, the *Historia* was written in Latin by one of their own and presented as sober historical fact,[39] so that schoolmen were forced to confront the product of an actual union between a mortal woman and an incubus-demon—Merlin, the celebrated British seer and adviser to kings. Geoffrey is surely being disingenuous when he has one of Vortigern's councillors tell the king that "in the books of our philosophers and in many histories I have found that many men were engendered in this way,"[40] for William of Auvergne, when he came to tackle the topic a hundred years later, could find only one other written source: Jordanes's *History of the Goth*s, cited as evidence that the Huns traced their origins back to incubi.[41] An additional rumor [*fama*], no doubt brought back by crusaders, that the Cypriots boasted a similar ancestry adds little to his case, and William's best evidence for demonic fecundity is clearly Merlin himself: "so from all these things you may not improbably infer that the well-known rumor, popularly believed, that a certain man, who is said to have been the son of an incubus-demon in Greater Britain, is not impossible" [ex his igitur omnibus colligere potes non improbabiliter, sermonem famosum, opinione vulgatum, de quodam, qui in majori Britannia filius daemonis incubi fuisse dicitur, non esse impossibilem].[42] William never mentions Merlin by name, but the fact that he goes on to discuss this man's prophesies makes it clear whom he is talking about.

William denies the possibility that demons can impregnate mortal women, but he remains uncertain how to account for cases like Merlin's. Even in his own day, however, the germ of an explanation was beginning to form. Caesarius of Heisterbach, discussing *Merlinus propheta Britannorum ex incubo daemone . . . generatu*s, credits a certain educated man ("a quodam literato homine") with the theory that demons can make use of human seed that is unnaturally shed ("crementum humanum quod contra naturam funditur") to make themselves bodies with which to impregnate humans.[43] Incidentally, Caesarius augments the cases of Merlin and the Huns with that of the reigning kings of England, said to be descended from a female fairy ("de matre phantastica descendisse referuntur")—presumably an allusion to Gerald of Wales's account of Henry II's mother.[44] Stephen Langton's rejection some thirty years earlier (in the course of a discussion of Merlin's parentage) of the notion that demons can transport human seed from elsewhere ("non poterant aliunde portare") proves that such ideas were not new.⁴⁵ By the middle of the thirteenth century, however, the scientifically minded Albertus Magnus had paved the way for what was to become the standard account by arguing that the ability of skillful demons to preserve human semen at its natural temperature (*calori naturale*) might solve the difficulties raised by the widespread story of Merlin's father ("rumor publicus de Merlino filio incubi").⁴⁶ This final explanation, as found in Aquinas and Bonaventure,⁴⁷ was to be passed down to the early modern witch-hunters.⁴⁸ Here, then, is Bonaventure's version, as given by the fifteenth-century Spanish Franciscan Alphonse de Spina: "For demons in the form of women first lie with men and take from them polluted semen and by a certain natural artfulness keep that same semen in its active state, and afterwards become incubi and with God's permission transfuse it into a woman's womb, from which transfusion humans can be generated, but those thus generated are the children of man not demons. [*De Spina adds*]: In this way Merlin was said to have been begotten."⁴⁹ It is time to return to Geoffrey of Monmouth to see what caused all this scholastic kerfuffle.⁵⁰

Since Geoffrey's account was to form the basis of all subsequent discussions of Merlin's engendering and since its fairy dimension is still not generally appreciated,⁵¹ it is worth examining in detail here. King Vortigern, losing his war against the invading Saxons, Hengist and Horsa, decides to build a fortress in a remote part of his kingdom and to take his stand there. He selects a suitable location, but every time he lays down the foundations they collapse overnight. Having been advised that only by obtaining a child without a father ("iuuenem sine patre") and by sprinkling the foundations with its blood will he succeed in getting the walls to stand firm, Vortigern sends envoys all over Britain to find such a child. In Carmarthen they come upon a group of boys squabbling over a ball game, and when one insults the other—"No one knows who you are since you have no father" [de te autem nescitur quis sis cum patrem non habeas]—they visit the child's mother and ask her to explain his paternity to Vortigern. "On my immortal soul, and on yours, my lord king," she says,

> I have known no one who begot him upon me. The one thing I do know is that when I was among my attendants in our bed-chamber someone would appear to me in the shape of a very handsome young man and often straining me in his arms he would kiss me. And when he had dallied a while with me, he would suddenly

disappear, so that I might see nothing of him. Also he conversed with me many times, while I sat in private, but was nowhere visible. And when he had attended me in this way, he often coupled with me in the form of a man and left me pregnant. You must know, my prudent lord, that other than this I have known no man who might have begotten this boy.[52]

When the king turns to Maugentius (one of his advisers) for his opinion, Maugentius says, "In the books of our philosophers and in many histories I have found many men who were engendered in this way. For, as Apuleius says in *De Deo Socratis*, between the moon and the earth live spirits whom we call incubi-demons. In part their nature is human and in part angelic, and when they wish they take on human shape and couple with women. Perhaps one of these appeared to this woman and begot this young man on her."[53]

Whether or not Geoffrey of Monmouth had actually read *De Deo Socratis* (there is nothing in this passage that he could not have deduced from Saint Augustine's refutation in *The City of God* of its claim that demons act as intermediaries between human beings and the gods [book 8] or from the speculations about incubi [book 15]),[54] it is interesting that he chose not to refer to the far better-known work here. By citing Apuleius rather than Augustine, Geoffrey gives his 'middle spirits' a distinctly neoplatonic (as opposed to patristic) caste.[55]

Geoffrey of Monmouth did not weave this passage out of whole cloth. He was embroidering a hint he had found in "Nennius,"[56] where a similar search for a boy with no father leads Vortigern's envoys to the mother of Ambrosius/Merlin: "I do not know how he was conceived in my womb," she tells them, "but one thing I do know is that I have never known a man" [nescio quomodo in utero meo conceptus est, sed unum scio, quia virum non cognovi umquam], and she swears to them that her son had no father ("et iuravit illis patrem non habere").[57] It is not difficult to see how this passage might have suggested a fairy lover to Geoffrey, particularly since there seems to have been a popular belief that sex with incubi posed no threat to a woman's virginity. In the mid-thirteenth century the confessor of a young nun reported her insistence that despite having had an extended and lurid sexual relationship with an incubus ("diuque a demone incubo fedissime polluta omnibus modis detestande libidinis"), she, like Merlin's mother, believed herself to be still a virgin: "she did not think that she had lost her virginity in the flesh since she knew that she had lived without knowing a man [non putabat se carnis virginitatem amisisse quare nouit se ab homine incongnitam exitisse]."⁵⁸ In the fifteenth century Saint Lidwina treated a woman making a similar claim to ringing sarcasm: "Supervacuo titulo tanti nominis, ut timeo, gloriaris: & si scire volueris, viginti quinque tales virgines, cujusmodi tu ipsa existis, super unam molam piperariam libere chorizare possent" [I fear you are enjoying an empty title to such an illustrious status [*virgo intacta*], and if you really want to know, twenty-five virgins of your sort could easily dance on a pepper mill].⁵⁹

To see how the term 'incubus' (and indeed the word 'demon') might have been understood by Geoffrey, and by many of his contemporaries, we might look at the way his account was handled by his immediate successors. By 1155, only twenty years or so after its composition, Geoffrey's history had been translated into Anglo-Norman by Wace.⁶⁰ Wace makes a number of changes to Merlin's mother's account of her seduction and to Maugentius's explanation of it: in the first place, he makes the mother a nun, where Geoffrey had only said, ambiguously, that she lived among nuns (*inter monachas degebat*);⁶¹ but far more importantly he makes her seducer completely invisible:

> Se Deus, dist ele, me aït,
> Unches ne cunui ne ne vi
> Ki cest vallet engenüi. (lines 7414–16)
>
> [So God help me, she said, I never knew nor saw who engendered this boy.]

Wace then goes on to tell us that she did not know whether or not she had been visited by an apparition: "Ne sai se fu fantosmerie" (line 7422). As for Maugentius's explanation, it omits any specific reference to Apuleius but contains a far more significant addition; speaking of incubi, Wace says.

> Ne püent mie grant mal faire;
> Ne püent mie mult noisir
> Fors de gaber e d'escharnir. (lines 7448–50)
>
> [They cannot do great wickedness; they cannot cause much harm, except to deceive and deride.]

This view survives in Robert Mannyng's account of Merlin's father in his *Story of England*: "Mykel skathe do they nought; / Drecchynge by tymes haue they wrought" (lines 8079–80).[62] The ultimate source for this idea seems to be Cassian's remark about "those whom the people also call fauns" [*quos etiam Faunos vulgus appellat*] in his *Seventh Collation*: "de risu tantummodo et illusione contenti, fatigari eos potius studeant quam nocere" [content merely with joking and deception, they strive rather to annoy (passersby) than to harm them].[63] Walter Map has the fairy companion of Eudo say much the same thing: "We can do anything that makes for laughter, but nothing that makes for tears."[64]

A couple of generations later, the English poet Layamon makes still more changes, describing Merlin's mother's encounter with her mysterious lover in a passage of great beauty. Each night, she says, she dreamed of "þe fæireste þing þat wes iboren, / swulc hit weore a muchel cniht, al of golde idiht" [the fairest thing that was born, just like a sturdy young man, all dressed in gold]. It glided before her, glittering with gold: "ofte hit me custe, ofte hit me clupte, / ofte hit me to-bæh, & eode me swiðe neh" [often it kissed me, often it embraced me, often it bowed to me, and came very near me]. Still dreaming ("mi mæte"), she came to perceive her own body as something alien ("me wes læ[ð] mine limes uncuð"), and finally understood that she was pregnant ("Þa anȝæt ich on ænde, þat ich was mid childe").[65] Wace's "fantosmerie" has been transformed here into a vivid and recurrent dream of a handsome and rich young man, and one, even more strikingly, who is clearly mortal: "þe fæireste þing *þat wes iboren*." In Layamon's version, the explanation that Maugentius offers Vortigern goes even further: these creatures, he says, dwell in the air where they will remain until Doomsday ("þa þer scullen bilæfuen þat Domes-dæi cume liðen"); some of them are noble, and some do bad things ("Summe heo beoð aðele & summe heo uuel wurcheð"); and they have many human descendants ("Þer-on is swiðe muchel cun þa cumeð imong monnen"). As in Wace, they are largely harmless tricksters ("Ne doð heo noht muchel scaðe bute hokerieð þan folke"), but Layamon adds that in addition to getting women pregnant they cause nightmares ("monine mon o[n] sweuene, ofte heo swencheð") and lead children astray with their magic ("monies godes monnes child heo bicharreð þurh wigeling").[66] In all but name, then, Layamon's incubi-demons are fairies.

Before the middle of the thirteenth century, Geoffrey of Monmouth's *Historia* was turned into Latin dactylic hexameters by an anonymous Breton poet, who goes out of his way to emphasize that Merlin's mother's sexual intrigue was entirely consensual.⁶⁷ Handsome in appearance but mild in bearing ("sub specie iuuenis, pulcherrimus ore, / In cunctis placidus"), he gives her repeated kisses and wrestles with her playfully ("repetita michi dare basia, deinde iocose / Luctari mecum"):

> Uicta—non inuite—subcumbens uim paciebar,
> Sed gratam passe uiolate non uiolatam.
> Inde recedebat tenues dilapsus in auras,
> More reuersurus solito, sed tardus amanti.
>
> [Conquered, not reluctantly, I yielded submissively to his strength—it was not duress, for I was glad to experience his forcefulness. Then he would withdraw, melting into thin air, and though he would reappear in the usual way, it seemed an age to his lover.]

The author seems likely to have been a cleric, but his apparition in this passage reads far more like the fairy lover of masculine wish fulfillment than the demon of clerical disapproval.

One final adaptation of this section of Geoffrey's *Historia*, a thirteenth-century Anglo-Norman poem, *coment Merlyn fu nee e sa nessaunce de sa mere*, is worth mentioning here for a remarkable addition it makes to the list of the lover's attributes. Merlin's mother confesses that when she was alone in her chamber saying her prayers,

> vn oyselet i soleyt entrer.
> Eyns deuynt a vn beu Bacheler,
> Souuente feyce moy acola
> E souuente foyz moy beysa.
> . . . .
> Mes apres aveunt taunt ala,
> Ke il ouueke moy se cocha
> Ausi cum humme, e io consu.⁶⁸
>
> [a little bird used to enter. Straightway, it turned into a fine young squire—many times he embraced me, and many times he kissed me. . . . But after having gone on like this, he lay with me as a man, and I conceived.]

This figure bears so strong a resemblance to the fairy lover in Marie de France's *Yonec* that the author may have felt that any further elucidation was unnecessary; in any event his version completely discards the episode with Maugentius.

All the versions of this scene that we have looked at so far except the last describe Merlin's father as an incubus-demon, but there is more than circumstantial evidence to show that this term actually was taken to denote a fairy. We have already seen that one scribe of Wace's *Roman de Brut* substitutes *luiton* for *incubi*,[69] but another early manuscript (Durham Cathedral, MS C.iv.27.1) goes one better. This version contains a complete rewriting of the passage on Merlin's conception and birth. By and large it brings it into far closer proximity with Geoffrey of Monmouth's original account; Merlin's mother is no longer a nun, for instance, and Apuleius's name is restored. But there is one glaring alteration: where Geoffrey had written "spiritus quos incubos demones appellamus" [spirits we call incubi-demons] this manuscript has the words "Faez sunt, car formes faees / Prenent suvent si devienent fees" [they are fairies because they often take on magical forms and so become fairies].[70]

The English equivalent of *fée* in this period was 'elf,'[71] and the late thirteenth-century chronicler Robert of Gloucester in his treatment of this same episode makes quite clear what he imagines incubi to be. Here is his version of Maugentius's explanation:

> He [Vortigern] esste at is clerkes . were it to leue were.
> Þe clerkes sede þat it is . in philosofie yfounde .
> Þat þer beþ in þe eyr an hey . ver fram þe grounde .
> As a maner gostes . wiȝtes as it be .
> And me may ȝem ofte an erþe . in wilde studes yse .
> ofte in mannes forme . wommen hii comeþ to .
> & ofte in wimmen forme . hii comeþ to men al so .
> Þat men clupeþ eluene. (lines 2746–543)[72]

[He asked his clerks whether it was credible. The clerks said that it is found in philosophy that there are in the air, far from the ground, certain kinds of spirit, creatures as it were, and they can often be seen on earth in wild places, and they often come to women in man's form, and also they often come to men in woman's form. And they are called elves.]

Further details of these *elvene* may be gleaned from a description of the ranks of the fallen angels in a closely related text,[73] *The South English Legendary*:

> And ofte in forme of womman . in moni deorne weie
> Me sicþ of hom gret companie . boþe hoppe & pleie
> Þat eleuene beoþ icluped . þat ofte comeþ to toune
> And bi daie muche in wode beoþ . & biniȝte upe heie doune.
>   (lines 253–56)[74]

[And often in woman's form, along many a secret path, great companies of them may be seen dancing and playing; they are called elves; they often visit human dwellings, and by day they spend much time in the woods and at night upon the high downs.]

For Robert of Gloucester, then, Merlin's father was clearly an elf, and right down to the end of the Middle Ages this reading would survive in other versions of his chronicle: in one fifteenth-century prose redaction, for instance, we find, "and som men calle hem elves fer from the grounde,"[75] and in another, "and men calleth hem noweadays Elves."[76]

Merlin's fame as a prophet—even William of Auvergne concedes that many of his predictions came true—made it vital for the church that the popular myths surrounding his birth should be thoroughly exploded. It was a comparatively simple matter for clerics to demonize his fairy origins (though, as we shall see, beliefs about supernatural insemination would prove much harder to eradicate). The process began very early. The so-called first variant version, which seems to have been produced shortly after the first appearance of the *Historia* in 1138, in fact while Geoffrey of Monmouth was still alive,[77] makes two significant changes to Maugentius's speech: for the simple "spirits [*spiritus*] we call incubi-demons" of Geoffrey's original, the first variant version reads, "evil spirits" [*spiritus immundi*]; and where the original reads, "Forsitan unus ex eis huic mulieri apparuit" [perhaps one of these appeared to this woman], the revision reads, "Forsitan aliquis eorum huic mulieri stuprum intulit" [perhaps one of them fornicated with this woman]. Similarly, William of Newburgh, one of Geoffrey's most strident critics, writes of Merlin's prophesies, "[Geoffrey] was ashamed to insert 'Thus saith the devil' as should have been appropriate to a prophet who was the son of a demonic incubus,"[78] and some early vernacular works strike the same note. The Anglo-Norman *Brut* in B.L. MS Royal 13. A. XXI, for instance, calls Merlin a "son of a whore, of base descent" [*fiz a putein de pute lin*] and also substitutes the far stronger word 'devil' for the 'demon' of Maugentius's explanation: "Uns diables qui incube unt nun."[79]

By the early fourteenth century the clerical interpretation of Merlin's father had become standard in the chronicle tradition; "Þe quilk spirites, amange vs alle, / Moniks, deuells and fendes we calle," says Castleford's version of the *Brut* (ca. 1327).[80] Those unwilling to enter this contentious arena had the choice of either disenchantment or open skepticism. Thus the popular standard version of the English prose *Brut* (perhaps first compiled around 1333) leaves us with the strong impression that Merlin was the son of a single mother, in a rather less exotic sense of that term:

> "but, sire" quod shee, "as y was a ȝonge maiden in my faderes chambre, and oþere of grete lynage were in my company, þat ofte were wont to play and to solacen, I belefte allone in my chaumbre of my fader, & wolde nouȝt goñ out, for brennyng of þe sone. And uppoñ a tyme þere come a faire bachiler, and entrede into my chaumbre þere þat I was allone; but how he come into me, & wher, I wiste neuer, ne ȝitte wote, for þe dorres were fast barrede; and wiþ me he dede game of loue, I nade noþer myȝt ne power him to defende fro me; and oft he come to me in the forsaide maner, so þat he bigate one me þis same childe; but neuer myȝt y wete of him what he was, ne whens he come, ne what was his name."[81]

No sudden vanishings, no invisible conversations here—merely a handsome young man with a short way with locked doors. And instead of Maugentius's elaborate explanation of the mystery, we have only a curt remark from Merlin himself: "sire, how y was bigeten axe ȝe no more, for hit falleþ nouȝt to ȝow ne to none oþere forto wete." Ranulph Higden, however, expresses open skepticism in his *Polychronicon* (after 1327): "moreover, I would have included what is contained in a single British book about the fantastic engendering of Merlin, if I had thought it supported by the truth" [Caeterum quae ... de fantastica Merlini genitura ... in solo Britannico libro continetur, praesenti historiae addidissem, si ea veritate suffulta credidissem]; his view was repeated by John Trevisa (by no means always a slavish translator) later in the century (1387): "and I wolde putte it to þis storie ȝif I trowed þat it be i-holpe by soþenesse."[82] This skepticism is even found in the metrical chronicle of John Harding (begun around 1440), though in other respects he was a great admirer of the Arthurian story:

> Ne of his [Merlin's] birth that many menne on wounder
> Of that werke, bothe aboue and vnder,
> That no father had, ne of his prophecye ,
> I cannot wryte of suche affirmably.[83]

The old story of Merlin's fairy parentage was clearly subject to considerable clerical pressure.

The single most important source of such pressure was a poem, now surviving only in a single fragment (though the rest is preserved in an early prose redaction), composed around 1200 by a shadowy Burgundian called Robert de Boron.[84] The narrative of Merlin's conception in the Arthurian Vulgate Cycle is derived from this version. (One further source, the non-cyclic *Lancelot do Lac*, presents us with an even more diabolic Merlin, but this does not seem to have been widely known in England.)[85] Geoffrey of Monmouth's account of Merlin's parentage (implying, as it does, an impious virgin birth) may well have shocked de Boron, but in any event, by seeking to bring it within the compass of his own rather eccentric theological horizons, he gives it a radical new twist. The poem begins with a council of devils selecting one of their number to go to earth in order to engender the Antichrist. The chosen devil so depraves Merlin's grandmother that she brings upon her family a series of disasters, including the deaths of her husband, her son, her middle daughter, and (by suicide) herself; her youngest daughter becomes a prostitute, and only the eldest daughter, Merlin's mother, holds out against him—and then only because a holy hermit instructs her to keep a candle burning in her chamber every night and to make the sign of the cross before going to bed. One night, when she is out of charity with her sister, she forgets these elementary precautions, and the devil slips into her bed and makes her pregnant, but his plans for the birth of the Antichrist are subsequently thwarted by her own penitence and the good offices of the hermit.

Although apparently not widely circulated in England before the fifteenth century (only one of the fifty-two surviving manuscripts of the French prose version is known to have been copied there),[86] around the year 1300 de Boron's version of Merlin's conception was incorporated into a popular

Middle English romance called *Of Arthour and of Merlin* (copied at least three times and printed once), and after 1400 two further English versions appeared, one in prose and the other in verse. Both seem to be the work of Londoners, and the second was translated by a respectable (if somewhat verbose) citizen, a skinner named Henry Lovelich.[87] Toward the end of the century (certainly after 1482), however, the owner of one prose *Brut* (Lambeth Palace, MS 84) decided to revise his manuscript in the light of other books he had read, and his account is worth quoting as an illustration of the degree to which the clerical demonization of Merlin's father had almost entirely buried the older tradition by this period.

While he omits de Boron's backstory of the council of devils and its emissary, this reviser does give Merlin's mother two sisters (though here she is the youngest and both her siblings are still alive). These sisters do not approve of her living as a poor virgin and take her to task for it:

> So thus of þat one reprefe, & of þat oþer, sche went home in gret hevynes, wepyyng, & shet her dorys, & leyde her on her bedde & wepte tyl sche fyl on slepe. Than þe Devyl, hauyng envy at her perfyt lyfe, & entryd in-to þe deede body of a fayre young man, & cam in-to her chambyr & oppressyd her, lyeng on her bed, and begat on her a chylde, & so departyd sodeynly from her ayen. And aftyrward, whan sche vndirstode & perseyuyd þat sche was consyuyd with childe, sche yede vnto þe Heremyte & tolde hym how þat, her dorys beyng fast schet, ther come yn a goodly young man vnto her—sche wist neuer how—& oppressyd her sore, ayenst her wyl, & begat her with childe & sodenly departyt from her ageyne—sche wist neuer how. Than þe Heremyte seyde it was sothe, but he woolde not discomfort her, in so-moche at yt was doon ayenst her wyl by þe envy of þe Devyl.[88]

This incubus is our most diabolic yet: a "Devyl . . . [in] þe deede body of a fayre young man." Fairy beliefs concerning the dead are particularly difficult to penetrate (as we shall see in Chapter 5), but the notion, as the *Lucydarye* has it, that "spyrytes and elues . . . that men say þat they se by nyght, they often ben deuylles that put theym in fourme of some deed body"[89] seems to be an importation from the learned tradition. At any rate, it was to feature later in the fervid imaginings of witch-hunters such as Henri Boguet and Nicholas Rémy."[90]

When it becomes generally known that she is pregnant, Merlin's mother is arrested for fornication and condemned to be stoned to death after the birth: "& as soone as yt was born, he ranne from þe mydwyfe, & woolde haue done & fulfyllyd þe wylle of þe Devyl, his fadyr, for he was begottyn to haue destroyed al þe worlde. But God, þat is þe wel of al goodnesse & correcter of alle wykkydnes, shewyd vnto þe Heremyte þe malycyus wyl of þe Devyl, the chyldys fadyr. And because he was born of a cristyn woman, almyhty God tolde þe Heremyte how he shulde cristyn hym. And be þe uertu of that holy sacrament his wekydnesse shulde be take from hym." The first act of this reformed infant is to save his mother from death. But even though he fails to fulfill "þe wylle of þe Devyl, his fadyr," this Merlin bears little resemblance to the ambiguous incubus-demon of Geoffrey of Monmouth. Sired by the devil, he is rescued from his father's clutches only by the timely intervention of the sacramental church.

Before we leave this topic, one final example of the campaign to demonize Merlin's father is worth noting. The English romance *Sir Gowther* (though not its French counterpart *Robert le diable*, whose most obvious intertext is the Breton lai *Tydorel*) is explicitly linked to the story of Merlin. Gowther's mother, the Duchess of Austria, barren after ten years of marriage, prays that God and Mary will give her a child by whatever means—"on what maner scho ne roghth" (line 63).[91] She conceives after an al fresco coupling with a being she believes to be her own husband:

> In hur orchard, apon a day,
> Ho meyt a mon, tho sothe to say,
> That hur of luffe besoghth;
> As lyke hur lorde as he myght be—
> He leyd hur down undur a tre,
> With hur is wyll he wroghtth. (lines 64–69)

The echo of Uther's begetting of Arthur in the guise of Igraine's husband is obvious here, but there is an even closer parallel in John of Tynemouth's *Historia Aurea*, repeated in Thomas Walsingham's *Historia Anglicana*. There we are told that in 1337 a woman coupled with an incubus in the forest of Woolmer, believing it to be her human lover (a forester); the consequences of her tryst, however, are rather different: three days later she swells up, turns black, and dies, and eight men can barely carry her coffin.[92] Similarly the poet of *Sir Gowther* leaves us in no doubt that the father of the Duchess of Austria's child is really a devil: "A felturd fende he start up son, / And stode and hur beheld" (lines 71–72). Not only that, but Merlin had earlier been cited as an example of how such pregnancies might come about:

> Sumtyme the fende hadde postee
> For to dele with ladies free
> In liknesse of here fere;
> So that he bigat Merlyng and mo,
> And wrought ladies so mikil wo
> That ferly it is to here. (lines 7–12)

In fact we are told that the same devil was at work in both cases and that the future Sir Gowther will be none other than Merlin's half-brother:

> This chyld within hur was non odur,
> Bot eyvon Marlyon halfe brodur,
> For won fynd gatte hom bothe." (lines 97–99)

When young Gowther turns out to be a monster, then, we know just who to blame. Interestingly, despite its apparent conformity with clerical standards, this account is provided with just such a temporal cushion as we often find in true fairy romances: "*Sumtyme* the fende hadde postee"; the license of devils to harm mortals is given a similar gloss in *Of Arthour and of Merlin*: "Ac whilom more þan now."[93]

By the end of the Middle Ages, then, the great tradition could count the progressive demonization of the fairy lover as one of its successes, but its explanation of the mechanics of supernatural impregnation seems to have been less widely accepted. In both the chronicle and romance traditions, Merlin, even where he is not the son of a fairy, is still, in the biological sense, the son of a demon. The devils' parliament of Robert de Boron's poem (as well as its prose adaptation) selects an emissary who has the ability to father human children:

> Nous avuns
> Cilec un des nos compeignuns
> Qui fourme d'omme puet avoir
> Et femme de lui concevoir. (lines 171–74)[94]

[There is one of our fellows here who can assume a human shape and can make women pregnant.]

I know of only one vernacular author who promotes a fully orthodox line on this topic. The first book of Ranulph Higden's universal history is a geographical survey of the known world, and when he comes to describe Wales, he offers us a versified paraphrase of Gerald of Wales's *Itinerarium Cambriae*. At one point Gerald had been forced to explain that there were two Merlins: one called Ambrosius, a prophet under King Vortigern, who had been begotten by an incubus and found in Carmarthen ("ab incubo genitus, et apud Kaermerdyn inventus"); and the other being Merlin Silvestris.[95] This passage Higden renders almost word for word, but his English translator John Trevisa is having none of it: "What wight wolde wene," he asks indignantly, "Þat a fend my3t now gete a childe?" He then goes on to try to show how the trick is done:

> Wiþ wonder dede
> Boþ men and wommen sede
> Fendes wyl kepe
> Wiþ craft, and bringe in on hepe.
> So fendes wilde
> May make wommen bere childe;
> 3it neuere in mynde
> Was childe of fendes kynde.[96]

It is true that the author of *Sir Gowther* does at least seem to recognize that there is a problem: "A selcowgh thyng that is to here," he says, "A fend nyeght wemen nere, / And makyd hom with chyld" (lines 13–15), but he decides against going into details: "Therof seyus clerkus, Y wotte how, / That schall not be rehersyd now" (lines 19–20). Its French counterpart *Robert le diable*, on the other hand, neatly sidesteps the whole issue: the duchess is made pregnant by her own husband, and it is only because she had earlier prayed to the devil for a child that her pregnancy is compromised.[97]

To this point we have concentrated on male incubi, but there is no doubt that in the popular imagination human/fairy miscegenation might quite as easily involve female incubi (or succubi, as they came to be called): "Ofte in mannes forme . wommen hii comeþ to," writes Robert of Gloucester, "& ofte in wimmen forme . hii comeþ to men al so."[98] Even Trevisa acknowledges, that

> That fend þat gooth a ny3t,
> Wommen wel ofte to begile.

Incubus hatte be ry3t;
And gileþ men oþer while,
Succubus is þat wight.⁹⁹

Romance has no difficulty with this brand of fairy/mortal interbreeding—not only the Lusignans, but also the English house of Plantagenet owed their origins to it—but it presented the great tradition with an obvious problem. Ingenious demons might be able to transport male semen at body temperature, but portable uteruses were quite another matter.¹⁰⁰ In actual fact, however, the church's real reason for its comparative neglect of the female fairy lover was probably its unreflective misogyny (reinforced by the patrilineal anxieties of its patrons), for once we reverse the gender polarities, we find ourselves in an entirely different cultural landscape.

Augustine's 'birth certificate of the medieval incubus' casts incubi as male (as silvans or pans always ready to accomplish their lustful desire to have intercourse with women),¹⁰¹ but it is striking how many of his scholarly followers are eager to reimagine such incubi as female. To take one obvious example, Gervase of Tilbury immediately after citing Augustine goes on to discuss apparently reliable reports of how lovers of spirits of this kind ("quosdam huiusmodi laruarum . . . amatores"), fairies, in other words ("quas fadas nominant"), died as soon as they contemplated marrying other women ("ad aliarum feminarum matrimonia se transtuleru*nt*").¹⁰² So too Thomas of Cantimpré, writing of the *dusii* about whom the most glorious Augustine has written explicitly ("de quibus gloriosissimus augustinus in libro de ciuitate dei euidentissime scribit"), says that they suddenly snatch the bodies of living men from among mankind, as for Diana ("hominum uiuentium corpora vt dyane subito ex hominibus rapiebant").¹⁰³ Walter Map has several stories of love affairs between humans and supernatural creatures, but generally the human lover is the male and the fairy is the female partner. Not only Eadric the Wild but also Gwestin Gwestiniog, Henno *cum dentibus*, and Gerbert/Silvester II all conform to this pattern, though perhaps this is predictable in an author whose antimatrimonial tract *Valerius ad Ruffinum* was clearly written for a male audience.

A similar pattern is also apparent (as we shall see) in vernacular romance, whose aristocratic preoccupations are reflected in this conspicuously masculine form of wish fulfillment.¹⁰⁴ Not that male fairy lovers never appear in romance, but it is striking how often they are merely the nameless progenitors of the real stories' male heroes—Yonec, Tydorel, and Degaré, for example. However, as Diane Purkiss has written, "if we follow medieval minds into the fairy forest, we will see that men and women take separate paths,"[105] and it is surely no coincidence that the most fully developed of such male fairy lovers, the father of Yonec, should have been created by a female poet, Marie de France. Furthermore, the tension between the twin roles of the fairy mistress (as object of erotic desire and as agent of capricious power) is deeply gendered.[106] We have seen it reflected in Chaucer's *Wife of Bath's Tale*, and we will meet it again in *Partonope of Blois*; its origins are to be sought, I suggest, in the deepest recesses of Purkiss's fairy forest, where, according to one version of the *Seven Sages of Rome*, there bubbles a spring which has the property of changing men into women and women into men.[107] Perhaps when William of Auvergne thanks God that no one has ever heard of fairies being homosexual,[108] he is reacting instinctively to a threat to orthodox power structures posed by fairy eroticism.

Another characteristic of female, as opposed to male, fairy lovers, then, is that they must be sought at the untamed edges of the human lifeworld. Except where their potential partners inhabit monastic cells (in which case predatory succubi are quite prepared to pay house calls),[109] they are generally encountered, as Robert of Gloucester puts it, "in wilde studes." Burchard of Worms's sylvans, "who are said to be corporeal and, when they wish, show themselves to their lovers, and take pleasure with them," were a feature of the countryside ("agrestes femine"),[110] and Walter Map's Eadric the Wild, as his name implies ("quod est silvestris"), was a frequenter of the woods where his fairy bride resided. William of Auvergne gives a vivid picture of the kind of delusion about which, he says, many stories were told in the western regions, particularly Brittany: "someone seems to find himself in a magnificent and beautiful palace, with a most beautiful woman, regal in dress and adornments, by his side, and he attends the most splendid banquets with her, and afterwards passes the whole night with her in sexual delights. But when all this suddenly vanishes he realizes that he has spent the entire night in the foul mud" [videtur sibi aliquis esse in palatio magnifico, atque pulchro, & videre sibi mulierem speciosissimam in apparatu regio & ornatu, esseque in epulis splendendissimis cum ipsa, & postmodum in lecto venereis deliciis tota nocte cum ipsa. Huiusmodi autem subito evanescentibus deprehendit se fuisse in luto sordidissimo tota nocte].[111]

Although William accounts for such experiences as delusory dreams, their open-air setting makes them much harder to rationalize than, say, Merlin's mother's trysts. Yet the fact that Burchard includes these *agrestes femine* in his confessional handbook implies that a belief in their existence was widespread, and William of Auvergne confirms that they were an almost constant topic of conversation among the people of Brittany: "in ore hominum regionis illius pene assiduis narrationibus creberrimum" [often in the mouths of the men of that region with their almost incessant stories]. Particularly striking is the fact that he reports having (almost) met a man who had had the experience: "Et memini me videre potuisse virum cui illusio ista acciderat; non autem vidi propter negligenciam meam, atque desidiam" [I recall that I could have seen a man who suffered from this delusion, but I missed seeing him because of my own carelessness and sloth]. Predictably enough, clerical writers were keen to warn that liaisons with fairy mistresses would never end well (and that any children begotten with them were bound to turn out badly). Here, for example, is the *South English Legendary*:

And mani fol hom liþ so by in wode and eke in mede
Ac þer nis non þat so deþ þat ne acoreþ þe dede
Hore membres toswelleþ somme & somme ofscapeþ vnneþe
And somme fordwineþ al awei forte hi be[o] ibroȝt to deþe
More wonder it is iwis hou eni ofscapeþe of liue
For an attri þing it is to lemman oþer to wiue (lines 247–52)[112]

[And many a fool lies with them thus in woods and meadows, but everyone who does so pays for it: the members of some of them swell up, some scarcely break free, and some fade away and die; it is more wonder that any of them escape alive, for it is a foul thing to take one as a lover or a wife].

Gervase of Tilbury too suggests that those who take fairy lovers risk losing "even the solace of a wretched life" [*etiam misere vite solatium*]. It seems that for William of Auvergne's Breton dreamer, merely wallowing in *luto sordidissimo* was the least of his worries.

The writers of vernacular romance, on the other hand, express no such concerns. In Breton lais (and longer romances, such as *Partonope of Blois*) liaisons with fairy mistresses are invariably exotic and exciting. It is here that the correlation of the marvelous with the erotic, ubiquitous in medieval romance, is at its most transparent.[113] Though such liaisons may be hedged about with prohibitions and taboos, and though they are not always conducted in an atmosphere of untroubled harmony, they offer a vision of frank sexual gratification that lies beyond the reach of stifling patrilineal regulation or ecclesiastical repression; there is no place in fairyland for an Emily making her sacrifice in Diana's temple or a Cecilia wearing a hair shirt beneath her wedding dress. Among the English Breton lais, *Sir Launfal* most clearly embodies this ethos. Resting at the edge of a wood, the impoverished Launfal is approached by two maidens who invite him to come and speak with their mistress, Dame Triamour, in her pavilion.[114] There, in a luxurious setting, he finds the daughter of the "kyng of Fayrye" ready to place herself entirely at his disposal:

> Jn þe pauyloun he fond a bed of prys
> Jheled wyth purpur bys,
> Þat semylé was of sy3te:
> Þerjnne lay þat lady gent
> (Þat after Syr Launfal hedde ysent),
> Þat lefsom lemede bry3t.
> For hete her cloþes down sche dede
> Almest to her gerdylstede:
> Þan lay sche vncovert.
> Sche was as whyt as lylye yn May,
> Or snow þat sneweth yn wynterys day—
> He seygh neuer non so pert. (lines 283–94)

Naked to the waist (surely "pert" here is punning on the sense 'exposed'), she exploits the (male) audience's sexual fantasies as she invites Launfal's eager gaze, and only a few lines later she is informing him that "Þer nys no man yn Cristenté" (line 304) whom she loves as much as him and offering to make him rich—"Yf þou wylt truly to me take" (line 315). Untold wealth (particularly attractive to the penniless Launfal) is another common benefit of taking a fairy lover. After a sumptuous supper, they go to bed:

> Whan þey had sowpeþ, & þe day was gon,
> Þey wente to bedde, & þat anoon,
> Launfal & sche yn fere.
> For play lytyll þey sclepte þat ny3t,
> Tyll on morn hyt was dayly3t. (lines 346–50)

She promises to come to him in secret whenever he wishes it, but inevitably there is to be a condition—he is to mention her name to no one—and, equally inevitably, he will later break it and lose her goodwill. After a period of penance, however, Triamour forgives him, and Launfal is "take ynto Fayrye" (line 1035)—"Fer ynto a jolyf ile, / Olyroun that hyghte" (lines 1021–22)—where presumably the two of them remain in bliss to this day.

Several French *lais féeriques* share with *Launfal* this obvious strand of masculine wish fulfillment. In both *Graelent* and *Guingamor* the heroes first encounter their fairy lovers bathing naked in forest pools and in order to prolong their voyeuristic recreation steal their clothes.[115] (Interestingly the fabliau *Le Chevalier qui fist parler les cons* begins with just such a scenario, and it is in exchange for their clothes that the fairies endow him with his improbable talent.) While Guingamor's lady grants him her love willingly, Graelent's conquest has every appearance of rape: "En l'espece de la forest / a fait de li ce que li plest" [in the depths of the forest he did with her what he pleased] (lines 281–82). Désiré too, encountering a fairy *pucele* in a wood, threatens to rape her, but he is talked out of it when she offers to take him to see her even more beautiful mistress, whom he finds ensconced in a woodland bower.[116] As in *Launfal* there is a strong element of voyeurism:

> Veïstes vus unk si bel vis,
> si beles meins, ne si beus braz,
> ne si gent cors vestu a laz,
> plus beus chevoils ne plus dulgez
> plus asssemezne meuz treciez?
> Unques ne fu si belle nee. (lines 188–93)

[Have you ever seen so beautiful a face, such beautiful hands, such beautiful arms, so fair a body in a robe adorned with laces, more beautiful hair, finer or better arranged and coiffed? Never was born so beautiful a creature.]

Désiré is the only one of these three lovers to have children with his fairy mistress, but his son and daughter are far from being the monsters envisaged by the great tradition: "Beles esteient sanz mesure / de cors, de vis e de feiture" [they were exceptionally fair of body, of face, and of demeanor] (lines 691–92). Graelent, Guingamor, and Désiré (like Lanval) all inevitably break their mistresses' solemn prohibitions (Désiré, significantly, by confessing his love to a hermit), but all are eventually forgiven, and all end up living out their days in fairyland. Only when one comes to understand this dimension of the traditional fairy romance can the rich comedy of Chaucer's Sir

Thopas, setting out to find himself an "elf-queene" to "slepe under [his] goore" (lines 788–89), be fully appreciated.

Perhaps the most fascinating romance from this point of view is *Partonopeu de Blois* (written in the early 1180s),[117] together with its mid-fifteenth-century English translation.[118] The plot, at least up to the breaking of the prohibition, follows closely the pattern of the Breton lais that we have been considering (*Lanval* in particular), though it is developed at a far more leisurely pace. Partonope is carried in a boat, manned by an invisible crew (as in Marie de France's *Guigamer*), to a handsome city set in a fertile and prosperous landscape and dominated by a splendid castle, but nowhere does he see any inhabitants. After a fine supper, served by invisible attendants, he retires to bed, where he is visited by an invisible lady who, after an extended exchange, grants him her sexual favors.[119] The prohibition is an odd one: he is to make no attempt to pierce her veil of invisibility for two and a half years. In return the lady, whose name is Melior, gives him the run of her castle; supplies him with clothing, food, and drink—"Whatte he wolde haue, a-none was fette" (line 2090)—and leaves him his days free to be passed in hunting and hawking. Each night he spends in Melior's bed:

> He made hym redy wyth-owte moo
> Streyte in-to þe bedde to goo
> And when he was in bedde layde,
> Sone aftyr, wyth-In a lytelle brayde,
> Comethe his ladye fayre and ffre.
> Her In hys Armes þen takethe he,
> And kyssethe her, and makethe her feste,
> And wyth her doþe what euer hym leste. (lines 2107–14)

As if all this is not enough, when after a year he returns to France to fight in his king's cause, Melior sends along with him twelve packhorses loaded with treasure, "To mayntayne yowr warres, and that in armes / Ye shulde be worchyppfull" (lines 2534–35).

Everything about this abundance, sexual and otherwise, suggests that Melior is a fairy. This indeed is what Partonope himself supposes from the very beginning: "This is a Shyppe of ffarye" (line 743), he says to himself when first he is spirited away, and on arriving in Melior's country, "He thouȝte he was but in fayre" (line 887). When, back in France, he tells his mother about Melior, she goes off to inform the king,

In Arderne a-monge þe wylde bestes,
Ther drewe to hym a þynge of ffeyre,
As þowe hyt had ben a woman or a ladye." (lines 5071–73)

The disenchantment that the poet attempts to effect under these circumstances is far more transparent than anything in Chrétien de Troyes. It turns out that in reality she is no fairy but rather, as she tells Partonope after he has broken her prohibition, the only child of the Emperor of Constantinople educated in the seven liberal arts, in medicine, and in divinity. "[T]o Nygromancy sette I was," she says, "Then I lerned Enchawntemente[s], / To knowe þe crafte of experimente[s]" (lines 5933–35). She is, in other words, a sorceress, and everything—the ship, the marvelous land, the invisible servants—were all an illusion.

The author of the non-cyclic *Lancelot* works the same trick (indeed he may well have learned it from *Partonopeu*), but his sleight of hand is no more convincing in the case of the Lady of the Lake (who, as Elspeth Kennedy puts it, "is a fairy by education, not by nature or heredity")[120] than in Melior's.[121] Similarly, Chaucer's Franklin, a male narrator, it should be noted, substitutes "magyk natureel" for the fairy enchantment we should normally expect to find in a Breton lai (*The Franklin's Tale*, line 1125).[122] From this point of view *The Wife of Bath's Tale* offers a significantly better example of the genre than does *The Franklin's Tale*. Chaucer's contemporary Jean d'Outremeuse comes close to trying to explain all fairy phenomena as nigromantic, but while he lists Partonope's lover along with Virgil, Mahomet, and Merlin as one of those who possessed "la science de faire les faieriez" [the expertise to perform wonders], he is also careful to stress her orthodoxy: "chelle s[av]oit plus de faierie que femme qui fust en monde, et fasoit ches invocacion des eperis par les hals nom de Dieu" [she knew more about wonders than any mortal woman, and she invoked spirits with the holy name of God].[123]

Partonope's mother has no such charitable view of her son's lover and sets out to free him from Melior's power. She first employs a love potion in a bid to get Partonope to marry the king's niece, but since he recovers his wits before the marriage is consummated, Melior forgives his lapse. Her second attempt proves more successful: she gets the Archbishop of Paris to convince her son that his liaison with Melior is sinful and then procures a magic lantern that will penetrate her cloak of invisibility. Had Melior remained a fairy (as she had clearly been in an earlier version of the story), this employment of magic against her would have been entirely understandable, but as it is, the idea that a powerful sorceress, able to conjure an entire kingdom out of thin air, should be tricked by a simple magic lantern rings rather hollow. More disturbing is the way the romance departs at this point from the traditional pattern we have seen in the other *lais féeriques*. In the typical lai it is only at the moment when the hero breaks his fairy lover's prohibition that her full power becomes manifest; he falls entirely under her control and sometimes, as in *Lanval*, his very life is at stake. In *Partonopeu*, by contrast, the breaking of the prohibition leads to Melior losing all her magic powers, becoming in effect the standard courtly mistress, angry and resentful but bound entirely by the traditions of *fin amour*. As a result the air seems to go out of the poem—the second half is far more orthodox than the first. From a powerful and seductive woman Melior is reduced to a bland and passive romance heroine, forced to await the outcome of a tournament to discover whether she can offer her hand to Partonope. Indeed at one point she launches into a lengthy excursus on the powerlessness of women to follow their own inclinations:

> And yite [I] wote, if I shuld hym sewe,
> That were a thing done of þe newe,
> For womanhode wole not þat it be so. (lines 10743–45)[124]

Dynastic and theocratic pressures have transformed Melior from a Triamour into an Emilye.

But that is not quite the whole story; Partonope's mother's employment of magic arts against her son's lover changes the rules of the game in a way that is particularly appropriate to this member of the "garants de la *doxa*," as Gingras calls her (p. 394). This is even clearer in the fifteenth-century English translation, which differs from its twelfth-century original in both the frequency with which Melior repeats her prohibition and the specific terms in which she frames it. Partonopeu, says the original, must inquire after no skill ("par vos ne soit *engiens* quis" or "ne soit *ars* quise") by which she might be seen,[125] but in English this skill is explicitly spelled out as nigromancy:

> And o thyng, my loue, y praye yowe
> That yn no wyse ye ne besy yowe howe
> By craffte of nygromansy me to see.
> For it wolle be for yowr worse be. (lines 2423–26; cf. line 1872)

Nigromancy is of course a learned discipline, a creature of the great tradition; its ethos is predominantly masculine,[126] and the spirits it deals with are ostensibly demons, not fairies. Even so, despite the masculine assumptions and values that dominate it, its essential complicity with the fairy world meant that the Middle Ages might still occasionally associate it with female practitioners. Melior, after all, had gone to school to learn nigromancy (line 1593), and she was not alone in this; so too had Niniene in *Lancelot do Lac* (Merlin was her tutor), the wicked stepmother in *William of Palerne*, and even Bertrand du Guesclin's wife, Tiffany. Nevertheless this book-magic has little in common with the predominantly feminine magic of the *lais féeriques*, which draws its nourishment from much deeper roots—from the long-standing association of fairies with the natural world, with the Dame Abundance whose cult so alarmed William of Auvergne. Male wish fulfillment helps to account for the popularity of sexually aggressive fairy heroines such as Melior among contemporary audiences, but at a deeper level their appeal derives from their enchantment of the natural world they inhabit—though in reality, of course, fairies do not merely inhabit this world, they also exercise dominion over it: Tyolet inherits from a fairy the art of catching wild animals merely by whistling for them; and Melior gives Partonopeu a magic horn to take hunting with him. To offend the fairies (as happens with the rape at the beginning of *The Elucidation*) is to risk turning this world into a wasteland; to submit to their will (the lesson that Lanval, Guingamor, Graelent, and Désiré all must learn) is to enjoy wealth and plenty.

Nigromancy turns this world on its head. As Michael Bailey has argued, by making female magic appear passive, by privileging masculine "intellectual striving" over feminine "susceptibility to temptation,"[127] it promotes a process of demonization that will contribute to the witch-hunting mentality of the early modern period. A process whose beginnings can already be detected in the late twelfth-century *Partonopeu* is well advanced in the fifteenth-century English *Partonope*. From the moment that nigromancy is employed against her, Melior becomes powerless, no longer agent but patient, fearful that the sexuality that was once the source of her potency must now be her undoing.

Reginald Scot, a great debunker of all things numinous, writing of necromancers or conjurers in 1584, explains that "these are no small fooles, they go not to worke with a baggage [*nasty*] tode, or a cat, as witches doo; but with a kind of majestie, and with authoritie they call vp by name . . . seventie and nine principall princelie diuels."[128] It is hardly surprising then that we should be able to detect a strong sexist bias in their activities or discover, for instance, that their stock in trade should have included a spell "to fetch vnto thee the fairie Sibylia":

> I coniure thee Sibylia, O gentle virgine of fairies, . . . by the king and queene of fairies, and their virtues, and by the faith and obedience that thou bearest vnto them . . . by the bloud that ranne out of the side of our Lord Iesus Christ crucified, and by the opening of heaven . . . to appeare in that circle before me visible, in the forme and shape of a beautifull woman in a bright and [white vesture], adorned and garnished most faire, and to appeare to me quicklie without deceipt or tarrieng; and that thou faile not to fulfill my will & desire effectuallie. For I will choose thee to be my blessed virgine, & will haue common copulation with thee.[129]

It is all too easy to assume that Scot is simply having fun with the witch-hunters here, that no one could possibly have taken such an incantation seriously, but several apparently genuine spells of the same kind survive, and they contain elements that evidently go back some way.[130] Since there could hardly be a better illustration of the misogynist assumptions underlying the learned demonization of the medieval fairy lover, we will conclude this chapter with four such spells preserved on a late sixteenth-century vellum sheet in the Folger Library (MS Xd 234).

It is impossible to date these spells (they are certainly older than 1600), but their male fantasies are timeless. Two of them (spells 2 and 3) concern arranging for sexual liaisons with fairies: "heare followethe þe waye & manor howe youe shall call one of theese vergins of fayres aforenamed at onces vnto thy beed when[e]vere thoue liste & haue her at pleasuer."[131] There can be little doubt that they were intended in all seriousness; there is no smoke screen of allegory or irony here to confuse the issue. After a great deal of preparatory mumbo jumbo, the crucial conjuration in spell 2 reads as follows:

> I conniore þe blessed & bountyfull virgynes all þe Ryall names & wordes afore Reacited, & charge þe to apeare in this cyrcle vysyble in the forme and shape of a bountyfull maide & virgine befor me in a grene gowne & bewtyfule [*appar*]elle & most fayreste to be holde, & to apeare quycklye & pleasantlye wᵗ owᵗ [*lette*] or tarryenge, and you fayle not to fullfyle my wile & desier effectuallye for I shall [*chose*] the & haue the to be my blessed virgine & Ioye: maike haste & spede to come to me & apeare before me for I wile haue a carnall copulacion wᵗʰ the therfore maike haste and come by the vertewe of the father the Sone, & the hollye gooste. (p. 342)

Particularly striking is the inclusion of the Trinity in this invocation (paralleling Reginald Scot's blood from Christ's side). While this might possibly be construed as an instance of Carlo Ginzburg's "cultural compromise formation,"[132] it seems more likely, given the esoteric nature of the document itself, that the author is merely ventriloquizing the kind of magical discourse that permeated much late medieval Christianity,[133] a reaction that Gramsci would have found perfectly understandable.

Even more remarkably, spell 3 contains a set of instructions on how to proceed after the conjuration has been successfully effected:

> This said goo to thy naked beed wth her but laye youe one to þ[e] Ryght syde & lett lye one her lefte syde & do wth her what soo ever you pleasse or canste doo for wthow^{t} doute shee is a woman + & you needeste not to feare her for shee shall haue no power to hurte the, beinge so bownde as is afore to the prescribed, nor the nether [*thou never?*] in the lyf hadiste soo pleasante a creature or lyvelye woman in beed wth the for bewtye & bountye nether quene nor empres in all the all worlde is able to countervaile her for I haue dyveres tymes provede her & haue had her wth me amen. (p. 344)

"I have diverse times proved her and had her with me": I can think of no better illustration of the historically contingent nature of the unstable boundary between fact and fiction nor any better way to satisfy C. S. Lewis's injunction to try to imagine "what it would feel like to witness, or think we had witnessed, or merely to believe in" the *ferlies* of medieval romance.[134]

CHAPTER 4

Christ the Changeling

> That the Fairies would steale away young children and putt others in their places: verily believed by old woemen of those dayes: and by some yet living.
>
> —John Aubrey, *Remains of Gentilisme*

In a 2001 article in the *Journal of the History of Behavioral Science*, C. F. Goodey and T. Stainton suggest that the concept of the fairy changeling had little, if any, general currency in the Middle Ages, arguing counterintuitively that the handful of surviving medieval references to the belief indicate that it was the product of a learned rather than a popular tradition.[1] Tempting as it is for medievalists to deprecate this amateurish foray into their terrain,[2] the fact remains that though changelings abound in later folklore, they are indeed something of a rarity in works written before 1500. Even a widely read folklorist such as J. A. MacCulloch can write that "the belief in fairy changelings is not found as such in medieval records."[3] In what follows I hope to correct the misapprehension that the idea of the changeling was foreign to the Middle Ages, especially the vernacular Middle Ages, and also to explain why it is that medieval records, if not entirely silent on this topic, are often equivocal. In addition I explore how popular notions of the changeling and similar fairy stereotypes might be used to subvert expressions of official culture—the English mystery plays offering a particularly rich source of evidence for such subversion.

First, however, we must be clear about what we mean by a 'changeling.' It is always risky to assume that any folkloric belief ever takes on a single and immutable form ("folklore," wrote Antonio Gramsci, "is much more unstable and fluctuating than language"),[4] and doubtless different regions at different periods held a variety of attitudes toward changelings and ascribed various qualities to them. It is possible to draw a fairly clear general picture, however. Changelings are fairies who have been substituted for their human counterparts. Usually these are children, though adult changelings can appear.[5] Changeling children are generally unattractive, bad tempered, sickly, and difficult to raise; often a lapse in parental vigilance, or a failure to take the proper precautions, is thought to have given the fairies an opportunity to make the substitution, and this can then be reversed only by performing elaborate rituals. Later folklorists have recorded a number of explanations for why fairies should wish to exchange their children for those of human parents,[6] but such explicit rationalization is not found in works from the Middle Ages.

Fairy intercourse with the world of mortals, in both the Middle Ages and more recent times, could take many different forms, and it is important to distinguish changelings from the participants in three closely related situations. One is straightforward fairy abduction. Fairies often abduct mortals—generally speaking, adults such as Sir Orfeo's wife (Heurodis) or Guingamor or Thomas of Erceldoune—but no living fairy substitutes are left behind in the mortal world as replacements for them. The well-known account in Ralph of Coggeshall's *Chronicon Anglicanum* of the human child called Malkin, apparently stolen by the fairies when her parents left her unguarded in the corner of a field at harvest time, is sometimes cited as evidence for a belief in changelings.[7] Malkin revisits the mortal world (much to the chagrin of her guardians) and converses with the family of Sir Osbern de Bradwell in Suffolk. Though generally invisible, she shows herself to one of the chambermaids in the form of "a very small child dressed in a white frock" [in specie parvissimi infantis, quae induebatur quadam alba tunica]. Her human nature is manifest in her visits to a chapel and in her demands for food and drink. However, while she does reveal that she has spent seven years in her new home, and still has seven more left to serve, she makes no mention of any fairy child left behind in her place, so that there is no reason to suppose that we are dealing here with anything other than a simple abduction. We do know that some mothers of "childeren þat been new boren or þai been cristunned" performed elaborate protective rituals for them "because of wicked wiʒthes,"[8] but this evidence is not easy to interpret. One of these rituals, tying the child to a stool or bench, need hardly be taken to imply anything more than a fear of abduction, though others, such as placing the baby in a sieve with some bread and cheese or alternatively with its father's underwear—"of þe fadur of þe childe sum preuy clooth"—might indeed be construed as protection against changelings: we shall see that an assertion of the child's claim on the family's food as well as a demonstration of its legitimate paternity could both be taken to be ways of warding off such fairy predation.

A second situation that invites comparison with that of the changeling is the child who has been 'elf-shot,' that is, afflicted with a sickness caused by the fairies.[9] As with the changeling, elaborate rituals might be required to effect a cure for the elf-shot child. In the late sixteenth century, for example, a twenty-year-old woman named Catherine Fenwicke deposed before the ecclesiastical court in Durham that her cousin had had a sick child and that one Jenkyn Pereson's wife had asked after it and suggested that the cousin consult her about the child: "And upon the same this deponent went unto hir; and the said Pereson wyfe said the child was taken with the farye, and bad hir sent 2 for southrowninge [south-running] water, and theis 2 shull not speke by the waye, and that the child shuld be washed in that water, and dib the shirt in the water, and so hang it upon a hedge all that night, and on the morowe the shirt shuld be gone and the child shuld recover health; but the shirt was not gone, as she said. And this deponent paid to Pereson wyfe 3d. for hir paynes."[10] While it is certainly possible that Jenkyn Pereson's wife is here trying to recover a changeling from the fairies, it seems more likely that all she is really doing is seeking to appease the fairies who have caused the child's sickness. So too we learn that as a child the Suffolk cunning woman Marion Clerk had had her neck twisted awry as a result of conversing with the elves and that she had been healed by an old man, though no details of his healing rituals are given.[11] Thus when Bernard Gui, the early fourteenth-century inquisitor, suggests that suspected female heretics should be asked "what they know, or have known, or have done about boys [*pueris*] or infants who were *fatatis* ['fairied'] or who 'had to be unfairied' [*defatandis*],"[12] it is impossible to tell whether he is referring to those who were imagined to be changelings, 'elf-shot,' or simply 'fated' in some way.

Last, there are the offspring of mortals and fairies (the incubi of clerical writers). We have seen that the most famous of such medieval hybrids was Merlin, but they were certainly not restricted to Arthurian romance. While it is not uncommon for such fairy parentage to manifest itself in some kind of physical abnormality, continual wailing, an insatiable appetite, and a failure to put on weight are not typical symptoms. Matthew Paris reports that the Welsh son of an *incuba* had all his teeth by six months but that, far from failing to thrive, by his teenage years he had grown to be unusually tall (a *gigantulus*, in fact).[13] Similarly, Tydorel, the son of a fairy, is unable to sleep (a characteristic that accompanies him into adulthood), but in other respects he is superior to his fellows. Many of Melusine's offspring betray their fairy parentage with odd traits (one eye higher than the other, unusually large ears, a tuft of hair on the end of the nose), but only her last, the aptly named Horrible, might possibly have been mistaken for a demon. Clearly, routine clerical demonization of fairies is responsible for the resemblance of Horrible to a changeling: "he was so euyl & so cruel that at the fourethe yere of his age he slew two of hys nourryces";[14] and this is equally true of Sir Gowther: "Be twelfe-monethys was gon, / Nyne norsus had he slon" (lines 114–15).[15] In the same way, Donegild in Chaucer's *Man of Law's Tale* misrepresents her daughter-in-law Constance as a fairy and her grandchild as being "so horrible a feendly creature" that no one could bear to be near it (lines 751–53).[16] Though such hybrid children can sometimes be represented as ugly and malicious, then, it is important to distinguish them from true changelings, all the more so since they *were* sometimes so confused in the Middle Ages and later. One reason for this is that both changelings and hybrid children raised a similar theological problem: devils, whatever other powers they may possess, cannot be credited with the God-given ability to procreate, either among themselves or with mortals. Another reason is that fairy hybrids, like changelings, might raise difficult questions of paternity and legitimacy; however, since hybrids were not necessarily insinuated into the family unit—some (such as Gowther) were, and others (such as Merlin) were not—they posed a less immediate threat to the patriarchy than did changelings.

    The general functionalist account that a belief in fairies offers "an explanation of happenings which apparently go against the natural and expected course of things"[17] has been widely accepted by folklorists writing about changelings, and a number of attempts have been made to identify the specific disability, such as 'failure to thrive,' that might have led to a child's being labeled a changeling in the Middle Ages.[18] Given the nature of the evidence (even for the post-medieval world), such attempts can take us only so far, but John Lindow's skillful analysis of the cultural pressures underlying changeling stories offers a far more promising line of investigation.[19] Lindow makes three important points: first, that direct descriptions of changelings are almost always made by educated observers who will inevitably attempt to explain away the simple beliefs of the poor and uneducated (this is as true of some recent commentators as of Carl Linnaeus, who examined a changeling in 1741); second, that changelings are overwhelmingly male;[20] and third, that accounts of both the behavior of the changelings and the rituals performed to reverse the exchange are often associated with the production, preparation, and consumption of food. The conclusion he draws from all this is that "[the changeling] was an extra mouth to feed, while at the same time, his illness deprived the household of a worker. In that sense the illness indeed made an exchange: a productive worker for an unproductive dependent. Legends of changelings mapped that unarticulated exchange onto the articulated exchange of a supernatural being" (p. 223).

The fullest medieval discussion of a belief in changelings is that of William of Auvergne from the early thirteenth century. It comes at the end of a lengthy refutation of those who credit demons with possessing procreative powers, since William is keen to prove not only that demons cannot interbreed with humans but also that they cannot breed among themselves:

> I must not pass over the little children [*parvulos*] whom the ignorant people call *cambiones*, and of whom the most ignorant old-wives' tales [*vulgarissimi sermones aniles*] report that they are the sons of *incubi demons* substituted by the demons with women so that they may be brought up by them as if they were their own sons, for which reason they are called *cambiones*, from *cambiti*, that is "having been exchanged," and substituted with female parents in place of their own sons. They say they are skinny and always wailing, and such milk-drinkers that four nurses do not supply a sufficient quantity of milk to feed one. These appeared to have remained with their nurses for many years, and afterwards to have flown away, or rather vanished. Thus I say that my earlier pronouncement [about the inability of demons to procreate] needs no modification: for it is easy for evil spirits to take on the appearance of this kind of child and seem to be exchanged with humans, whenever divine goodness permits things of this kind. . . . That children of this kind seemed for so long almost to have drained the breasts of nurses or consumed other kinds of nourishment was therefore only a deceptive vision and not the truth, which is why they vanished, leaving no trace of their former existence.[21]

We should note that William regards changelings as predominantly male [*filii daemonum incuborum*], that he regards a voracious appetite as their main characteristic, and that as a learned commentator he feels compelled to explain them away as a demonic illusion visited upon the ignorant.

Though William's account was to become the standard scholastic explanation for changelings throughout the Middle Ages (it was reused by Ranulph Higden in the mid-fourteenth century and by an anonymous German demonologist early in the fifteenth, and was still being echoed as late as the *Malleus Maleficarum*),[22] it leaves one gaping hole. If changelings are demonic doubles substituted for real children, what then becomes of the original infants? Where do they go? Folk belief, unlike scholastic theology, has no difficulty with such a question since fairyland is imagined as a real and potentially accessible location, a place to which human children (and indeed adults) may easily be abducted. But demons have no such hospitable homeland to which they can carry off their prizes. Jean-Claude Schmitt has drawn our attention to three saints' lives, those of Lawrence, Bartholomew, and Stephen, whose early scenes are evidently fashioned around a changeling motif—though Stephen only partially fits the model since, after he is stolen from his cradle, an effigy (an *idolum*), not a wailing, voracious demon, is left in his place.[23] However, following the theft, all three, *faute de mieux*, must then be abandoned as foundlings to be brought up by (human) strangers: Lawrence is left in the woods, Bartholomew on a rock, and Stephen, with an irony apparently lost on the hagiographer, on the doorstep of a bishop. In due course they will make their way back to their birth parents and evict their usurpers, but this essential period of exile in fairyland has clearly frustrated clerical attempts to provide it with a simple and politically correct topographical correlative.

Self-evidently, a medical explanation of changelings raises far fewer difficulties than a pastoral one does. William of Canterbury has left us a remarkably detailed description of the kind of disability that might be ascribed to a fairy exchange in his account of Thomas à Becket's miraculous cure of a boy called Augustine:[24]

> Within six months of his birth he was wasted with such great emaciation and gauntness, that he exhibited a wretched appearance, having less flesh on his whole body than an able-bodied person has on one of his fingers. A severe affliction, caused by a pulmonary injury, or the noise of his wailing, or various other reasons recognized by the medical profession [*aliis causis quas physicus assignat*], had consumed his bodily substance.... His spine jutted out so that his ribs and vertebrae showed clearly. His arms hung

down haphazardly, just like twigs from the middle of a branch. His face was wretched, more a mask than a face—as it were, a life without vitality, a substance without form, a body without structure. The exhaustion of his essential fluids and an ugly desiccation (a mere heap of bones) refuted his claim to humanity, but on the other hand his wailings and his facial movements hinted at something human.[25]

William's careful enumeration of these medical symptoms seems designed to counter any possibility of attributing Augustine's disease to supernatural influence, and indeed he inserts into the middle of it the pointed remark that "no one of balanced mind believes the fanciful absurdities of the common people, who think that boys are exchanged or transformed [*pueri supponi putat aut transformari*]."

Despite William of Auvergne's assurance that changelings were really devils who would vanish of their own accord given time, or William of Canterbury's insistence that they were simply real children suffering from a medical condition best left to the doctors (or to the intercession of a saint), laypeople evidently had their own ways of dealing with the problem. The only extended medieval description of a ritual of recovery, discussed at length in a famous study by Jean-Claude Schmitt, is found in Étienne de Bourbon's story of the cult of Saint Guinefort, the holy greyhound. The death of this faithful dog, unjustly killed after defending his master's infant son from a snake, was the subject of an ancient and well-known exemplum (it is one of the oldest tales in the popular collection known as *The Seven Sages of Rome*),[26] but in a village near Lyon in the early thirteenth century this dog's supposed tomb became a site for performing a ritual to recover changelings from the fairies (Étienne's term for them is *fauni*).

Schmitt's study is so thorough that there might seem to be little left to add, but I might remark in passing that exposing infants to snakes seems sometimes to have been regarded as a paternity test: "And when þer childer war born, þai wolde put þies serpentis in þe creduls with þaim, at þai mot prufe whethur þai wer þer trew fadurs or nay."[27] This tradition goes back at least as far as Pliny's *Natural History* (7.2.14), which locates the practice in Africa, as does Bartholomaeus Anglicus,[28] but others situate it in the Mediterranean—the *Golden Legend* in Mytilene and *Mandeville's Travels* on Sicily.[29] Some such folk belief seems to lie behind the story of Caradoc's almost having the life sucked out of him by a snake soon after discovering that the king who had raised him was not his real father,[30] or the odd incident in the *Cheuelere Assigne* when a boy called Aeneas, who is fighting a judicial duel to vindicate his mother and demonstrate his own legitimacy, is aided by an adder that "springs" from his shield.[31] We shall see that notions of the changeling were deeply implicated with issues of legitimacy, and it is surely no coincidence that a serpent-killing dog should become the patron saint of fairy abductees.

Here, then, is Étienne de Bourbon's account of the ritual recovery of an exchanged child as effected by Saint Guinefort:

> But the peasants, hearing of the dog's noble act and of how it had died guiltlessly . . . visited the place, honoured the dog as a martyr, prayed to it when they were sick or in need of something. . . . Above all, though, women who had weak or sickly boys [*pueros*] . . . would find an old woman who might teach them how to perform the rite and make offerings to the demons and invoke them, and who might lead them to the place. When they arrived there, they would make offerings of salt and other things and hang their boy's little garments [*panniculos pueri*] on the bushes round about; they would drive a needle into a tree-trunk that had grown in this place; they would pass the naked boy [*puerum*] between the trunks of two trees—the mother, on one side, held the boy and threw it nine times to the old woman, who was on the other side. After a demonic invocation, they called upon the fauns in the forest of Rimite to take the sick and feeble boy, which, they said, was theirs, and to bring back to them their own (whom the fauns were detaining), fat and well, safe and sound. Having done this, the murderous women[32] took the boy and laid him naked at the foot of the tree on straw from the cradle; then, using the light they had brought with them, they lit two candles, each an inch long, one on each side of the child's head and fixed them in the trunk above it. Then they withdrew until the candles had burnt out, so as not to see the boy nor hear him wail. . . . If, however, returning to the boy, they should find him still alive, they would carry him to a certain fast-flowing river nearby, called the Chalaronne, and immerse him in it nine times.[33]

This ritual is suspiciously elaborate, more likely a composite account from several witnesses melded into a formalized demonic rite conforming to Dominican expectations than a true reflection of the actual bricolage of folk custom. We might for instance compare it with the following from late sixteenth-century Hertfordshire:

> Mary Pennyfather, of Hippollettes, hath a woman childe of the age of fower yeares which could nether goe nor speke, whome she caryed to Thomas Harden, because it is noysed in the country that he is a wyse man and can skyll in many thinges, who tolde her that the childe was a changelinge, but wold in tyme helpe her. The next tyme she came unto hym he bade her to take a nutt and to picke out the curnell and fiyll yt with quicksilver, and to stoppe the hole with waxe and to bynd a thred a crosse over the nutte and to lay yt under a pyllow wher the chylde shoulde lye, and that shoulde helpe yt. Her chylde having therby noe helpe, she repared to him againe and then he bad her to sett the child upon a chare uppon a dungell by the space of an houer uppon a sonny day, which she did and the childe had no helpe.[34]

Rituals designed to reverse a fairy exchange are often harsh or brutal, so it is quite possible that prohibitions against placing children on roofs or in ovens as a cure for fever in a number of early Penitentials really refer to attempts to recover changelings from the fairies;[35] if so, it is particularly interesting that female children are sometimes specified ("mulier, si qua ponit filiam suam supra tectum vel in fornacem").[36] Of course the possibility remains that such children were simply thought to be elf-shot, suffering from a sickness caused by fairies.[37]

With Étienne de Bourbon's holy greyhound, we have almost come to the end of medieval scholastic accounts of changelings, but one allusion in the *Sermones Vulgares* of Étienne's predecessor Jacques de Vitry directs us toward a rather more intriguing line of investigation: the changeling in vernacular discourse. We saw that when William of Auvergne referred to changelings, he used the term *cambiones* (clearly a Latin calque, not a vernacular term at all), but Jacques de Vitry brings us far closer to the living language when he compares those who hear the word of God but fail to act on it "to the boy [*puero*] whom the French call a *chamium* whose breast-feeding exhausts many nurses but who never thrives nor grows, but has a hard and distended belly, though his body can never be induced to put on weight."[38] *Chamium* is the form of the word given in Paris, B.N., MS Latin 17509 (the copy text used by T. F. Crane, de Vitry's editor), but elsewhere it appears as *chamion* (in Cambridge, Mass.,

Harvard University, MS Riant 35, f. 67ʳ) and as *chamjon vel chanjon* (in Cambrai, MS 534).³⁹ There is indeed a Francien word, *chanjon* or *changon,* meaning 'changeling,' but in writing at least it seems to have been very rare. Godefroy's *Dictionnaire de l'ancienne langue française* supplies one instance from a letter of remission of 1427, and Tobler-Lommatzsch's *Altfranzösisches Wörterbuch* supplies another from Villon; there is a third instance in Martin le Franc's *Champion des Dames*. The *Altfranzösisches Wörterbuch* glosses *chanjon* as *Wechselbalg* [changeling], but in some ways the word's connotations are more interesting than its denotation; Godefroy glosses the 1427 instance as a "terme injurieux," while the *Französisches etymologisches Wörterbuch* says that Villon is using a word meaning 'enfant substitué' "*als schimpfwort*" [as an obscenity].

It is worth looking more closely at these instances. The first in particular gives a vivid picture of the word in actual use.⁴⁰ The petitioner, one Jean Rossignol, seeking release from prison, explains that he and William Tirant had been playing cards together quite amicably for a pint of wine and that after Tirant had lost, Jean asked to be paid his wine; thereupon Tirant, growing angry, had called him a *changon* and other bad words ("autres dures parolles"), and Jean had replied that he certainly was not a *changon* ("il n'estoit point changon") and threatened to do him an injury before he was very much older. Accordingly, having discovered that Tirant had stored some goods in a nearby house, Jean had helped himself to a piece of cloth (of equivalent value to his pint of wine?) and was promptly arrested. Now, if a man in 1427 felt that the authorities would understand that being called a *changon* might incite someone to petty theft, we can hardly suppose that, in oral use at least, *changon* was either a rare or an insignificant word. How then do we explain the fact that almost no one chose to commit it to writing? The obvious answer is that it must have been a taboo word, rarely written down because of its shameful connotations. There is, in fact, a rather obvious reason why *changon* should have acquired this status in medieval France: in a patrilineal society, where doubts as to paternity could have major consequences, *changon*, like 'bastard,' offered a serious threat to one's social standing. To call someone 'the son of a fairy' or perhaps, by this period, 'the son of a demon' was evidently a very serious matter.

There is a dramatic illustration of this from the Italian *Historiae romanae fragmenta*. In the late 1350s, when the papal legate Gil d'Albornoz was besieging the ruthless condottiere, Francesco Ordelaffi in the city of Forli, the chronicler tells us, Ordelaffi's son Lodovico made a sensible appeal to his father to give up his hopeless struggle with the church and offer the legate honorable terms. This produced an outraged eruption from his irascible parent: "You are a bastard [*biscione*], or else you were changed on me at the font [*mi fusti scagnato alli fonti*]."⁴¹ When the son turned away, his infuriated father stabbed him in the back and killed him. Even if this is a calumny invented by the chronicler (he earlier calls Ordelaffi, "a perfidious patarine dog"), it suggests how closely issues of fairy exchange were associated with questions of legitimacy and how easily *changon* might become a taboo word.

Most scholars, if they had to pick the one medieval French poet likely to flout such a taboo, would probably settle on François Villon, so it is perhaps unsurprising to find him writing in the *Lais*:

> Et a ce malostru changeon,
> Moutonnier, qui le tient en procés,
> Laisse troys coups d'un escourgon. (lines 141–43)⁴²

So rare a word is *changeon* that more than one editor has mistaken it for a proper name here, but it is clear that these lines actually mean "And to that foulmouthed changeling, Moutonnier, who is involved in a lawsuit with him [the Seigneur de Grigny], I leave three lashes of the whip." It would be easy to dismiss this particular appearance of *changeon* as merely an undifferentiated 'terme injurieux,' but since one manuscript gives Moutonnier in the (metrically more appropriate) form of Mouton and Villon is known to have taken the alias of Michel Mouton after becoming involved in the fatal stabbing of a priest called Philippe Sermoise in 1455, it is tempting to see something more in these lines than simply a generalized insult. If *changeon* here were meant as an ironic reference to the poet himself, the *malostru* Villon would then be revealed as a changeling not only in the sense of having adopted another personality (something he may well have come to regret) but also in light of his own obscure parentage. The fact that, after being raised by a chaplain called Guillaume de Villon, the young François de Montcorbier took his foster father's name has been taken by some to mean that he was in fact illegitimate. After all, he does refer to himself elsewhere as the son of a fairy: his parentage, he suggests, will allow him to bestow on one Maistre Lomer (probably a priest entrusted with cleaning up prostitution in Paris) the gift of being loved by all women:

> Item, donne a maistre Lomer
> Comme extraict que je suis de fee,
> Qu'il soit bien amé. (1896–98)⁴³

[Item, as the son of a fairy, I bestow on Master Lomer the gift of being widely loved].

Villon's older contemporary Martin le Franc seems to be using the word in a rather less loaded sense in a passage satirizing the fashions of the nobility in his *Champion des Dames*, but even here it is quite clear that *canjon* is no generalized insult. The context makes it obvious that members of the nobility are behaving like changelings because they are constantly changing their appearance. Democritus, he says, used to smile at the follies of the world, but now he would have to laugh out loud at the disorder and the dissoluteness of the nobles' apparel, which, just like the *canjon*, is always changing: "En laquelle mutacion / Les grans ensuivent les canjons" (4:15463–64).

The word *changeon* may make only rare appearances in France, but we encounter a very different state of affairs across the English Channel. Unlike the word *changeling* itself, which is not recorded before the sixteenth century,[44] the Middle English cognate of *changon* (early, *cangun*; later, *conjeoun*) seems to have been a fairly common word (the MED gives twenty-one citations, and these could be quite easily augmented).[45] Evidently no comparable taboo operated in England, but as the strange story of Edward II and John of Powderham illustrates, that can hardly mean that the threat that changelings posed to the patriarchy was any less real there than in France or Italy.[46]

According to the *Lanercost Chronicle*, a man called John of Powderham appeared in Oxford in June 1318 asserting that he was the true king of England and that he had been switched in his cradle with the man who now claimed to be Edward II. Edward himself seems to have regarded the whole thing as rather a joke (the *Anonimalle Chronicle* says that he presented Powderham with a fool's bauble),[47] but his council took a far more serious view of the matter, and Powderham was hanged in Northampton at the end of July. Three chroniclers (those of Meaulx, Bridlington, and Oseney) sought to rationalize the story by implying that the switch was believed to have been made by the royal nurses, but the vast majority saw the hand of the devil at work.[48] We do not need a great deal of imagination to detect here the routine demonization of a fairy motif—in this particular case, that of the fairy changeling. The *Lanercost Chronicle* supplies us with a classic account of a spirit who had appeared to Powderham in dreams (and once, while he was walking alone in the country, in person) and had granted him riches, fleshly pleasures, and other things he desired.[49] Moreover three details reinforce the impression that what really lay behind Powderham's claim was the belief that

Edward II was a fairy changeling: the fact that the queen was reported to have been angry beyond words (maternal carelessness is a frequent feature of changeling tales);[50] that Powderham's real parents were apparently sent for and questioned (a move that would have served to refute any putative sojourn in fairyland);[51] and the scandalized tone in which the *Anonimalle Chronicle* reports Powderham's claim: "People asked him how this might be, and he told them how and in what manner—which will not be put down in writing nor repeated by me" [La gent li demaunderent coment ceo poiet estre, et il lour dist coment et en quel manere qe pur moi ne sera mis en escripte ne reherce] (p. 94). Significantly, Edward II seems not to have been the only royal prince suspected of being a changeling. Henry VI's son Edward suffered a similar calumny: "whose noble mother susteynyd not a little dysclaunder and obsequye [?obloquy] of the common people, sayinge that he was not the naturall sone of kynge Henrye, but chaungyd in the cradell, to hyr great dyshonour and heuynesse, whiche I ouer passe."[52]

The vernacular term that those who believed Powderham's story would no doubt have employed when referring to Edward II was *conjeoun*. This word had been in the language a long time; its form, with the initial velar stop /k/ (as opposed to the affricate /tʃ/ or fricative /ʃ/) shows that it must have come in with the Normans (Martin le Franc, a Norman, was still using this form on the Continent in the fifteenth century). Unfortunately the *Middle English Dictionary* (s.v. "conjŏun" [n.]) completely obscures its primary denotation, 'changeling,' by glossing only its connotations: 1) "A fool, a nincompoop; a worthless person, a rascal"; 2) "A person possessed by a devil, a lunatic"; and 3) "A dwarf or very small person, a brat." This is like defining 'bastard' as "a term of abuse for a man or boy" and missing its root sense of "one begotten and born out of wedlock; an illegitimate or natural child" (OED). Of course derived senses can sometimes drive out the root sense altogether: the primary meaning of 'idiot,' for instance, "a person without learning; an ignorant, uneducated man," has not been used in English since the middle of the seventeenth century, though examples of what must originally have been a subsidiary sense, such as "a person so deficient in mental or intellectual faculty as to be incapable of ordinary acts of reasoning or rational conduct" (OED), are actually recorded earlier than the root ones. Nevertheless it is not difficult to show that, as is the case with 'bastard' now, most people were well aware of *conjeoun*'s original denotation throughout the Middle Ages. Since it has been claimed that the first recorded use of the word 'changeling' in early sixteenth-century England actually marks the arrival of the concept of the fairy changeling from France,[53] a brief philological digression on its Middle English precursor may be in order here.

Perhaps the strongest evidence for Middle English *conjeoun*'s denoting a 'changeling' is a passage from the early thirteenth-century *Ancrene Wisse*: "*Filia fatua in deminoratione erit*. þis is Salomones sahe; þet hit limpe to ei of ow, Godd ne leue neauer. 'Cang dohter i-wurð as mone i wonunge'; þriueð as the cangun, se lengre se wurse" (2:902–5).[54] In other words: "Solomon says that 'a foolish daughter shall to his [her father's] loss' [*Ecclus*, 22:3]; God grant that it never happen to any of you. 'A foolish daughter is like the moon in its waning,' she thrives like the *cangun*, the longer, the worse." It is quite clear that the *cangun* here is the typical 'changeling' who, as in Jacques de Vitry, never puts on weight however much, and for however long, it is fed. The *Ancrene Wisse*'s usage may well have undergone some semantic contamination from the word *cang* (meaning "foolish"), a word which is etymologically quite distinct from it; however, *cang* was a far rarer word than *cangun* (indeed it appears to be restricted to the Katherine group, and later manuscripts of the *Ancrene Wisse* sometimes substitute *cangun* for it), so there is no reason to imagine that such contamination was widespread.

One of the most striking instances of the word occurs in *Of Arthour and of Merlin*, since it confirms that medieval fairies could exchange adults as well as children. When an envoy from a demonic conclave sets about preparing a mortal woman on whom to engender the Antichrist (as we have seen, Merlin's birth results from the miscarriage of this project), he begins by substituting a changeling for the wife of a rich man with a son and three daughters:

> Bi þat day was a riche man
> Þat hadde to wiue a fair wiman
> Bi whom he hadde a sone fre
> And wel fair douhtren þre;
> A forseyd deuel liȝt adoun
> And of þat wiif made a conioun
> To don alle his volunte
> Wharþurth in hem he had entre
> And brouȝt hem in chideing and fiȝt. (lines 675–83)

[At that time there was a rich man who was married to a beautiful woman by whom he had a noble son and three very beautiful daughters; the aforesaid devil came down and made a *conjoun* of the woman to do all his will, by which means he had access to [the family] and brought them to whining and brawling.]

This substitution seems to be only temporary, for after this *conioun* has given the devil access to her children ("Þe Deuel sche tauȝt hir biȝate" [line 686]), an action which results in her son being killed, the mother—presumably the restored flesh-and-blood mother—commits suicide.[55]

I certainly do not mean to suggest that *conjoun* invariably denotes a 'changeling' in Middle English, for there are clearly contexts in which it seems to function as a generalized term of abuse. There seems no reason to suppose that the *cammede kongons* who "cryen after 'col, col!' " in the lyric "Swarte Smekyd Smethes,"[56] for instance, are being characterized as 'changelings' sensu stricto. However, when examined in context, it is surprising how often uses of the word *conjoun* turn out to evoke issues of child rearing, fostering, and paternity. For example, when a truculent young lord abuses Saint John the Apostle in the Laud version of the *South English Legendary:* " 'Loke,' he seide, 'þis olde conIoun: in his olde liue, / Þat men holdez swuch prophete: alle oþur men to schriue! / wel bi-trufleth he þat folk,' "[57] it is easy to miss the detail that at the time the saint is carrying a young partridge on his wrist. Indeed it is this very fact that seems to so incense the young man: "here men miȝhten i-seo / hou he pleiȝez with þis ȝongue brid: he ne miȝhte nouȝt wys beo" (lines 323–24). Now, in bestiary lore the partridge steals other birds' eggs and raises the chicks as her own (thus if not herself a changeling, she is participating in an analogous process), so it is not difficult to understand why a hostile onlooker should associate Saint John and his pet partridge with *conjeouns*, and thus with false prophets. There is a similar instance in the late fourteenth-century *Richard the Redeles*, where the author figures Richard II as a partridge—"a *congion* with a grey cote,"[58] who will inevitably be rejected by his nestlings when they realize that he is not their legitimate father. Obviously, *conjoun* is not being used in a narrowly technical sense here, but I would argue that it has been chosen as a term of abuse precisely because of its associations with substitution and illegitimacy.

Similar examples of the use of *conjoun* attesting to the survival of its original denotation are to be found elsewhere in *Of Arthour and of Merlin*, as well as in *Kyng Alisaunder* and in *Generides*. Of the remaining four occurrences of the word in the Auchinleck version of *Of Arthour and of Merlin*, one seems only marginally relevant (King Moyne is called a *conjoun* by his followers because of his cowardice in avoiding battle),⁵⁹ but the other three are more significant in that they all concern illegitimate birth. Merlin's mother is threatened with being buried alive for fornication since she cannot produce a father for her son (*Of Arthour and of Merlin* follows Robert de Boron, rather than Geoffrey of Monmouth, in making Merlin's father a devil). The precocious child (he is two years old at the time) defends his mother in court by turning the tables on the judge—"Ich wot wele who mi fader is / Ac þou knowest nouȝt þine ywis" (lines 1063–64); he then reveals that her accuser is the son of a local priest (line 1104). The judge responds by calling Merlin himself a *conjoun* (line 1071), and the judge's mother adds that no one but a *conjoun* would believe him (line 1110). The first of these insults at least appears to confound the true changeling with the related concept of the fairy hybrid, but the key to this exchange may well be the understanding that priests' bastards were often passed off as fairy children, or more loosely, changelings. Medieval sources, no doubt reflecting their clerical bias, discreetly avoid this topic, but in the mid-seventeenth century, the Anglican bishop of Norwich, Richard Corbet, wrote with gentle irony of the passing of the old world:

> Lament, lament old Abbies
> The Fairies lost command.
> They did but change Priests babies,
> But some have chang'd your land;
> And all your children stolne from thence
> Are now growne puritanes,
> Who live as changelings ever since
> For love of your demaines.⁶⁰

A little later in *Of Arthour and of Merlin*, the well-known story of Merlin's discovery by Vortigern's messengers shows Merlin himself using *conjoun* to deflect questions of legitimacy. The messengers are seeking "a child with no father" for a sacrifice and overhear one of Merlin's playmates mocking him for just this shortcoming:

> Merlin schoke his heued and louȝ
> He was of fiue winter eld
> And he spac wordes swiþe beld
> "Yuel þe bifalle þou conioun!
> Þou hast yseyd to loude þi roun." (lines 1214–18)

[Merlin shook his head and laughed; he was five years old and he spoke very boldly: "Evil befall you, conjoun, you have spoken your secret too loudly."]

In other words, when his playfellow accuses Merlin of being a bastard, Merlin goes one better, retorting ironically that *he* is a fairy- (or, more probably, a devil-) child. We might note that Merlin's speech here is described as *beld,* or "daring"—if English *conjoun* is not perhaps as strong a taboo word as its French cognate, it remains nevertheless a loaded term.

The medieval Alexander, like Merlin, was of dubious parentage, since the magician Nectabanus in the form of a dragon had fathered him on Philip's queen, Olympias. Philip had exiled his wife after her infidelity had become public, and this scandal is clearly what Darius is referring to in his letter to the young king in *Kyng Alisaunder*:

Darrye, kyng of all kynges . . .
Sendeþ gretyng wiþouten amoure
To a ȝonge fals robboure.
Alisaunder, þou *conion* wood,
Jn þe spilleþ þi faye blood![61]

Pace Smithers, the text's editor, the word *faye* here seems more likely to mean 'fairy' (MED, s.v. "faie") than 'fated' (MED, s.v. "fei(e") here: "you crazy *conjoun*, your fairy blood churns within you."

The hero of the romance *Generides* is begotten by King Aufreus of India on the fairylike princess Sereyne and brought up in secret by his mother. When he reaches maturity, he sets off to find his father and is taken into service in the royal court, but he quickly falls afoul of the queen and her lover, the king's steward. Although the vengeful steward is unaware at this point of Generides's true parentage, the terms in which he addresses him are deeply ironic:

The steward tho lift vp his staf,
And seid, "thou mysproude quengeouñ,
Whi answerest [th]ou not to my reasouñ?"
He drew him bi the here that stound,
And threw him douñ to the ground
That both mouth and noyse blede.[62]

There is no possibility that *conjoun* here is simply meant as an allusion to Generides's unprepossessing appearance since he had earlier been described as an exceptionally tall and well-favored youth (lines 790–98); the nature of the insult does, however, help explain why King Aufreus (who *is* aware that Generides is his son) should react to his steward's insult by hurling a knife at him.

Still other uses of *conjoun* seem intended to exploit its connotations of incongruity, of something or someone out of place. In the earliest *South English Legendary*'s version of the life of Saint Catherine,[63] for example, it is presumably the inappropriateness of a simple woman offering to dispute with a panel of learned men—"And me-self to desputy a-ȝeines heom: þat nam bote a fol wenche" (line 90)—that leads one of them to call her a *conjoun*: "Seie, dame con*I*oun, ȝwat artþou?": þis o legistre seide, / "Þenchestþou speke a-ȝein ore clergie?: turne þi þouȝt, ich rede!" (lines 95–96) ["Tell us who you are, Dame *Conjoun*," said one of the philosophers; "Do you intend to quarrel with our learning? I advise you to think again!"]. Interestingly, some later texts of the *Legendary* change *dame* here to *quene*, 'prostitute.'[64] Similarly, in the eleventh passus of the A text of *Piers Plowman*, Dame Study turns on the hapless dreamer: "And now comiþ a conyon & wolde cacche of my wittes / What is dowel fro dobet; now def mote he worþe.[65] Since she has just been fulminating against those laymen who seek to meddle in the mysteries of the faith—

> For now is iche boy bold, & he be riche,
> To tellen of þe trinite to be holden a sire,
> And fyndiþ forþ fantasies oure feiþ to apeire (lines 61–63)—

Dame Study is clearly attacking Long Will here for aspiring to knowledge that is improper for him to possess; both Saint Catherine and Langland's dreamer, then, warrant the epithet *conjoun* because they are seen as impostors, illegitimate substitutes for real clerks. Certainly not every occurrence of the word *conjoun* in Middle English can be glossed in this way, but I hope that by now enough has been said to show that when medieval English people used the word, they were well aware of its root denotation 'changeling' and were sometimes quite consciously exploiting this sense.

We turn finally to one particular set of uses of *conjoun* whose associative resonances are particularly rich, its appearance in the English mystery plays. Five of the MED's twenty-one citations for *conjoun* come from the York mystery plays, and the *Chester Plays* furnish two further examples. This is perhaps not surprising in itself, since the word evidently belongs in a demotic register and the mystery plays come closer than most other medieval literary genres to preserving the flavor of common speech, but the context in which the word is used *is* somewhat surprising: three times in the *Chester Plays* and once in the *York Plays*, Christ is called a 'changeling,' and there is also an allusion to the same motif (though the actual word *conjoun* is not used) in connection with Christ's nativity in the *Towneley Plays*; furthermore in the *Chester Plays*, Abel, a type of Christ, is called a *conjoun* by his brother; and finally, a related term, *mare*, is used of Christ in the Towneley *Coliphizacio*.

The most dramatic of these instances occurs in the Chester *Three Kings* when Herod, alerted by the magi to the birth of Christ, reacts violently to hearing the Doctor expound prophesies of the Messiah:

> Alas, what presumption should move that pevish page
> or any elvish godlinge to take from me my crowne?
> Cast downe the sword.
> But, by Mahound, that boye, for all his greate outrage
> shall die under my hand, that elfe and vile [congion].
> (8:325–28)[66]

Here, whatever one makes of Darius's letter in *Kyng Alisaunder*, is an indisputable verbal association of *conjouns* and fairies: Christ is an "elvish godlinge" and an "elfe and vile *conjoun*." I hope the full significance of calling Christ a 'little fairy God' and a 'foul fairy changeling' will emerge later, but first I wish to draw attention to three other examples. In the Chester *Slaughter of the Innocents*, Herod again refers to Christ as a 'vile conjoun'; urging his soldiers on to the massacre, he shouts,

> Dryve downe the dyrtie-arses all bedeene,
> and soone that there were slayne!
> So shall I keepe that vyle [congeon]
> that would reave mee of my crowne. (10:143–46)[67]

This term is echoed by one of his soldiers a few lines later: "But for to kyll such a conjoyne / mee shames sore" (10:166–67). In the course of the massacre, Herod's soldiers twice refer to the Innocents as *conjouns*—"manye a smale congeon" (10:196) and "these congeons in there clowtes" (10:209)—proof, if any were needed, that the term was still firmly associated with young children at this period. Finally, in the second Chester play a disgruntled Cain says to his younger brother Abel (a common type of Christ), "Say, thou caytiffe, thou congeon, / weneste thou to passe mee of renowne?" (2:601–2). Once again we find *conjoun* implying doubts about legitimacy, though in this freshly postlapsarian world what kind of alternative paternity might be imagined for Abel, other than a fallen angel/fairy,[68] is unclear.

The motif of Jesus as a fairy interloper appears in the York and Towneley cycles as well. In the York *Remorse of Judas*, the high priest Anna complains of "Jesus þat japer":

He marres oure men in all þat he may,
His merueylis full mekill is mustered emelle vs,
That faitoure so false.
He dois many derffe dedis on oure Sabotte day,
That vnconnand *conjeon*, he castis hym to quelle vs. (32:45–49)[69]

Notice that Christ is here called not just an ignorant *conjoun* but also a *faitour*, 'an impostor,' and is treated as an alien, an outsider, as well as a threat to the established order. The epithet *conjoun* here is of a piece with the *York Plays'* regular employment of the term *warlowe* to refer to Jesus throughout the sequence of pageants dealing with his trial and crucifixion (Plays 29 to 36). All in all Pilate, Anna, Caiphas, and the servants and soldiers of Pilate and Herod use this term no fewer than eighteen times; Pilate's "What, wenys þat woode warlowe ouere-wyn vs þus [w]ightly? / A begger of Bedlem, borne as a bastard?" (32:105–6) is typical. We should not be too quick to assume that *warlowe* (one of the more slippery terms in this general semantic cluster) means simply a male witch; it could also refer to a spirit or 'an evil creature': Sir Gowther, for instance, is described as "a warlocke greytt" (line 22), and after his reclamation the pope promises,

Now art thou Goddus chyld;
The thar not dowt [you need not fear] tho warlocke wyld:
Ther waryd [*cursed*] mot he bee. (lines 667–69)

This is an apparent reference to his demon/fairy father.[70]

The Towneley plays never describe Christ as either a *conjoun* or a *warlowe*, but Caiphas does use an interesting analogous term of him. Throughout the *Buffeting* Anna and Caiphas play at good cop/bad cop, and at one point

Caiphas regrets the priestly vocation that prevents him from joining in to give Christ a good beating:

> Els myght I haue made vp wark
> Of yond harlot and mare,
> Perdé! (21:449–51)

Mare, surviving in the English word 'nightmare' (and in the French *cauchemar* and the German *Nachtmahr*), is, as we have seen, a very old term for the incubus fairy that oppresses us while we sleep,[71] but despite the relatively few entries for it in the MED, we need not suppose that it was a rare word among the burghers of Wakefield, York, and Chester. When Robin Hood arrives in nearby Nottingham disguised as a potter,

> Yn the medys of the towne,
> There he schowed hes ware;
> "Potys! Potys!" he gan crey foll sone,
> "Haffe hansell ffor the mare!"[72]

The *hansell* (in French, *étrenne*) was a term used of the first sale of the business day, and evidently merchants were prepared to offer generous discounts and bonuses in order to enjoy the good luck that a successful handsel might bring;[73] the various superstitions that were attached to this handsel, however, attracted the disapproval of the church,[74] and the *Fasciculus Morum* describes as "false, vain, and superstitious" those people "who believe in first gifts, which are called year's gifts or handsells."[75] Robin Hood may have been a better outlaw than a salesman, but as even he knew, one of these superstitions was that a good handsel was an antidote to the *mare*; from Peter Idley we learn that salesmen commonly advertised their bargains with the cry of "Away, the mare!":

> Metyng ne handsell causeth noo welfare,
> Neither wicchecraft ne sorcerie, I the ensure;
> Ne crieng among chepmen, "away the mare!"
> All theise be verrily the deuelis lure.[76]

We may well suppose, then, that the guildsmen who mounted the mystery plays, and who were in the habit of promoting the first bargain of their day as a way to banish the night terror, would have fully appreciated how grimly appropriate was Caiphas's use of the term *mare* for the *fatur* (line 243) who has got him up in the middle of the night.

Another of the Towneley pageants that evokes this magical universe is the *Second Shepherds' Play*. Linda Marshall has argued that this play juxtaposes the positive and negative typologies of Christ and Antichrist, using Mak and Gill's parodic inversion of the holy family to deepen the Christmas story with darker eschatological overtones; Cain, she argues at one point, is a type of the Antichrist (just as Abel is a type of Christ), and she points out that Mak's name is literally an inversion of Cain's—*Cam* (the Towneley spelling of his name) written backward.[77] But more links Towneley's Cain with Mak the sheep stealer than learned typological allusions; on a far more homely level both are shown to inhabit a magical landscape, a landscape that over two hundred years earlier Robert de Boron too had associated with the Antichrist. That Cain and Abel, only the second generation of humans to inhabit a pristine world, should walk beside angels, and even God himself, is unsurprising, but Cain's particular reaction to this magical setting is striking. When the two brothers first fall out over their sacrifice, God calls down, "Cam, whi art thou so rebell / Agans thi brother Abell?" (2:293–94); and Cain responds with the richly comic lines, "Whi, who is that hob ouer the wall? / We! who was that that piped so small?" (2:299–300). For Cain, God is a hob, an irritating fairy intruding on his domestic peace.

The setting of the Towneley *Second Shepherds' Play* darkens and obscures this world—literally, since the play opens at night in "spytus" weather with "wyndys ful kene" (13:84). Its unearthliness is evoked by Daw (the *tertius pastor*):

> We that walk on the nyghtys,
> Oure catell to kepe,
> We se sodan syghtys
> When other men slepe. (13:196–99)

Mak moves about this world not merely as a thief and trickster but as a sorcerer: in a homespun anticipation of the last act of the *Tempest*, where Prospero invokes the aid of "elves of hills, brooks, standing lakes and groves" (5.1.33) to draw a magic circle about the stupefied Neapolitan courtiers, Mak binds the shepherds in place:

> Bot abowte you a serkyll
> As rownde as a moyn,

> To I haue done that I wyll,
> Tyll that it be noyn,
> That ye lyg stone-styll
> To that I haue doyne. (13:400–405)

Such circles are commonplace in manuals of learned magic: for instance, Richard Kieckheffer describes one spell in a German grimoire that begins with the magician's going to a field out of town and tracing a circle on the ground; he then conjures various spirits, one of whom he forces to bring him a cap of invisibility.[78] Here, Mak needs the shepherds to fall into a deep sleep so he can steal one of their sheep, and accordingly he recites a sleeping spell over them:

> And I shall say thertyll
> Of good wordys a foyne:
> On hight,
> Ouer youre heydys, my hand I lyft:
> "Outt go youre een! Fordo youre syght!" (13:406–10)

When the shepherds come looking for their stolen sheep the next morning, Mak's wife, in one of the most celebrated scenes in the English medieval theater, hides it in the cradle and tries to pass it off as their newborn child (a parodic nativity whose force cannot have been lost on even the most obtuse spectator). The trick almost works, but when it is discovered ("What the dewill is this? / He has a long snowte!"), Mak and Gill make one last desperate attempt to bluff it out:

> *Mak:* I tell you, syrs, hark!—
>   Hys noyse was brokyn.
>   Sythen told me a clerk
>   That he was forspokyn. (13:883–86)

Their child, says Mak, has been bewitched,[79] and Gill elaborates:

> *Vxor:* He was takyn with an elfe,
>   I saw it myself;
>   When the clok stroke twelf
>   Was he forshapyn. (13:890–93)

Gill's "He was takyn with an elfe" might possibly signify that her lamb/child is an actual changeling, since the phrasal verb 'taken with' could mean 'taken by' in the fifteenth century.[80] A more natural reading, however, is that the child is suffering a deformity or sickness caused by the elves. Thomas Elyot's *Dictionary* of 1538 defines *Lamiae* as "women, wyche beholdynge chyldren, or gyuyng to theym gyftes, doo alter the fourme of them, which children be afterwarde called elfes, or taken with the fayrye."[81] Even so, this sickness may still have been associated in the audience's mind with the idea of the changeling; the MED's entry on 'elf-taken' (s.v. "elf" [n.] 2. [e]) cites two medical texts, one of which appears to refer to the condition now known as 'failure to thrive' that was popularly associated with changelings: "a chylde that ys elfe y-take and may nat broke hys mete, that his mouthe ys donne [?doune]."[82] Thus the phrase "takyn with an elfe" (together with the sleight of hand that has placed the sheep in the cradle in the first place and the explicit references we have noted in the *Chester Plays*) implies that Gill may be here trying to pass off her own parodic Lamb of God as a counterfeit "elvish godlinge."

What are we to make of the mystery plays' association of Christ with the *conjoun*, and his first cousins the *warlowe* and the *mare*? The first thing to point out is that this association occurs within a wider context of witchcraft and sorcery in the plays. The significance of witchcraft, particularly in the trial scenes, has long been noticed; in 1974 John Gardner aptly described the Towneley *Buffeting* as "a burlesque witch trial in which Christ is viewed as witch and the witches play judge."[83] Here, for example, the two torturers attribute Christ's miracles to sorcery and witchcraft:

> He rases men that dees—
> Thay seke hym be myles—
> And euer thrugh his soceres
> Oure Sabate-day defyles. (21:121–25)[84]

and

> Sir, Lazare can he rase—
> That men may persaue—
> When he had lyne iiii dayes
> Ded in his graue.
> All men hym prase,

> Both master and knaue,
> Such wychcraft he mase. (21:144–50)

However, a similar case could be easily made for York and Chester and even the N-Town cycles. In the York *Christ Before Pilate 1*, Jesus's opponents represent his miracles as evidence of either sinister witchcraft or clever trickery. Anna says,

> Yha, thurgh his fantome and falshed and fendescraft
> He has wroght many wondir where he walked full wyde;
> Wherfore, my lorde, it wer leeffull his liffe were hym rafte.
>   (30:298–300)

Caiphas later adds,

> The deffe and þe dome he delyuered fro doole
> By wicchecrafte, I warande, his wittis schall waste;
> For þe farles þat he farith with, loo how þei folowe yone fole.
>   (30:442–45)

Similarly, in the Chester *Resurrection* Anna complains, "I sawe him and his companye / rayse men with sorcerye" (18:59–60). A glance at the Infancy Gospels might suggest how naturally Jesus was associated in the popular imagination with such 'faring with ferlies.'[85] At one point, for example, he makes a dozen toy sparrows out of clay and then brings them to life and watches them fly away; at another he stretches a board that his carpenter father has carelessly cut too short in order to make it fit the work (there is a cruel parody of this incident in the York *Crucifixio Christi* [35:105–50]). Pilate's surmise, "Yhis, his fadir with som farlis gan fare, / And has lered þis ladde of his la[i]e," is charmingly ironic, then, just as Anna's response, "Nay, nay sir, [we wiste þat] he was but a write, / No sotelté he schewed þat any segge saw" (30:502–5), is obtusely literal minded. The second witness in the N-Town's *Trial Before Herod* adds his voice to this chorus:

> Ȝa, be fals crafte of soserye
> wrowth opynly to þe pepyll Alle
> and be sotyl poyntys of nygramancye
> many thousandys fro our lawe be falle.[86]

Perhaps the most dramatic employment of this motif, however, is Chester's conception of the resurrection as the effect of sorcery. In a late manuscript of the *Crucifixio* (B.L., MS Harley 2124), Pilate releases Christ's body to Joseph of Arimathea with the direction, "But look thou make no sigaldry / to rayse hym up agayne" (lines 95–96),[87] and in the *Resurrection* Anna laments, "This foolish prophet that we all torent / though his witchcrafte ys stollen awaye" (18:296–97).

In such a context, what kind of cultural work should we suppose that Christ the changeling is doing? Members of the great tradition who were ready to hear the plays speaking with the church's voice could certainly have found perfectly orthodox ways of understanding this particular motif. From their point of view the crazed rantings of a stock villain like Herod or the rustic antics of such comic figures as Coll, Gyb, and Daw convey an obvious moral message. Only a monster or a simpleton, the argument might run, could confuse the profound truths of the incarnation with so patent an absurdity as a belief in changelings. No one but a fool could suppose that Christ is not God-made-man, but a fairy castoff slipped into the manger in Bethlehem as a substitute for the real Messiah—an "elvish godlinge," a "vile [conjoun]." Indeed the author of the *Second Shepherds' Play*, perhaps responding with indirection to the danger inherent in his subject matter, might be thought to have gone one better: where Chester's Herod turns Christ into a changeling, Towneley's antitype of Christ, Mak, substitutes a literal sheep for the Lamb of God and then tries to pass *that* off as a fairy; Mak, in other words, would offer us a changeling for a changeling. By this account the medieval audience is being invited to recognize the fact that it shares its own unreflective assumptions about fairies with monsters and crooks.

Certainly such a move can be seen elsewhere. At the end of Capgrave's *Life of Saint Katherine*, Emperor Maxentius forbids anyone to give her martyred body burial. When he finds that his friend Porphiry has disobeyed him, he launches into a long tirade against Christianity cast in precisely these terms:

> My Porphirie, my knyth, thus is he lost,
> So deceyved of witchcraft that he begynnyth rave.
> . . . .
> Ten dayes I graunt thee or ellis twelve.
> Leve this Crysten cumpany, forsake that elve
> Jhesu of Nazareth—He dede nevyr man good.
> . . . .

> Who caused him thus sone to reneye
> The holy religion, the eld trew wey
> Whech that oure faderes kept withoute mynd? (5:1612–27)

Capgrave works a particularly clever sleight of hand here: were there any danger that his audience might be tempted to associate "the eld trew wey" with a traditional belief in fairies, he completely short-circuits it by making this pagan emperor treat Christianity itself as a fairy fantasy; 'that elf, Jesus of Nazareth,' says Maxentius, 'he never did man good!' Earlier the King of the Medes had made a similar point:

> "Your God Cryst," he seyd, "is know full wyd
> That He was a wyche and so was His dame,
> And the grettest in wycchecrafte as is the fame.
> Fye on swyche wysdam! Fye on swyche feyth!" (4:1067–70)

Like William Langland before him ("'*Crucifige*!' quod a Cachepol, '[he kan of wicchecraft]!'"),[88] John Capgrave was clearly writing with the authority of the orthodox expositor. This point of view, however, becomes rather more difficult to sustain in the mystery plays.

A typological schema of the kind imagined by Linda Marshall and Rosemary Woolf[89] undoubtedly gave shape to several individual plays, and even (as V. A. Kolve suggested many years ago) provided a basic structure for the cycles themselves,[90] but except where such a schema was furnished with the crude device of an expositor (a device peculiar to the Chester cycle), it is rather hard to see how they can have made much of an impression in actual performance.[91] D. W. Robertson's promotion of a tropological model at the expense of a typological one in the plays has at least the advantage of making the dramatized "events in both the Old and New Testaments immediately and practically relevant to the daily life of the observer,"[92] and from this perspective it is possible to see Christ the changeling doing a somewhat different kind of pedagogical work. In contrast to the mystery plays' stock bogeyman Mahoun, references to the denizens of fairyland are strikingly apposite: Jesus, the supernatural child insinuated into a human family, is not unreasonably called a *conjoun*. So too Christ the miracle worker might well appear to be a *warlowe*, a practitioner of *wicchecrafte* and *sigaldry*. And Caiphas, woken in the middle of the night to deal with an arraigned criminal, could be forgiven for regarding him as a *mare*. This is anachronism working to make the mysteries of the Old and

New Testaments comprehensible in terms that even the simplest member of the audience might understand, and it is possible to imagine that such references were the work of enlightened clerics seeking to render the Christian story in vivid and immediate terms. If so, these playwrights were not alone; a parallel case is found in the way popular songs (some with obvious fairy allusions) were picked up by medieval preachers. Siegfried Wenzel has persuasively argued that the haunting lyric "Maiden in the mor lay," which provided the tune for a Latin hymn in the Red Book of Ossery and an illustration of the Golden Age in a mid-fourteenth-century sermon, must have had its roots in "a figure of medieval folk belief, perhaps some woodland or water sprite or *fée*."[93] So too the lyric "Sey me viit in þe brom,"[94] an exchange between a woman and a woodland spirit [*O spiritus in mericis*],[95] survives in three manuscripts, all of them preachers' collections, and another verse with strong fairy overtones, "At a sprynge-wel vnder a þorn / . . . Þer by-syde stant a mayde,"[96] is preserved in a collection of "exempla moraliter exposita."[97]

The problem is that once such doctrinally ambiguous figures were brought onto the stage there was always a danger that they might get out of hand. At the end of the Chester Innkeepers' play of *The Harrowing of Hell* (Play 17), for instance, after Christ has led the saved souls out of hell, a female brewer is left onstage to boast of how she has adulterated her ale and wine and cheated her customers. She is welcomed back into hell by Satan and two of his demons ("welcome, deare darlinge, to endles bale / . . . nowe thou shall have a feaste!" [lines 333–36]), but there is almost nothing in the bare text—other than her lines "Therefore I may my handes wringe, / shake my cuppes and kannes ring" (lines 297–98)—to indicate that this was actually the occasion for a popular game (whose precise details remain obscure) known as "cups and cans." So well received was this game that the Innkeepers reprised it as their contribution to Chester's Midsummer Show,[98] which is where we learn that it involved a woman on a horse, two demons, gunpowder, and a lot of broken crockery.[99] Likewise the Chester Butchers, who were responsible for the *Temptation* (Play 12), seem to have transferred the popular figure of the "devill in his fethers" from their Whitsun play to the Midsummer pageant. In 1600 the Chester mayor, Henry Hardware the younger, "a godlye, ouer-zealous man," attempted to suppress both of these displays (along with the "Gyauntes," the "dragon and Naked boyes," and the particularly enigmatic figure of "god in stringes"),[100] though his efforts were not everywhere appreciated: "howsoeuar the vulgar [or baser sorte] of people did oppose themselues against the reformation."[101] As this incident proves, some Chester citizens were far from averse to embellishing the official play text (or "Regenall") with traditional elements of their own.

While it is quite possible, then, to rationalize the grounds on which a didactic playwright might have chosen to present Christ as a changeling, such rationalization means closing our ears to the possibility of another, and potentially more subversive, note. Recent criticism of these plays has begun to move away from treating them as primarily dramatized pedagogy and to restore to them the long-suppressed voices of the little tradition. Perhaps the most forceful statement of this position is James Simpson's: "Typological instruction and devotional responsiveness cannot convincingly account for the project of these plays; they are not, therefore, simple examples of the Church's instruction of the laity. The cycles are not 'instructional' at all. Instead they offered a space in which the members of many institutions could reflect on their own practice in the active life."[102] From this point of view, it is worth wondering whether, when one of the cycle villains associates Christ with a *conjoun*, an elf, a warlock, or a *mare*, he may not be reinforcing rather than undermining traditional beliefs.

The radical shift, so well documented by John van Engen, in the historiography of the medieval church that has occurred over the last few decades can now make the totalizing claims of Rosemarie Woolf and D. W. Robertson seem to belong to a distant time before the *annalistes* taught us to see the hollowness of an imagined "Age of Faith." Against Rosemarie Woolf's confident assurance that Isaac as a type of Christ "was part of the small stock of knowledge which the common people might be expected to have received,"[103] we might set Keith Thomas's contention that "a medieval peasant's knowledge of Biblical history or Church doctrine was, as far as one can tell, extremely slight."[104] John Bromyard tells of a traveler who asks a shepherd he meets whether he knows anything of the Father, the Son, and the Holy Spirit: "I know the father and the son," he replies, "because I look after their sheep, but not the third one; there's no one with that name in our village" [bene, inquit, novi patrem, & filium, quia oves illorum custodio, sed illum tertium non novi, quia nemo est in villa nostra, qui tale nomen habeat].[105] There is no reason to think that things had changed much two hundred years later; here is a sixteenth-century report of a minister's interrogation of a respectable parishioner on his deathbed: "Being demanded what he thought of God, he answers that he was a good old man; and what of Christ, that he was a towardly youth; and of his soul, that it was a great bone in his body; and what should become of his soul after he was dead, that if he had done well he should be put in a pleasant green meadow."¹⁰⁶ John Bromyard's contemporary Robert Mannyng says that some common people had so little grasp of the basics of their faith that they were even unsure whether or not the Jews were saved:

> Ofte we here þe lewed men seye,
> And erre ful moche out of þe weye,
> Þat of þe Iewes seye sum oun
> "Þey ne wote wheþer þey be saued or noun." (lines 9523–26)¹⁰⁷

Some went even further; a list of "articles in which modern heretics err" from southwestern France around the end of the thirteenth century (possibly compiled from the records of the inquisitor, and later pope, Jacques Fournier) includes the axiom that "the law of Jews is better than the law of Christians."¹⁰⁸ Fournier reported a man as saying that "one should not do ill to heretics or Jews or Saracens, no more than to a person who worked well. It was a sin to do ill to heretics, Jews and Saracens if they worked well and earned their living."¹⁰⁹ I cite this remarkable statement because it brings to mind Simpson's dramatic claim that the mystery cycles "mounted a theology of labour at whose center stands the practice of mercy in the active life" (p. 513), since it is only from some such standpoint, I believe, that we can fully understand the paradox of Christ the changeling.

The latent hostility of some of the cycle plays to institutionalized ideology is not difficult to demonstrate. In both the Towneley and York cycles the high priests Caiphas (the "pontificall prince of all prestis" [York, 30:206]) and Anna are represented as unscrupulous canon lawyers seeking to convict Christ in what is essentially a travesty of an ecclesiastical court. In the York *Christ Before Anna and Caiaphas*, Caiphas begins,

> By connyng of clergy and casting of witte
> Full wisely my wordis I welde at my will,
> So semely in seete me semys for to sitte,
> And þe lawe for to lerne you, and lede it by skill.
> . . . .
> Ther is nowder lorde ne lady lerned in þe lawe,
> Ne bisshoppe ne prelate that preued is for pris,
> Nor clerke in þe courte þat connyng will knawe,
> With wisdam may were [defend] hym in worlde is so wise. (29:5–17)

As purveyors of justice, then, these medieval churchmen do not come off well, and as we watch their attempts to frame Christ—"With wicche-crafte he fares withall" (York, 29:58); "With wicchecrafte þis wile has he wrought" (30:299)—we might recall that fifteenth-century England witnessed a dramatic increase in prosecutions for witchcraft and similar superstitious practices[110] and ask ourselves whether what we are seeing here might not be something like popular resistance to the church's increasing regulation of traditional culture. York's *Christ Before Pilate 2* reaches its climax with a farcical interlude in which the soldiers instinctively salute Christ as he enters the court by dipping their standards: "Ʒa, ther cursed knyghtes by crafte lete them croke [bow down], / To worshippe þis warlowe vnworthy in wede" (33:170–71). When they protest that they have acted involuntarily, the enraged Anna and Caiphas replace them with "right bigg men and strange" (line 217), but all to no avail; Christ's second entrance not only produces the same result but even makes Pilate himself leap to his feet: "I vpstritt, I m[e] myght noȝt abstene / To wirschip hym" (lines 274–75). For Anna and Caiphas this is the final proof of Christ's guilt, and to Pilate's admission that he fears to offend Christ, they reply:

> *Anna.* þan oure lawe were laght till an ende;
>   To his tales if ȝe treuly attende,
>   He enchaunted and charmed oure knyghtis.
> *Cayphas.* Be his sorcery, ser, youreselffe þe soth sawe,
>   He charme[d] oure chyualers and with myscheffe enchaunted.
>   To reuerence hym ryally we rase all on rowe;
>   Doutles we endure not of þis dastard be daunted. (33:285–91)

These trials of Christ with their torture and brutality remind Simpson of Archbishop Arundel's examination of the lollard William Thorpe, but if any such parallel is to be invoked, I cannot help wondering whether the legal harassment of townsmen and women hauled up before the archdeacons' courts for sorcery and *sortilegium* does not provide a closer analogue.[111]

In fifteenth-century England witchcraft was rarely punished by death, and certainly at a local level it seems often to have been treated with a considerable degree of leniency, but there is no denying the fact that official intolerance of traditional practices was on the increase. The theology faculty of the University of Paris in 1398 had determined that it was an error to regard as licit the use of magical arts for a good end [quod licitum est uti magicis artibus . . pro quocumque bono fine],[112] and even white magic was now falling under the archdeacon's jaundiced eye: Peter Idley claims clerical authority for the assertion that conjuring (even *by thi Pater noster*) or doing *mervelous werkis* (even *by hooly wordis*) is plain heresy.[113] Reliable evidence from what Lawrence Poos has called "lower ecclesiastical jurisdiction" in fifteenth-century England is somewhat restricted,[114] but nevertheless cases involving charges of sorcery are not hard to find: the court of the Prior and Convent of Durham heard six of them in a twenty-year period (1435–55), for instance.[115] As we might expect, such cases were not necessarily concerned with *maleficium*: in 1463/4 two men, Robert Mabley and John Whitlamb, of Wisbech in Cambridgeshire were accused of witchcraft for casting spells (presumably for good luck) on fishing nets (*incantando recia piscum*), and, unsurprisingly, neither had any trouble finding neighbors to swear to his innocence.[116] More pertinently, Marion Clerk of Suffolk was tried in 1499 for employing "the gracious fairies" to help with her healing and fortune-telling (as we saw in Chapter 1), but in the same record we encounter three similar cases, only one of which was clearly concerned with *maleficium*.[117] In 1438, when one Alice Hancock appeared before the bishop of Bath and Wells accused of *sortilegium* for, among other things, claiming that she could heal boys who had been touched or harmed by the spirits of the air who are commonly called fairies [quod ipsa profitetur se sanare pueros tactos vel lesos a spiritibus aeris, quos vulgus 'feyry' appellant], she was forced to abjure.[118] We cannot know what precise form was taken by the nigromancy practiced by Thomas Hull in Hertford in 1457, but it is interesting to find that his servant was forced to abjure as a potential heretic: "I abiure and forswer all maner of heresies and errours, & promyt that I shal never (in tyme to come) yef ayde, help, sucour, nor favour, nor counsell to any that holdeth heresies or vseth nigromancy in tyme to come."[119]

Popular opposition to such official harassment may well have been exacerbated by the conviction that clerics themselves practiced their own forms of witchcraft or *gramerie* (think, for instance, of Chaucer's Pardoner's "sholderboon of an hooly Jewes sheep" and his magical mitten that ensures a good harvest).[120] Ironically ("the witches play judge"), in the N-Town's *Christ Before the Doctors* the First Doctor had earlier boasted of his skill in "calculation and negremauncye" (p. 178), and he is far from the only learned figure to be treated skeptically in the plays. In the Chester *Innocents*, it is a doctor who advises Herod to undertake the massacre: "Deeme them, lord, for to be dead; / for that is best, as I eate bread" (10:126–27), and later on another doctor advises the Antichrist on how to deal with Enoke and Helias: "This is my counsell and my reade, / yonder heretikes for to spill" (23:438–39).

From this perspective, then, the real scapegoats of Caiphas and Anna's inquisition are the elves, *congeons, warlowes,* and *mares* of popular tradition. Mak's tossing in a blanket is often represented as a humane alternative to the gallows that awaited anyone convicted of stealing a sheep—indeed it is this quintessentially merciful act that lies at the heart of Simpson's theology of labor—but we should recall that Mak's is no simple theft, that it has been compounded by sorcery. Not only has he cast a spell on the sleeping shepherds, but he has also sought to transform their sheep into a child and then tried to blame the elves for having changed it back. By tossing Mak in a blanket, then, the shepherds are not merely thumbing their noses at the king's law; they are flouting the church courts as well. In light of such evidence, we might think of the elvish Christ of the miracle plays as representing folkloric resistance to an increasingly authoritarian church as it sought to extend its control over traditional practices and beliefs.

As a counter to a reading of the mystery plays filtered through the ideology of the great tradition, it is useful to try to imagine how they might have been received by the *lewed* who must have made up a majority of their original audience. Consider, for example, the Sibyl's prophesy of Christ's nativity (Chester, 6). No doubt it would have seemed unexceptionable to those educated audience members who had read of Aeneas's encounter with the Cumean Sibyl in *Aeneid 6* (or more pertinently Virgil's evocation of her in *Eclogue* 4) or who were familiar with Augustine's translation of the apocalyptic hymn "Iudicii signum tellus sudore madescet," attributed to the Erythraean Sibyl. Somewhat lower down the educational ladder, some laymen and women with vernacular literacy could well have encountered support for Chester's story of the Tiburtine Sibyl's prophesying Christ's birth to Augustus in any number of pastoral works, such as John Mirk's *Festial* or the popular *Alphabet of Tales*. But what of the members of the little tradition? Sibyl the sage and her prophesy must have appeared in an entirely different light to them. Sibyl had long been a generic name for any female seer:

"Sibile" erent nomees
E sages apellees
Tutes femmes savantes
Ki erent devinantes.[121]

[All learned women who could foretell the future were called Sibyl and labeled wise.]

Or as Ranulph Higden puts it, "as a man þat propheciaþ is i-cleped a prophete, so a womman þat propheciaþ is i-cleped Sibil."¹²² Moreover in England, because of the episode in Geoffrey of Monmouth where King Alan learns of Cadwallader's approaching death, the Sibyl's name was frequently linked with Merlin's: "Þe king alein let þo anon in is bokes aspye / Boþe of sybile þe sage & of merlines prophecye."¹²³ It is hardly surprising, then, that Sibyls came to be regarded as fairies; as Josiane Haffen writes, "just like the medieval fairy, the Sibyl lives at the edge of the human lifeworld . . . she has the gift of prophesy, and she enjoys, if not immortality, a remarkable longevity."¹²⁴ Unsurprisingly fairies are given the name Sibyl in a number of French romances;¹²⁵ among the fairy names of the gossips in *Les Évangiles des quenouilles* (including Dame Abonde and Dame Berthe) we find a "Sebile des Mares,"¹²⁶ and Antoine de la Sale conceived his *Paradis de la reine Sibylle* in terms of fairyland. Moreover (as we saw in the last chapter), Reginald Scot parodies a conjurer's spell that is intended "to fetch vnto thee the fairie Sibylia." So when the Chester Sibyl— "Sybell the sage, that well fayre maye," as Nuntius describes her (6:179)—tells Augustus, "I tell you sicker that born ys hee / that passeth thee of postee" (6:645–46), there must have been some members of the audience to whom she looked rather more like a fairy godmother than a Virgilian pythoness. If this was how the playwright sought to bring the meaning of the nativity alive to the less educated, then he was certainly playing with fire. The puritan observer Christopher Goodman, who watched the Chester plays in 1572, must have thought so, for he complained that "Sybill is brought in so superstitious a manner as is not commendable."¹²⁷

In much the same way, the appearance of Helyas in the Chester *Antichrist* (Play 23) may have provoked conflicting responses. Again, the educated would have had no difficulty in recognizing the prophet Elijah and his traditional role in medieval eschatology, but Elyas is also a common name in medieval romance. The Swan-Knight, the *Chevalier au Cygne* (in his earliest manifestation, in *Dolopathos*, quite plainly the son of a fairy), is usually called Helyas,¹²⁸ but the name also turns up for one of King Mark's enemies, for one of the grail keepers, and even, in Malory, for one of Morgan le Fay's knights.¹²⁹ The prophet Helyas and his companion Enock were celebrated for never having died (indeed they furnish the answer to a widely circulated scholastic riddle: "quis fuit natus et non mortuus?"),¹³⁰ but so too were King Arthur and a number of other heroes popularly believed to be still living in fairyland, ready to return at a time of dire need (a motif to be explored in the next chapter). When Enock announces that he has "lyved in great likynge . . . in paradice withowt anoye" along with his brother Helye, who "was after sent to mee," and that the two of them have come back to fight "this champion [Antichrist] . . . that nowe in the worlde walketh wide" (23:270–82), can we be certain that none in the audience would have been reminded of the once and future king of their Welsh neighbors? The Chester *Prophets*, surely the least dramatic of all the mystery plays, seems in part designed to head off such a misinterpretation (22:245–60). Again, Christopher Goodman offers proof that at least one member of the audience found the picture of "Enoch and Elias living in paradise in the flesh & the abiding there for a time" offensive.[131]

The Chester *Antichrist*, a particularly difficult piece whose doctrinal project seems to point in one direction while its dramatic realization takes it in quite another, embodies these contradictions. At its heart lies a battle between Antechriste and the two patriarchs Enock and Helyas for the hearts and minds of four kings. Each side accuses the other of *fantasie* (23:28, 526) and of *faiterie* (23:349, 353), and at stake is the right to proclaim one's own orthodoxy. "I put you owt of heresye / to leeve me upon" (lines 87–88), boasts Antechriste, and after Helyas has finally exposed his chicanery, Primus Rex expostulates, "thou hast us lead in heresye / Fye on thy workes eychone!" (lines 599–600). But the heresy that the Chester *Antichrist* presents us with looks nothing like Lollardy or even Protestantism (the Peniarth manuscript proves that the play had taken on its current form long before Luther's theses): "Fye on thee, fellonne, fye on thee, fye! / For all thy wytchcrafte and sorcerye" (lines 488–89), cries Helyas, and Primus Rex echoes him, "Thou fayture feard with fantasye, / with sorcerye, wytchcraft, and nygromancye" (lines 597–98). This is hardly heresy in any narrow theological sense (the only doctor to appear in the play, predictably on the side of Antechriste, can think of no better weapon against his master's enemies than to curse them). Antechriste, an inveterate ventriloquist, calls Helyas a wizard (Peniarth MS:371), but then from his own retinue he summons Ragnell (line 647), a demon with strong fairy associations.[132]

Doctrinally, of course, the Chester *Antichrist* is unexceptional, representing a well-established medieval tradition reaching back to Adso,[133] but it is impossible to ignore its populist overtones. We have already noticed that Enock and Helyas, taken off to live in the earthly paradise until Doomsday, bear a strong resemblance to heroes like Arthur who live on in fairyland, but even more striking is the threefold repetition of the death-and-rebirth motif: not only does the necromancer Antechriste stage a spurious revival of three dead men to prove his own triumph over the grave, but he then engineers his own ludicrous death and resurrection ("I dy, I dye, Nowe am I dead! . . . I ryse!

Nowe reverence dose to mee" [lines 133–65]), and finally Enock and Helyas themselves die at Antechriste's hands only to be revived seventy lines later by Michael. As with other mystery plays, the stage directions can do no more than hint at a farcical dimension to the actual performance: "Tunc Michael occidet Antechristum et in occidendo clamat Antechristus [Then Michael kills Antechriste and, while being killed, Antechriste calls out] 'Helpe, helpe, helpe, helpe!' " (lines 644f.), and "resurgens Enok and Helias ab antechristo [coesi] et auditoribus status suos commonstrabunt [Enock and Helyas, having been killed by Antechriste, rising up shall together demonstrate their state to the audience]" (lines 686f. [*recte* 696f.]). Their speeches at this point ("for dead I was and nowe lyve I" [line 713]) make Enock and Helyas sound more like the heroes of a mummers' play of Saint George than the central actors in a solemn liturgical drama. Medieval fairies, after all, had their own version of the death-and-rebirth figure (think of *Sir Orfeo* or the opening scene of *Sir Gawain and the Green Knight*), and it is surely not too much of a stretch to imagine some members of the Chester audience taking the *Antichrist* as a satire on the church's hypocritical proscription of "nygromancye" and a confirmation of their own traditional beliefs.

Scholars who have linked the demise of the mystery plays in England with the emergence of a surveillant society have generally done so in the context of the Protestant reformation.[134] (Even James Paxton, who cleverly opposes sixteenth-century witch-hunting to the irreverent "artificial demonic" of the mystery plays, makes this connection).[135] However, it is all too easy to turn a deaf ear to a much older set of oppositions. Richard Emmerson, after summarizing the doctrinal differences between Protestants and Catholics over the question of the Antichrist, invites us to imagine how various sixteenth-century puritan audiences might have received the Chester plays,[136] but we can now document the actual response of one specific puritan, Christopher Goodman, to the Chester *Antichrist*. The man who objected to the presentation of Enock and Helyas and "Antichrist to die & rise again" also objected to magical devices, to "turning of trees upwards," and to "Elias blessing bread with the sign of the cross" in order to expose Antechriste's resurrection of the dead men as a fraud.[137] Certainly, Goodman's list contains a number of theological objections, but not all his complaints are so easily pigeonholed. "[T]he unreverent speaking of the shepherds," their "foolish descanting . . . upon Gloria in excelsis," and, above all, "their vain offerings to move laughter & to maintain Superstition,"[138] these are hardly doctrinally motivated. And in any case, what is so superstitious about the shepherds' offerings? Can it be that Garcius presents the Christ child with "a payre of my wyves ould hose" (7:591) in order to safeguard it from fairies? After all, we have already seen that mothers sometimes placed in their cradles "of þe fadur . . . sum preuy clooth" to protect their babies from "wicked wiȝthes."[139] Catholics certainly held no monopoly on superstition (though Protestant polemicists such as Reginald Scot and Samuel Harsnett may have wished to believe this): the decline of civic drama in the Kentish port of Rye seems to have coincided, as elsewhere, with the increasing influence of the town's puritan faction.[140] But when rumors of witchcraft circulated there in 1607 (it seems that someone had been conjuring fairies to help her find buried treasure), it was a prominent puritan, Anne Taylor, who became the focus of the investigation. The threat that Christ the changeling posed to those who sought to regulate early modern civic life, in other words, had its roots in attitudes far more deeply entrenched than anything specifically propounded by reformation theologians.

This chapter began with my suggesting that the learned tradition remained stubbornly silent about changelings throughout much of the Middle Ages, or, at least, that only rarely did it pay direct attention to this popular belief. We should certainly not conclude from the clerical elite's apparent indifference that it felt such popular beliefs were little threat to its hegemony, however; anyone seeking theoretical support for such an assertion can find it in the work of the great Marxist thinker Antonio Gramsci, one of the few theorists to give proper weight to the subversive potential of folklore. Literary critics have been much preoccupied with textual silences and the anxieties they are held to conceal, and I have tried to show here that a similar approach might profitably be extended to a reading of medieval vernacular culture. If we listen carefully, the margins of medieval civic drama offer a rare opportunity for us to hear, however muted and indirect, the raised voices of the common people themselves.

CHAPTER 5

Living in Fairyland

Nay, sure, he's not in hell! He's in Arthur's bosom, if ever man went to Arthur's bosom.
—Shakespeare, *Henry V*

Arthur and Avalon

When Geoffrey of Monmouth suggested that Merlin was the product of human/fairy miscegenation, he put the cat among the clerical pigeons. Confronted with a second potential clerical gaffe, however, he showed himself far more circumspect. In many ways the popular belief that King Arthur was still alive and living on in Avalon would prove to be even more disturbing to clerical sensibilities, and the author of the *Historia Regum Britanniae* was quite properly reluctant to broach this topic too openly; in fact, in the *Historia* he hardly goes further than making Merlin predict that Arthur's death will be 'uncertain' ("exitus eius dubius erit").[1] While he does allow rather more space to this question in his later *Vita Merlini*, even there Geoffrey is careful to hedge his bets. The bard Taliesin, after describing the Isle of Apples as an earthly paradise, tells Merlin, "It was there that we took Arthur after the battle of Camlann, where he had been wounded. . . . Morgen received us with due honour. She put the king in her chamber upon a golden bed, uncovered his wound with her noble hand and looked long at it. At length she said he could only be cured if he stayed with her a long while and accepted her treatment. We therefore happily committed the king to her care."[2] Merlin then laments the disasters that have befallen the land since Arthur's departure, and Taliesin replies, "Then our people must send someone to call on our leader to return . . .

to re-establish the nation in its old state of peace" (p. 103). Merlin, however, denies this as a possibility. Later he alludes to Taliesin's story in terms much closer to the account in the *Historia*: "on that field the king was mortally wounded [*letali vulnere lesus*] and left the kingdom. As you [Taliesin] have described, he sailed with you over the water and came to the palace of the nymphs [*nimpharum venit ad aulam*]."[3] While it is quite obvious that Geoffrey of Monmouth was familiar with tales of Arthur's return, it is equally clear that he was reluctant to repeat them too openly.

If Geoffrey was unwilling to discuss the question of Arthur's return, his French adapter Wace was only slightly less circumspect. True, he does say that Arthur is still in Avalon ("encore i est") and specifically mentions that the Britons await his return. He also makes explicit that Geoffrey's 'doubts' about his death means doubts as to whether or not he still lives ("se il est morz u il est vis"). But he also stresses that he himself has no views on the matter and would prefer not to speculate about Merlin's ambiguous statement:

> Arthur, si la geste ne ment,
> Fud el cors nafrez mortelment;
> En Avalon se fist porter
> Pur ses plaies mediciner.
> Encore i est, Bretun l'atendent,
> Si cum il dient e entendent,
> De la vendra, encor puet vivre.
> Maistre Wace, qui fist cest livre,
> Ne volt plus dire de sa fin
> Qu'en dist li prophetes Merlin;
> Merlin dist d'Arthur, si ot dreit,
> Que sa mort dutuse serreit.
> Li prophetes dis verité;
> Tut tens en ad l'um puis duté,
> E dutera, ço crei, tut dis,
> Se il est morz u il est vis. (13275–90)[4]

[Arthur, if the stories are true, was mortally wounded in the body. He had himself carried to Avalon for his wounds to be treated. He is still there; the Britons await him, as they say and believe: thence will he come, and he may live once more. Master Wace, who wrote this book, wishes to say nothing more of his end than the prophet

Merlin has said. Merlin rightly said of Arthur that his death would
be doubtful. The prophet spoke truly; every age since has had
its doubts about the man, and I believe that they always
will—whether he is dead, or whether he lives.]

Stories of Arthur's survival and future return were clearly circulating orally even before Geoffrey of Monmouth's time. William of Malmesbury, writing a dozen years or so before the relevant section of the *Historia* was composed, says that, since King Arthur's tomb is nowhere to be found, old tales feign that he is yet to return ("adhuc eum venturum fabulatur"),[5] and other texts suggest that such a legend might count on fierce partisan support at the time. Hermann of Tournai tells an amusing story about some monks from Laon visiting the Cornish town of Bodmin in 1113, one of whom fell out with a local man over the question of whether Arthur still lived: a considerable brawl arose, many armed men attacked the church, and bloodshed was only narrowly averted by the intervention of a local cleric called Algard ("unde non parvo tumultu exorto, cum armis ecclesiam irruunt plurimi, et nisi praefatus Algardus clericus obstitisset, paene usque ad sanguinis effusionem ventum fuisset").[6] A commentary on the *Prophesies of Merlin* doubtfully attributed to Alan of Lille indicates that such loyalties were just as strong later in the century: if you doubt that men differ over whether or not Arthur still lives, says the author, try going to Brittany and announcing in the marketplaces and villages that Arthur is dead just like other dead men ("more ceterum mortuorum mortuum esse"); should you manage to get away from there with a whole skin, at the very least you will be assaulted by the curses of your listeners or more likely pelted with rocks ("si tamen immunis evadere inde potueris, quin aut maledictis audientium opprimaris, aut certe lapidibus obruaris").[7]

If this opinion was so strongly held at the time he was writing, why was Geoffrey of Monmouth (and following him, Wace) so reluctant to discuss it openly? The usual explanation is that the early years of King Stephen's reign witnessed a resurgence of Welsh nationalism and that Geoffrey was being careful not to stir up further trouble between the English and the Welsh,[8] but this I suspect is at best only a partial answer. It is difficult to believe that many of the English can have been seriously worried about Arthur's possible reappearance after a six-hundred-year absence. Certainly the very idea of Arthur at the head of a fairy army is ridiculed in the poem *Draco Normannicus*.[9] Indeed there is clear evidence that, at least outside Wales, the West Country, and Brittany,[10] the skeptical view of Arthur's return had developed a proverbial ring to it, a medieval equivalent of "when Hell freezes over" or "if pigs could fly." Thus, Peter of Blois describes Reginald Prince of Antioch, waiting vainly for relief at the siege of Tyre: "sed vereor ne sic eam [gentem bellicosam] praestoletur, ut Britones Arturum et Judaei Messiam" [but I fear he awaited his military compatriots, just like the Britons waiting for Arthur, or the Jews, the Messiah]; moreover, Peter uses variant forms of the doublet *ut Britones Arturum et Judaei Messiam* to express disappointed hopes elsewhere,[11] and this phrase is also echoed by Gerald of Wales.[12] Joseph of Exeter says of the Lesbians awaiting the return of the drowned Castor and Pollux: "Sic Britonum ridenda fides et credulus error Arturum expectat exspectabitque perenne" [just so is the laughable credulity and mistaken belief of the Britons who await the return of King Arthur now and will always do so].[13] Even as far away as Italy (and before the end of the twelfth century), "'Arturum exspectare' had become a proverbial phrase for expecting the impossible,"[14] as when the Florentine Henry the Pauper wrote, "Et prius Arturus veniet vetus ille Britannus, / Quam ferat adversis falsus amicus opem" [and that old Briton Arthur will arrive sooner than a false friend would offer help to his rivals].[15]

But something more than Celtic naïveté is being mocked by Peter of Blois and Gerald of Wales. John Gillingham has argued persuasively that we should read Geoffrey of Monmouth's *History* against "the background of a . . . growing fashion for dismissing the Celtic peoples as barbarians" and that his work is in essence a defense of Welsh civilization: "Geoffrey, in other words, asserts not only that the Britons had a long and heroic history of migration and successful war, but that they had long been civilized."[16] From this perspective, the story of Arthur's return was a serious embarrassment, something Geoffrey was unwilling to broadcast too openly. The Englishman William of Newburgh, for one, was not going to let him get away with it; his motive in writing, says William, was "a desire to please the Britons, most of whom are considered to be so barbaric that they are said to be still awaiting the future coming of Arthur, nor can they bear to hear talk of his death" [gratia placendi Britonibus, quorum plurimi tam bruti esse feruntur ut adhuc Arturum tanquam venturum exspectare dicantur, eumque mortuum nec audire patiantur].[17] How William relishes his crude pun on *Bruti*—their very name showing them to be uncivilized brutes! But what, we might wonder, is particularly uncivilized (as opposed to naive) about waiting for Arthur to return? Unsurprisingly, the answer has to do with fairyland.

With the possible exception of Geoffrey's own reference to the *aula nimpharum* on the Isle of Apples in the *Vita Merlini*,[18] the reworking of the *Historia*

Regum Britannie to associate Avalon explicitly with fairyland is Layamon's. In a speech of great power, he has the wounded Arthur say,

> And ich wulle uaren to Aualun, to uairest alre maidene,
> to Argante þere quene, aluen swiðe sceone;
> & heo s[c]al mine wunden makien alle isunde.
> al hal me makien mid haleweiʒe drenchen.
> And seoðe ich cumen wulle to mine kineriche
> and wunien mid Brutten, mid muchelere wunne.[19]

[I will journey to Avalon, to the most lovely of all maidens, to Argante its queen, a very radiant fairy; and she will heal my wounds completely and restore me to health with wholesome draughts. And afterward I will come to my kingdom and live among the Britons in great joy.]

At this point a small boat arrives, driven by the waves and containing two women 'wondrously adorned'; Layamon then describes how they laid Arthur softly in the boat and carried him off, adding, "Bruttes ileueð ʒete þat he bon on liue, / and wunnien in Aualun, mid fairest alre aluen" [Britons still believe that he is alive and dwelling in Avalon with the most lovely of all fairies] (lines 14292–93). Given the national rivalries that are claimed to underlie stories of Arthur's return, Layamon's concluding remark is particularly telling; Merlin, he says, was a wise man, and he prophesied truly "þat an Arður sculde ʒete cum Anglen to fulste" [that Arthur should yet come to aid the English] (line 14297). This is of a piece with Layamon's earlier promise "þet he wolde of Engle þa æðelæn tellen" [that [his work] would tell of the English nobility] (line 7) and suggests that within some seventy years of the *Historia*'s being written, even in the Welsh marches Arthur might be regarded as not just a British hero but an English one.

In some ways the parallel passage in the *Gesta Regum Britannie*, the early thirteenth-century metrical paraphrase of Geoffrey's *Historia*, is even more remarkable.[20] Here again ambiguity is reduced: "Uiuo rege tamen, cui mortis ianua clausa / Creditur Arturo" [But King Arthur, to whom the door of death is believed to be closed, lives]. Its lengthy description of the remarkable island to which Arthur is taken has sometimes been compared with the Isle of Apples in Geoffrey's *Vita Merlini*,[21] but the effect of the two is rather different. While the *Vita*'s island is a kind of Land of Cockayne, where an abundance of food is produced without any labor, the *memorabilis insula* of the *Gesta Regum Britannie* resembles nothing so much as a vision of the heavenly paradise.[22]

In fact the parallels with Peter Damian's great Christian hymn *Ad perennis vitae fontem*[23] are so close that it is difficult to believe that the author of the *Gesta* is not consciously imitating it. The *Gesta* describes a land that winter never chills and summer never burns ("non nix, non bruma, nec estas / Immoderata furit" [lines 298–89]), one that basks in a temperate climate where spring flowers coexist eternally with autumnal fruits:

> Uer tepit eternum; nec flos nec lilia desunt
> Nec rosa nec viole flores et poma sub una
> Fronde gerit pomus. (lines 300–302)

> [An eternal spring warms; neither blossom nor lilies are lacking, neither rose nor violets. The apple tree bears blossom and fruit upon a single branch.]

These are also qualities that are present in the heavenly kingdom depicted in *Ad perennis vitae fontem*:

> Hiems horrens, aestus torrens illic numquam saeviunt;
> Flos perpetuus rosarum ver agit perpetuum,
> Candent lilia, rubescit crocus . . .
> . . . .
> Pendent poma floridorum non lapsura nemorum. (lines 13–18)

> [Shivering winter, burning summer never rage there. A perpetual flowering ushers in a perpetual spring: lilies shine, the crocus blushes. . . . The apples of the flowering groves hang down, never to fall.]

So too the *Gesta* describes a land of perpetual harmony ("pax et concordia perpes" [line 302]) whose inhabitants live free from disease and old age, experience no bodily desires, and hold everything in common:

> Habitant sine labe pudoris
> Semper ibi iuuenis cum uirgine. Nulla senectus,

Nullaque uis morbi, nullus dolor, omnia plena
Leticie. Proprium nichil hic, communia queque. (lines 302–5)

[Youths and the virgins dwell there forever with no shameful blemish. There is no old age, and no threat of disease, no sadness; all things are filled with joy. There is no ownership here, everything is common.]

And again, these are all qualities to be found in Peter Damian's poem: "Cleansed of every blemish, they know no wars of the flesh" [Omni labi defaecati carnis bella nesciunt] (line 25); "The healthy are free of disease, the young of old age" [Absunt morbi semper sanis, senectus iuvenibus] (line 33); and "Thus individual belongings become common to all" [Proprium sic singulorum commune fit omnium] (line 42). Like its Arthurian counterpart, Peter Damian's paradise is imagined as a reward for the weary soldier (though this soldier has been long warring against spiritual foes), but there the similarities end. Instead of Christ (the *palma bellatorum*), it is a royal virgin (*regia virgo*), a most lovely nymph surrounded by her lovely virgins ("Uirginibus stipata suis pulcerrima pulcris / Nimpha" [307–9]), who presides over this paradise—and this despite the fact that there is mention of a king, and it is in his hall, the *aulam regis Auallonis*,[24] that the royal virgin tends to Arthur's wounds.

What are we to make of this remarkable passage whose devotional echoes can barely disguise its doctrinal heterodoxy? Indeed they might even be argued to accentuate it. Though the author was probably a Breton and says he is writing only for a British audience ("solis hec scribo Britannis" [10:492]), he is no obscure village priest composing in the vernacular like Layamon. His work is written in the dactylic hexameters of the schoolman and dedicated to a bishop. (Not that even episcopal rank innoculated one against such beliefs of course: Peter des Roches, Bishop of Winchester (1205–38) was fond of recounting how he had once encountered King Arthur while he was out hunting, and had been entertained by him in a castle deep in the woods.)[25] Elsewhere, however, the author shows a markedly greater interest in religious matters than his source does, and even as he describes the magical healing of a man "to whom the door of death is believed to be closed," he dates Arthur's arrival in Avalon to "the five hundred and forty-second year after the Word was made flesh without a father's seed" [post incarnatum sine patris semine verbum] (9:312–13). It is difficult to detect much irony here, however, and only the telltale phrase *si credere fas est* suggests that the author is aware of the inappropriateness of his own description:

> uirgo regia uulnus
> Illius tractans, sanati membra reseruat
> Ipsa sibi; uiuuntque simul, si credere fas est.

> [the royal virgin, treating his wound, saves the limbs of the restored man for herself, and they live on together—if it is right to believe it] (9:315–17).

For this Breton author, I suspect, pride in local tradition trumps even doctrinal propriety.

Whatever precisely we make of it, then, there can be no doubt that this passage sets Arthur's survival in direct opposition to orthodox belief. To be writing approximately seven hundred years after the Battle of Camlann (an event the poem carefully dates) and to claim that the British leader lives on, inhabiting a feminized simulacrum of the Christian heaven, cannot but have raised the soteriological hackles of an orthodox reader. In *Draco Normannicus*, for example, a fictional Henry II says that he will gladly leave Arthur to his own brand of *vita perennis* so long as he himself can enjoy the prospect of true eternal life *sub Christi iure*.[26] So too in a poetic dialogue between a courtier and a detractor of court life written by Peter of Blois,[27] the detractor warns the courtier that he is risking eternal punishment by indulging in the worldly pleasures of the court, but the courtier replies,

> sompniator animus
> respuens presencia
> gaudeat inanibus—
> quibus si crederis
> exspectare poteris
> Arturum cum Britonibus. (st. 8)

> [Let the dreaming mind, rejecting reality, rejoice in follies; if you believe in such things you are capable of waiting for Arthur alongside the Britons.]

The foolish courtier, Peter implies, can see no difference between the truths of the Christian faith and British fairy tales; it is a throwaway remark, but its implication is unmistakable: Arthur's Avalon stands as a direct contravention of orthodox belief for the unwary.

When Gerald of Wales raises concerns about this same issue, he does so in the context of the supposed discovery of Arthur's tomb at Glastonbury around 1191. As regards other aspects of fairy belief Gerald was certainly no knee-jerk skeptic: he concludes a detailed account of the priest Eliodor's boyhood visits to a subterranean kingdom—where he learned, among other things, that the fairies speak a language not dissimilar to Greek—by saying that he is unable either to affirm or deny such things.[28] However, Gerald draws the line at believing that Arthur can be still alive in Avalon. Before this discovery, he writes scornfully in *de Principis Instructione* (ca. 1196), preposterous tales had circulated that "at the end Arthur's body like a sort of phantasm was carried far away by some kind of spirits and became immune to death" [huius autem corpus quod quasi phantasticum in fine et tanquam per spiritus ad longinqua translatum, neque morti obnoxium fabulae confinxerant].[29] So too in his *Speculum Ecclesiae* (ca. 1219) he describes Morgan as a type of outlandish goddess (*dea quaedam phantastica*) and pours scorn on the overimaginative (*fabulosi*) Britons who say that she has taken Arthur to Avalon to heal him of his wounds. His greatest disdain, however, he reserves for the so-called British hope: "they expect that he will still come, just like the Jews with their Messiah, deluded by an even greater folly and misery, along with their lack of faith" [ipsum exspectant adhuc venturum, sicut Judaei Messiam suum, maiori etiam fatuitate et infelicitate, simul ac infidelitate decepti].[30]

The opening of a grave reputedly belonging to Arthur by the monks of Glastonbury around the year 1191 has been much discussed. Despite archaeological evidence for the graveyard's having been disturbed at about the right period,[31] most historians have assumed that this exhumation was a self-interested subterfuge, perpetrated in the wake of a major fire in the abbey, either to win the king's favor or to attract visitors. "There is not much doubt," writes Richard Barber, "that the coffin and its contents . . . were produced by the monks in order to raise money for the rebuilding of the abbey."[32] The argument that Arthur's tomb would have constituted a tourist attraction seems to me a weak one (Arthur and Guinevere were no miracle-working saints at whose shrine grateful pilgrims might have been expected to leave offerings), but clearly the discovery raised serious questions about the British hope, and as such may possibly have been welcomed by the English Crown. William of Malmesbury had said that the absence of a body encouraged the Welsh in their belief that Arthur would return, and (as we shall see later) that the materiality of corpses posed a serious difficulty (though not necessarily an insuperable one) for those who might choose to believe that their relatives were still alive in fairyland.

Walter Map tells the story of Triunein, the son of Gwestin Gwestiniog and a fairy, whose body was missing after a battle between two Welsh kings and who local legend held had been saved by his mother and was living with her at the bottom of a lake; "I think it must even be called a lie," concludes Map skeptically, "for such a fiction could easily be invented about a man who was missing."[33] While it may well be, then, that the monks of Glastonbury were happy to curry favor with the English Crown by publicizing their new discovery,[34] we need not assume that their motives were wholly cynical. They must have seen the belief of their credulous Welsh neighbors in a living Arthur as a serious doctrinal lapse, a genuine threat to their hope of salvation, so that it is possible that by fabricating his tomb (if fabricated it was) they believed they were doing God's work, performing an action analogous to the forging of monastic charters so dexterously defended by Giles Constable.[35] This is certainly the spirit in which Gerald of Wales, a lover of his country and a man dismayed by the manifest *infidelitas* of his countrymen on this point, understood the discovery. His are by far the longest and most detailed accounts of the exhumation, and he might well have hoped that their diffusion would help to set his fellow Welshmen back on the true path and spare them the mockery of men such as William of Newburgh.

There exists, in fact, a tract in Welsh, drawn mainly from Gerald's *Speculum Ecclesie* but with two interpolated passages from his *de Principis Instructione*, that was clearly intended to counter the legend of the British hope among the people of Wales. Four manuscripts of this tract, *de Sepultura Arthuri Regis*, survive (two of them postmedieval); in the earliest (Aberystwyth, National Library of Wales, MS Llanstephan 4), *de Sepultura Arthuri* is bound up, significantly (as we shall see), with the *Visio Pauli* and *St Patrick's Purgatory*.[36] The opening sentence sets out its position unequivocally: "This is the information of the books which is clearer than that which the brut says concerning the end of King Arthur for the purpose of recognizing the truth concerning tales and false imaginings" (p. 437). At a number of points the force of Gerald's original is heavily underlined: for instance, where Arthur's skull is described as exhibiting ten old wounds, only one of which seemed to be lethal ("quodque solum letale fuisse videbatur"), the Welsh reads, "In the bone of his head there were sixteen wounds and each of those had closed and healed firmly except one and that one was open and it was an extensive wound so that it was undoubted that it was from that one that he had died" (p. 439). And the phrase "fabulosis exsufflatis" [with fabled matters cleared away] is upgraded to "until those untrue tales are abandoned and cease to be and have disappeared" (p. 443). The portrait of Morgan the healer is darkened considerably; instead of a *nobilis matrona* she is described as an "old dame," and the, admittedly ambiguous, phrase *dea phantastica* is rendered as "a goddess of the netherworld" (p. 443). Perhaps the most interesting passage comes at the very end, where Gerald's Latin manuscript (damaged in the Cottonian fire) is defective: Arthur, says the tract, enriched the church in Glastonbury, aided by "the just judgment of God, the one who rewards bountifully and without any doubt, every good deed that is done; and that, not only in heaven itself but also on earth, both the living and the dead, and after death in the life eternal" (p. 451). Gerald, and following him his Welsh apologist, leaves us in no doubt about what has happened to Arthur's immortal soul, and it has nothing to do with some kind of deathless existence, lived out in the company of a phantasmagorical goddess on an outlandish Apple Island.

The earliest accounts of the British hope leave us with the impression that Arthur awaits his return to this world as the sole mortal in a kingdom populated by fairies, but later texts, some of which clearly reflect local traditions, imply something far more sociable: an Arthur accompanied by his old companions in arms. Chaucer, for example, was evidently aware of a tradition that made Gawain, "with his olde curteisye," Arthur's companion, for "though he were comen ayeyn out of Fairye" (*The Squire's Tale*, lines 95–96)[37] must mean that he too was an inhabitant of fairyland. In addition, according to Jean d'Outremeuse's *Myreur des histors*, Avalon contained not only Arthur and Gawain but also two other mortals; Morgan, he writes, "oit deleis li des pucieles asseis, et oit IIII hommez tant sorlement: Artus, Gawain, Ogier et Alberon" [gathered several maidens about her, and she had four men only: Arthur, Gawain, Ogier and Oberon].[38] Despite his name, this Oberon is apparently mortal (the son of Morgan and Meliadus, and thus Tristan's half brother and Gawain's cousin); Ogier the Dane, an account of whose shipwreck on the island occasions this description,[39] is only a temporary resident, but the others are destined to live there in perpetual youth (and chastity) until Judgment Day. (Incidentally, Jean places this island in the Mediterranean, for despite Gerald of Wales's best efforts to make Glastonbury the official Avalon, Arthur's haven continued to adapt its topography to local contingencies for centuries to come, located not only on distant islands but also on mountaintops and even under the sea.)[40] Elsewhere, Arthur is accompanied by all his old comrades; in the *Disputation Between a Christian and a Jew*, the disputants encounter "al þe rounde table good" in fairyland,⁴¹ and Lydgate writes of "How kyng Arthour, flour of cheualrie, / Rit [rides] with his knihtis & lyueth in Fairye."⁴² Étienne de Bourbon offers the *familia Arthuri* as an alternative to the *familia Allequini* when describing the mysterious troop of huntsmen or warriors who were sometimes encountered after dark (we shall return to Herlequin's ride later); he tells of a peasant who once encountered near *Montem Cati* (probably the *Mont du Chat* in Savoie) an infinite number of men on foot and on horseback, "et cum quereret ab uno illorum qui essent repondit quod essent de familia regis Arthuri" [and when he asked one of them who they were, he replied that they were members of Arthur's household].⁴³ Gervase of Tilbury reports that such huntsmen were believed to be "of the company and household of Arthur" [*de sosietate et familia Arturi*] in both Britain and Brittany.⁴⁴

It may even be that popular tradition regularly assigned those who had disappeared on the battlefield a place in fairyland. William of Auvergne, for instance, considers briefly the question of whether the fairy horde might be made up of those who had been lost in battle, "disgladiatos eos vulgus vocat" [the common people call them 'sword-killed'].⁴⁵ We have already noted Walter Map's reference to Triunein, and nearly five hundred years later, in 1576, Bessie Dunlop, a Scottish cunning woman accused of witchcraft, told the court that her fairy accomplice had been killed at the Battle of Pinkie Cleugh twenty-nine years earlier ("quha deit at Pinkye, as he himselff affirmit").⁴⁶

A particularly intriguing account of fairyland as the abode of past heroes appears in the *Fasciculus Morum*, a preacher's handbook written in the early fourteenth century by an English Franciscan: "But I ask, what shall we say of those superstitious wretches who [have claimed] that at night they see dancing the most beautiful queens and other girls, who in our native tongue are called *elves*? . . . And they believe that these can change both men and women into other beings and carry them with them to *elvenland* where there are already, as they say, those strong champions like Onewyn and Wade and others. All this is nothing but phantoms shown them by [an evil] spirit" (pp. 578–79).⁴⁷ A later manuscript substitutes "King Arthur with his troops" [*rex Arthuri cum suis militibus*] for "Onewyn and Wade."⁴⁸ Very little is known of Wade, the father of Weland the Smith; he appears in the Anglo-Saxon poem *Widsith* (line 22),⁴⁹ and Speght's apparent disinclination to elucidate

Chaucer's allusion to "Wades boot" (*The Merchant's Tale*, line 1424)[50]—"because the matter is long and fabulous, I passe it over"—has caused generations of scholars to tear their hair out.[51] Onewyn, however, is even more obscure.[52] He too is mentioned in *Widsith* (line 114), where he is said to be the son of Ostrogotha, and a late medieval chronicle alludes to a *Gesta Unwini*, whose hero is among those who "were famous in arms and military affairs" [*armis et rebus bellicis claruerunt*],[53] but other than this his exploits are entirely lost to history. There can be few starker reminders of how thin our knowledge of medieval vernacular culture really is. Generations of literate clerics parrot an ostensibly popular belief that Arthur is the main, perhaps the only, mortal denizen of fairyland, and meanwhile here is a West Country Franciscan calmly informing us that there were people who believed that there were other heroes quite as ancient as Arthur (heroes whose stories we can only guess at) sharing his refuge.[54]

Needless to say, stories such as these were not approved of by the church. Citing Gratian for justification, the *Fasciculus Morum* proclaims that "those who believe in such things ... are more faithless and worse than heathens," fit to be "cursed every single day by the servants of holy church" (pp. 580–81). Jean d'Outremeuse remarks, "Ch'est une chouse la sainte Englise n'ajouste point de foit; mais ilh le croit qui veut, et qui veut, ilh le lait" [It is a thing that Holy Church puts no faith in; but let he who wishes, believe it, and if he wishes, leave it] (p. 53). Nevertheless it was not always possible to insulate orthodox teaching from such beliefs, as the remarkable story of the appearance of Thomas of Canterbury to support Simon de Montfort at the Battle of Lewes in 1264 demonstrates: "Also a certain boy, working in the Canterbury region, had seen in his sleep the blessed Thomas rise up from his tomb. The boy asked him, 'What are you doing, blessed Thomas, and how is it you arise now? I believed you to be dead.' 'I was not dead,' the blessed Thomas told him, 'but I rested in peace. But now it is necessary for me to rise up and fight for my homeland, England'" [*Quidam etiam puer in partibus Cantuariae agens, in somnis viderat beatum Thomam de suo feretro surgentem, cui dicit puer, "Quid facis, beate Thoma, qualiter modo surgis? Credebam te mortuum fuisse." Cui Beatus Thomas, "Non fui," inquit, "mortuus, sed quievi in pace; sed iam necesse habeo surgere et pugnare pro patria mea Angliae"*].[55] For some people, it seems, fairyland contained not only King Arthur and King Herla, or Wade and Onwyn, but Thomas à Becket as well.[56] (We shall see later how such popular beliefs might spill over into orthodox accounts of purgatory.)

The Living and the Dead

As the story of Saint Thomas implies ("non fui mortuus"), we should be careful about seeing fairyland, whether in Avalon or elsewhere, as simply a land of the dead. King Arthur, "to whom the door of death is believed to be closed," is emphatically alive, and indeed to claim otherwise could apparently get you into a fight in twelfth-century Brittany. The point is made with particular clarity in a late thirteenth-century romance called *Floriant and Florete*; Floriant, a protégé of Morgan, is described as a contemporary of King Arthur and in fact precedes him into Morgan's safekeeping. In the final episode, set in Sicily, Floriant finds himself mysteriously transported to Morgan's castle while out hunting a white stag—lured there, Morgan informs him, to save him from his impending death:

> Amis, vous devïez mourir
> Et de cest siecle departir;
> Nus ne vous i pëust aidier,
> Mecinne n'i ëust mestier,
> Pour itant vous fis ci venir.
> Sachiés de voir et sanz mentir
> Que cist chastiaus si est feez,
> Sachiés que ço est veritez,
> Nus hone ne puet çaienz morir.
> Li rois Artus, au defenir,
> Mes freres, i ert amenez
> Quant il sera a mort navrez.[57]

[My friend, you would have died and departed this world; no one could have helped you, no medicine could have saved you, and for that reason I made you come here. Know truly and without any lie that this castle is so enchanted (you must know that this is the truth) that no one can die within it. My brother King Arthur at the end will be brought here when he shall be wounded unto death.]

This news saddens Floriant, who fears it means he is to be separated from his love Florete, but Morgan immediately sends three fairies to bring her to his side, and the romance ends happily with the couple facing a deathless future together in fairyland.

Floriant and Florete are unusually lucky to find themselves united in fairyland. In a handful of romances, most conspicuously *Sir Orfeo*, a sojourn in fairyland separates, rather than unites, lovers, and it is quite understandable that the sense of loss that this generates should evoke thoughts of death. However, unlike Hamlet's undiscovered country, the bourn that separates fairyland from our own world is far from impassable. Nocturnal travelers (homeward-bound huntsmen such as Map's Eadric the Wild or late-night revelers such as William of Newburgh's *rusticus*) might stumble upon a fairy feast and escape unscathed; innocent children like Gerald of Wales's Eliodor might wander about in fairyland and return to tell the tale, while others, like Ralph of Coggeshall's Malkin, despite being taken there against their will, might expect to be returned after a set period; even those who follow their fairy lovers into the otherworld might make occasional return visits, such as Sir Launfal, or even return for good, such as Thomas of Erceldoune. Certainly the passage into and out of fairyland is perilous, and anyone seeking to rescue a mortal from the clutches of the fairies must face daunting and difficult tests, but the fact remains that for human denizens of the fairy world, even for Walter Map's King Herla, the possibility of a return to this world can never be completely ruled out. It is vital then that we distinguish between the extended life of human beings taken to live among the fairies and the finality of biological death. "Upto now," says the inscription on a mysterious tomb in Chrétien de Troyes's *Knight of the Cart*, "no one has ever returned [from the land of Gorre]" [*N'ancor n'an est nus retornez*] (line 1918), but we would be mistaken were we to take this to mean that Gorre is a land of the dead, for when Lancelot first defeats Melegeant and rescues Guinevere, we learn,

> Tel costume el païs avoit
> Que, puis que li uns s'an issoit,
> Que tuit li autre s'an issoient. (lines 3917–19)

> [It was the custom in this country that when one captive escaped, all the others were free to leave.]⁵⁸

Indeed the mysterious episode in the Christian graveyard (lines 1141–2022) seems to offer the possibility of the merciful relief of mortality to those freed from the deathless clutches of Gorre.

The motif of a recovery from fairyland, typically suppressed and rationalized by Chrétien de Troyes, is employed transparently in the romance of

Reinbrun, a coda to *Guy of Warwick*: the episode in which Reinbrun delivers his father's friend Amis from the castle of the fairy knight called Sir Gayere is related with almost no interference from the great tradition. Passing through "Mechel Arderne" (the Ardennes) on his way back to England from Africa, Guy's son Reinbrun and his tutor Heraud arrive at Amis's castle, only to learn that its lord has disappeared while out hunting and that his grieving wife attributes this to the enmity of "a fairy kniȝt herin is / Þat is of meche miȝt" (stanza 74, lines 4–5).[59] The next day Reinbrun sets out alone to rescue Amis. He first passes through a set of gates in a hillside and then, after riding in darkness for half a mile, comes upon a splendid castle on the far side of a formidable river, which he manages to cross on the back of his swimming horse—a curious double barrier that is reminiscent of the ambiguous boundary of Gorre in Chrétien's *Chevalier de la charete*.[60] This castle seems at first to be deserted, but once inside, Reinbrun discovers Amis, a disconsolate prisoner, who informs him that it belongs to a fairy knight ("Hit is a kniȝtes of fayri") and has the property of freezing time:

> Þis paleys is of swiche miȝt,
> Her schal no man elde apliȝt,
> Be he her neuer so longe.
> Þei he wer her a þosand ȝer,
> In is heued schel hore non her,
> Ne non elde fonge. (86:1–6)

Amis further informs Reinbrun that his jailer, whose name is Sir Gayere, is impervious to all weapons ("noþing ne schel him dere") except for a sword that is hanging on a nearby pillar, and this sword accordingly Reinbrun takes along with him. In the ensuing battle, it is made quite clear that Gayere is mortal ("His heued benome him he hadde / Ner it þat he merci gradde"), and Reinbrun spares his life on condition that he release not only Amis but also all his other prisoners. Like the Knight of the Cart whose defeat of Melegeant redeems all those held captive in Gorre,

> R[e]inbroun glad & bliþe is:
> He hadde deliuered sire Amis,
> Þre hondred kniȝtes & mo. (95:7–9)

Amis's exile in fairyland may have meant that he was effectively dead to the lady he had left behind, but there is no sense in which the poem shows him as having experienced literal death. Magical it may have been, but the land from which Reinbrun rescues his father's friend is a land of the living, not a land of the dead. Nevertheless it is not difficult to see how some of those who were carried off to live in fairyland (rather than in a Christian version of the afterlife) might have been thought of as dead by those left behind. Some such economy must underlie a strange story found in a poem on the wonders of Ireland from a manuscript of about 1200.[61] A man, described as good and truthful (*bonus et verax*), is said to have thrown a stone at some birds as he was walking beside a river and managed to hit a swan; running to catch the wounded bird, he finds to his surprise a naked and still breathing woman. He asks her who she is, what has happened to her, and from what time she comes:

Haec, "infirma fui," inquit ei, "et tunc proxima morti,
Atque putata meis sum quod defuncta videbar,
Daemonibus sed rapta fui cum carne repente."[62]

[She told him, "I was sick and on the point of death and it was thought by my family that I seemed dead, but I was suddenly snatched away in the flesh by demons."]

After he has fed and clothed her, he returns her to her family, who are scarcely able to credit what has happened, since they believed that they had laid her in the grave: "Tradidit atque suis credentibus esse sepultam." As we have come to recognize, these demons must be fairies (and the woman's transformation to a swan may possibly be related to some legend similar to the *Chevalier Assigne*),[63] but the real puzzle is how she might have been imagined to be living on *cum carne*, after her relatives thought they had buried her. We are not dealing here with an Arthur or a Triunein, whose bodies were never found. What, in other words, did her relatives think they had buried?

One answer (perhaps a clerical rationalization of a popular belief) is to be found in a remarkable passage in Thomas of Cantimpré's *Bonum Universale de Apibus*, which Dorena Allen first drew to the attention of scholars in an important article on *Sir Orfeo*.[64] Thomas, in fact, has a whole section on "*dusii* demons and how they substitute something for a body they have abducted" [De Dusiis daemonibus, & quomodo uno corpore sublato aliud substitutant].[65] These demons, he explains, are the same *dusii* that Augustine writes about in his *City of God* (15:23), but we find nothing in Augustine resembling this particular aspect of their activities:

They have suddenly snatched the bodies of living people from among men, as if for Diana, and, since deluded men have seen those (who at home were thought to be dead) carried off by her into other regions, they now believed them to be made immortal and adjudged them to be numbered with the gods. And in just the same way we have frequently heard even in our own day and age that women, caught in the throes of death, were suddenly snatched away, and simulacra put in their place by demons (these same simulacra closely resembled the stolen bodies) and buried as if they were corpses; but afterward the women were seen, and consorted with men.[66]

Thomas first tackles the question of fairy abduction in general, citing an instance given, he says, by Albertus Magnus in a disputation held before an unnamed Bishop of Paris (possibly William of Auvergne). A daughter of the Count of Schwalenberg was being abducted by demons for a certain period of the night, and her brother, rather like Orfeo surrounding Queen Heurodis with his *scheltrom*,[67] sought to protect her; though he clasped his sister to his bosom and held her tightly in his arms ("sororem suam in gremio, & brachiis eam fortissime strinxit, ac tenuit"), she was still dragged from his hands and rendered invisible and impalpable ("de manibus tenentis invisibiliter & incontrectabiliter tollebatur"). Such an experience, says Thomas, was quite likely to drive the victim mad, and those who were restored to the human world would never be the same again. Orfeo's description of Heurodis after her first encounter with the fairy king,

> Allas! þi rode, þat was so red,
> Is al wan, as þou were ded;
> . . . .
> Allas! þi louesom ey3en to
> Lokeþ so man doþ on his fo! (*Sir Orfeo*, lines 107–12)

is strongly reminiscent of Thomas's portrait of such survivors: "Quod quidem referunt, qui viderunt, facies sic raptarum, quae pallide sunt semper macie & lividae, & occuli magis instabiles, quam in non raptis" [Indeed, those who have seen them say that the faces of women abducted in this way, which are always of a pallid thinness, are livid, and their eyes less steady than those of non-abductees].

Even more remarkable are the two stories Thomas then goes on to tell of the simulacra (his word is *figmenta*) that demons leave behind so that the relatives of those they have abducted, believing them to be dead, may bury their corpses. The first account takes place in the town of Merchtem near Brussels. A young man is on the point of asking for the hand of a local girl when he learns that she has died of a fever, but to his amazement, while he is walking disconsolately in the woods, he encounters the girl herself who says she had been led there by a man. After taking her back to his house, he goes to her parents and asks for her hand; they promise wryly that if he can bring her back to life he can marry her, and they take him to see her corpse: "Mox iuvenis, cum relevasset linteum, quo cooperta putabatur, figmentum mirabile, quale a nullo hominum fieri potuit, invenerunt" [As soon as the young man had pulled back the shroud with which she was believed to be covered, they found a wondrous simulacrum, such as could be made by no human hand]. The young man subsequently marries the girl, who, says Thomas, is still alive and well at the time of writing: "usque ad tempora nostra incolumis perduravit." The second story, which takes place in Flanders, is similar except that the abducted girl is found wandering on the seashore by her brother, who secretly brings her home and then, to everyone's horror, proceeds to cut up his sister's supposed corpse with his sword. This rescued girl too is said to be still living. Thomas professes himself uncertain about how to take such stories ("nec inficior, nec confirmo") and says that he had consulted Albertus Magnus on the subject but that the great man was evasive and reluctant to commit himself ("sed ille dissimulavit, & noluit aliquid definire").

What precisely, we might ask, does Thomas intend us to understand by these simulacra (*figmenta*)? In the Merchtem case he actually offers us a detailed description of the kind of thing that was involved: "Dicitur autem ab his, qui figmenta huiusmodi diabolica inspexerunt, ea esse interius putrido ligno similia, levi exterius pellicula superducta" [It is said by those who have examined devilish simulacra of this kind, that they are like putrid wood within, and covered on the outside with a thin hide]. Despite the fact that it can be paralleled elsewhere, however,[68] this account reads like a clerical rationalization, for it is difficult to believe that adherents of the little tradition could have supposed that fairies were really driven to so complicated an expedient. Fairies were dab hands at shape-shifting, and for creatures that had no trouble convincing Sir Gowther's mother that she was actually sleeping with her husband, impersonating the corpse of an abducted girl would have been a comparatively simple matter. After all, the whole changeling tradition depends on a similar subterfuge. A somewhat different solution to this problem is offered in the romance of *Amadas and Ydoine*. There, Ydoine is given a ring by her fairy suitor that makes her appear to be dead to those around her; his plan is to take her from the grave, remove the ring, and carry her off with him, but he is thwarted by the grief-stricken Amadas, who has mounted a guard over her tomb.[69]

Death is not the only context in which the stubborn materiality of bodies left behind could pose a problem for those who believed in fairy transference. True, the canon *Episcopi* had poured such scorn on the naïveté of those who believed that women were able to traverse great distances by night in order to be present at gatherings in honor of Diana that it was not until the period of the early modern witch hunts that schoolmen were forced to confront the contradiction that those who were accused of being present at satanic sabbats had been observed sleeping soundly beside their husbands all the time.[70] It seems likely that such 'transvection' was still popularly accepted, however, as the fifteenth-century English sermon with which we began this book implies: people believe, it says, that *Eluysche folke* "possunt . . . alios pro se dimittere et illos secum adducere ad *Eluenlond*" [can . . . leave others in their place and carry (men and women) with them to Elfland].[71] The story about Saint Germain told by Étienne de Bourbon shows how this problem might be encountered in a slightly different context.[72] The saint, visiting Britain to combat heresy, lodges in a house where he notices his hosts leaving food out on the table before they go to bed. Told that the 'Good Things' often gathered there and that it was not fitting to leave them unprovided for ("quod bone res frequenter ibi conveniebant nec erat dignum quod mensam invenierent inmunitam cum a[limento]"), Germain keeps watch and observes a great number of men and women assemble at the table. He commands them in Christ's name to remain as they are until he gives the word ("precepit eis in virtute Christi ut sic starent ut erant usque ad preceptum eius") and then rouses his fellow guests to come and look at them. On being informed that several of them were well-known neighbors, he sends men to fetch the actual neighbors to come and confront their look-alikes: "Quod cum fecissent, viderunt eos per omnia similes demonibus in eorum similitudinibus transfiguratis" [When they had done this, they saw that they were in every way similar to the demons that were transfigured into their likenesses]. The fraud exposed, the saint then banishes the demons for good.

Though Dorena Allen does not go so far as to employ Thomas of Cantimpré's simulacra to explicate the difficult passage in *Sir Orfeo* where the hero encounters what appears to be a collection of corpses, some grotesquely maimed, in the courtyard before the Fairy King's hall (lines 386–408), such an association is difficult to avoid. Many critics have found this passage deeply troubling, and Bruce Mitchell even goes so far as to suggest that it is a later interpolation on the grounds of its divergence from the overall tone of the poem: "all the evidence of the poem apart from the courtyard scene suggests that the faery world is a pleasant place."[73] Two facts are clear: 1) the collection is made up of mortals who have been carried off to fairyland ("Of folk þat were þider y-brouȝt" [line 299]) just as they were at the moment of their taking ("Eche was þus in þis warld y-nome" [line 403]); and 2) despite the fact that these mortals appear to be dead ("& þouȝt dede" [line 389]), they are in fact merely taking a siesta ("Riȝt as þai slepe her vnder-tides" [line 402]). It is natural to assume that men and women who have been beheaded, mutilated, skewered, choked, drowned, and burned are dead, but the poet takes care to assure us that they are very much alive: "& þouȝt dede, *& nare nouȝt*" (line 389). Presumably they are also able to enjoy all the pleasures of fairyland since at least one of them, Heurodis, has just returned from an elegant hunting party. It is surely significant that while Orfeo had recognized his wife instantly when he saw her out hawking, in the courtyard he could identify her only by her dress ("Bi her cloþes he knewe þat it was he" [line 408]). These double-images, then, look very like some form of Thomas's abductee-and-*figmentum*, which are reported elsewhere in the British Isles[74] and (as we shall see) have their parallels in late medieval England. One explanation for their presence on the threshold of the fairy king's hall is that they act as a kind of test, a final challenge to those seeking to recover their loved ones from fairyland. If so, Orfeo, undeterred by encountering the apparent form of his dead queen, succeeds triumphantly: he demands his wife in fulfillment of the fairy king's rash promise and leads back to the world of mortals a Heurodis once more made whole.

Several recent critics of *Sir Orfeo* have shown themselves aware of the poem's failure to accommodate itself to the tenets of orthodox Christianity, and even of the potential dangers of such failure; "the elaboration of meaning in other contexts and according to other codes," writes Jeff Rider, "was difficult, dangerous, or at least problematic, because Christianity was both hegemonic and imperialist."[75] Nevertheless the difficulty we find in escaping such hegemonic constraints, even now, has meant that these interpretations have tended to find only indeterminacy, ambiguity, and even incoherence in the poem. "Faerie," according to Rider, represents the force the artist must confront in order to liberate the poem "from the sterile frozen state in which the unmastered imp of interpretation would captivate it" (p. 366); Alan Fletcher, writing of the competing discourses of *Orfeo* (they include the discourses of Christianity and of fairyland), concludes that they are "incapable of containing chaos in one totalizing explanation";[76] and Neil Cartlidge reads the poem as "prompting so many different registers of interpretation at once, without actually authorizing any of them," that it brings us "to the brink of moral and interpretative entropy."[77] At the risk of appearing obtusely reductive, however, I am tempted to ask what precisely the discourse of Christianity in *Sir Orfeo* consists of.

There are, by my count, only eight explicit gestures toward orthodox belief (by no means all of which are unambiguous) in the entire poem.[78] The poet twice underlines his hero's dramatic situation with the exclamation "Lord!" (lines 263 and 590), and when Orfeo first sees the party of ladies out hawking (and before he has recognized Heurodis) he says, "Þider ichil, bi Godes name!" (line 316). It is difficult to read deep significance into any of these exclamations. So, too, the description of the fairy king's throne as "a tabernacle" (line 412) need carry no religious overtones since the MED provides us with plenty of secular instances of its meaning simply 'a canopied dais.' The unmistakable echo of *The Book of Ruth* (1:16) at lines 129–30, "Whider þou gost ichil wiþ þe, / & whider y go þou shalt wiþ me," is an appropriate and moving expression of Orfeo's devoted commitment to his wife, though none but a die-hard Robertsonian would be tempted to read it allegorically in the context.[79] This leaves us with only three rather more significant instances. Orfeo introduces himself to the fairy king as "an harpour of heþenisse" (line 513), and though Bliss offers 'from foreign parts' as a possible gloss, there does seem to be a definite implication that the hero is non-Christian here. While there is nothing surprising about this (we had earlier learned that "His fader was comen of King Pluto, / & his moder of King Juno, / Þat sum-time were as godes y-hold" [lines 43–45]), such cultural distancing might well be read as a self-protective move on the poet's part. On the other hand, the poem's two references to *Paradis* (particularly the second) might appear more provocative: anyone listening to Orfeo's harping, says the poet, "schuld þenche þat he were / In on of þe ioies of Paradis" (lines 36–37), and anyone encountering the "riche werk" of the fairy king's palace, "Bi al þing him þink þat it is / Þe proude court of Paradis" (lines 375–76). This last comparison so disturbed the scribes of the Harley and Ashmole versions of the poem that they left out these lines altogether.

Another way to highlight *Sir Orfeo*'s ideological position is to contrast it with one of its closest analogues, *Amadas et Ydoine*. Neil Cartlidge has claimed that "*Amadas and Ydoine* is triumphantly subversive of the established order of moral authority" (p. 222), but, if anything, such a judgment seems to me to apply better to *Sir Orfeo*. Quite apart from Ydoine's conspicuous sexual propriety (Amadas is allowed no premarital license, even when the couple find themselves alone in a deserted graveyard), the hero's combat with his fairy rival is couched in conventional Christian terms. The epithet regularly used of the fairy knight is *maufé* (for example, line 7681), etymologically an 'evil-fairy,' but here unmistakably a 'demon':

> Adont pense com gentil ber
> Que, se d'infer tuit li mauffé
> Estoient illoec assemblé,
> N'aroient il, n'a droit n'a tort,
> Le cors s'amie sans la mort. (lines 5606–10)

[Then, like a wellborn nobleman, he thought that if all the demons of hell were assembled there, they should never live to take away his love's body, come what may.]

As with many such vernacular romances, however, the demonization of its fairy archetype is only skin-deep. When the 'demon' knight first encounters his rival beside the tomb, he begins well enough, demanding to know, by the God in whom Amadas claims to believe ("par la foi que tu dois / A icel Diu en qui tu crois" [lines 5709–10]), what he is doing there; but only three lines later he is himself repeating his demand in God's name ("de la part Dé"), an imprecation that reassures Amadas ("por ce se rasseüre" [line 5720]). Like other mortals encountering fairies (Partonopeu, for example, or Yonec's mother), Amadas is heartened to hear his adversary speak of God. In another departure from Christian orthodoxy, Amadas's demonic (and thus deathless) opponent proves to be vulnerable and potentially mortal; Amadas wounds him in the head and then cuts off his right hand, so that, weak from loss of blood, he is forced to sue for mercy (lines 6311–32). *Sir Orfeo*, by contrast, makes no obvious accommodations with the dominant ideology, and compared with *Amadas and Ydoine* the English poem shows itself remarkably unembarrassed in its espousal of a fairyland ethos.

For all that the traditional position seems to have been that those taken by the fairies lived on in a deathless paradise, the notion (no doubt ultimately plausible to both laity and clerics alike) that fairyland was really a land of the dead came gradually to undermine it. Unlike Heurodis, Ydoine is explicitly said to have been rescued from the dead:

Bien savés qu'il avint de moi
Par un maufé que morte fui;
Par la grand prouece de lui
Sui venue de morte a vie. (lines 7674–77)

[You well know that a demon brought about my death; and by [Amadas's] great valor I have returned from death to life.]

One might have supposed it to be no less sacrilegious to bring one's heroine back from the dead than to show her living on in fairyland: if Heurodis is no Enoch, surely Ydoine is no Lazarus. However, this is one area where the lines between the great and the little traditions can hardly ever have been clearcut. While some must have chosen to believe that their departed had been taken to fairyland, others would surely have been prepared to accept that they were truly dead. It is easy to interpret Sir Thomas Malory's famous account of the death of Arthur as the work of a man trying to have it both ways, that in accordance with the little tradition, like Layamon, he allows his king to live ("'Comforte thyselff,' seyde the kynge, . . . 'For I muste into the vale of Avylyon to hele me of my grevous wounde'"), while at the same time, like Gerald of Wales, he bows to the authority of the great tradition by having him killed off ("'Ala[s]!' seyde sir Bedyvere, '[th]at was my lo[r]de kynge Arthur, whych lyethe here gravyn in thys chapell'").[80] But it is also possible that vernacular culture was able to embrace both these incompatible accounts, and that when Malory writes, "Yet I woll nat say that hit shall be so, but rather I wolde sey: here in thys worlde he chaunged hys lyff" (3:1242), he is not prevaricating so much as expressing genuine perplexity. One indication of such cultural ambivalence is the permeability of the boundary between fairy tale and ghost story in the late Middle Ages.

When Walter Map, for instance, tells of a man who rescues an apparently long-dead wife from the fairies and subsequently enjoys many years of married life with her, he expresses a similar perplexity: "This would be an incredible and portentous breach of nature's laws, did not trustworthy evidence of its truth exist."⁸¹ The German demonologist Johann Georg Gödelmann (1559–1611), who says that he learned the story from the scholar Georg Sabinus (1508–60), gives an even clearer illustration of how easily tales of fairy abduction might mutate into ghost stories:

> [Sabinus says] a man born to a noble family in Bavaria felt such great grief in his heart at the death of his wife that he could accept no consolation and passed his life in solitude. Finally, when he could set no term to his grief, his wife, raised from the dead, appeared and said that she had indeed finished the course of her life as assigned by nature once, and was commanded by God to resume the way of life that she had long enjoyed up to that point, but on this condition and stipulation, that her marriage, terminated by death, should again be instituted by a priest in a solemn ceremony, and that henceforth he should abstain from berating people with the blasphemous words he had been accustomed to employ, for she had been delivered to him for the sake of these things, and she would be once more deprived of life when first he uttered any word of this kind. These things being done, she returned to her domestic duties as before and even gave birth to several children, though she was always sad and pale. After many years, however, her husband got drunk one evening and angered by a servant girl, uttered the words he was not supposed to speak; in that moment [his wife] disappeared from the little room where she would go to fetch apples for her husband, and she left her gown, just as it had been draping her body, like a phantom, beside the chest where the apples were kept. Sabinus said he had heard these things from many reliable informants who claimed that the Duke of Bavaria had assured the Duke of Saxony that they were true.⁸²

The Christian influence is far clearer in this story than in *Orfeo*: the woman returns from the dead at God's commandment, for instance (and then only to teach a moral lesson), and the resumed marriage must first be consecrated by a priest. Nevertheless its fairy pedigree is unmistakable: the children of this resumed marriage (in what ghost story does a revenant ever become pregnant?) and, above all, the inevitably broken prohibition (bizarrely moralizing though it is) prove that this can only be a late reworking of an older fairy motif.

This brings us to one of the most difficult associations of fairies with the land of the dead: the origins of the household of King Herlequin or King Hellequin. During his ten-year sojourn in the wilderness, and just before his meeting with Heurodis and her hawking party, Sir Orfeo witnesses three other incursions from the fairy world. The first is a mysterious hunt:

> Þe king o fairy wiþ his rout
> Com to hunt him al about
> Wiþ dim cri and bloweing,
> & houndes also with him berking;
> Ac no best þai no nome; (lines 283–87),

the second is a great army riding to war ('displayed banners' and 'drawn swords' were universally recognized as signifying hostile intentions):

> a gret ost bi him te,
> Wele atourned, ten hundred kniȝtes,
> Ich y-armed to his riȝtes,
> Of cuntenaunce stout & fers,
> Wiþ mani desplaid baners,
> And ich his swerd y-drawe hold; (lines 290–95),

and the third, which need not delay us here, is a band of knights and ladies dancing (lines 297–302). In context, all three confirm the tendency of fairy society to mimic its counterpart in the human lifeworld.[83] But from a different perspective (and although these fairy bands ride by day and through the woods, rather than across the night sky), they are clearly manifestations of the *familia Herlequini* or *la mesnie Hellequin*, a term which, as Claude Lecouteux has shown, might encompass a wide variety of disparate phenomena;[84] in fact, these particular examples comprise, respectively, the wild hunt (*die wilde Jagt*) and the wild horde (*das wildes Heer*), distinct motifs which are all too often lumped uncritically together. While it is certainly not my intention here to try to rationalize or reduce the various phenomena comprehended in the *familia Herlequini*, one generalization accepted by almost all authorities (including Lecouteux)[85] does seem to me in serious need of qualification: that the *familia Herlequini* always and everywhere represented a troop of the dead.

The problem is that the earliest explicit reference to the *familia Herlequini* in Orderic Vitalis's *Ecclesiastical History* (1130s) connects it quite specifically with the dead. Orderic relates at length the story of a Norman priest called Walchelin, who describes his encounter on New Year's night in 1091 with a mysterious procession of knights, ladies, priests, monks, and commoners, "like the movement of a great army," among whom he recognized "many of his neighbours who had recently died."[86] At one point Walchelin says to himself, "Haec sine dubio familia Herlechini est" [Without a doubt this is Herlequin's household] (p. 243). There are two particularly striking features of this procession. In the first place, its members are solidly material: at one point Walchelin grabs one of their horses by the reins and experiences an intense burning (p. 245), and at another, one of the knights seizes him by the throat (p. 247), leaving a scar which he carries to the grave (p. 249). Second, all the members of the procession suffer penitential torments for their former sins: one of the knights, for instance, tells Walchelin: "The arms which we bear are red-hot, and offend us with an appalling stench, weighing us down with intolerable weight, and burning with everlasting fire" (p. 249). There is hardly anything in Orderic's account to connect this *familia Herlequini* with fairyland.

The other early description of Herlequin's ride, written some fifty years later, is from Walter Map's *De Nugis Curialium*.[87] Here a Welsh king called Herla encounters a diminutive Pan-like creature who predicts his future marriage and then strikes a bargain with him: he will attend Herla's wedding on condition that the king help him celebrate his own wedding a year later. This creature, who is never named, turns out to be royal and shows up at Herla's wedding with a splendid retinue bearing lavish gifts. The return visit, which involves passing through "a cave in a high cliff" (p. 28), is equally successful, but when the time comes for him to leave, Herla's host presents him with a small dog, with the instruction that none of his retinue is to dismount until the dog jumps down to the ground. He returns to his kingdom only to discover that hundreds of years have passed. Inevitably, some of his company dismount before the dog jumps down and are promptly turned to dust: "The King, comprehending the reason of their dissolution, warned the rest under pain of a like death not to touch the earth before the alighting of the dog. The dog has not yet alighted. And the story says that King Herla still holds on his mad course [*circuitus vesanos*] with his band in eternal wanderings, without stop or stay" (p. 31). Later, Map refers to this band as "phalanges noctivage quas Herlethingi dicebant" [night-wandering battalions which they say are Herlething's] or simply the "Herlethingi familia" [Herlething's household] (pp. 370–71). In contrast to Orderic's version, the fairy elements in Map's account (the foretelling of the future, the underground kingdom entered through a cave, the disruption in the passage of time, the magical prohibition) could hardly be more obvious (the parallels with the ending of *Guingamor*, for instance, are particularly striking). Moreover, Herla's household is not expiating its former sins; it suffers merely for breaching a seemingly arbitrary injunction. There are also clear indications that the story has an etiological function—sudden and violent storms being explained as the riding of Herla's host across the sky, an element that is certainly present in other accounts of Hellequin.[88] Finally, and most importantly, Herla and his companions are emphatically not dead. They are held in a seemingly endless state of suspended animation; death will come to them only if they dismount.

In order to adjudicate between these two accounts, we should begin by recognizing that the legend itself probably predates them both, possibly by a considerable time, and that any attempt to recover a hypothetical 'original' is by now quite futile. Both accounts are, as Lecouteux recognizes, etiological, and our task is less to decide which description is the more authentic, but rather which explanation—one Christian, the other folkloric—is the more feasible.

Orderic's near silence on the fairy question is inherently suspicious since later Christian writers do acknowledge it, explicitly or otherwise. William of Auvergne, for example, moves seamlessly from a discussion of nocturnal apparitions riding to battle to "other deceptions of evil spirits which they sometimes practice in groves and in charming places with leafy trees, where they appear in the likeness of girls or women in radiant feminine garments" [aliae ludificationes malignorum spirituum, quas faciunt interdum in nemoribus et locis amoenis et frondosis arboribus, ubi apparent in similitudine puellarum aut matronarum ornatu muliebri et candido].[89] In a late thirteenth-century poem on confession, the priest is instructed to ask, "Creïs tu . . . / Ne [le luiton] ne la masnée / Herllequin, ne genes ne fees?" [Do you not believe . . . in the goblin, in the household of Herlequin, in witches, and fairies?],[90] and an early fourteenth-century Dominican redaction of the *Elucidarium*, known as the *Second Lucidaire*, makes a similar association when it speaks (in the early sixteenth-century English translation) of "elues, gobelyns, & helquins þe whiche men se by nyght, as men of armes trottynge on horsebacke with grete assembles."[91] Another fourteenth-century author, Raoul de Presles, commenting on Augustine's discussion of *incubi demones* in *The City of God*, recommends that his readers consult William of Auvergne on the topic, "and also he speaks in that place of Hellekin's household and of Lady Abundance and of the spirits that they call fairies, which appear in stables and woods" [et aussi parle il en celle partie de la maisnie de hellequin et de dame habonde et des esperis quilz appellent faes qui apperent es estables et es arbres].[92] Finally, when the author of *Richard the Redeless*, referring no doubt to the *duketti* created by Richard II in 1397, writes, "Oþer hobbis ȝe hadden / of Hurlewaynis kynne," he explicitly associates Herlequin with hobs or fairies (his use of the wild horde to satirize court folly has a long history, going back to Walter Map and Peter of Blois).[93] Few of these passages give us any reason to suppose that Herlequin or Hellequin was automatically associated with the realms of the dead.

Perhaps the clearest illustration of this point comes from Adam de la Halle's brilliant farce *Le Jeu de la feuillée* (ca. 1255). The action of the play takes place in Arras on a feast day (perhaps May Day or possibly Midsummer's Eve)[94] and concerns a banquet held in honor of the fairies. The sound of bells leads a character called Gillot to anticipate the imminent arrival of "le maisnie Hellekin," and when another character asks, "will the fairies be following him?" [*venront dont les fees après*], Gillot assures her that they will (lines 578–83).[95] In the event, Hellequin himself does not appear but later sends a messenger to Morgan (one of the three fairies who do) with a love letter (lines 604–9); at first she spurns his offer, but after learning that her current beau, the Arrageois Robert Sommeillons, has been cheating on her, she regrets having rejected so peremptorily "the greatest prince in fairyland" [le graigneur / Prinche ki soit en faerie] (lines 758–59). Though described as a king and shown to be in some sense the leader of a fairy troupe, Hellekin does not appear to be an actual fairy. In any event, there is nothing in this life-affirming, bawdy farce to connect Hellequin with death; as a potential lover for Morgan he looks far more like a mortal king living in fairyland—a counterpart, as Étienne de Bourbon implies, of King Arthur ("in the likeness of knights hunting or jousting, commonly known as the household of Hellequin or of Arthur"),[96] in other words, someone far more like Walter Map's King Herla than the shadowy figure who presides over Orderic Vitalis's procession.

Before Morgan and her sisters can appear, a monk has to be hustled offstage: "We'd have seen the wonders of fairyland here some time ago if it hadn't been for you" [se pour vous ne fust / Ke piech'a chi endroit eüst / Grant merveille de faerie] (lines 561–63). The play takes for granted a mutual antipathy between clerks and fairies, and it is hardly surprising that Orderic Vitalis's portrait of the *familia Herlequini* should be so lurid. Of course even in popular culture fairies were not always benevolent, and Orderic seems eager to exploit their malignant side when he includes in his description "a great army of knights, in which no colour was visible save blackness and flickering fire. All rode upon huge horses, fully armed as if they were galloping to battle and carrying jet black standards" (p. 243). These knights resemble William of Auvergne's demons, "terrible in size, with arms and horses, and also with torches, or firebrands, or other kinds of flame" [*terribiles magnitudine armis et equis, apparent eciam cum facibus seu faculis seu aliis ignibus*],[97] and the "knights, all black, with burning, flaming lances" [*chevaliers toz noirs; et avoient glaives ardanz et enflambez*], who surround Perlesvaus's sister in the romance of *Perlesvaus*.[98] Étienne de Bourbon even supplies the vernacular term for them: *arzei* "as if burning or fire-bearing" [*quasi succensi vel flammigeri*];[99] quite possibly this is a reference to the folkoric *feu-follet* or will-o'-the-wisp. In view of this, it would be certainly rash to claim that medieval people never associated figures such as King Herla with death, or that when clerical texts portrayed the wild horde as a ride of the dead they always ran counter to popular notions (indeed in the passage just referred to, Perlesvaus's sister is sheltering in a graveyard, and her fiery assailants are said to be the spirits of dead knights who had not been buried in hallowed ground). My point is simply that such a view was not universal, and moreover that a realignment of the *familia Herlequini* with Arthur's Avalon offers us a powerful expository tool.

If I am right, it becomes immediately obvious why Orderic Vitalis and other clerical commentators should wish to present the *familia Herlequini* in the way they do. People could hardly be allowed to believe that Herla and his followers (or King Arthur and his court) were living happily in fairyland, a kind of secular travesty of Enoch and Elias, especially when they apparently continued to enjoy the very pastimes (hunting, jousting, making war, even making love) that had preoccupied them in this world. Thus the crowd of armed knights that appeared in the vicinity of Worms in 1123, emerging from a mountain and apparently riding to a tournament, led the Bavarian chronicler Ekkard von Aura, Orderic's contemporary, to explain that their arms and their horses were really a means of torture ("materia tormenti"), even though it did not look that way ("quamvis id vos corporalibus oculis discernere non possitis").[100] A hundred years later Helinand of Froidmont makes his own motive for denigrating Hellequin and his followers perfectly transparent. He denounces Virgil's description of dead heroes in Hades—"quae gratia currum / armorumque fuit uiuis, quae cura nitentes / pascere equos, eadem sequitur tellure repostos" [the pleasure the living took in chariots and armor, the care they took to feed their glossy horses, follows them when they are concealed in earth] (*Aeneid*, 6:653–55)—as "a false conjecture or a conjectural falsehood" [*falsitas opinionis vel opinio falsitatis*].[101] He then tells three stories, each designed to show that, far from being pleasurable, participation in the *familia Hellequini* involved excruciating torments for the souls of the departed. Like Orderic Vitalis and Ekkard von Aura, then, Helinand regards the wild horde as a penitential vehicle, and his view—quoted verbatim in Vincent of Beauvais's influential *Speculum Historiale* (29:118–20)—became the standard clerical one throughout the Middle Ages.

Not that all authorities were uncritical of it. William of Auvergne devotes much of a chapter of *De Universo* to investigating the problem of substances appearing in the likeness of knights and warriors hastening to battle and in the likeness of innumerable armies (in all but name a discussion of the *familia Hellequini*),[102] and in particular, the reason why they should appear in the likeness of men who were famous in this world and in this life ("de substantiis apparentibus in similitudine equitantium & bellatorum, in praelium currentium, & in similitudinem exercituum innumerabilium . . . quam ob causam in similitudines hominum qui noti fuerant in mundo isto, & in vita ista?").[103] William toys with the idea that this activity is penitential: "creduntur autem poenitentiam agere in armis, quoniam in armis peccaverunt" [they are believed to do penance in arms because they sinned in arms],[104] but this solution clearly does not satisfy him fully, mainly because he prefers to believe that such apparitions are not actual mortal souls but merely demonic impersonations of them. This certainly accords well with his idea of demons/fairies fighting among themselves—in an earlier chapter William had given a remarkably Hobbesian account of their ceaseless war of each against all;[105] but since he regards them as both immortal and invulnerable to weapons, he can explain their use of arms and armor only by suggesting that they are engaged in play fighting, a kind of jousting or *hastiludium*—an odd activity for spirits doomed to eternal punishment to engage in![106] (Hardly surprisingly, William does not even try to account for the wild hunt.) He finally concludes that God permits such visions as a warning to the living not to commit similar abuses: "quia non est possibile ut poenas patiuntur quae non nisi agentes talia pati possunt, signa tamen sunt ex consequenti poenarum, quas talibus actionibus dum essent in corporibus, meruerunt" [because it is not possible that they should suffer punishments which they can suffer only by doing such things, yet they are still signs of the resulting punishments, which they deserved by doing such actions while they were in the flesh].[107] This somewhat lame conclusion, which raises more problems than it settles, seems to arise from William's own conception of purgatory,[108] for him a far less harsh and punitive concept than that first made popular by such radical later twelfth-century works as the *Vision of Tundale* and *St Patrick's Purgatory*.

Fairyland and Purgatory

Jacques Le Goff's important study *La naissance du Purgatoire* (1981) has hardly escaped criticism: questions have been raised about its structuralist methodology; about the validity of both Le Goff's original binary order (heaven and hell) and even the ternary one (heaven, purgatory, and hell) that, he claims, superseded it in the late twelfth century; and about his rigidly 'nominalist' dating, which denies the possibility of purgatory's existence before the first recorded use of the word *purgatorium* around the year 1170.[109] As long as the possibility of an earlier date (perhaps as early as the end of the eleventh century) is granted, however, many would agree that Le Goff does indeed put his finger on a genuine social and theological phenomenon, that the idea of postmortem purgation does take on a new importance in the course of the twelfth century, and that a preoccupation with both the process and the location of such purgation does extend to a far wider audience. It is not my intention to rehash any of this here or to try to follow Le Goff into the thorny thickets of Parisian and Cistercian soteriology, but it does seem to me that there remains something more to be said about the vernacular dimension of his birth of purgatory. Le Goff himself would certainly have been sympathetic to such a venture, for he was quite ready to acknowledge that popular Celtic and Germanic aspects of medieval culture contributed to the imaginary representation of purgatory, though he seems to have found the methodological problems of disentangling them daunting.[110] In fact Alan E. Bernstein, one of his reviewers, feels that the idea of "a popular need for a 'third place' . . . lying latent in *l'imaginaire*" is implicit in Le Goff's study—as indeed is its corollary that, "embarrassed by this strong advance in folklore, theologians felt compelled to 'purge' the new concept, to correct popular tendencies with orthodox teaching."[111] While I would certainly not presume to try and rewrite Le Goff's *grand récit* here, it does seem to me that some of its implications will bear reexamination. Ingeld may have had nothing to do with Christ, but it is harder to believe that Avalon had nothing to do with purgatory.

Evidence for such a proposition comes from three interrelated stories from the first half of the thirteenth century. Le Goff must have known all three, since they are discussed by Arturo Graf in a chapter that he cites,[112] but he himself considers only the first and the last, and the inference he draws from them strikes me as problematic.

The first is Gervase of Tilbury's account of the Bishop of Catania's groom's recovery of his master's errant horse from King Arthur's court in a hidden recess of Mount Etna. Gervase may well have heard the story during his stay in Sicily in the early 1190s, but its appearance in the *Otia Imperialia* must date to around 1215.[113] The servant, finding a path among the dark places of the mountain ("circa montis opaca"), comes out "onto an immensely wide and beautiful plain, full of delights of every kind; there in a palace constructed with marvellous workmanship, he found Arthur reclining on a couch of royal splendour." After returning his master's horse to him, Arthur informs the groom that he has been living there for a long time, ever since being wounded in his ancient battle with Mordred. Nothing about this, apart from the passing remark that his old wounds reopen every year ("vulneribus quotannis recrudescentibus") is remotely purgatorial.

Less than ten years later the Cistercian Caesarius of Heisterbach gives a rather different version of the same story. He tells of a dean of Palermo, a German, who sends his servant to look for a lost horse. The servant is informed by an old man he meets along the way that the horse is on Mount Gyber (a form of the Arabic name for Etna): "my lord King Arthur has it there (this same mountain belches flames like Vulcano)" [ibi eum habet dominus meus Rex Arcturus. Idem mons flammas evomit sicut Vulcanus].[114] He is further instructed to summon his master to attend Arthur's august court ("ad curiam eius sollemnem") in fourteen days' time; the dean laughs off this summons, however, only to sicken and die on the appointed day. Caesarius says that he got this story from a canon in Bonn, and certainly the variants between his version and Gervase's suggest that it was circulating orally. This is not quite all there is to it, however, for at the end of the next chapter, the novice for whose benefit the story is told asks what is known about such mountains and whether they are the site of hell or purgatory. His master replies that they are said to be the mouth of hell, for only the wicked, not the chosen, are sent there ("Os dicuntur esse inferni, quia nullus electorum sed reprobi tantum in eos mittuntur").

The final version, from the 1250s, is Étienne de Bourbon's. The motif of the servant's looking for his master's lost horse on a Sicilian mountain (here a mountain "next to Vulcano" [*iuxta Vulcanum*]) is common to all three, but in Étienne's account the master is not specifically said to be an ecclesiastic.[115] A new character, a gatekeeper who warns the servant not to eat any of the food he is offered, is introduced, and Arthur's court is transformed into a large and populous city. Arthur is never named; he becomes merely "a prince surrounded by his men" [*principem suis circumvallatum*]. As in Gervase, the horse is returned to the servant; and as in Caesarius, its owner is summoned to appear at a later date. Étienne says that he got the story from an Apulian friar called John (presumably a fellow Dominican), and all indications are that this version too was taken from oral circulation. The one major innovation is that the mountain is here reputed to be the site of purgatory ("ubi dicitur locus purgatorii").

For Jacques Le Goff, the differences between Gervase's and Étienne's versions epitomize a significant stage in the development of attitudes to the afterlife: the "infernalization" of purgatory.[116] However, this deduction hardly seems warranted. Whatever literal infernalization there is, is restricted to Caesarius's account (which Le Goff does not discuss); and if anything is being infernalized in Étienne de Bourbon version, it is surely not purgatory but rather fairyland. A clear survival of its suppressed original can be seen in the porter's warning "quod caveret ne comederet de aliquo ferculo quod ei daretur" [that he should beware of eating any dish he might be offered]. So on his way to fairyland, Thomas of Erceldoune is checked by the queen:

> He pressede to pulle frowte with his hande,
> Als mane for fude þat was nere faynt;
> Scho sayde, "Thomas, þou layte þame stande,
> Or ellis þe fende the will atteynt."[117]

The peasant who stumbles on a fairy feast in William of Newburgh's *History* wisely refuses to drink from the cup he is offered, pours its contents on the floor, and flees: "consulte noluit bibere, sed effuso contento . . . concitus abiit."[118] Returning to his homeland, Guingamor is warned by his fairy mistress, "que ne bevez ne ne mengiez / por nule fain que vos aiez" [do not drink or eat, however hungry or thirsty you are],[119] for in Sir John Mandeville's words, "no man dar taken of that frute, for it is a thing of fayrye."[120] The fairy world is hedged about with prohibitions against eating and drinking, then, but it is not clear why these same prohibitions should apply to purgatory. Evidently what Étienne is really doing here is not rendering purgatory infernal but fairyland purgatorial.

The echoes of fairyland in these accounts of a Sicilian gateway to purgatory are even more marked when we turn to medieval reports of purgatory's main entrance—on Station Island in the Irish lake of Lough Derg. The *Tractatus de Purgatorio Sancti Patricii* (ca. 1180), which describes the purgatorial journey of an English knight called Owein, furnishes the classic account of this site.[121] At least 150 manuscripts of the Latin *Tractatus* survive,[122] and not without reason Le Goff has called it a central text ("texte décisif") in the birth of purgatory.[123] Nevertheless (as we shall see) this carefully crafted product of Cistercian orthodoxy is not without its fairy reverberations, and some of its spin-offs, both in Latin and in the vernacular, appear even more elvish.

The popular *Visiones Georgii*, for instance,[124] which purport to record the experiences of a Hungarian knight called George Grissaphan, who visited Lough Derg in 1353, show him encountering Saint Patrick's version of the wild horde: "he came to a certain open space where he saw coming towards him two thousand knights, men-at-arms, soldiers, and noblemen, many of whom had the appearance of soldiers and noblemen he had known in this life" [venit ad quendam locum satis spaciosum, ubi inuenit sibi obuiam veniencia duo milia equitum, hominum armatorum et militum et baronum, quorum multi in effigiebus multorum baronum et militum, quos in hac vita nouerat].[125] These knights profess some strikingly heretical beliefs, informing him that Christ was a mortal sinner of no particular worth ("Jhesus Christus mortuus est tamquam homo peccator et nullius valoris"), that he was quite properly condemned to a shameful death ("fuit iustissime iudicatus et ad morte turpissimam condemnatus"), and that they have renounced their faith in him ("negauimus ipsum et fidem illius"). The description they give of their existence is strongly reminiscent of Arthur's Avalon: "we came to this world after our death, made most powerful and strong, even immortal, and in this noble condition, without death or injury, with no wounds or diseases, without hunger or thirst, we perform together chivalrous and martial exercises in tournaments and jousts for eternity" [post mortem nostram venimus in hunc mundum, facti potentissimi, fortissimi, et eciam immortales, exercentes iugiter actus nobiles et bellicos in torneamentis et hastiludijs, in eternum in hac nobilitate sine morte et sine aliqua lesione, sine aliquo vulnere et sine aliqua infirmitate, sine fame et siti] (*Visiones Georgii*, pp. 112–13).

In his next vision, George encounters a strikingly handsome woman ("pulcherrima vultu et corpore") dressed in the richest scarlet ("nobilissimo et ditissimo scharleto") and wearing a splendid crown bedecked with jewels ("coronam pulcherrimam diuersis lapidum preciosorum generibus adornatam"). She too denies the divinity of Christ and, offering George her hand in marriage, tempts him with the prospect of ruling over her agreeable land forever; "Crede igitur mihi," she concludes, "et dimitte fatuitates tuas atque vanissimam fidem tuam" [Believe then in me. . . . Put aside your follies and your completely vacuous faith]. Lest we should be tempted to think of this queen as a fairy, however, the author is careful to point out that she has cloven hooves (*Visiones Georgii,* pp. 115–17). In another Saint Patrick's Purgatory narrative, however, the *Visio Ludovico de Francia* (dated to 1360), the penitent, though warned that he is about to encounter demons ("Ecce demones venient"), has a series of visions of unblemished female beauty.[126] A group of dancing teenagers ("in etate XVI vel XVII annorum") with snowy foreheads, creamy complexions, teeth like ivory, lips like coral, and breasts like apples, who represent themselves to him as powerful and immortal goddesses possessed of great wealth ("dee immortales habentes potestatem magnam multasque divitias"), are succeeded by five further groups of women, each more captivating than the last, who offer him delicious dishes, untold wealth, and of course sex. Along with some alluring nuns ("monasterium pulcherimarum dominarum"), they include a weeping girl with a bag of silver and gold sitting beside a fountain and three ladies playing chess beneath a beautiful tree. Sonia Barillari is surely right to associate these "signore del purgatorio" with the fairies of medieval folklore.[127]

Visions such as those of George Grissaphan and Louis of France are sometimes lumped in with the *Tractatus de Purgatorio Sancti Patricii* and treated as popular counterparts of Dante's *Inferno* and *Purgatorio,* but there is a major difference. Unlike Owein, George and Louis are not passive observers of the horrors of hell or the trials of purgatory; they are active participants in what can only be described as a perilous quest. The demons of Saint Patrick's Purgatory take on alluring forms in order to win them over to their cause, and they survive only by rigid adherence to protective rituals. This aspect of their visions is barely touched on in the *Tractatus,* where the demons appear in propria persona, though (as we shall see) it can be detected in some of the vernacular versions of *Owayne Miles.* Thus the underlying structure of these variant narratives is that of the quest romance, and it is surely no coincidence that their protagonists should be drawn from the knightly class. One of the earliest and strangest of these ancillary Saint Patrick's Purgatory narratives, Peter of Cornwall's story (ca. 1200) of an unnamed knight who had visited Lough Derg thirty years earlier,[128] renders this romance underpinning completely transparent. Once he has entered purgatory this knight comes upon the hall of a huntsman-king called Gulinus, who immediately tenders him the hand of his beautiful daughter. That night in the throes of passion he opens his eyes only to discover that he is embracing an old withered tree and that his penis is trapped in a fissure in its trunk ("uirilem ipsius uirgam in quodam foramine facto in illo trunco coartam").[129] One of the king's servants hammers away at it with a spike, tightening the tree's grip and causing him excruciating pain, but when the king offers him the relief of a soothing warm bath, he promptly finds himself being boiled alive; predictably the subsequent offer of a cool bath to refresh him leads to his being plunged into freezing water and being lacerated with shards of ice. Ever trusting, he then accepts an invitation to visit the games room, where he is hung up by his feet and bounced like a ball from one abrasive wall to the next. In the morning the king and his servants have vanished and the knight finds himself alone in the entrance to purgatory. Even without Easting's suggestive association of King Gulinus with Herlewinus (pp. 406–7), there is plenty of evidence that we are dealing here with a barely Christianized account of the dangerous hospitality of the fairy folk.

To read the *Tractatus de Purgatorio Sancti Patricii*, or its English derivative *Owayne Miles*, after accounts such as these is to find oneself moving in a very different world. While far from being theologically watertight, its romance underpinnings are more thoroughly masked and its echoes of fairyland more deeply buried, so it is hardly surprising that this should be the version espoused by the great tradition. Nevertheless the underlying form of the quest romance cannot be wholly suppressed, and one particular detail (regarded with skepticism by some fourteenth-century writers, such as Nicholas Oresme and Jean Froissart)[130] underlines its pedigree: unlike many other accounts of journeys to the otherworld, Owayne's visit is still made in the flesh, not merely in the spirit—as the Auchinleck version puts it, "He was deliuerd from þe fendes turment / Quic man into þat place."[131] The parallel with actual visits to fairyland by romance heroes such as Sir Orfeo (also found in the Auchinleck manuscript) is unmistakable. Furthermore (as we shall see) other romance motifs such as the sword bridge, though suppressed in the *Tractatus*, reemerge alive and well in its vernacular reworkings.

Two features of the otherworld in the *Tractatus* stand out. The first, to use Le Goff's term, is the infernalization of its purgatory. Readers coming to it from Dante's *Purgatorio* will be shocked by its savage brutality, for only the fact that a limit is set to their duration seems to distinguish its torments from those of hell itself:[132]

> Somme wiþ irene rakeie . al furi honge an hey
> Somme bi armes & somme bi uet . & bi þe swure manion
> Anhonge were in stronge vure . of pich & of brymston
> Somme honge bi stronge oules . iput in eiþer eiȝe

Þoru þe þrote somme & somme [.] þoru eiþer ere wel heiӡe
Somme þoru hore deorne limes . & somme þoru hore tete
Þat hom were leuer þanne alle þe world . þat hi miӡte þat lif lete
Somme upe gridils of ire . yrosted were also
Somme as ges in spites of ire . þoru out hom ydo
Somme leie upward fram þe gronde . ӡonynge wel uaste
Þe deuelen walde led & bras . & in hore mouþ caste. (*South English Legendary*, lines 312–22)[133]

[Some hung on high from fiery iron chains; some by the arms, some by the feet, and many by the neck were hung in a strong fire of pitch and brimstone; some hung up high by iron hooks stuck in one of their eyes, or through their throats, or in one of their ears, or in their sexual organs or in their breasts, so that they wanted to die more than anything in the world; some were also roasted on iron grills, and some with iron spits stuck through them like geese; some lay on their backs gaping wide while devils poured lead and brass into their mouths.]

Furthermore the administering of such torments clearly required that purgatory be populated with demons, and though the *South English Legendary* version suggests that this was an unexceptional notion—"For in pultatorie þe ssrewen beoþ . as wel as in helle / And worþe forte þe day of dome . telle wat me telle" [for there are devils in purgatory, just as in hell, and will be till Doomsday; I report what men say] (lines 261–62)—it was far from being standard theology.[134] One of the duties of these demons is to impede Owayne's progress through purgatory and to force him to return, but though he is warned that they will employ torments, threats, and blandishments ("nec tormentis nec minis nec promissis eorum cesseris" [p. 54]), in the Latin *Tractatus* they rely almost exclusively on the first two.

However, when we turn to the vernacular versions of the *Tractatus* (there are three independent Middle English verse translations and four in Anglo-Norman, including one by Marie de France),[135] we encounter something much closer to the visions of George and Louis: 'demons' actually trying to recruit Owayne to their cause:

Þer uore we redeþ turn þi þoӡt . and do us her manrede
And we ssolleþ [þe] þane wei as þou come . al sauf aӡen lede

And þe tit an eorþe al þi lif . richesse & ioie also
For we ssolleþ þe euere finde inou . as riʒt is þat we do. (*South English Legendary*, lines 421–24)[136]

[Therefore we advise you to change your mind and do homage to us here and we shall safely lead you back the way you came, and wealth and joy await you on earth all your life, for we shall always provide for you as we ought to do.]

In the Latin *Tractatus* the primary role of the 'demons' is to try to make Owein turn back, but in Marie de France's *L'espurgatoire* they employ their threats to recruit him to their cause: "S'a nus ne vus volez tenir" (line 959); "se vus ne nus creez" (line 1028); "se vus ne cunsentez a nus" (line 1058); "S'a nus ne vus volez tenir" (line 1244).[137] Surrounded by scenes of desolation and torture, Owein might be forgiven for regarding this as a less than attractive proposition, but such offers are strongly reminiscent of the way demons/fairies are presented in pastoral literature elsewhere. In particular, it invites comparison with Thomas of Cantimpré's account of the German Dominican's visit to the hall of some *dusii*-demons deep in a mountain or with the Vernon Manuscript's *Disputation Between a Christian and a Jew*.[138]

The second striking feature of *Owayne Miles* is the prominence it gives to the terrestrial paradise, which occupies almost as much of the poem as purgatory does. Indeed, as Robert Easting has pointed out, from this perspective Le Goff's ternary system is in effect a quaternary one (adding the earthly paradise to heaven, hell, and purgatory).[139] Having traversed purgatory, Owayne crosses a perilous bridge over hell and arrives in the terrestrial paradise, from where he can see, but not enter, the gates to the celestial paradise. In terms of its role in the soteriological economy, however, the function of this terrestrial paradise is far from clear; it acts as a staging post along the road to eternal bliss, but even the two archbishops who act as Owayne's guides at this point seem unable to explain what precisely it is doing there or why the properly penitent should not proceed immediately to their heavenly reward (*South English Legendary*, lines 571–604). Again, though *Owayne Miles*'s position could count on only lukewarm theological support,[140] the role of this properly salvific earthly paradise in neutralizing a popular fairy belief was clearly paramount. Medieval descriptions of paradise, of the Fortunate Isles, and of Avalon all depended so heavily on the classical topos of the *locus amoenus*[141] that it was natural that all three locations should become confused in the popular imagination: as Bartholomaeus Anglicus writes of the Fortunate Isles, "þere þe grounde bereþ all manere of fruyt withoute tilyng. [Þere] on dounes treen ben alweye ycloþede with greene twigges and spray and with swete fruyt and gode. Þer corne groweþ as herbes and gras. Þerfore erroure of naciouns and dyte of secular poetes, for godenesse of the grounde mened þat þis ilondes be Paradys; and þat is errour."[142] Howard Patch has already delineated the extensive parallels between Avalon and the earthly paradise, and there is no point in repeating his work here,[143] but it is important to stress that these connections go beyond the merely rhetorical. For some people, the earthly paradise was actually populated by fairies.

The text that demonstrates this most explicitly is an early fourteenth-century *Roman d'Ogier*. The earliest verse versions of this *roman* have never been edited, but a faithful fifteenth-century prose rendering is easier to consult.[144] This contains an episode in which Ogier the Dane is shipwrecked on a voyage to India only to find himself "pres du chasteau . . . d'Auallon qui nest gueres deca paradis terrestre, la ou furent rauis en vne raye de feu Enoc & helye, & là ou estoit morgue la faye" [near the castle of Avalon which is just this side of the earthly paradise. There Enock and Helyas were transported in a fiery beam and there was Morgan le Fay] (p. 267). After spending a night in the castle accompanied by only a fairy horse, Ogier "followed a little path which took him to a garden which was so beautiful and pleasing that it was a little paradise to the eye. And in it there were such fine trees bearing fruit of all kinds" [suiuit vne petite sente que le mena en vng vergier tant bel & tant plaisant que cestoit vn petit paradis a veoir. Et leans auoit [t]ant de beaux arbres portans fruites de toutes sortes] (p. 270). Foolishly he eats an apple, falls ill, and is saved only by the appearance of a lady dressed in white, whom he first takes to be the Virgin Mary but who turns out to be Morgan le Fay; it is she who has brought him to Avalon, where, she says, he will be able to see the finest nobility in the world and amuse himself among the ladies ("la vous esbatrez a faire passer le temps aux dames" [p. 271]). There can be no question that this castle and its adjacent garden represent fairyland—Ogier meets King Arthur and King Oberon there, and he is given magic gifts (a ring that restores his youth, a crown that confers perpetual contentment, and a firebrand that protects his health)—but at the same time its association with the earthly paradise is always in view.[145] When in due course Ogier is transported back to France (where he discovers that two hundred years have passed), he tells the lord of a castle that had once belonged to him that he has spent the intervening time in the earthly paradise ("iay de puis este en paradis terrestre" [pp. 284–85]), and he later makes the same claim at an abbey where he is staying the night: "si leur dist comme il auoit este sans nulle faulte en paradis terrestre" [he told them how without fail he had been in the earthly paradise] (p. 286). In a remarkable scene the next morning, he makes a full confession to the abbot but quite deliberately conceals from him the secrets of fairyland: "& puis luy dist & confessa la vraie verite de son cas et conscience *sauf et excepte tout le secret de fairie quil garda secretement*" [my italics] (p. 286).

This idea—that fairies inhabited the terrestrial paradise—is even implied by the *South English Legendary,* the text that includes the first English translation of the *Tractatus de Purgatorio Sancti Patricii.* Speaking of the neutral angels (a little later in the text to be associated explicitly with elves), it says, "In eor[þ]lich parais somme beoþ also / And in oþer studes an eorþe hore penance to do" [some are also in the earthly paradise and in other places on earth, in order to perform their penance].[146] Indeed the *Legendary*'s remark, quoted above, about "þe ssrewen" that are "in pultatorie" may derive ultimately from some popular account of them ("wat me telle") as penitents rather than as tormentors. Given such associations, it is little wonder that the action of *Owayne Miles* should invite comparison with fairy romances.

To enter the fairy world in the Middle Ages was not as straightforward as simply stepping into a wardrobe. We have already noted that the precise point at which Lancelot crosses into the land of Gorre in Chrétien's *Chevalier de la charete* is unclear (though Douglas Kelly's suggestion that it is after he has left the mysterious cemetery and long before he reaches the famous sword bridge seems plausible), but the larger point is that fairyland is often conceived of as being a kind of peripheral zone or hinterland surrounding a central nucleus, usually a castle, and that journeys to fairyland thus entail three stages: 1) an initial crossing of the boundary between the fairy world and that of mortals; 2) a perilous journey through an uncanny territory; and 3) a second crossing into the fairy heartland. This pattern is present in Reinbrun's rescue of Amis from fairyland, but *Thomas of Erceldoune* offers an even clearer instance. His fairy lover leads Thomas "in at Eldon hill, / Vndir nether a derne lee" (lines 169–70);[147] they then travel in darkness "the montenans of dayes three" (line 173), wading through knee-deep water, until they arrive at a beautiful garden, where Thomas is warned not to touch any of the fruit "Or ells þe fende the will atteynt" (line 188); it is only at this point that he is shown five paths, one of which leads to a "faire castelle, / . . . In erthe is none lyke it vn till" (lines 217–20). It is worth pointing out that this perilous journey, as in Gawain's ride through the *wyldrenesse of Wyrale* "in peryle and payne and plytes ful harde" (line 733) or Orfeo's sojourn in the *wildernes*—"Lord! who may telle þe sore / Þis king sufferd ten ȝere & more?" (lines 263–64)—often takes on a penitential aspect.

It will be immediately obvious that the journey in *Owayne Miles*, with its entrance through a hole in the ground, its progression through purgatory in the face of hostile opposition, and its perilous crossing into the earthly paradise, closely mimics this pattern. Moreover some of its specific details, not merely the entrance through a hole but the presence of an unearthly underground light and the crossing of a perilous bridge, are fairy commonplaces, though such parallels are sometimes clearer in the vernacular renderings than they are in the original *Tractatus*. For instance, none of the English versions calls the entrance to Saint Patrick's Purgatory a cave, perhaps because the "fossa rotunda" of the *Tractatus* implies that it is not a natural formation,[148] but the description of the Auchinleck version is considerably more uncanny than the Latin:

> Þer was an hole michel apert,
> Þat griseliche was of siȝt.
> Round it was about and blak;
> In alle þe warlde no was his mack,
> So griseliche entring. (sts. 11–12)

The perilous bridge, one of the most ubiquitous feature of journeys to both the afterlife and to fairyland (as Patch has shown), is given an interesting twist in many of the vernacular versions of *St Patrick's Purgatory*. The Latin *Tractatus* (in both α and β versions) assigns three qualities to this bridge: it is slippery (*lubricus*); it is narrow (*strictus et gracilis*); and it is dizzyingly high,[149] and this is how it is described by both Marie de France and the *South English Legendary* ("narȝ & slider & hey"). On the other hand, the Auchinleck version describes it as "scharpe as a rasour" (st. 121), the Cotton MS of *Owayne Miles 2* calls it "kener þen ony glasse" (line 414), the Yale MS, "as scharp as ony sw[e]rd," and another of the Anglo-Norman versions, as "trechant cum un rasur."[150] Moreover, in the *Visiones Georgii* this bridge is "acutissimus et ... scindentissimus ad modum ensis" [exceedingly sharp and keen like a sword] (p. 190), in one manuscript of the *Visio Ludovici* it is "amplum velut talentum cutelli" [as wide as the blade of a knife],[151] and in the *Vision of William of Stranton* the rungs of a ladder, which is substituted for the bridge, are "sharper þan ony rasor."[152] Thus we are left with the distinct impression that, despite the *Tractatus*, popular feeling supported the notion that the main peril of all such perilous bridges should be their honed edges. One obvious way to account for this is direct interference from Lancelot's celebrated sword bridge in Chrétien de Troyes's *Chevalier de la charrette* (lines 3017–155), the earliest and best-known example of this motif.[153] A last instance of this kind of contamination occurs in the Yale MS of *Owayne Miles* 2: after he has crossed over the bridge into the earthly paradise, Owayne

> sey kynggys and emprorys,
> Devkys, castelys and towerys,
> And women he sey on euery syde
> That merthys maden yn þat tyde. (lines 542–45)

For the second line here the Cotton MS reads (unmetrically), "And dukes þat hadde casteles and tourres," but even if this is the original reading (and even if it means 'dukes that had once had . . .'), the fact remains that the Yale scribe must have imagined an earthly paradise that, like fairyland, contained castles and towers.

All these motifs are combined in a remarkable scene in the Dutch *Roman van Walewein* (ca. 1230–60). Walewein (Gawain) rides in quest of a lady called Ysabele, who is being held captive in Endi (India) by her father, King Assentijn; father and daughter reside in a formidable castle that has a pleasure garden containing a fountain of youth whose waters flow from the earthly paradise.[154] When Gawain first spies this castle, it is on the far side of a river whose waters burn like fire and which can be crossed only on a bridge that is sharper than a razor; his first reaction is striking: "is it the enchantment of elves or magic / that I see?" [*Eist elfs ghedrochte of toverie / Dat ic zie*] (lines 5012–13). Eventually he is shown a way past this barrier by a speaking fox (who turns out to be a prince, bewitched by a wicked stepmother); the fox shows him a hidden hole leading to a tunnel that emerges on the far side of the burning river (lines 6044–97). On the way there, his guide explains to Gawain that this river

> is the true purgatory [*vaghevier*].
> All souls, having departed from the body,
> Must come here to bathe. (lines 5825–27)

Gawain observes black birds plunging into the river only to emerge whiter than snow, and he is told that the river's source is in "the depths of hell" (line 5953).

This wonderful gallimaufry of questing knights and imprisoned princesses, of impregnable castles and paradisal gardens, of secret holes and underground passages, of burning rivers and sword bridges (not to mention talking foxes) demonstrates how thoroughly the discourses of fairyland and purgatory had interpenetrated one another by the middle of the thirteenth century.

Medieval visions of the afterlife often involve priests or monks, but even where the visionaries are secular (as with Fursey, Tundale, or the visitors to Saint Patrick's Purgatory), their accounts must often have been vetted by the authorities. There is, however, one remarkable exception: the report of a near-death experience in 1465, *The Vision of Edmund Leversedge*.[155] Leversedge, the youngest son of a Somerset gentleman, was clearly literate and, judging from the aspersions he casts on the morals and learning of several local priests (lines 583–609), a man of independent religious views; his vision is strikingly idiosyncratic. It begins conventionally enough: after Leversedge has been "smytone with þe plage of pestylence" (p. 83), suffered the torments of two devils "disfigurid foule and lothesome" (p. 85), and been given up for dead by his companions, his soul is led by his good angel "into a grett playn valey, where was noþer mone ne sonne ne stere þat gaffe any liȝt" (p. 85). The devils that now assail him, however, are distinctly unusual: "Þe going of þe seyd devyllys . . . was in schort gownes and dowblettes, closse hosyn, longe heere upon here browes, pykes on þer shon of a foot in lengh and more, hyghe bonettes as myself sumetyme usid, and þes prowid peple þat callis þemselfe galantes ȝit usid" (p. 86). These devils, we later learn, are "spirites þat God had gifin powar and commaundement to persecute and smyt þe people, for þe synne þat dayly renyth among þem, with þe infirmyte and plage of pestilence" (p. 96). Since Leversedge sees his own abiding sin as personal vanity, he projects this onto his assailants, but nonetheless they resemble the elegant denizens of the fairy world far more than they do the grotesque fiends of *Owayne Miles*.

Leversedge's good angel then leads his soul to the top of a hill by way of a ladder, out of reach of the devils, and there he meets "a woman of longe stature, þe fayrest in fayrnes, bewte and favor in visage þat ever God mad, þe most mekest in cowntenaunce and speche; and as þe snowe excedith þe bewate of alle women in whittnes, in lyke wise excedith þat blissid woman and lady al oþer women" (p. 94). On her head she wears a white kerchief and a gold crown, and her body is covered with a black mantle, "myche like unto þes mantelles of þes ladyes þat have takyn þe mantil and þe ring weren" (that is, wives and widows, who have taken a vow of chastity). This woman is never identified (the fact that she refers to the Virgin in the third person suggests that she is not herself Mary), though she might be compared with the far less fully described "faire woman" who appears at the top of a tower at the end of William of Stranton's vision. Two of this woman's actions, however, link her with a fairy counterpart. First, she gives Leversedge's soul an (unconsciously ironic) out-of-body experience: "Sho showid my saule also þe towne and wallis of Oxforth, with þe ryvers and medeues pertei[ni]ng þerto" (p. 95)—in this his experience resembles that of Marion Clerk, who claimed to have visited Canterbury "by the power of the fairies."[156] Second, she predicts the future: "sho told me of suche of my kynne þat shuld die, as my moþer, and also þat al my enmyes shuld be deed or þat I come home into my contrey" (p. 96). However, by far the most remarkable fairy correspondence in the whole vision occurs when Leversedge first meets this woman; the devils complain from the bottom of the hill that she has wronged them by depriving them of Leversedge's soul: "And þey schewid a similitude and shappis of the facion of my pykis, bolstirs, stuffid dowblettes, schort gownes, hygh bonettes, long heere and of al þe inordinate aray þat ever I usyd, and shoke hit and schuvid hit up to þe hille and seid of very right my saule aught to be þers" (pp. 91–92). The *similitude* of Edmund Leversedge that the devils shake to prove their right to his soul must surely belong to the same category as the *figmenta* that Thomas of Cantimpré discusses at such length and which I earlier compared to the folk that "þou3t [seemed] dede, & nare nou3t" (line 389) outside the fairy king's hall in *Sir Orfeo*—in other words, it is one of the model corpses that fairies were supposed to be able to construct in order to mislead bereaved relatives into believing that their loved ones were truly dead and buried. Anyone approaching this *similitude* exclusively through the discourse of purgatory will find it disconcertingly opaque; only in the discourse of fairyland is its meaning plainly revealed.

For some medievalists, the idea that the discourse of purgatory should have been modeled on that of fairyland, or at least should have been sedulously promoted as a corrective to it, will seem a travesty. Thomas of Erceldoune may have mistaken a fairy for the Virgin Mary, but surely no one could have mistaken the Virgin for a fairy.[157] There is, however, one feature shared by both versions of the otherworld where the direction of influence looks to be incontrovertible—their heterochronology. Le Goff has called the contrast between purgatorial time, where one year can seem like a thousand,[158] and time in what he calls the Celtic otherworld, where the passing years are experienced as days, as a "play of inversions" and offers it as "one proof the presence of folklore at the heart of the genesis of Purgatory."[159] It is entirely understandable that Le Goff should see the relationship between the great tradition and the little tradition here as an adversarial one—even though, as he points out, parodic inversion is usually a weapon employed by the weak against the strong, not the other way around—but I will conclude this chapter with a rather different instance of heterochronology, one where the church appears to be colluding with, rather than resisting, popular tradition.

The story of the monk and the bird was one of the most popular of medieval exempla.[160] A vernacular English version of it appears in *The Northern Homily Cycle* (in the Vernon Manuscript),[161] but it is given here in Jacques de Vitry's conveniently succinct account:

> We read of a certain very pious abbot that when he was contemplating the last things and what might happen to him after this present life, among other things he began to ponder the joys of paradise and how it was that the saints could spend so long in one place without being bored. And immediately, while he was in a garden near the abbey, a most beautiful bird appeared to him, with which he began to play and in whose most charming song he took particular delight. Coming to himself once more, he arrived at the gate of the abbey and found everything changed; he did not recognize the doorkeeper, nor could anyone in the monastery identify who he was. And when he said, "I am the abbot of this monastery who just now went out to the garden to meditate," they, dubious and confounded, consulted a book in which were written the names of the former abbots, and found that three hundred years had passed since the monastery had recorded his abbacy.[162]

In some versions the bird is said to be an angel in the guise of a bird,[163] and De Vitry's account ends with a quote from Psalm 89:4, but the fairy origins of this story cannot be disguised either by turning its spirit/bird into an angel or by alluding to the swift passage of "a thousand years in [God's] sight"; if nothing else, the bemused return of the central character to a world unrecognizably changed (as with Herla, Guingamor, or Ogier the Dane) makes such origins self-evident. Moreover the terrestrial paradise (associated, as we have seen, with fairyland in the popular imagination) generated similar accounts.[164] Indeed the tale survived as an actual fairy story in Wales down to the nineteenth century.[165]

The extremely wide distribution of the exemplum of the monk and the bird implies something more than the ubiquity of fairy beliefs in the Middle Ages, however. It suggests that traffic between learned and vernacular traditions did not all flow in one direction, and that the church was sometimes prepared to temporize with fairy beliefs in order to win over the other estates to its cause. Certainly if we project back from the witch hunts of the sixteenth and seventeenth centuries we may be led to assume an attitude of unrelenting and violent hostility toward all popular superstition on the part of the medieval elite, but *Owayne Miles* hints at another possibility. Caesarius of Heisterbach's novice had been unsure whether to understand Avalon as purgatory or hell, and though *Owayne Miles*'s infernalized purgatory seems to vacillate between each of these unappetizing prospects, its portrayal of the earthly paradise appears to offer something rather more inclusive. The land on the far side of its sword bridge contains the gateway to the heavenly kingdom, and if some people envisioned this land as fairyland, perhaps their error need not be wholly wrongheaded; like the abbot's enchanting birdsong, Avalon might usefully be reclaimed for doctrinal purposes. Such an enlightened attitude was never the dominant one in the Middle Ages, but that it can be detected at all makes the savagely repressive campaigns of the early modern church, both Catholic and Protestant, seem all the more repugnant.

Postscript

> More strange than true: I never may believe
> These antique fables, nor these fairy toys.
> —Shakespeare, *A Midsummer Night's Dream*

This book began with C. S. Lewis and it will end with him. In his *Discarded Image*, Lewis noted a curious anomaly in the Renaissance attitude to fairies: "within the same island and same century Spenser could compliment Elizabeth I by identifying her with the Faerie Queene and a woman could be burned at Edinburgh in 1576 for 'repairing with' the fairies and the 'Queene of Elfame'" (p. 124). In what follows, I will explore Lewis's anomaly, partly as a way of wrapping up a topic that has been touched on several times in this study—the way the medieval church's longstanding campaign against vernacular superstition culminated in the witch hunting of the early modern period—and partly to argue for an aspect of Geoffrey Chaucer's legacy to sixteenth-century England that has remained unappreciated. First, however, it will be necessary to emphasize something that would have seemed less contentious in Lewis's day than in our own: that the discourse of early modern witchcraft was riddled with medieval fairy lore.

On Saturday, 20 April 1610 the self-styled physician Simon Forman went to the Globe Theatre in London to see a performance of *Macbeth*: "Ther was to be obserued, firste, howe Mackbeth and Bancko, 2 noble men of Scotland, Ridinge thorowe a wod, the(r) stode before them 3 women feiries or Nimphes, And Saluted Mackbeth, sayinge, 3 tyms vnto him, haille Makcbeth, king of Codon; for thou shalt be a Kinge, but shalt beget No kinges, &c. then said Bancko, What all to mackbeth And nothing to me. yes, said the nimphes, Haille to thee, Banko, thou shalt beget kings, yet be no kinge."[1] To the modern eye Forman's apparent identification of *Macbeth*'s witches as "feiries or Nimphes" looks distinctly odd—witches, we assume, are human beings, and fairies are not—but in his own time such a conflation seems to have been commonplace. Bishop Thomas Cooper in his *Thesaurus linguae Romanae & Britannicae* (1565), for instance, glosses *strix* as "a witche that chaungeth the fauour of children: a hegge or fairie," a definition echoed by John Baret in his *Aluearie or triple dictionarie, in Englishe, Latin, and French* (1574).[2] As John Swan explains in a marginal note to his *Speculum Mundi* (1635), "The Scriechowl. which the Latines understand by the word Strix. . . . Some (in old time) have fabled strange things of this bird, . . . whereupon some have used the same word for a witch, a fairie, or hagge."[3] The same kind of conflation occurs with the word *mare*: for example, John Higgins's translation of Adrianus Junius's *The nomenclator* (of 1585) glosses *incubus* as "ephialtes, . . . a kinde of disease called the night mare or witch."[4] Things do not seem to have been very different on the Continent. Florio's *Worlde of Wordes*, the first Italian/English dictionary (1598), for instance, glosses *Fata* as "a fairie, a witch, an enchantres, an elfe" and *Strega* as "a witch, a sorceresse, a charmer, a hag or fairie," and a year later Richard Percival's *Dictionarie in Spanish and English* glosses *Estantigua* as "a hag, a hobgoblin."[5] Nor is this conflation restricted to the dictionaries: William Barlow, in a translation of three sermons by Ludwig Lavater (1596), for instance, raises "a question often discussed and muche debated, both by learned men and Idiottes: Whether *Sorserers or Witches, Faries or Spirites* (call them by what name you will) can raise anie tempests, or bring downe such Hayle as wee oft see."[6]

The basis of such a conflation is not far to seek: if witches were the efficient cause of magical activity, fairy potency must sometimes have appeared to constitute its material cause. We have seen that when an archiepiscopal court in 1499 accused the Suffolk wise-woman Marion Clerk of having "the art of healing people of various diseases," she defended herself by saying that she had received this art "from God and the Blessed Virgin and the gracious fairies,"[7] and when a cunning man named John Walsh was asked in 1566 "how he knoweth when anye man is bewytched," he answered "that he knew it partlye by the Feries."[8] "Our common wizards," wrote William Vaughan in 1630, "auerre, that they walke euery weeke with the Fayries."[9] For those who had been cured of a malady after paying a visit to such cunning folk, then, it would have amounted to much the same thing whether their recovery were attributed to the actions of a witch or a fairy.[10] From a less sympathetic perspective, of course, the fairies themselves might be seen as the cause of malevolent effects: a skeptical John Gaule, while asserting that "the principall Efficient of a Witch is the Devill," rejects one of "the Plebeian traditions" that the devil's "chiefely begotten Children" might include "Fairies, Elfes, and Changelings."[11] From this perspective the wise-woman's primary role was to counter, not exploit, fairy power. Thus the physician William Bullein, writing in 1562, tells of a "false witch" from Suffolk who a few years earlier "had no small resort of foolysh women, when their Chyldren were syck. To thys lame Wytch they resorted, to haue the Fairie charmed, and the Spyrite coniured away."[12] Perhaps it was professional jealousy that led him to exclaim, "Oh! That damnable witches be suffred to liue vnpunished & so many blessed men burned!" George Gifford gives a far less hostile account of a local wisewoman (in 1596): "There was another of my neighbours had his wife much troubled, and he went to her, and shee tolde him, his wife was haunted with a Fairy. I cannot tell what shee bad him doe, but the woman is mery at this howre."[13] Clearly, the relationship between cunning folk and fairies remained ambivalent well into the early modern period.

In recent years the historiography of early modern witchcraft has had little time for any such fairy dimension. No doubt reacting against the discredited theories of Margaret Murray,[14] modern scholarship has by and large shied away from studying witchcraft 'from below,' preferring rather to characterize it as the creature of a persecuting society, a set of beliefs that had little coherence, possibly even little real existence, outside the fertile imaginations of the inquisitor and the witch-hunter.[15] For instance, one would have to search long and hard in Stuart Clark's monumental *Thinking with Demons* (it is over eight hundred pages in length) to find any reference to fairies. True, a number of local studies of witchcraft in countries around the European periphery (such as Scotland, Hungary, Sicily, and Spain) have explored the fairy element in early modern witch beliefs,[16] but with the honorable exception of Carlo Ginzburg,[17] few prominent historians have chosen to venture far into this territory. However, Ginzburg's argument in *Ecstacies* that a learned perversion of earlier folk rituals furnishes at least part of the explanation for the witches' sabbat would hardly have seemed far-fetched to an Elizabethan skeptic such as Reginald Scot. In his *Discouerie of Witchcraft* (1584), Scot dismisses the idea of witches as "old women which danse with the fairies, &c."; he wonders dryly what becomes of the fat ox and the butt of Malmsey, "after they haue delicatelie banketted with the divell and the ladie of the fairies"; and he treats as a fable the story of Saint Germain, "who watched the fairies or witches, being at a reere banket." He does, however, concede that some witches are imagined to enter pacts with the devil, "wherevnto they consent priuilie, and come not into the fairies assemblie."[18] Reginald Scot's was, of course, one of the few voices to be raised against the persecution of witches, but lest we assume that only skeptics might have characterized the witches' sabbat as a fairy dance, here is Henri Boguet's *Discours des Sorciers* (1606), as nasty and credulous a treatise as any: "Sometimes, but rarely," he writes of the sabbat, "they dance two-by-two, and sometime with one on one side and one on the other—such dances resembling those of the fairies, true corporeal devils, who reigned not long ago" [*semblables à celles des fees, vrays Diables incorporez qui regnoient il ny'y a pas long-temps*].[19] Stuart Clark may have had little interest in the role of fairies in witchcraft, but a much earlier, and equally weighty, historian, Balthasar Bekker, in *The World Bewitched* (1691–93), seems to have found their participation self-evident.[20] Or as the clergyman Thomas Cooper put it in 1617: "This *conuersing of Satan* with the *Witch*, hath beene the ground of all these *Conceits of Fairies*."[21]

One of the most puzzling questions in the historiography of the early modern witch hunts is why the persecution of witches varied widely in intensity at different periods and in different parts of Europe. Brian Levack has offered a number of reasons for "the relative tameness of witch-hunting in Britain" (as opposed to France, Germany, and Switzerland);[22] most of them are judicial—the absence of papal inquisitors, the sparing use of torture, and the practice of trying witches by jury (to which one might add a highly centralized criminal justice system and a greater emphasis on empirical evidence)—but the one to be explored here is less tangible: the fact that witch-hunting "received only reluctant and half-hearted support from the administrative and ruling elite in England" (p. 201). Stephen Greenblatt has argued that a rhetoric of possession drove the European conquest of the New World,[23] and I am making an analogous argument here—that one of the reasons for the comparative mildness of the English witch hunt was an attitude of amused skepticism on the part of the ruling elite toward such popular superstitions as fairy belief and, further, that this attitude owes much to the cultural prestige of *The Canterbury Tales*.

It has not always been noticed how unusual Chaucer's attitude to fairies is. He puts no faith in the truth of Lancelot's story (*The Nun's Priest's Tale*, lines 3211–13),[24] nor does he expect Gawain to return from Avalon (*The Squire's Tale*, lines 95–96); he calls alchemy—a vocation he clearly regards as fraudulent—*elvysshe* (*The Canon's Yeoman's Tale*, lines 751, 842),[25] and when he applies the same adjective to himself (whatever its precise denotation), he does so in a spirit of self-mockery (*The Tale of Sir Thopas*, line 703).[26] The Wife of Bath, even though she tells a story about a fairy transformation, affects skepticism about the ability of elves to survive the depredations of modern mendicants (*The Wife of Bath's Tale*, lines 864–72), and in *The Man of Law's Tale* the attempt to represent Constance as a fairy succubus is a malicious invention on the part of her mother-in-law (*The Man of Law's Tale*, line 754). Finally, elves make two broadly comic appearances in *The Canterbury Tales*: in Sir Thopas's erotic fantasy of an elf queen to sleep under his "goore" (*The Tale of Sir Thopas*, line 789); and in the *dii ex machina*, Pluto and Proserpina, who interrupt May's "strugle" with Damian in a pear tree (*The Merchant's Tale*, lines 2219ff.). None of this suggests that Chaucer took fairies seriously, as either the mysterious denizens of a green world or the demons whom Satan employs to try to undermine Christendom. Though perfectly prepared to exploit its imaginative possibilities, Chaucer plainly regards fairyland as an absurd delusion, and in this he differs from the *Gawain* poet (who offers us one of the least self-conscious fairy romances in the canon), from Gower (who frequently classicizes his fairies as nymphs or fauns—as in the tales of *Calistona* or *Hercules and Faunus*), and from Langland (who makes *Gobelyne* one of Satan's supporters in the Harrowing of Hell scene [B text, 18:293] and regularly uses the term *pouke* to designate Satan himself). If any medieval English author aestheticizes (to borrow Le Goff's term) fairyland, it is Chaucer.

It would be difficult to overestimate the regard in which Chaucer was held in sixteenth-century England ("As Homer is reputed the Prince of Greek Poets; and Petrarch of Italian Poets: so Chaucer is accounted the God of English Poets," wrote Francis Meres),[27] but this is not to say that he was necessarily admired for the same qualities that recommend him now. One of his *Canterbury Tales* that evidently enjoyed a somewhat surprising level of popularity was *The Tale of Sir Thopas*.[28] Sir Thomas Wyatt seems to imply that Henry VIII's courtiers valued it more highly than *The Knight's Tale*, though of course his self-portrait as a plain-speaking man, unwilling to "Praysse Syr Thopas for a nobyll talle, / And skorne the story that the knyght tolld," should be taken with a grain of salt.[29] Perhaps, in fact, Wyatt is commenting on the vulgarity of court life, since Puttenham associated *The Tale of Sir Thopas* with "olde Romances or historicall rymes, made purposely for recreation of the common people."[30] Another use of *Sir Thopas* that is difficult to parse is Prince Arthur's dream in book 1 of Spenser's *Faerie Queene* (canto 9:12–15). The influence is unmistakable—in John Burrow's words, "like Thopas, Arthur rides out into a forest. Growing weary, he dismounts and falls asleep with his head pillowed on his helmet. He too dreams of a fairy queen, falls in love and sets off in search of his beloved" (p. 84)—but is Spenser, as Burrow speculates, really missing the joke? Perhaps what he is actually responding to, as Matthew Woodcock has argued, are "the self-consciously literary" elements in

Chaucer's poem.[31] *Sir Thopas* offered him all the aesthetic resources of fairyland with none of its historical baggage.

As is well known, the idea of associating Elizabeth I with the fairy queen did not originate with Spenser. We cannot be sure exactly when the queen's champion and organizer of the Accession Day tilts, Sir Henry Lee, first hit on the idea, since the records are far from continuous, but it features prominently in an entertainment with which he welcomed Elizabeth to Woodstock (supposed by some in the sixteenth century to be Chaucer's birthplace) in 1575; "we are here probably close to the living springs in living pageantry whence both Sidney's *Arcadia* and Spenser's *Faerie Queene* drew their emotional nourishment," writes Frances Yates.[32] Nevertheless, since the fairy queen was certainly a feature of some of the later tilts that Lee was to organize, she could well have appeared earlier. At any rate there can be no doubt that "fairy played a significant and recurrent part in one of the central dramatic vehicles for Elizabethan mythmaking."[33] There is no direct evidence that Lee drew his inspiration from Chaucer (though, since he received his education from his uncle Sir Thomas Wyatt, it is inconceivable that he should not have been familiar with the poet), but there is certainly a rustic cast to his fairy queen that is more reminiscent of *Sir Thopas* than "the story that the knyght tolld"; perhaps this is because the annual Accession Day tilts were part of a wider campaign to promote the Elizabethan political program at a popular level,[34] and we know that the common people were invited to witness this "worship of Elizabeth by her knights."[35] There can be no question of Queen Elizabeth's not wholeheartedly encouraging the cult; after "The Speech of the Fairye Quene to her Majestie," delivered on the last day of the *Entertainment at Elvetham* (1591), "This spectacle and musicke so delighted her Majesty, that shee commanded to heare it sung and to be danced three times over, and called for divers Lords and Ladies to behold it."[36]

When Lewis contrasts the cult of Elizabeth as fairy queen with a witch burning in Edinburgh, we might suppose that the two are so far apart rhetorically as to be entirely incommensurable, but the old clerical concept of fairies is occasionally to be found lurking even in the margins of Elizabethan courtly triumphs. In the early *Queens Entertainment at Suffolk and Norfolk* (1578), for instance, Mercury describes how

> The water nymphes, and feyries streight appears
> In uncouth formes, and fashion strange to view:
> The hagges of hell, that hateful are of kind,
> To please the time, had learnd a nature new.[37]

It is particularly striking, then, to find that a Protestant divine, Thomas Holland, felt himself obliged to defend Elizabeth's Accession Day celebrations against Catholic polemicists who he claimed objected not only to "the ringing of bells that day, the bone-fires, and other signes of ioy vsed by the faithfull people of the land" but also to "the triumphs vsed now yeerely before White-Hall" (that is, the tilts). Although the Elizabethan fairy myth is not directly addressed, it is certainly implied. According to Holland, Catholics complain "that these exercises upon [open] a window to reduce people backe againe to heathenish Paganisme, extinguished already by the light of the gospell, . . . that [they] are meere parasitical devises, and voide of religion, as they are performed in th*e* Realme, . . . [and that they] haue no better grounde, then the *i*dolatrous rites and pastimes exhibited by the Heathen to *Iupiter, Mars, Hercules, &c.*"[38] This is certainly the kind of thinking that was eager to identify fairy beliefs with witchcraft, so it is particularly ironic that Holland's own sister-in-law, Anne Gunter, should have claimed that she was the victim of witches in 1605. Holland was rector of Exeter College in Oxford at the time and three years earlier had preached a sermon at St. Paul's Cross in support of the church's moderate position on witchcraft;[39] it is significant, then, that he should have remained aloof at the trial of those accused of bewitching Anne Gunter, even though his wife and several of the dons in his college gave evidence for the prosecution.

Thomas Holland certainly knew his Chaucer—in a sermon on the Queen of Sheba, printed along with his defense of the Accession Day festivities, he quotes, "the greatest clarkes are not the wisest men" (f. F2^r) from Chaucer's *Reeve's Tale* (line 4054)—but in this respect he is outdone by another Anglican divine, one who would go on to far greater eminence and one, moreover, who took an active role in exonerating the women accused by Anne Gunter—Samuel Harsnett. In *A declaration of egregious popish impostures to with-draw the harts of her Maiesties subiects from their allegeance, and from the truth of Christian religion professed in England, vnder the pretence of casting out deuils*, printed in 1603 but evidently written some time earlier, Harsnett turns from those "that haue their braines baited, and their fancies distempered with the imaginations, and apprehensions of Witches, Coniurers, and Fayries, and all that Lymphatical Chimaera" to a fount of common sense: "And *Geoffry Chaucer*, who had his two eyes, wit, and learning in his head, spying that all these brainlesse immaginations, of witchings, possessings, house-hanting, and the rest, were the forgeries, cosenages, Imposturs, and legerdemaine of craftie priests, and leacherous Friers, . . . writes in good plaine termes of the holy Couent of Friers thus:

> For there as wont to walken was an *Elfe*,
> There walketh now the *Limitor* himselfe:
> In euery bush, and vnder euery tree,
> There nis none other *Iucubus* but hee."[40]

Harsnett is well known to literary scholars for providing Shakespeare with a list of outlandish names for devils to be used by Poor Tom in *King Lear*, but another of Shakespeare's sources, Reginald Scot (who apparently supplied some of the fairy lore for *A Midsummer Night's Dream*), was also an admirer of Chaucer. Scot ends book 4 of his *Discouerie of Witchcraft* (which treats of "bawdie Incubus and Succubus, and whether the action of venerie may be performed between witches and divells") with a much longer (fifteen-line) quotation from the opening of *The Wife of Bath's Tale*: "Now will I (after all this long discourse of abhominable cloked knaveries) here conclude with certeine of G. Chaucers verses, who as he smelt out the absurdities of poperie, so found he the priests knaverie in this matter of incubus and (as the time would suffer him) he derided their follie and falsehood."[41] (Incidentally, the enthusiasm with which these Protestant apologists embrace Chaucer as an ally is partially explained by the fact that in the sixteenth century *The Plowman's Tale* was accepted as part of the canon.)

As a late sixteenth-century promoter of the Elizabethan fairy myth Shakespeare was certainly less prominent than Spenser, but the image of fairyland presented by *A Midsummer Night's Dream* (as well as the ending of *The Merry Wives of Windsor* and Mercutio's Queen Mab speech in *Romeo and Juliet*) is no less aestheticized. It is also, as several critics have pointed out, similarly indebted to Chaucer. While the most obvious intertext of *A Midsummer Night's Dream* is *The Knight's Tale*, Tyrwhitt long ago suggested that Shakespeare modeled Oberon and Titania on Pluto and Proserpina in *The Merchant's Tale*, and recent criticism has expanded this insight.[42] *The Tale of Sir Thopas* has been proposed as another Chaucerian intertext for the play, either as a pattern for the homespun parody of the play within a play[43] or, intriguingly, as a springboard for Bottom's adventure: "the only suggestion [Shakespeare] could have got for this amazing mésalliance is from the extravagant love of the doughty Sir Thopas for his unknown elf-queen."[44]

So thoroughly does the fairy ethos permeate late sixteenth- and early seventeenth-century English courtly verse and so clearly can we see the hand of Chaucer in it that it would be possible to discuss several other examples, but for the sake of brevity I mention just two here. In the charming lyric "Hark, all you ladies that do sleep!" not only does Thomas Campion call his fairy queen Proserpina—a clear echo of *The Merchant's Tale*—but like Chaucer, he enlists her in the advancement of female sensual pleasure:

> All you that love or loved before,
> The fairy-queen Proserpina
> Bids you increase that loving humour more (lines 29–31).[45]

There are some suggestions that this song may have been written for a masque, but if so, it could hardly have been one intended for performance before the Virgin Queen. Michael Drayton, author of *Nymphidia*, one of the most deft of early modern fairy poems, reveals an obvious debt to *Sir Thopas* in the poem's first line:

> Olde Chaucer doth of Topas tell,
> Mad Rablais of Pantagruell,
> A latter third of Dowsabell,
> With such poore trifles playing.

He then contrasts these with "another sort . . . that will / Be talking of the fayries still."[46] Those who miss the joke that *Sir Thopas* actually *is* about fairies (and *Pantagruell* about giants) will probably also fail to twig that the "latter third" is Drayton himself (*Dowsabell* is a slightly smutty pastoral, written in the meter of *Sir Thopas*, who is also mentioned in its first stanza).[47] But the Chaucerian echoes do not end here. The fairy knight Pigwiggen has a love affair with Queen Mab, much to the annoyance of King Oberon, and finds himself forced to fight a joust with her husband; bloodshed is avoided only by the intervention of Proserpina, who envelops the combatants in infernal fog and then commands peace in Pluto's name. The allusions, not only to *Sir Thopas* but also to *The Knight's Tale* and *The Merchant's Tale*, are impossible to ignore.

Nymphidia is so self-consciously artificial and fantastic that it is easy to forget that some of Drayton's contemporaries still took fairies seriously. In the summer of 1597 the London theaters were closed because of the plague, and the Lord Chamberlain's Men (Shakespeare's company), in the course of a tour of southeast England, visited the town of Rye.[48] We cannot know what they performed there (it would be nice to think that they played *A Midsummer Night's Dream*—the dates certainly fit), but in any event we do know that ten years later a woman named Susan Swaffer was accused of witchcraft in the local court for "counselling with, entertaining and feeding evil and wicked spirits with the intention of acquiring treasure," along with her landlady, Anne Taylor, who was charged with aiding and abetting her.[49] These spirits, as the subsequent interrogation made clear, were imagined as fairies. A few months after Anne Taylor was finally released from prison (in June 1609), the court of chancery heard a far more bizarre case. In a suit between Thomas Rogers and Sir Anthony Ashley and his brother, it was alleged that the Ashleys had hired a man called Greene to swindle Rogers out of five or six pounds on the pretense that Greene was able to arrange an advantageous marriage for him with the queen of fairies.[50] C. J. Sisson's argument that this case is the source of the farcical scenes in Ben Jonson's *Alchemist* involving Abel Drugger and his aunt, the 'Queen of Fairy,' has been strongly challenged by Richard Levin, who draws attention to an earlier lawsuit: in 1595 a cunning woman, Judith Phillips, was arraigned "at the Sessions house without New-gate" for cheating "a rich churle in Hampshire" out of fourteen pounds by offering to enlist the help of the queen of fairies to reveal the whereabouts of treasure buried on his farm.[51] Levin argues that Judith Phillips's case should no more be considered a source for *The Alchemist* than Thomas Rogers's, but for our purposes both serve to show that fairy beliefs were alive and well in Shakespeare's day and that they were sometimes met with open mockery, not merely by sophisticated playwrights like Jonson but also by the two anonymous pamphleteers who chronicled Judith Phillips's chicanery. Pamphlets such as *The brideling, sadling and ryding, of a rich churle in Hampshire, by the subtill practise of one Iudeth Philips, a professed cunning woman*[52] and *A quest of enquirie, / by women to know, / whether the tripe-wife were trimmed / by Doll yea or no / Gathered by Oliuer Oat-meale*[53] might seem to take us well beyond the influence of Geoffrey Chaucer, but the case of Brian Walker (1635) proves that the poet might turn up in some surprising places. Walker was hauled up before an ecclesiastical court in Durham "for utteringe blasphemous woordes" and is reported to have said, "I doe not beleive there is eyther God or devill, neyther will I beleive anie thinge but what I see." In the course of the trial one of the witnesses testified to hearing Walker "conferr and speake of the booke called Chawcer, which booke he verie much commended, and saide he did beleive the same as well as he did the Bible, or woordes to the same effect."[54]

The other half of Lewis's early modern anomaly is the woman "burned at Edinburgh in 1576 for 'repairing with' the fairies and the 'Queene of Elfame.'" We have already met this woman in the person of Bessie Dunlop, who, along with a number of other 'witches' tried in Scotland (such as Jonet Boyman, Andro Man, and Isobel Gowdie), furnishes some of our best evidence for early Scottish fairy beliefs.[55] However, the fact that, in Levack's words, "prosecutions [for witchcraft] were much more intense in Scotland than in England" (p. 202), taken along with Chaucer's extensive influence on sixteenth-century Scottish writers, would seem to undermine the case I have been making for the ameliorating effects of his legacy on witch-hunting. Of course other factors must be taken into account: torture was employed more extensively in Scotland than in England; James VI (in strong contrast to Elizabeth I) was a published demonologist who strongly disapproved of the "kinde of Spirite called the Phairie"; and a reading of Robert Kirk's *Secret Commonwealth* suggests that early modern Scottish fairy beliefs were far more deeply entrenched than their English equivalent. Even so, the literary prominence of "the Scottish Chaucerians" obviously complicates my argument.

On closer examination, however, Chaucer's skepticism about fairy beliefs does not seem to have made much of an impression on this school. Henryson's *Orpheus and Eurydice*, for instance, has Orpheus's wife carried off by fairies: "Allace, Erudices 3our quene," reports her maid, "Is with the fary tane befor myne ene!" and later: "the quene of fary / Claucht hir wp sone and furth with hir can cary."[56] In this it resembles the Middle English *Sir Orfeo*, whose tradition seems to have enjoyed a longer life in Scotland than in England; a late sixteenth-century manuscript, apparently owned by a gentry family (either the Cockburns or the Sinclairs), contains a fragmentary *King Orphius* in which the queen laments, "ye king of pharie vill me haif / yair may na erdlie thing me saif."[57] Henryson's choice is all the stranger because he later follows Chaucer's lead in *The Knight's Tale* by turning the Greek pantheon into planets. However, lest we suppose it is only Erudices's maid who talks of fairies, when Orpheus finally encounters his wife, "Lene and dedelike, pitouse and pale of hewe" (line 349), in Hades, it is Pluto who explains that "thouch scho be like ane elf, / Thare is na cause to plenye" (lines 359–60). Gavin Douglas, on the other hand, as befits a future bishop of Dunkeld, is far more circumspect: at the beginning of book 6 of his translation of the *Aeneid* (Aeneas's visit to the underworld) he counters the criticism of those who complain,

"All is bot gaist*is* and elrich fantasyis,
Of browneis *and* of bogillis ful *th*is buke:
Owt on *th*ir wandrand sperit*is*, wow!"

with the familiar argument that Virgil was a virtuous pagan whose work anticipates the Christian gospel, but in the prologue to book 10 (which includes a council of the gods) he takes good care to dissociate himself from any taint of paganism:

Lat Virgill hald hys mawme*nt*is to hym self;
I wirschip no*w*der *y*doll, stok, nor elf,
*Th*ocht furth I write so as myne auto*u*r dois.[58]

William Dunbar might seem to come closest to the Chaucerian spirit in his poem to "Schir Thomas Norny," a burlesque clearly modeled on *The Tale of Sir Thopas*, but even here the butt of the joke is not actual fairy belief. Written as an attack on an upstart court fool, the poem treats fairyland as a source of insult rather than fantasy (as in "The Flyting of Dunbar and Kennedie," where his opponent had twice called Dunbar an elf), so that instead of setting out in quest of an elf queen, Norny turns out to be the progeny of one:

Quhais father was ane giand keyne—
His mother was ane farie queyne
Gottin be sossery.[59]

No doubt the general attitude to fairies in Scotland acted as a constraint on these "Scottish Chaucerians," but this in turn suggests that Chaucer's English legacy might better be seen as both cause and effect of the very different atmosphere across the border. In other words, if Chaucer did indeed contribute to what I have called a rhetoric of amused skepticism, he could have done so only in a cultural climate that was already receptive to it—a climate that was only partly inflected by confessional pressures.[60] As this book has repeatedly attempted to demonstrate, vernacular beliefs, whether in fairies or witches, are best understood by seeking to examine them not only from above but also from below.

NOTES

INTRODUCTION

1. Cambridge University Library, MS KK IV 24, ff. 240–41ra. See Siegfried Wenzel, *Latin Sermon Collections from Later Medieval England: Orthodox Preaching in the Age of Wyclif* (Cambridge: Cambridge University Press, 2005), pp. 136–39, 415–23 [B/a 58].

2. "Sunt et alii qui dicunt se de nocte videre mulieres et puellas tripudiantes quos vocant *Eluysche folke* et credunt quod tales possunt tam homines quam mulieres transformare vel alios pro se dimittere et illos secum adducere ad *Eluenlond* que omnia non sunt nisi fantastica et a maligno spiritu illis donata, quare, quando diabolus anima*m* alicuius talis ad talia credendum subiugavit, seipsum alium transformat, modo in formam angeli, modo in formam hominis, modo mulieris, modo aliarum creaturarum, modo in coreis et aliis ludis et sic per incredulitatem animarum tal*es* [MS: talis] miseri deluduntur. Hi vero qui in predictis credunt vel pertinaciter defendunt et do*c*ent [MS: dolent] maxime cum veritatem audierint sunt infideles et paganis deteriores et maledicti a domino et sancta ecclesia quarter in anno . . . sciant se a fide christi apostatasse et suum baptismatum prevaricasse ac iram domini et eius inimicitiam incurrisse"; see CUL MS KK IV 24 f. 241ra–rb.

3. *Fasciculus Morum: A Fourteenth-Century Preacher's Handbook*, ed. and trans. Siegfried Wenzel (University Park: Pennsylvania State University Press, 1989), pp. 581–82.

4. Carlo Ginzburg, *Ecstasies: Deciphering the Witches' Sabbath*, trans. Raymond Rosenthal (New York: Pantheon Books, 1991), p. 11.

5. See Diane Purkiss, *At the Bottom of the Garden: A Dark History of Fairies, Hobgoblins, and Other Troublesome Things* (New York: New York University Press, 2000), p. 8.

6. Simon Young, "Against Taxonomy: Fairy Families in Cornwall," *Cornish Studies* 21 (2013):223–37.

7. [Thomas of Cantimpré], *Thomae Cantipratani, Bonum Universale de Apibus*, ed. George Colvener (Douai: Balthazar Beller, 1627), 2:55 (pp. 531–94).

8. "Silvans and Pans, who are commonly called *incubi*, often misbehaved towards women and . . . certain demons, termed *Dusii* by the Gauls, constantly attempt and perpetrate this foulness"; see Saint Augustine, *The City of God Against the Pagan*s, ed. and trans. William M. Greene et al., 7 vols. (Cambridge, Mass.: Harvard University Press, 1957–72), 4:548–49 (15:23).

9. Another (possibly folk) etymology connects them with *nuit* [night]: "gobelins, ce sont petis dyablotz que l'en appelle en moult de pais netuins, c'est a dire choses qui vont par nuit"; see [*Second Lucidaire*], ed. Doris Ruhe, in *Gelehrtes Wissen, 'Aberglaube' und pastorale Praxis im französischen Spätmittelalter: Der Second Lucidaire und seine Rezeption, 14.–17. Jahrhundert: Untersuchung und Edition* (Wiesbaden: Reichert, 1993), p. 294B.

10. See the chapter "*De neptunis qui homines deludunt* 'Neptunes Which Delude Human Beings,' " in Gervase of Tilbury, *Otia imperialia: Recreation for an Emperor*, ed. and trans. S. E. Banks and J. W. Binns (Oxford: Clarendon Press, 2002), 3:61 (pp. 674–77).

11. The suggestion that the English expression 'What the Deuce!' derives from it (cf. A. L. Mayhew, "The Etymology of 'Deuce': Interjectional and Imprecatory," *Academy*, 30 January 1892:111–12) looks like a folk etymology; it seems more likely to come from dicing. For other possible reflexes, see Claude Lecouteux, *Les Nains et les elfes* (Paris: Imago, 1988), p. 170.

12. *Early Modern Witches: Witchcraft Cases in Contemporary Writing*, ed. Marion Gibson (London: Routledge, 2000), p. 29.

13. James Wade, "Abduction, Surgery, Madness: An Account of a Little Red Man in Thomas Walsingham's *Chronica Maiora*," *Medium Aevum* 77 (2008):10–29.

14. Katharine Mary Briggs, *The Fairies in English Tradition and Literature* (Chicago: University of Chicago Press, 1967); Lecouteux, *Les Nains et les elfes*.

15. W. B. Yeats gave the rather fustian term "trooping fairies" to such creatures; see D. L. Ashliman, *Fairy Lore: A Handbook* (Westport, Conn.: Greenwood Press, 2006), p. 55.

16. See Alaric Hall, *Elves in Anglo-Saxon England: Matters of Belief, Health, Gender and Identity* (Woodbridge: Boydell Press, 2007).

17. *Anglo-Norman Medicine II: Shorter Treatises*, ed. Tony Hunt (Cambridge: D. S. Brewer, 1997), p. 224.

18. The word *fairy* in Middle English regularly refers to a place or region, the abode of those creatures known to the French as *fées* (Latin, *fata*): *fées*, in other words, live in *fée-erie*. Though *fairy*, influenced perhaps by the native word *ferli*, might also have been used as a synonym for a 'marvel' or 'wonder' and sometimes in a more generalized sense as 'magic,' it does not seem to have been used to denote an actual creature, a *fairy*, much before the middle of the fifteenth century. Nor, so far as I can see, is it used unambiguously as an adjective: in Middle English one referred to a *fairy knight* much as we now refer to a 'New York policeman'—that is to say, *fairy* in such phrases was primarily appositional, not adjectival.

19. See Richard M. Dorson, *The British Folklorists: A History* (London: Routledge, 1968), pp. 392–439.

20. W. Y. Evans-Wentz, *The Fairy Faith in Celtic Countries* (London: Oxford University Press, 1911), is probably the best-known advocate of this position.

21. *Waltharius* and *Ruodlieb*, ed. and trans. Dennis M. Katz (New York: Garland, 1984), pp. 38–39 (lines 756–79).

22. Gareth Morgan, "Walther the Woodsprite," *Medium Aevum* 41 (1972):17.

23. Admittedly, Walter mocks Ekivrid's "Celtic tongue" [*celtica lingua*], but as the context makes clear, it is a Celtic love of puns, not an obsession with fairies, that prompts his remark. In any case *celtica lingua* here seems more likely to be referring to Gaulish than to the direct predecessor of any present-day Celtic language; see David Dumville, "Ekiurid's Celtic Lingua: An Ethnological Difficulty in Waltharius," *Cambridge Medieval Celtic Studies* 6 (1983):87–93.

24. *Waltharius*, ed. Karl Strecker (1947; Hildesheim: Weidmannsche Verlagsbuchhandlung, 1987), pp. 7–8. Paris, B.N., MS Lat. 8488A dates from the middle of the thirteenth century; see Elisabeth Pellegrin, "Membra disiecta Floriacensia," *Bibliothèque de l'École des chartes* 117 (1959):25–43.

25. Dorena Allen, "Orpheus and Orfeo: The Dead and the Taken," *Medium Aevum* 33 (1964):107.

26. *The Oxford Book of Medieval Latin Verse*, ed. F. J. E. Raby (Oxford: Clarendon Press, 1959), pp. 170–71 (no. 121).

27. The strongest advocate of this position, derived from Arthurian romance, was Roger Sherman Loomis, but it continues to be widely accepted, even outside the tradition of Anglophone scholarship (Jacques Le Goff entertains a version of it). For a recent instance, see Carolyne Larrington, "The Fairy Mistress in Medieval Literary Fantasy," in *Writing and Fantasy*, ed. Ceri Sullivan and Barbara White (London: Longman, 1999), pp. 32–47, esp. pp. 35–36.

28. Valdimar Th. Hafstein, "The Elves' Point of View: Cultural Identity in Contemporary Elf-Tradition," *Fabula* 41 (2000):98.

29. Alberto Cirese, "Gramsci's Observations on Folklore," in *Approaches to Gramsci*, ed. Anne Slowstack Sassoon (London: Writers and Readers, 1982), pp. 221–47.

30. Stephen O. Gencarella, "Gramsci, Good Sense, and Critical Folklore Studies," *Journal of Folklore Research* 47 (2010):221–52.

31. See Kate A. F. Crehan, *Gramsci, Culture and Anthropology* (Berkeley: University of California Press, 2002), pp. 119–23.

32. Purkiss, *At the Bottom of the Garden*, p. 4.

33. R. I. Moore, *The Formation of a Persecuting Society: Authority and Deviance in Western Europe, 950–1250*, 2nd ed. (1987; Oxford: Blackwell, 2007).

CHAPTER I

1. C. S. Lewis, "De Audiendis Poetis," in *Studies in Medieval and Renaissance Literature*, collected by Walter Hooper (Cambridge: Cambridge University Press, 1966), p. 17.

2. Francis Dubost, *Aspects fantastiques de la littérature narrative médiévale, XIIème–XIIIème siècles: L'autre, l'ailleurs, l'autrefois*, 2 vols. (Geneva: Slatkine, 1991), 1:217. Dubost draws a crucial distinction between the fantastic and the marvelous, but this generalization applies to both.

3. Helen Cooper, *The English Romance in Time: Transforming Motifs from Geoffrey of Monmouth to the Death of Shakespeare* (Oxford: Oxford University Press, 2004); Corinne Saunders, *Magic and the Supernatural in Medieval English Romance* (Woodbridge: D. S. Brewer, 2010); James Wade, *Fairies in Medieval Romance* (New York: Palgrave Macmillan, 2011).

4. See, for example, Daniel Poirion, *Le merveilleux dans la littérature française du moyen âge* (Paris: Presses universitaires de France, 1982); Laurence Harf-Lancner, *Les fées au moyen âge: Morgane et Mélusine; la naissance des fées* (Geneva: Slatkine, 1984); Dubost, *Aspects fantastiques* (1991); Claude Lecouteux, *Au-delà du merveilleux: Des croyances du moyen âge* (Paris: Presses de l'Université de Paris-Sorbonne, 1995); Jean-René Valette, *La poétique du merveilleux dans le Lancelot en prose* (Paris: Champion, 1998); Christine Ferlampin-Acher, *Fées, bestes et luitons: Croyances et merveilles dans les romans français en prose (XIIIe–XIVe siècles)* (Paris: Presses de l'Université de Paris-Sorbonne, 2002); Francis Gingras, *Erotisme et merveilles dans le récit français des XIIe et XIIIe siècles* (Paris: Champion, 2002). There is a useful overview of work on *le merveilleux* in Francis Dubost, "Merveilleux et fantastique au moyen âge: Positions et propositions," *Revue des langues romanes* 100.2 (1996):1–35.

5. Jeffrey Jerome Cohen, *Of Giants: Sex, Monsters, and the Middle Ages* (Minneapolis: University of Minnesota Press, 1999); Jeffrey Jerome Cohen, *Hybridity, Identity, and Monstrosity in Medieval Britain* (New York: Palgrave Macmillan, 2006); Geraldine Heng, *Empire of Magic: Medieval Romance and the Politics of Cultural Fantasy* (New York: Columbia University Press, 2003). Patricia Clare Ingham, *Sovereign Fantasies: Arthurian Romance and the Making of Britain* (Philadelphia: University of Pennsylvania Press, 2001), gives a more narrowly focused political reading of the role of romance fantasy.

6. See particularly Jacques Le Goff, *L'imaginaire médiéval: Essais* (Paris: Gallimard, 1985); Jacques Le Goff, *Pour un autre moyen âge* (Paris: Gallimard, 1977); and Jean-Claude Schmitt, *Le saint Lévrier: Guinefort, guérisseur d'enfants depuis le XIIIe siècle* (Paris: Flammarion, 1979).

7. Keith Thomas, *Religion and the Decline of Magic: Studies in Popular Beliefs in Sixteenth and Seventeenth Century England* (London: Weidenfeld & Nicolson, 1971); Ronald Hutton, *The Rise and Fall of Merry England: The Ritual Year, 1400–1700* (Oxford: Oxford University Press, 1994); Stephen Wilson, *The Magical Universe: Everyday Ritual and Magic in Pre-modern Europe* (London: Hambledon and London, 2000); Walter Stephens, *Demon Lovers: Witchcraft, Sex, and the Crisis of Belief* (Chicago: University of Chicago Press, 2002); Carl S. Watkins, *History and the Supernatural in Medieval England* (Cambridge: Cambridge University Press, 2007); Robert Bartlett, *The Natural and the Supernatural in the Middle Ages* (Cambridge: Cambridge University Press, 2008); Euan Cameron, *Enchanted Europe: Superstition, Reason, and Religion, 1250–1750* (Oxford: Oxford University Press, 2010); Catherine Rider, *Magic and Religion in Medieval England* (London: Reaktion Books, 2012).

8. Michelle Sweeney, *Magic in Medieval Romance from Chrétien de Troyes to Geoffrey Chaucer* (Dublin: Four Courts Press, 2000), p. 19.

9. One French exception is Ferlampin-Acher, *Fées, bestes et luitons*, pp. 19–28; cf. Dubost, *Aspects fantastiques*, 1:142–64.

10. Fredric Jameson, "Magical Narratives: Romance as Genre," *New Literary History* 7 (1975):142; cf. Larrington, "The Fairy Mistress."

11. M. W. Latham, *The Elizabethan Fairies* (New York: Columbia University Press, 1930), p. 13.

12. "Alii vero, qui prope homines in collibus habitant, magis sunt familiares et non ita malefici nisi injuriis nescio quibus affecti fuerint ad nequitias provocati. Utrique sane incredibili subtilitate corporum videntur praediti, cum etiam montes et colles putentur penetrare. Utrique sunt nobis invisibiles, nisi cum ipsi sponte volunt apparere; sunt tamen quorundam hominum oculi natura sua et malo fato ita Lyncei, ut nunquam possint ulla spectra praesentia visum eorum subterfugere. Utriusque norunt mille technas et stratagemata infinita, quibus homines miseris exagitant modis. Sed posteriores et statura et vestitu et victu quoque persimili cum vicinis hominibus uti credentur et coitu quoque humano magnopere delectari. Nec desunt exempla aliquot nebulonum, qui foeminas subterraneas dicuntur impraegnasse et statis temporibus, vel quotiescunque libuerit, eas accessisse. Et vicissim compressae sunt nostrates foeminae ab istis terrigenis raptique multoties innocentes pueri, puellae et utriusque sexus juvenes et adolescentes, quorum nonnulli restituti sunt salvi et illaesi post dies aliquot et interdum post aliquot septimanas, aliqui vero nunquam deinceps visi et quidam inventi semianimes etc. Sed taedet in ista commemoratione plus operae insumere; sive enim haec contingant fraudibus, imposturis et illusionibus Satanae, quae fere videntur esse omnium saniorum sententia, sive sint aliquae eiusmodi mixti generis inter spiritus et animalia creaturae, ut quidam conjiciunt, tamen certum est non in sola Islandia vulgares fuisse istorum spectrorum apparitiones, sed in aliis etiam regionibus compluribus, ut frustra assumatur hoc argumentum ad stabiliendas illas nugas de inferno confictas"; see [Oddur Einarsson, Bishop of Skálholt], *Qualiscunque Descriptio Islandiae: Nach der Handschrift der Hamburger Staats- und Universitäts-Bibliothek*, ed. Fritz Burg (Hamburg: Selbstverlag der Staats- und Universitäts- Bibliothek, 1928), pp. 14–15.

13. For the *fraus Sathanae*, see below. The theory of the *genus mixtum* is attributed to Albertus Magnus by Johannes Nider in his *Theologi Preceptorium* (of 1438): in answer to the question "an verum sit, quod aliqui homines sint siluestres" [whether it be true that certain

men may be (wood) fairies], he writes, "Aliquando sunt Pigmei, quod animal secundum Albertus in De Animalibus, vbi prius est multum simile homini, quia erecte incedit, manibus vtitur ad opera quaedam, loquitur lingua. Et tamen simpliciter plus est bestia quam homo: licet sit nobilius animalium infra hominem. Aliquando etiam daemones in siluis apparent esse homines vel feminae, vt decipiant incautores" [Sometimes they are Pigmies, which, according to Albertus Magnus in *De Animalibus,* is a kind of animal much like a man, because it walks upright, uses its hands for certain tasks, and employs language; and yet it is clearly more beast than man, although more noble than the other animals below man. Also sometimes they are demons who appear to be men or women in the woods, in order to deceive the unwary]; see [John Nider], *Praeceptorium* (Douai: Bogarde, 1611), pp. 71–72 (I.xi.9). Albertus, in [Albertus Magnus], *De animalibus,* ed. Hermann Stadler, 2 vols., Lib. II, tract. 1, cap. 4 (Münster: Aschendorffsache, 1916, 1920), 1:244, describes the capture of a pair of them in his own day; he says that the male was conspicuously lecherous. See also [William of Auvergne], *De Universo,* II. iii, 8, in *Guillielmi Alverni Opera Omnia,* 2 vols. (Paris: Pralard, 1674),1:1029bD.

14. Konrad Murer, "Die Hölle auf Island," *Zeitschrift des Vereins für Volkskunde* 4 (1894):256–69.

15. C. S. Lewis, *The Discarded Image: An Introduction to Medieval and Renaissance Literature* (Cambridge: Cambridge University Press, 1964), pp. 137–38.

16. For instance, in the Anglo-Saxon remedy, "wiþ ælfcynne & nihtgengan & þam mannum þe deofel mid hæmð" [against elfkind and night-travelers, and for those who have intercourse with the devil]; see *Leechdoms, Wortcunning, and Starcraft of Early England,* ed. Thomas Oswald Cocayne, 2 vols. (London: Longman, Green, 1864), 2:344 (no. 61).

17. *Patrologia Latina,* 172:1109A–76D. See Yves Le Fèvre, *L'Elucidarium et les Lucidaires: Contribution, par l'histoire d'un texte, à l'histoire des croyances religieuses en France au moyen âge* (Paris: E. de Boccard, 1954); Aron Gurevich, *Medieval Popular Culture: Problems of Belief and Perception,* trans. Janos M. Bak and Paul A. Hollingsworth (Cambridge: Cambridge University Press, 1988), pp. 152–75 (chap. 5).

18. Valerie Flint, "Heinricus of Augsberg and Honorius Augustodunensis: Are They the Same Person?" *Revue Bénédictine* 92 (1982):148–58.

19. [Burchard of Worms], *Die Bussordnungen der abendländischen Kirche,* ed. F. W. H. Wasserschleben (Halle: Graeger, 1851), p. 658 (cap. 140). See also *Patrologia Latina,* 140:971C.

20. London: B.L., MS Cotton Faustina A. VII, f. 33a. Thomas Wright attributes this passage to Bartholomew of Exeter (see *Reliquiae Antiquae,* ed. Thomas Wright and J. O. Halliwell, 2 vols. [London: Pickering, 1841, 1843], 1:286), but it is evidently a later (thirteenth-century) interpolation; see Adrian Morey, *Bartholomew of Exeter: Bishop and Canonist* (Cambridge: Cambridge University Press, 1937), p. 166. For Burchard's original, see [Burchard of Worms], *Bussordnungen,* ed. Wasserschleen, p. 150 (cap. 91); *Patrologia Latina,* 140:965C.

21. [*Second Lucidaire*], ed. Monika Türk, in *"Lucidaire de grant sapientie": Untersuchung und Edition der altfranzösischen Übersetzung 1 des "Elucidarium" von Honorius Augustodunensis,* ed. Monika Türk (Tübingen: Max Niemeyer Verlag, 2000). This redaction was itself augmented and revised more than once in the late middle ages; see Doris Ruhe, *Gelehrtes Wissen,* Sections 162–63, pp. 284–99.

22. *The Late Middle English* Lucydarye, ed. Stephen Morrison (Turnhout: Brepols, 2013), p. 53. This is Andrew Chertsey's translation (printed twice by Wynkyn de Worde in ca. 1505 and 1523) of a 1480 French incunabulum of the *Second lucidaire*; see Ernstpeter Ruhe, *Elucidarium und Lucidaires: Zur Rezeption des Werks von Honorius Augustodunensis in der Romania und in England* (Wiesbaden: L. Reichert, 1993), p. 292.

23. Paris, B.M. MS Latin 15970, f. 413a (col. 1). A condensed version of the same story is told in the *Golden Legend (Jacobi a Voragine Legenda aurea)*, ed. Theodor Graesse, 2nd ed. (Leipzig: Arnold, 1850), p. 449 (chap. 107). For an account of similar fairy gatherings as *phantasmata*, see the *Fasciculus Morum*, ed. Wenzel, pp. 579–81.

24. Augustine, *City of God*, 4:548–49 (15:23).

25. Apparently Conrad of Marburg, the notorious German inquisitor, who was murdered in 1233. See Malcolm Lambert, *The Cathars* (Oxford: Blackwell, 1998), pp. 118–22.

26. Conrad of Höxter, or Conrad of Germany; Victor F. O'Daniel, *The First Disciples of Saint Dominic* (New York: Pustet, 1928), pp. 169–73. He was a Doctor of Canon Law and the author of a confessional manual, the *Summula Magistri Conradi*; see *Trois sommes de pénitence de la première moitié du XIIIe siècle*, ed. Jean-Pierre Renard (Louvain-la-Neuve: Centre Cerfaux-Lefort, 1989).

27. "Anno ab incarnatione domini M.CC.XXXI. predicante in Theutonia magistro Conrado contra hereticos et ab eisdem felici morte perempto, hereticus quidam—ut per fratrem Conradum, Provincialem fratrum predicatorum per Theutoniam, ante annos multos acccepi—seductus a demonibus fratrem quemdam ordinis predicatorum ad heresim invitabat. Quem cum videret instantissime renitentem, dixit fratri: 'Pertinax valde es in fide tua nec tamen de hac, nisi per scripta quedam, aliquod certius inspexisti. Credere autem si velles dictis meis Christum tibi et matrem eius ac sanctos oculata fide monstrarem.' Mox ille illusionem demonum suspicatus volens tandem probare quid esset, 'Non immerito,' inquit: 'tibi tunc crederem si promissa duceres ad effectum.' Gavisus hereticus diem fratri statuit. Frater vero pixidem cum sacramento corporis Christi clam secum sub cappa portavit. Duxit ergo fratrem hereticus in specu ciuisdam montis in amplum valde palatium quod claritate mirabili relucebat. Nec mora, ubi in inferiorem partem palacii pervenerunt, viderunt thronos positos quasi ex auro purissimo, in quibus sedebat rex fulgore corusco circumdatus & iuxta eum regina sereno vultu pulcherrima et ex utraque parte sedilia in quibus seniores quasi patriarche vel velut aposotoli astante permaxima multitudine angelorum et hi omnes luce siderea coruscantes, ut nihil minus quam demones putarentur. Hos, mox ut vidit hereticus, cadens in faciem adoravit. Dictus autem frater immotus stetit sed tanto spectaculo vehementer obstupuit et mox ad eum conversus hereticus: 'quare,' inquit, 'dei filium intuens non adoras? Pronus accedens adora quem vides et ab ore eius fidei nostre secreta suscipies'" (pp. 553–54) (spelling and punctuation modernized).

28. Jean Gobi, *La Scala Coeli*, ed. Marie-Anne Polo de Beaulieu (Paris: Centre de la Recherche Scientifique, 1991), p. 325 (no. 374).

29. *Sir Orfeo*, ed. A. J. Bliss, 2nd ed. (Oxford: Clarendon Press, 1966), lines 347–76; *Thomas of Erceldoune*, ed. Ingeborge Nixon, 2 vols. (Copenhagen: Akademisk Forlag, 1980, 1983), 1:38–42 (lines 169–220); *The Romance of Guy of Warwick (Auchinleck and Caius MSS.)*, ed. Julius Zupitza, EETS ES 42, 49, 59 (reprinted as one vol.) (1883–91; London: Early English Text Society, 1966), stanzas 78–81; *The Romance of Guy of Warwick (The 15th-Century Version)*, ed. J. Zupitza, EETS ES 25, 26 (reprinted as one vol.) (1875–76; London: Early English Text Society, 1966), lines 11379–416.

30. For instance, Bernard Gui's instruction to inquisitors to ask anyone suspected of sorcery about "female fairies, who are called *good things*, and who are said to travel by night" [de fatis mulieribus quas vocant bonas res, que, ut dicunt vadunt de nocte]; see Bernardus Gui, *Manuel de l'inquisiteur*, ed. and trans. G. Mollat, 2 vols. (Paris: Champion, 1926, 1927), 2:22.

31. Margaret Alice Murray, *The Witch-Cult in Western Europe: A Study in Anthropology* (Oxford: Clarendon Press, 1921); Margaret Alice Murray, *The God of the Witches* (London: Faber and Faber, 1931).

32. A similar case has been made for the so-called heresies of the Cathars and the Waldensians; see Moore, *Formation of a Persecuting Society*, pp. 174–77. Also, Sonia Maura Barillari, *Protostoria della Strega. Le Fonti Medievali Latine e Romanze* (Aicurzio: Castel Negrino, 2014), pp. 153–57.

33. Conrad of Marburg's own investigations, in fact, led him to construct what Lambert calls "an artificial heresy, that of the Luciferians" (*The Cathars*, p. 120); its overheated fantasies are reflected in the decretal *Vox in Rama* issued by Gregory IX in 1233 (see Edward Peters, *The Magician, the Witch, and the Law* [Philadelphia: University of Pennsylvania Press, 1978], pp. 156–57).

34. See *Middle English Debate Poetry*, ed. John W. Conlee (East Lansing, Mich.: Colleagues Press, 1991), pp. 178–91.

35. Carleton Brown, in "The Vernon Disputisoun bytwene a Christenmon and a Jew," *Modern Language Notes* 25 (1910):141–44, argues for Thomas of Cantimpré's direct influence on the poem.

36. See Roseanna Cross, "'Heterochronia' in Thomas of Erceldoune, Guingamor, 'The Tale of King Herla,' and the Story of Meriadoc, King of Cambria," *Neophilologus* 92 (2008):162–75.

37. Cf. Maria Panzona's testimony in Ginzburg, *Ecstacies*, p. 100.

38. *The Register of John Morton, Archbishop of Canterbury, 1486–1500, III*, ed. Christopher Harper-Bill (Woodbridge: Boydell & Brewer, 2000), p. 215 (no. 661).

39. John Bromyard, *Summa Predicantium*, 2 vols. (Venice, 1586), 2:371b (S. XI. 8; s.v. "sortilegium").

40. Annabel Gregory, *Rye Spirits: Faith, Faction, and Fairies in a Seventeenth-Century English Town* (London: Hedge Press, 2013), p. 114.

41. *Oxford Book of Medieval Latin Verse*, ed. Raby, pp. 170–71 (no. 121).

42. John Capgrave, *The Life of Saint Katherine*, ed. Karen A. Winstead (Kalamazoo, Mich.: Medieval Institute Publications, 1999).

43. See Matt. 10:19–22; Luke 21:12–15; Mark 13:11–13.

44. Peter Idley, *Peter Idley's Instructions to His Son*, ed. Charlotte D'Evelyn (Boston: Modern Language Association of America, 1935), p. 114 (lines 381–83).

45. *The English Register of Godstow Nunnery*, ed. Andrew Clark (London: Early English Text Society, 1911), p. 1.

46. Bromyard, *Summa Predicantium* (1586), 2:373 (S. XI. 10 (s.v. "sortilegium").

47. Kew, National Archives, KB 27/755, m.75 (Rex, m. 4). For an English translation of the whole entry, see Alexander L. Kauffman, *The Historical Literature of the Jack Cade Rebellion* (Farnham: Ashgate, 2009), pp. 178–79; as in other references to this record, *de ffeyre* should be rendered as 'of Fairyland,' not 'of the fairies.'

48. *Six Town Chronicles of England*, ed. Ralph Flenley (Oxford: Clarendon Press, 1911), p. 127.

49. *Kent Records: Documents Illustrative of Medieval Kentish Society*, ed. F. R. H. Du Boulay (Ashford: Kent Archaeological Society, 1964), p. 255.

50. Michael J. Bennett, "Henry VII and the Northern Rising of 1489," *English Historical Review* 105 (1990):35.

51. *Paston Letters and Papers of the Fifteenth Century*, pts. 1 and 2, ed. Norman Davis (Oxford: Clarendon Press, 1971, 1976); pt. 3, ed. Richard Beadle and Colin Richmond, EETS SS 22 (Oxford: Oxford University Press, 2005), 1:659.

52. I am grateful to Simon Young for drawing my attention to both the Paston reference and the Derbyshire place-name.

53. Cf. E. P. Thompson, *Whigs and Hunters: The Origin of the Black Act* (New York: Pantheon Books, 1975); and Peter Sahlins, *Forest Rites: The War of the Demoiselles in Nineteenth-Century France* (Cambridge, Mass.: Harvard University Press, 1994).

54. Gervase of Tilbury, *Otia imperialia*, ed. Banks and Binns, p. 731.

55. Caesarii Heisterbacensis, *Dialogus Miraculorum*, ed. Joseph Strange, 2 vols. (Cologne: Heberle, 1851, 1852), 1:319–21. See Dyan Elliott, *Fallen Bodies: Pollution, Sexuality, and Demonology in the Middle Ages* (Philadelphia: University of Pennsylvania Press, 1999), p. 138.

56. Thomas Chestre, *Sir Launfal*, ed. A. J. Bliss (London: Nelson, 1960), lines 326–27, 375–93, 580–94, etc.

57. M. Dando, "Les anges neutres," *Cahiers d'études Cathares* 27 (1976):20.

58. W. P. Ker, "The Craven Angels," *Modern Language Review* 6 (1911):85–87; Lewis, *Discarded Image*, pp. 135–36; Wade, *Fairies in Medieval Romance*, pp. 14–15.

59. *Middle English Religious Prose*, ed. Norman F. Blake (London: Edward Arnold, 1972), pp. 106–7.

60. *The South English Legendary*, ed. Charlotte D'Evelyn and Anna J. Mill, 3 vols., EETS OS 335, 336, 344 (London: Oxford University Press, 1956, 1959), 2:408–10.

61. Jean d'Arras, *Melusine*, ed. A. K. Donald, EETS ES 68 (London: Kegan Paul, 1895), p. 316.

62. Dando, "Anges neutres," pp. 3–4, 24–25.

63. For a Thomist understanding of this concept, see John Freccero, "Dante and the Neutral Angels," *Romanic Review* 51 (1960):3–14.

64. Walter Map, *De nugis curialium: Courtiers' Trifles*, ed. and trans. M. R. James, rev. C. N. L. Brooke and R. A. B. Mynors (Oxford: Clarendon Press, 1983), p. 355.

65. Jean-Patrice Boudet, "Les Condamnation de la magie à Paris en 1398," *Revue Mabillon*, n.s. 11/12 (2000–2001):151 (no. 25).

66. *Esclarmonde, Clarisse et Florent, Yde et Olive: Drei Fortsetzungen der Chanson von Huon de Bordeaux*, ed. Max Schweigel (Marburg: Elwert, 1889), pp. 118–20.

67. *The Boke of Duke Huon of Burdeux*, ed. S. L. Lee, 4 vols., EETS OS 40, 41, 43, 50 (London: Trübner, 1882–87), 2:592.

68. Harf-Lancner, *Fées au moyen âge*, p. 408.

69. The same motif appears in *Les Merveilles de Rigomer* and in *Ogier le Danois*; see Harf-Lancner, *Fées au moyen âge*, pp. 385–86.

70. *Thomas of Erceldoune*, ed. Nixon, 1:34 (Thornton MS).

71. For a similar scene, see Gerald of Wales, *Itinerarium Kambriae* (1:5), in [Gerald of Wales], *Giraldi Cambrensis Opera*, ed. J. S. Brewer, James F. Dimock, and George F. Warner, 8 vols., Rolls Series 21 (London: HMSO, 1861–91), 5:57.

72. *The English and Scottish Popular Ballads*, ed. Francis James Child, 5 vols., 2nd. corr. ed., ed. Mark F. Heiman and Laura Saxton Heiman (1883–98; Northfield, Minn.: Loomis House Press, 2001–11), no. 37A, sts. 12–14.

73. *Sidrak and Bokkus: A Parallel-Text Edition*, ed. T. L. Burton, EETS 311, 312 (Oxford: Oxford University Press, 1998, 1999), 2:546 (lines 8189–90). This is an addition to the French original: *Sydrac le philosophe: Le livre de la fontaine de toutes sciences*, ed. Ernstpeter Ruhe (Wiesbaden: Dr. Ludwig Reichert Verlag, 2000), p. 176 (para. 433).

74. Le Goff, *Imaginaire médiéval*, p. 104.

75. Sir John Mandeville, *Mandeville's Travels*, ed. M. C. Seymour (Oxford: Clarendon Press, 1967), p. 122 (chap. 17).

76. *Procès en nullité de la condamnation de Jeanne d'Arc*, ed. Pierre Duparc, 5 vols. (Paris: Société de l'histoire de France, 1977–88), 1:244–315. On this episode, see particularly Madeleine Jeay, "Clercs et paysans au XVe siècle: Une relecture de l'épisode de l'arbre au fées dans les procès de Jeanne d'Arc," in *Normes et pouvoir à la fin du moyen âge*, ed. Marie-Claude Déprez-Masson (Montreal: Editions CERES, 1989), pp. 145–63; Karen Sullivan, *The Interrogation of Joan of Arc* (Minneapolis: University of Minnesota Press, 1999), pp. 1–20.

77. *Procès de Condamnation de Jeanne d'Arc*, ed. Pierre Tisset and Yvonne Lanhers, 3 vols. (Paris: Société de l'histoire de France, 1960–71), 1:65–66 [Latin] and 2:65–68 [French].

78. Gui, *Manuel*, ed. Mollat, 2:22.

79. The English translation (ca. 1500) is taken from Jean d'Arras, *Melusine*, ed. Donald, p. 4. For the French, see Jean d'Arras, *Mélusine, ou la noble histoire de Lusignan*, ed. Jean-Jacques Vicensini (Paris: Librairie générale Française, 2003), p. 116.

80. See Gervase of Tilbury, *Otia imperialia,* ed. Banks and Binns, pp. 730–31; the reference is to Ps. 35:6 [36:7]: *Iudicia Dei abbissus multa.*

81. Gervase of Tilbury, *Les Traductions Françaises des Otia Imperialia*, ed. Cinzia Pignatelli and Dominique Gerner (Geneva: Droz, 2006).

82. Léopold Delisle, *Recherches sur la librairie de Charles V, Pt. II* (Paris: Champion, 1907), p. 126* (no. 776). See also Le Goff, *Pour un autre moyen âge*, p. 314n11.

83. Jean d'Arras, *Melusine,* ed. Donald, pp. 370–71; Jean d'Arras, *Mélusine,* ed. Vicensini, pp. 814–16.

84. Jean d'Arras, *Melusine,* ed. Donald, p. 320; Jean d'Arras, *Mélusine,* ed. Vicensini, p. 704.

85. [Coudrette], *The Romans of Partenay, or of Lusignen, Otherwise Known as the Tale of Melusine*, ed. Walter W. Skeat, EETS OS 22 (London: Kegan Paul, 1866), p. 135 (line 3879); [Coudrette], *Le roman de Mélusine, ou histoire de Lusignan*, ed. Eleanor Roach (Paris: Klincksieck, 1982), p. 247 (lines 4220–21).

86. Jean d'Arras, *Melusine,* ed. Donald, p. 369.

87. Kenneth Fowler, *Medieval Mercenaries*, 1 vol. (Oxford: Blackwell, 2001–), 1:16, 70–71, 297–99.

88. See Françoise Lehoux, *Jean de France, duc de Berri, sa vie, son action politique (1340–1416)*, 3 vols. (Paris: A. et J. Picard, 1966–68), 1:334n5 (for the capture of Cresswell), 344 (for the surrender of Lusignan).

89. Interestingly, Guillaume Larchevêque, Lord of Parthenay, patron of Coudrette's version of *Mélusine*, was involved in the ransom negotiations; see Lehoux, *Jean de France, duc de Berri*, 1:337.

90. Jean d'Arras, *Mélusine,* ed. Vicensini, pp. 810–12.

91. This Evan ("Yvain de Galles") seems to have been fighting on the French side; see Donald's note in Jean d'Arras, *Melusine,* ed. Donald, p. 386.

92. *Li romans de Claris et Laris*, ed. Johann Alton (Tübingen: Litterarischer Verein in Stuttgart, 1884), pp. 90–91.

93. Jeff Rider, "The Other Worlds of Romance," in *The Cambridge Companion to Medieval Romance*, ed. Roberta L. Kruger (Cambridge: Cambridge University Press, 2000), p. 129.

94. Cooper, *English Romance in Time*, p. 137.

95. Arthur C. L. Brown, "A Note on the *Nugae* of G. H. Gerould's 'King Arthur and Politics,'" *Speculum* 2 (1927):449.

96. *Le Roman de Rou*, ed. A. J. Holden, 3 vols., Société des anciens textes français (Paris: Firmin Didot, 1970–73). Although the forms of *soloir* at lines 6379 and 6387 are in the present tense, Holden suggests that they carry a past sense; see note in 3:202–3, line 3116.

97. Chrétien de Troyes, *Yvain (le Chevalier au lion)*, ed. T. B. W. Reid (Manchester: Manchester University Press, 1942), p. 17.

98. Huon de Méri, *Le Torneiment Anticrist*, ed. Margaret O. Bender, Romance Monographs, 7 (Jackson: University of Mississippi Press, 1976), lines 1076–79 (pp. 86–87), lines 552–61 (p. 73).

99. [Jacques de Vitry], *Libri duo, quorum prior Orientalis, sive Hierosolymitanae: Alter, Occientalis Historiae nomine inscribitur* (Douai: Balthazar Beller, 1596), pp. 215, 217.

100. This reference is to Henry of Marsburg; in his youth he had been on crusade, and he later accompanied Louis IX to the Holy Land, dying on the return journey in 1254. See O'Daniel, *First Disciples*, pp. 442–48.

101. This is a reference to John of Wildeshausen; See O'Daniel, *First Disciples*, pp. 469–86.

102. "Fratrem Henricum Theutonicum, quondam Lectorem fratrum Predicatorum in Colonia, virum in omni scientia cum sanctitate conspicuum, de quo superius fecimus mentionem, attestantibus fratribus, narrantem quod subjungo audivi. Cum quidam frater nobilis genere et rebus pollens, de Britannie partibus, ordinem Predicatorum intrasset, apud Lugdunum Galliae cum fratribus morabatur; appropinquante autem tempore professionis suae petivit a priore suo redire ad terram suam, ut disponeret de rebus suis; et annuit prior, cum eoque iter arripuit. Cumque venissent in deserta Britannie, dixit frater novitius priori suo: 'Vultis videre antiquum illud Britannie miraculum?' Et prior: 'Quod est illud?' Et frater illum ducens ad fontem lucidissimum, super quem lapis, instar altaris, in columnis marmoreis locabatur, aquam protinus superfudit. Nec mora, contenebrato celo, coeperunt nubes concurrere, mugire tonitrua, imbres ruere, fulgura coruscare, statimque tanta inundatio facta est, ut circa locum ad leucam unam tota terra obrui videretur. Quod ut vidit prior miratus est, et audiente dicto fratre Henrico, magistro ordinis beate memorie, fratri Joanni Epicopo, et aliis pluribus fratris enarravit. Hoc idem audivi a patre meo ante annos quadraginta, qui illis in partibus sub rege Richardo Angliae militavit. Haec cum dictus frater Henricus mihi et multis aliis recitaret, quaesivi vnde ista fieri potuissent? Et respondit, quod arte magica, ignota modo hominibus, et ministerio demonum, qui ad tempestates et pluvias aera possunt impellere et concitare cum volunt, occulto tamen Dei iudicio permittente" (pp. 559–60).

103. Geoffrey Chaucer, *The Riverside Chaucer*, ed. Larry D. Benson et al. (Boston: Houghton Mifflin, 1987), p. 359.

104. *English Wycliffite Sermons, I*, ed. Anne Hudson (Oxford: Clarendon Press, 1983), p. 686.

105. Nicholas Orme, "An English Grammar School ca. 1450: Latin Exercises from Exeter (Caius College MS 417/447, Folios 16v–24v)," *Traditio* 50 (1995):280 (C20).

106. "Item, joignant la dicte fontayne y a une grosse pierre que on nomme le perron de Bellenton, et toutes les foiz que le seigneur de Monfort vient à la dicte fontayne et de l'eau d'icelle arouse et moulle le dit perron, quelque challeur temps assuré de pluye, quelque part que soit le vent et que chacun pourroit dire que le temps ne seroit aucunement disposé à pluye, tantost et en peu d'espace aucunes foiz plus tost que le dit seigneur ne aura peu recoupvrez son chasteau de Comper, aultres foiz tost plus tart, et que que soit ains que soit le fin d'icelui jour, pleut ou pays habundaument que la terre et les biens estans en ycelle en son arousez et moult leur prouffite"; see *Cartulaire de l'Abbaye de Redon en Bretagne*, ed. Aurélien de Courson (Paris: Imprimerie impériale, 1863), p. ccclxxxvi.

107. Roger Sherman Loomis, "Breton Folklore and Arthurian Romance," *Comparative Literature* 2 (1950):300.

108. "Denique hoc vasculum materiae incognitae, coloris insoliti, et formae inustitatae Henrico seniori Anglorum regi pro magno munere oblatum est, ac deinde fratri reginae, Davidi scilicet regi Scottorum contraditum annis plurimis in thesauris Scotiae servatum est; et ante annos aliquot, sicut veraci relatione cognovimus, Henrico secundo illud aspicere cupienti a rege Scottorum Willelmo resignatum est"; see William of Newburgh, *The History of English Affairs, Bk I*, ed. and trans. P. G. Walsh and M. J. Kennedy (Warminster: Aris & Phillips, 1988), pp. 120–21 (1:28).

109. Map, *De nugis curialium*, ed. James, pp. 156–57.

110. See Nancy Partner, *Serious Entertainments: The Writing of History in Twelfth-Century England* (Chicago: University of Chicago Press, 1977), pp. 114–40.

111. William of Newburgh, *History of English Affairs*, ed. Walsh and Kennedy, pp. 28–37 (*Proemium*).

112. Map, *De nugis curialium*, ed. James, pp. 154–55.

113. Antoine de la Sale, *Le Paradis de la Reine Sibylle*, ed. Fernand Desonay (Paris: Droz, 1930), p. 55 (the account of the German knight's visit is on pp. 23–41).

114. For a folklorist's comparison of the two sets of belief, see Peter M. Rojcewicz, "Between One Eye Blink and the Next: Fairies, UFOs and the Problems of Knowledge," in *The Good People: New Folklore Essays*, ed. Peter Narváez (1991; Lexington: University Press of Kentucky, 1997), pp. 479–514. For an excellent account of modern alien beliefs, see Susan A. Clancy, *Abducted: How People Come to Believe They Were Kidnapped by Aliens* (Cambridge, Mass.: Harvard University Press, 2005). James Wade prints a remarkable fourteenth-century fairy parallel in "Abduction, Surgery, Madness."

115. Purkiss, *At the Bottom of the Garden*, p. 3 (cf. pp. 319–20).

CHAPTER 2

1. Cf. John H. Arnold, *Belief and Unbelief in Medieval Europe* (London: Hodder, 2005), pp. 9–13.

2. Gurevich, *Medieval Popular Culture*, p. xv.

3. Peter Burke, *Popular Culture in Early Modern Europe*, rev. ed. (Aldershot: Scolar Press, 1994), pp. 23–24.

4. Le Goff, for one, seems prepared to accept such a model for the early Middle Ages: "although there were great differences in degree in the culture of clerics, it was a culture of a single kind, and the important division was between clerics and laymen"; see Jacques Le Goff, *Time, Work, & Culture in the Middle Ages*, trans. Arthur Goldhammer (1977; Chicago: University of Chicago Press, 1980), p. 155.

5. John Van Engen, "The Christian Middle Ages as an Historiographical Problem," *American Historical Review* 91 (1986):530.

6. See Jean-Claude Schmitt's response to Van Engen in *Religione, folklore e società nell'occidente medievale* (Bari: Laterza, 1988), pp. 1–20, conveniently available (trans. Lucia Carle) in *Debating the Middle Ages: Issues and Reading*, ed. Lester K. Little and Barbara H. Rosenwein (Malden, Mass.: Blackwell, 1999), pp. 376–87.

7. "Today's folklorists also view folklore as the unofficial culture *of any group*, not just the poor or old-fashioned"; see Carl Lindahl, "Folklore," in *Medieval Folklore: A Guide to Myths,*

Legends, Tales, Beliefs, and Customs, ed. Carl Lindahl, John McNamara, and John Lindow, 2 vols. (Oxford: Oxford University Press, 2002), 1:334.

8. Le Goff, *Pour un autre moyen âge,* p. 328. See also Jean-Claude Schmitt, "Les 'Superstitions,'" in *Histoire de la France religieuse, 1,* ed. Jacques Le Goff and René Rémond (Paris: Seuil, 1988), pp. 497–99.

9. Jan R. Veenstra, *Magic and Divination at the Courts of Burgundy and France* (New York: Brill, 1997), pp. 93, 122 n100. For a possible reading of the *Bal des suvages* as "a fictive recovery of wildness that actually enhances courtly status," see Susan Crane, *The Performance of Self: Ritual, Clothing, and Identity During the Hundred Years War* (Philadelphia: University of Pennsylvania Press, 2002), pp. 155–62.

10. William R. Jones, "Political Uses of Sorcery in Medieval Europe," *Historian* 34 (1972):670–87.

11. Angela Bourke, *The Burning of Bridget Cleary* (New York: Penguin, 2001). See also Simon Young, "Some Notes on Irish Fairy Changelings in Nineteenth-Century Newspapers," *Béascna* 8 (2013):34–47.

12. Augustine, *City of God,* 4:548–49 (15:23).

13. Gervase of Tilbury, *Otia imperialia,* ed. Banks and Binns, p. 729.

14. Gervase of Tilbury, *Traductions Françaises des Otia Imperialia,* ed. Pignatelli and Gerner, pp. 327, 328.

15. Gervase of Tilbury, *Otia imperialia,* ed. Banks and Binns, pp. 670–73.

16. A possible, though perhaps tendentious, translation of *antiquorum* 'people of old' might be 'the ancient ones'; [William of Auvergne], *De Universo,* II. iii, 12 (1674 ed., 1:1037a), tells us that in Spain the wild horde was known as the *exercitus antiquus,* 'the ancient army.'

17. He had been involved in the surrender of Saint-Maur (1371), Moncontour, Soubise (1372), Chizé, and Niort (1373) to du Guesclin; see Fowler, *Medieval Mercenaries,* 1:296–98.

18. *La chanson de Bertrand Du Guesclin de Cuvelier,* ed. Jean-Claude Faucon, 3 vols. (Toulouse: Editions universitaires du Sud, ca.1990), 1:58; the later MS variant *c'estoit destinee* (for *c'estoit une fee*) implies that she had merely learned from the fairies (see 2:200).

19. Antoine de la Sale, *Paradis de la Reine Sibylle,* ed. Desonay, p. 55.

20. *Procès en nullité,* ed. Duparc, 1:300–301.

21. There is no sign of a Peter Gravier in Georges Poull's *Le Château et les seigneurs de Bourlémont, 1149–1412* (Corbeil-Essonnes: private ed., 1962), nor of a woman called "Fée"; an early thirteenth-century Sieur de Bourlémont, Pierre II, had married someone called Felicité, however, and his son Joffroi's wife was called Sibylle.

22. Madeleine Jeay, "Clercs et paysans," p. 161, calls it an "avatar des légendes mélusiniennes," an example of "le bricolage culturel" at work.

23. *Procès en nullité,* ed. Duparc, 1:260, 267, 272, 283.

24. See Robert Bartlett, *England Under the Norman and Angevin Kings, 1075–1225* (Oxford: Clarendon Press, 2000), p. 692.

25. Ferlampin-Acher, *Fées, bestes et luitons,* p. 16.

26. Le Goff, *L'imaginaire médiéval,* p. 35.

27. Le Goff, *L'imaginaire médiéval,* pp. 103–6.

28. See Hall, *Elves in Anglo-Saxon England.*

29. See C. P. Wormald, "The Uses of Literacy in Anglo-Saxon England and Its Neighbours," *Transactions of the Royal Historical Society* 27 (1977):104–5.

30. Bernadette Filotas, *Pagan Survivals, Superstitions and Popular Cultures in Early Medieval Pastoral Literature* (Toronto: Pontifical Institute of Mediaeval Studies, 2005), p. 358.

31. Le Goff, *Time, Work, & Culture*, p. 185.

32. R. W. Southern, "Between Heaven and Hell: Review of Jacques le Goff, *La Naissance du Purgatoire*," *Times Literary Supplement*, 18 June, 1982, p. 652. Southern would date this shift rather earlier than Le Goff.

33. [William of Auvergne], *De Universo*, II. iii, 12 (1674 ed., 1:1036bF), 24 (p. 1066 bG), 25 (p. 1072bH).

34. Étienne de Bourbon says that this peasant "portaret facem lignorum ad lunum" [would have carried a bundle of wood to the moon]; see *Anecdotes historiques, légendes, et apologues tirés du recueil inédit d'Étienne de Bourbon*, ed. A. Lecoy de la Marche, Société de l'histoire de France (Paris: Renouard, 1877), p. 321. A popular verse quoted by Alexander Neckham may help explain this: *Rusticus in luna, quem sarcina deprimit una, / Monstrat per spinas nulli prodesse rapinas* [The man in the moon with his burden of wood, / learns from its prickles that thieving's no good]; see Neckam, *De Naturis rerum*, ed. Thomas Wright (London: Longman, 1863), p. 54.

35. [Étienne de Bourbon], *Anecdotes historiques,* ed. de la Marche, pp. 316, 321, 326.

36. Filotas, *Pagan Survivals*, p. 358.

37. Le Goff, *L'imaginaire médiéval*, pp. 35, 38.

38. Le Goff, *L'imaginaire médiéval*, p. 106.

39. See Schmitt, "Superstitions," pp. 510–23.

40. See Michael D. Bailey, *Fearful Spirits, Reasoned Follies: The Boundaries of Superstition in Late Medieval Europe* (Ithaca, N.Y.: Cornell University Press, 2013).

41. [Burchard of Worms], *Bussordnungen*, ed. Wasserschleben, p. 658 (no. 140). See also *Patrologia Latina*, 140:971C.

42. *Malleus maleficarum*, ed. and trans. Christopher S. Mackay, 2 vols. (Cambridge: Cambridge University Press, 2006), 2:366 (1:504).

43. Wade, *Fairies in Medieval Romance*, pp. 30–38.

44. David R. Carlson, *Chaucer's Jobs* (New York: Palgrave Macmillan, 2004).

45. *Partonopeu de Blois*, ed. Olivier Collet and Pierre-Marie Joris ([Paris]: Livre de poche, 2005), p. 276 (lines 3823–24); [*Partonope of Blois*], *The Middle English Versions of Partonope of Blois*, ed. A. Trampe Bödtker, EETS ES 109 (London: Kegan Paul, 1912), p. 188 (lines 5000–5001).

46. *The Elucidation: A Prologue to the Conte del Graal*, ed. Albert Wilder Thompson (New York: Institute of French Studies, 1931), pp. 88–89.

47. Cf. Alan Fletcher's analysis of the competing discourses in *Sir Orfeo* in "*Sir Orfeo* and the Flight from the Enchanters," *Studies in the Age of Chaucer* 22 (2000):141–78.

48. Chaucer, *Riverside Chaucer*, pp. 116–17.

49. Chaucer, *Riverside Chaucer*, pp. 124–25. D. W. Robertson's two explanations (folkloric and pastoral) for the devil's wearing green ("Why the Devil Wears Green," *Modern Language Notes* 69 [1954]:470–72) do not strike me as being incommensurable.

50. Przemyslaw Mroczkowski, "Incubi and Friars," *Kwartalnik Neofilologiczny* 8 (1961):191–92. There is a better text in Stephen L. Forte, "A Cambridge Dominican Collector of Exempla in the Thirteenth Century," *Archivum Fratrum Praedicatorum* 28 (1958):132 (no. 137).

51. Gobi, *Scala Coeli*, ed. Polo de Beaulieu, pp. 267–68 (no. 248).

52. *Liber exemplorum ad usum praedicantium saeculo XIII*, ed. A. G. Little (Aberdeen: Typis academicis, 1908), pp. 85–86. I am grateful to Alan Fletcher for bringing this passage to my attention.

53. See [William of Auvergne], *De Universo*, II. iii, 24 (1674 ed., 1:1065bBff.): Cujus modi sunt isti spiritus per modum exercitus apparentes?

54. *English Conquest of Ireland, A.D. 1166–1185, Mainly from the 'Expugnatio hibernica' of Giraldus Cambrensis*, ed. F. J. Furnivall, EETS OS 107 (London: Kegan Paul, 1896), p. 17.

55. John Capgrave, *Abbreuiacion of Chonicles*, ed. Peter J. Lucas, EETS 285 (London: Oxford University Press, 1983), p. 221.

56. *Liber exemplorum*, ed. Little, p. 86.

57. One of the fullest accounts of fairy activities written in England, for instance, is a chapter ("on the tricks of demons") in Ranulph Higden's treatment of the First Commandment: *Speculum Curatorum: A Mirror for Curates, Book I*, Dallas Medieval Texts and Translations, 13.1, ed. and trans. Eugene Crook and Margaret Jennings (Leuven: Peeters, 2012), pp. 124–37.

58. [Jean d'Outremeuse], *Ly Myreur des histors, chronique de Jean des Preis dit d'Outremeuse*, ed. Stanislas Bormans and Adolfe Borgnet, 7 vols. (Brussels: Académie royale de Belgique, 1877), 4:56.

59. Chaucer, *Riverside Chaucer*, p. 72.

60. E. T. Donaldson, "The Miller's Tale, A 3483–86," *Modern Language Notes* 69 (1954):310–13.

61. *Procès en nullité*, ed. Duparc, 1:254.

62. *Procès en nullité*, ed. Duparc, 1:286. Of those testifying in Domrémy, Stephen de Syon (a priest) and Louis de Martigny (a squire) also deny knowing anything, but they do not seem to have been locals (pp. 262–63, 265–66). More interesting is a third priest, Dominic Jacob, who, though no longer living there, seems to have been brought up in Domrémy; he recalls the dancing and picnicking at the tree but has nothing to say about fairies (p. 256).

63. This fact is only occasionally acknowledged; see, for example, J. A. MacCulloch, *Medieval Faith and Fable* (Boston: Jones, 1932), p. 28; Cameron, *Enchanted Europe*, p. 42.

64. [Caesarius of Heisterbach], *Dialogus miraculorum*, ed. Strange, 1:277 (5:2).

65. Chestre, *Launfal*, ed. Bliss, p. 61.

66. *Aucassin et Nicolette, chantefable du XIIIe siècle*, ed. Mario Roques (Paris: Champion, 1929), p. 23 (22:30–31).

67. *William of Palerne: An Electronic Edition*, ed. G. H. V. Bunt (Ann Arbor: University of Michigan Press, 2002), lines 229–30. In the French original (lines 423–24), it is because William is all alone that the emperor thinks he is a fairy; see *Guillaume de Palerne, roman du XIIIe siècle*, ed. Alexandre Micha (Geneva: Droz, 1990), p. 51.

68. "Mout bele e ascemee / Si resemble ben fee" (lines 511–12); see [*Lai du Cor*], *The Anglo-Norman Text of 'Le Lai du Cor,'* ed. C. T. Erickson, ANTS, 24 (Oxford: Blackwell, 1973), p. 46.

69. *Wars of Alexander: An Alliterative Romance*, ed. Walter W. Skeat, EETS ES 47 (London: Trübner, 1886), p. 263 (lines 5257–58).

70. John Gower, *The Complete Works of John Gower: The French Works*, ed. G. C. Macaulay (Oxford: Clarendon Press, 1899), p. 60 (*Balade*, 27, line 22).

71. "El fu si cointe et si tifee, / El resembloit deesse ou fee"; see *Le Roman de la rose*, ed. Daniel Poirion (Paris: Garnier-Flammarion, 1974), p. 124 (lines 3427–28). Cf. *The Romaunt of the Rose*, lines 3713–15 (Chaucer, *Riverside Chaucer*, p. 726). The goddesses who vie for the judgment of Paris in *The Seege or Batayle of Troye*, ed. Mary Elizabeth Barnicle, EETS OS 172 (London: Oxford University Press, 1927), p. 40, are described as "ffoure ladies of eluene land" (line 508).

72. Cf. Gower's description of Medea, "In sondri wise hir forme changeth, / Sche semeth faie and no wommman," in John Gower, *The English Works of John Gower*, ed. G. C. Macaulay, 2 vols., EETS ES 81, 82 (London: Oxford University Press, 1900, 1901), 2:58 (*Confessio Amantis*, bk. 4, line 4105).

73. *Thomas of Erceldoune*, ed. Nixon, 1:36 (Thornton MS, lines 139–40).

74. *Itinerarium Kambriae* (1:5), in [Gerald of Wales], *Giraldi Cambrensis Opera*, vol. 5, ed. James F. Dimock, Rolls Series 21 (London: HMSO, 1868), p. 57.

75. Interestingly, in a late manuscript of *Thomas of Erceldoune* (B.L., MS Lansdowne 762), the hero suspects a demonic delusion: "Sche woxe so grym and so stowte / The dewyll he wende she had be" (lines 143–44). The lady immediately denies it, however—"fende of hell am I none" (line 150)—and the fact that neither his conjuring at this point nor his prayers to Mary (Thornton and Cambridge MSS) and Jesus (Lansdowne and Cambridge MSS) a few lines later have any effect on her suggests that this view is the poet's.

76. See further Angelica Rieger, " 'Dame plus bele que fée': Une expression proverbiale et son histoire dans les littératures française et occitane du moyen âge," in *Die Welt der Feen im Mittlealter / Le monde des fées dans la culture mediévale*, ed. Danielle Buschinger and Wolfgang Spiewok, Greifswalder Beiträge zum Mittelalter 32 (Greifswald: Reineke-Verlag, 1994), pp. 143–61; Wade, *Fairies in Medieval Romance*, p. 154n9.

77. Technically, Melior is a sorceress rather than a fairy. This rather lame rationalization will be discussed in the next chapter.

78. [*Partonope of Blois*], *Middle English Versions of Partonope*, ed. Trampe Bödtker, p. 42. For the French original, which treats the scene as a whole more concisely, see *Partonopeu de Blois*, ed. Collet and Joris, pp. 134–35 (lines 1282–1301).

79. *Lay de Tydorel*, lines 69–71, in *Lais féeriques des XII*^{e} *et XIII*^{e} *siècles*, ed. Alexandre Micha (Paris: Flammarion, 1992), pp. 154–55.

80. *Lancelot do Lac: The Non-cyclic Old French Prose Romance*, ed. Elspeth Kennedy, 2 vols. (Oxford: Clarendon Press, 1980), 1:21.

81. [William of Auvergne], *De Universo*, II. iii, 2 (1674 ed., 1:1018aE).

82. *South English Legendary*, ed. D'Evelyn and Mill, 2:409.

83. Map, *De nugis curialium*, ed. James, pp. 158–59.

84. The author of *Lancelot do Lac* points out that Niniene could not have deceived Merlin when he was asleep if he had not been half-human: "car deiables ne puet dormir" (ed. Kennedy, 1:23).

85. *Le procès de Guichard, évêque de Troyes (1308–1313)*, ed. Abel Rigault (Paris: A. Picard, 1896), pp. 126–27. On the penchant of incubi demons for women with beautiful hair, see [William of Auvergne], *De Universo*, II. iii, 25 (1674 ed., 1:1072bE); Higden, *Speculum Curatorum*, ed. Crook and Jennings, pp. 134–35; Joseph Hansen, *Quellen und Untersuchungen zur des Hexenwahns* (Hildesheim: Georg Olms, 1963), p. 86.

86. Stephens, *Demon Lovers*, esp. pp. 63ff. See also Elliott, *Fallen Bodies*, p. 33; Maaike van der Lugt, *Le ver, le démon et la vierge: Les théories médiévales de la génération extraordinaire* (Paris: Les Belles Lettres, 2004), pp. 279ff. As we shall see in the next chapter, the theory did not originate with Aquinas.

87. Lewis, *Discarded Image*, p. 122.

88. Martianus Capella, *De nuptiis Philologiae et Mercurii*, ed. Adolfus Dick (Stuttgart: Teubner, 1969), p. 69 (lines 11–12); [Bernard Silvestris], *Bernardi Silvestris de Mundi Universitate*, ed. Carl Sigmund Barach and Johann Wrobel (Frankfurt: Unveränderter Nachdruck, 1964), p. 50 (7:116).

89. [Matthew Paris], *Matthæi Parisiensis, monachi Sancti Albani, Chronica Maiora*, ed. Henry R. Luard, 7 vols., Rolls Series (London: HMSO, 1872–83), 5:82. See also Matthew Paris, *Historia Anglorum* (London, B.L., MS Royal 14C. VII, f. 146^r): "Cuius mater in puerperio miserabiliter est exanimata."

90. Elioxe, despite having inherited nine cities and fifty castles from her father (lines 221–23), lives in a cave under a mountain—"Es cavernes del mont la ot abitement" (line 166)—and is specifically called a *fée* at line 1635; see *Elioxe*, ed. Emanuel J. Mickel, Jr., in *The Old French Crusade Cycle I: La naissance du Chevalier au cygne* ([Tuscaloosa]: University of Alabama Press, 1977), pp. 1–129.

91. *Boke of Duke Huon of Burdeux*, ed. Lee, 1:267. In the thirteenth-century verse original, Auberon says he does not wish to live longer—"je ne vuelz plux es ciecle demoreir" (line 10756)—nor does he choose to remain in fairyland—"En faerie ne veul plus arrester" (line 10760); see *Huon de Bordeaux, chanson de geste du XIIIe siècle*, ed. William W. Kibler, trans. François Suard (Paris: Champion, 2003), p. 592.

92. [William of Auvergne], *De Universo*, II. iii, 24 (1674 ed., 1:1029bD–30aE).

93. *Fatati* here evidently means something more than simply 'fated,' a sense William had discussed earlier; see [William of Auvergne], *De Universo* I. iii, 24 (1:791aD). Perhaps *milites fatati* resembled in some way the *benandanti* discussed by Carlo Ginzburg, *The Night Battles: Witchcraft and Agrarian Cults in the Sixteenth and Seventeenth Centuries*, trans. John and Anne Tedeschi (Baltimore: Johns Hopkins University Press, 1992).

94. [William of Auvergne], *De Universo*, II. iii, 24 (1674 ed., 1:1065bB–66bF).

95. [Ranulph Higden], *Polychronicon Ranulphi Higden monachi Cestrensis: Together with the English Translations of John Trevisa*, ed. Churchill Babington et al., 9 vols., Rolls Series (London: Longman, 1865–86), 1:421.

96. *Boke of Huon of Burdeux*, ed. Lee, 2:598–99.

97. Cf. *Esclarmonde*, ed. Schweigel, lines 2854–3139 (pp. 120–23).

98. She calls "l'immortalité . . . le privilège des êtres surnaturels"; see Harf-Lancner, *Fées au moyen âge*, p. 416.

99. *Lancelot do Lac*, ed. Kennedy, 1:21.

100. [John of Salisbury], *Frivolities of Courtiers and Footprints of Philosophers: Being a Translation of the First, Second, and Third Books and Selections from the Seventh and Eighth Books of the* Policraticus *of John of Salisbury*, trans. Joseph B. Pike (Minneapolis: University of Minnesota Press, 1938), p. 234.

101. William of Newburgh, *History of English Affairs*, ed. Walsh and Kennedy, pp. 28–31 (*Proemium*).

102. *Thomas of Erceldoune*, ed. Nixon, 1:50 (Thornton MS, lines 318–19).

103. "Als y yod on a Mounday," in Peter Langtoft, *The Chronicle*, ed. Thomas Wright, 2 vols., Rolls Series (London: Longmans, Green, 1866, 1868), 2:452–67. This poem is related to the later ballad "The Wee Wee Man" (in *English and Scottish Popular Ballads*, ed. Child, no. 38); see E. B. Lyle, "*The Wee Wee Man* and *Als y yod on a Mounday*," in *Ballad Studies*, ed. E. B. Lyle (Cambridge: D. S. Brewer, 1976), pp. 21–28.

104. Antoine de la Sale, *Le Paradis de la reine Sibylle*, ed. Desonay. "Sibile, distant relative of the ancient Sybil, is one of the guises of the medieval fairy"; see Anne Paupert, *Les Fileuses et le clerc: Une étude des Evangiles des Quenouilles* (Paris: Champion, 1990), p. 214.

105. [*Lucydarye*], *Late Middle English* Lucydarye, ed. Morrison, p. 53. Cf. "Les dittes fees disoient que les gens estoyent destinés les ungz a bien, les autres a mal selon le cours du ciel et de nature, comme se ung enfant naissoit de telle heure et en tel cours il luy estoit destiné qu'il seroit pendu ou neyé ou qu'il seroit riche ou povre ou qu'il espouseroit une telle femme, lesquelles choses sont faulce, car l'omme a en soy liberal arbitre et volunté franche de faire bien ou mal tellement que s'il veult, il ne fera pas chose pour quoy il soit pendu ne ne se mettra pas au dangier destre neyé, n'espousera ja femme s'il ne le veult faire; et ainsi ses destinacions seront

faulces. Et par ces raisons on n'y doit point adjouster de foy"; see [*Second Lucidaire*], ed. Ruhe, in *Gelehrtes Wissen,* p. 293 [Druck I].

106. Even if this attribution is false, the prophecies that bear his name were closely identified with the Augustinian priory of Bridlington; see A. G. Rigg, "John of Bridlington's *Prophesy*: A New Look," *Speculum* 63 (1988):596–613.

107. See *The Divination of Demons,* 7, in Saint Augustine, *Treatises of Marriage and Other Subjects,* ed. Roy J. Deferrari (New York: Fathers of the Church, 1955), p. 426. A more cautious position is taken in Augustine, *City of God,* 3:232–38 (9:22); and Saint Augustine, *De Doctrina Christiana,* 2:23 (Saint Augustine, *On Christian Doctrine,* trans. D. W. Robertson [New York: Bobbs-Merrill, 1958], pp. 58–59). See also Veenstra, *Magic and Divination,* pp. 249–53, for a summary of Augustine's views in an early fifteenth-century tract, *Le Traitié contre les divineurs,* 1, 7.

108. [William of Auvergne], *De Universo,* II. iii, 25 (1674 ed., 1:1072aH).

109. *Boke of Huon of Burdeux,* ed. Lee, 2:605. The romance contains even more bizarre conflations of Christian and fairy belief than this; see Albert Gier, "Comment on devient fée: La féerie chrétienne d'*Esclamonde*," in *Die Welt der Feen im Mittlealter / Le monde des fées dans la culture mediévale,* ed. Danielle Buschinger and Wolfgang Spiewok, Greifswalder Beiträge zum Mittelalter 32 (Greifswald: Reineke-Verlag, 1994), pp. 59–66.

110. Jean d'Arras, *Melusine,* ed. Donald, p. 316.

111. *Medieval English Romances,* ed. A. V. C. Schmidt and Nicolas Jacobs, 2 vols. (London: Hodder and Stoughton, 1980), 2:57–88.

112. *The Breton Lays in Middle English,* ed. Thomas C. Rumble (Detroit: Wayne State University Press, 1965), pp. 46–78.

113. *Sire Degarré,* ed. Gustav Schleich (Heidelberg: Carl Winter's Universitätsbuchhandlung, 1929), p. 62.

114. In the Cambridge manuscript this reads, "a paire of gloues / That were sende hur owt of Elues lande" (*Sire Degarré,* ed. Schleich, p. 68).

115. See Cooper, *English Romance in Time,* pp. 332–40.

116. *Lybeaus Desconus,* ed. M. Mills, EETS OS 261 (London: Oxford University Press, 1969).

117. Renaut de Beaujeu, *Le Bel Inconnu,* ed. G. Perrie Williams (Paris: Champion, 1929).

118. *Lybeaus Desconus,* ed. Mills, p. 75 (line 9).

119. *Lybeaus Desconus,* ed. Mills, p. 165 (lines 1485–96).

120. *Lybeaus Desconus,* ed. Mills, p. 164 (line 1432). The reading *fantasme* is partially supported by one other manuscript, Lincoln's Inn MS Hale 150, which reads *fantume* (*Lybeaus Desconus,* ed. Mills, p. 272).

121. It may even be observed in chronicle writing. Carl Watkins has recently shown how later redactions and manuscript copies of William of Newburgh, a writer interested in fairy material, tend to omit it or tone it down; see Carl Watkins, "Fascination and Anxiety in Medieval Wonder Stories," in *The Unorthodox Imagination in Late Medieval Britain,* ed. Sophie Page (Manchester: Manchester University Press, 2010), pp. 55–56.

122. Another example occurs in the Percy folio's version of *Sir Lambewell,* where the fact that Tryamour's father was "kyng of Fayrye" is omitted, as is the fact that she spirits her mortal lover off "ynto Fayrye" at the end. Cf. "He fond yn þe pauyloun, / Þe kynges douȝter of Olyroun, / Dame Tryamour þat hyȝte; / Her fader was kynge of Fayrye, / Of occient, fer & nyȝe, / A man of mochell myȝte" (Chestre, *Launfal,* ed. Bliss, lines 276–82) with "For sooth there was in that pavillion / The Kings daugter of Million" (*Sir Lambewell,* lines 113–14) and

"Þus Launfal, wythouten fable, / Þat noble kny3t of þe Rounde Table / Was take ynto Fayrye" (Chestre, *Launfal*, ed. Bliss, lines 1033–35) with "And shee brought Sir Lambewell from Carlile / Farr into a jolly iland / That clipped was Amilion" (*Sir Lambewell*, lines 618–20). See *Sir Lambewell*, in *The Percy Folio of Old English Ballads and Romances*, ed. Frederick James Furnivall and John Wesley Hales, 4 vols. (London: De la More, 1905–10), 1:81–98.

123. *A Royal Historie of the Excellent Knight Generide*s, ed. Frederick J. Furnivall (London: Roxburghe Club, 1865).

124. Sara Sturm, *The Lay of Guingamor: A Study* (Chapel Hill: University of North Carolina Press, 1968), p. 72. For *Guingamor* (line 393) and *Tydorel* (lines 434–36), see *Lais féeriques*, ed. Micha, pp. 86, 176.

125. Sarah-Grace Heller, "Obscure Lands and Obscured Hands: Fairy Embroidery and the Ambiguous Vocabulary of Medieval Textile Decoration," *Medieval Clothing and Textiles* 5 (2009):15–35.

126. *Chaucerian and Other Pieces (A Supplement to the Complete Works of Geoffrey Chaucer)*, ed. Walter W. Skeat (Oxford: Clarendon Press, 1897), p. 443. See also the passage from the *Roman de Troie* cited by Heller, "Obscure Lands," pp. 34–35. Professor Heller has suggested to me that the allusion may be to shot silk.

127. *The Saga of Tristram and Ísönd*, trans. Paul Schach (Lincoln: University of Nebraska Press, 1973), p. 95. Cf. *Le Roman de* Tristan *par Thomas*, ed. Joseph Bédier, 2 vols., Société des anciens textes français (Paris: Firmin Didot, 1902, 1905), 1:218–19.

128. Sir Thomas Malory, *Works*, ed. Eugène Vinaver, 2nd ed., 3 vols. (London: Oxford University Press, 1971), 1:348. Cf. "The Boy and the Mantle," in *English and Scottish Popular Ballads*, ed. Child, no. 29, sts. 11, 12.

129. See especially Roger Sherman Loomis, *Arthurian Tradition and Chrétien de Troyes* (New York: Columbia University Press, 1949).

130. Arthur C. L. Brown, "The Grail and the English *Sir Perceval*," *Modern Philology* 16 (1918–19):553–68; 17 (1919–20):361–82; 18 (1920–21):201–28, 661–73; 22 (1924–25):79–98, 113–32.

131. Lucienne Carasso-Bulow, *The Merveilleux in Chrétien de Troyes' Romances* (Geneva: Droz, 1976), p. 83.

132. *The High Book of the Grail*, trans. Nigel Bryant (Cambridge: D. S. Brewer, 1978), pp. 144, 177–78; *Le Haut Livre du Graal: Perlesvaus*, ed. William A. Nitze and T. Atkinson Jenkins, 2 vols. (Chicago: University of Chicago Press, 1932), 1:222, 277.

133. [Étienne de Bourbon], *Anecdotes historiques*, ed. Lecoy de la Marche, p. 321 (no. 365).

134. *The Elucidation*, ed. Thompson, pp. 87–89 (lines 29–113); see also Thompson's introduction, pp. 37–50.

135. Thomas, *Religion and the Decline of Magic*, p. 726.

136. From the prologue to the *Lay le Freyne* in the Auchinleck MS. A. J. Bliss has argued that these lines are scribal, not authorial (*Sir Orfeo*, ed. Bliss, pp. xlvii–viii), but for my purposes their source hardly matters.

137. *Lais féeriques*, ed. Micha, pp. 64, 106, 182.

138. *Sir Gowther*, in *Six Middle English Romances*, ed. Maldwyn Mills (London: J. M. Dent, 1973), pp. 148–68.

139. *Lais féeriques*, ed. Micha, pp. 152–79.

140. *Lancelot do Lac*, ed. Kennedy, 1:23.

141. [*Partonope of Blois*], *Middle English Versions of Partonope*, ed. Bödtker, p. 36 (lines 1341–47; cf. lines 1883–1906); *Boke of Huon of Burdeux*, ed. Lee, 1:76.

142. *Yonec*, lines 149–54, 162–63, in Marie de France, *Lais*, ed. Alfred Ewart, introd. Glyn S. Burgess (Bristol: Bristol Classical Press, 1995), pp. 85–86; *Lai de Désiré*, lines 387–90, in *Lais féeriques*, ed. Micha, p. 128.

143. Map, *De nugis curialium*, ed. James, pp. 348–49; cf. Gervase of Tilbury, *Otia imperialia*, ed. Banks and Binns, pp. 664–65.

144. [*Richard the Lionheart*], *Der mittelenglische Versroman über Richard Löwenherz*, ed. Karl Brunner (Vienna and Leipzig: Wilhelm Braumüller, 1913), p. 89, lines 185–94.

145. For other accounts, see Harf-Lancner, *Fées au moyen âge*, p. 392n28.

146. Cooper, *English Romance in Time*, p. 174.

147. See Linda Dégh, *Legend and Belief: Dialectics of a Folklore Genre* (Bloomington: Indiana University Press, 2001), pp. 6–9.

148. See Valette, *Poétique du merveilleux*, pp. 118–26.

149. Robin G. Collingwood, *The Philosophy of Enchantment: Studies in Folktale, Cultural Criticism, and Anthropology* (Oxford: Clarendon Press, 2005), p. 129.

150. Cooper, *English Romance in Time*, p. 178.

151. Hans-Robert Jauss, "Theorie der Gattungen und Literatur des Mittelalters," *Grundriss der romanischen Literaturen des Mittelalters* 1 (Generalités) (1972):124–25; the quotation is taken from the abridged translation in *Modern Genre Theory*, ed. David Duff (London: Longman, 2000), p. 132.

152. D. S. Brewer, "The Interpretation of Fairy Tales," in *A Companion to the Fairy Tale*, ed. Hilda Ellis Davidson and Anna Chaudhri (Woodbridge: D. S. Brewer, 2003), p. 16.

153. See, for example, Jan M. Ziolkowski, *Fairy Tales from Before Fairy Tales: The Medieval Latin Past of Wonderful Lies* (Ann Arbor: University of Michigan Press, 2007).

154. Jacob Grimm and Wilhelm Grimm, *Deutsche Sagen*, 2 vols. in one (Munich: Winkler, 1965), p. 7.

155. See Jacques Le Goff and Emmanuel Le Roy Ladurie, "Mélusine maternelle et défricheuse," *Annales: Économies, Sociétés, Civilisations* 26 (1971):594–95.

156. Gervase of Tilbury, *Otia Imperialia*, ed. Banks and Binns, pp. 88–90.

157. Paupert, *Les Fileuses*, p. 6.

158. Le Goff, *L'imaginaire médiéval*, pp. 104–5.

159. Cooper, *English Romance in Time*, p. 43.

160. "Each text," he continues, "would thus call for a reevaluation of the wonder, or at the very least of its position in the narrative or semantic structure fashioned by the story"; see Dubost, *Aspects fantastiques*, 1:64.

161. Gillian Bennett, *"Alas, Poor Ghost!": Traditions of Belief in Story and Discourse* (Logan: Utah State University Press, 1999), p. 3.

162. Dégh, *Legend and Belief*, p. 38.

163. Elliott Oring, *Folk Groups and Folklore Genres: An Introduction* (Logan: Utah State University Press, 1986), p. 125.

164. Dégh, *Legend and Belief*, 311.

165. E. P. Thompson, *Customs in Common* (New York: New Press, 1991), pp. 10–11.

166. Antonio Gramsci, *Selections from Cultural Writings*, ed. David Forgacs and Geoffrey Nowell-Smith, trans. William Boelhower (Cambridge, Mass.: Harvard University Press, 1985), p. 190.

167. Thomas Wright, ed., *A Selection of Latin Stories, from Manuscripts of the Thirteenth and Fourteenth Centuries* (London: Percy Society, 1842), p. 77.

168. Wright, *Selection of Latin Stories*, p. 110. Earlier English instances are to be found in *The Penitential of Bartholomew of Exeter*, in *Medieval Handbooks of Penance: A Translation of the Principal libri poenitentiales and Selections from Related Documents*, ed. and trans. John T. McNeill and Helena M. Gamer (New York: Columbia University Press, 1938), p. 350; [John of Salisbury], *Policraticus*, ed. K. S. B. Keats-Rohan, Corpus christianorum, 118 (Turnholt: Brepols, 1993), p. 67 (1:13); and the Anglo-Norman preacher's handbook, [*Le Manuel des péchés*], *Robert of Brunne's 'Handlyng Synne' with . . . William of Waddington's 'Manuel de Pechiez,'* ed. F. J. Furnivall, EETS OS 119 (London: Early English Text Society, 1901), p. 14 (unlike his original, Robert Mannyng does not explicitly mention the priest).

169. G. R. Owst, "Sortilegium in English Homiletic Literature of the Fourteenth Century," in *Studies Presented to Sir Hilary Jenkinson*, ed. J. Conway Davies (London: Oxford University Press, 1957), p. 299.

170. See George L. Kittredge, *Witchcraft in Old and New England* (Cambridge, Mass.: Harvard University Press, 1929), p. 44.

171. *Les Évangiles des quenouilles*, ed. Madeleine Jeay (Montreal: Presses de l'Université de Montréal, 1985), p. 109.

172. *Of Shrifte and Penance: The ME Prose Translation of Le Manuel des péchés*, ed. Klaus Bitterling (Heidelberg: Winter, 1998), p. 46.

173. Gramsci, *Selections from Cultural Writings*, p. 189.

174. Cf. "une étude des comportements culturels du peuple révèlent souvent 'une réla-tion de défiance et de défence à l'égard des messages dominants," in Le Goff, *L'imaginaire médiéval*, p. 106 (quoting Roger Chartier).

175. Gramsci, *Selections from Cultural Writings*, p. 191.

176. Marjorie Swann, "The Politics of Fairylore in Early Modern Literature," *Renaissance Quarterly* 53 (2000):450.

177. Aisling Byrne, "Fairy Lovers: Sexuality, Order and Narrative in Medieval Romance," in *Sexual Culture in the Literature of Medieval Britain*, ed. Amanda Hopkins, Robert Allen Rouse, and Cory James Rushton (Cambridge: D. S. Brewer, 2014), p. 102.

178. Antonio Gramsci, *Selections from the Prison Notebooks*, ed. and trans. Quintin Hoare and Geoffrey Nowell Smith (New York: International Publishers, 1971), p. 326n5.

179. John Speirs, *Medieval English Poetry: The Non-Chaucerian Tradition* (London: Faber and Faber, 1957), written in the shadow of an occultist modernism, associates his folkloric "non-Chaucerian tradition" with such Leavisite fetishes as T. S. Eliot and D. H. Lawrence, a very different ideological construct from the one I am contemplating here. See R. H. Robbins, "Middle English Misunderstood: Mr Speirs and the Goblins," *Anglia* 85 (1967):270–81.

180. [John Gerson]. *Joannis Gersonii Opera omnia nova ordine digesta, & in V. tomos distributa* (Antwerp: Sumptibus societatis, 1706), 1:206. See Françoise Bonney, "Autour de Jean Gerson: Opinions de théologiens sur les superstitions et la sorcellerie au début du XVe siècle," *Moyen Âge* 77 (1971):85–98.

CHAPTER 3

1. Guibert of Nogent, *Monodies* and *On the Relics of the Saints*, trans. Joseph McAlhany and Jay Rubenstein (London: Penguin Books, 2011), pp. 36–37 (*Monodies*, 1:13).

2. Clancy, *Abducted*, p. 34.

3. Clancy, *Abducted*, p. 35. Cf. O. Davies, "The Nightmare Experience, Sleep Paralysis, and Witchcraft Accusations," *Folklore* 114 (2003):181–203.

4. Higden, *Speculum Curatorum*, ed. Crook and Jennings, pp. 130–31.

5. James I, King of England, *Dæmonologie (1597); Newes from Scotland (1591)*, ed. G. B. Harrison (New York: E. P. Dutton, 1924), p. 69.

6. For this useful distinction, see David J. Hufford, *The Terror That Comes in the Night: An Experience-Centered Study of Supernatural Assault Traditions* (Philadelphia: University of Pennsylvania Press, 1982), p. 15.

7. For a useful overview of the medieval incubus, see Nicholas Kiessling, *The Incubus in English Literature: Provenance and Progeny* (Pullman: Washington State University Press, 1977).

8. See Hufford, *The Terror That Comes in the Night*, pp. 129–35, for an analogous confusion in the work of Ernest Jones.

9. Gervase of Tilbury, *Otia Imperialia*, ed. Banks and Binns, pp. 96–97.

10. Augustine, *City of God*, 3:548–49 (15:23); Le Goff, *Pour un autre moyen âge*, p. 228n17.

11. Gervase of Tilbury, *Otia Imperialia*, ed. Banks and Binns, p. 730.

12. Gervase of Tilbury, *Otia Imperialia*, ed. Banks and Binns, pp. xxix–xxx.

13. Map, *De nugis curialium*, ed. James, pp. 156, 158. Map is one of the earliest writers to use the term 'succubus,' a medieval Latin neologism (in classical Latin *incubus* is gender neutral).

14. *Le roman de Brut*, ed. Ivor Arnold, 2 vols., Société des anciens textes français (Paris: Firmin Didot, 1938, 1940), 1:394 (apparatus to line 7445).

15. Raoul de Presles, *de Civitate Dei*, liv. XV, chap. 23 (from Paris, MS B.N., Français 173, ff. 94r and 95r).

16. *Le roman de Troie*, ed. Léopold Constans, 6 vols., Société des anciens textes français (Paris: Firmin Didot, 1904–12), 1:358 (line 6751).

17. John Lydgate, *Troy Book*, ed. Henry Bergen, 4 vols., EETS ES 97, 103, 106, 126 (London: Kegan Paul, 1906–35), 1:147.

18. Lydgate, *Troy Book*, 1:364 (lines 7700–7703).

19. *Dives and Pauper*, ed. Priscilla H. Barnum, 2 vols. (in 3 pts.), EETS 275, 280, 323 (London: Oxford University Press, 1976–2004), 1, 2:118 (VI.xxi).

20. Hansen, *Quellen und Untersuchungen*, p. 84.

21. K. M. Briggs, "Some Seventeenth-Century Books of Magic," *Folklore* 64 (1953):448.

22. "Incubus quidam nominans se regem Goldemar adhaesit cuidam armigero dicto *Neveling de Hardenburg* in Comitatu de Marca prope flumen *Rure*. Incubus loquebatur cum hominibus, lusit in instrumento musicali, perceptibiliter lusit ad taxillos, pecunias exposuit, vinum bibit, visibiliter tamen multis tam religiosis quam secularibus responsa dedit, sed crebro religiosos, scelera eorum occulta recitando, confudit. Hospitem suum praedictum saepius ad inimicorum suorum adventum praemonuit, et contra eos consilia dedit. Manus duntaxat palpandas preaebuit, & manus erant graciles et molles, ac si quis tangeret murem vel ranam. . . . Haec omnia a multis audivi, & post, anno XXVI. ab ipso Nevelung plenius intellexi. Quem etiam docuit, ut hoc verso se signaret. *Increatus Pater, increatus Fillius, increatus Spritus S*. Et postquam triennio secum morabatur, sine cujusquam laesione recessit"; see [Dietrich Engelhus], *Chronicon Theodorici Engelhusii*, ed. Gottfried Wilhelm Leibniz, in *Scriptores Rerum Brunsvicensium*, vol. 2 (Hanover: Foerster, 1710), p. 1133.

23. See, for instance, [Thomas of Cantimpré], *Bonum Universale*, pp. 546–48, 556–57, 564–65.

24. *Acta Sanctorum Octobris, I (quo dies primus & secundus continentur)* (Antwerp: Plassche, 1765), p. 677F (99).

25. John Bromyard, *Summa Predicantium* (Venice, 1586), 2:371b (S. XI. 8; s.v. "sortilegium").

26. William of Newburgh, *History of English Affairs*, ed. Walsh and Kennedy, pp. 118–21 (1:28).

27. *The Life of St Hugh of Lincoln*, ed. Decima L. Douie and Hugh Farmer, 2 vols. (London: Nelson, 1961, 1962), 2:119–22.

28. The story may well be traditional; it is also the subject of one of the exempla in British Library, MS Royal 7 D I. (f. 116a). Cf. J. A. Herbert, *Catalogue of Romances in the Department of Manuscripts in the British Museum*, vol. 3 (London: Trustees of the British Museum, 1919), p. 495 (no. 206).

29. "In latin it is named *Incubus* and *Succubus*. In Englyshe it is named the Mare. And some say that it is kynd of spirites, the which doth infect and trouble men when they be in theyr beddes slepynge, as Saynt Augustine saythe . . . I haue red, as many more hath done, that can tell yf I do wryte true or false, there is an herbe named *fuga Demonum*, or as the Grecians do name it *Ipericon*. In Englyshe it [is] named saynt Johns worte, the which herbe is of that vertue that it doth repell suche malyfycyousnes or spirites"; see Andrew Borde, *The Fyrst Boke of the Introduction of Knowledge*, ed. F. J. Furnivall, EETS ES 10 (London: Trübner, 1870), pp. 78–79. See also Briggs, "Some Seventeenth-Century Books of Magic," p. 455.

30. In 1413 Jehan Perrot of Saint-Pourcain deposed that he had been lured from his bed by a female spirit who ordered him to spread his cloak on the ground: "il lui sembla qu'elle lui gettoit or et argent dussus icelle robe, at avec se lui sembloit qu'il en avoit plus qu'il n'en porroit porte" [it seemed to him that she threw down gold and silver on this cloak for him, and moreover there was more than he could possibly carry]; see Roger Vaultier, *Le Folklore pendant la guerre de Cent Ans* (Paris: Guénégaud, 1965), p. 232.

31. *The Life and Miracles of St William of Norwich*, ed. Augustus Jessop and Montague Rhodes James (Cambridge: Cambridge University Press, 1896), pp. 79–82 (bk. 2, chap. 7).

32. Forte, "Cambridge Dominican Collector of Exempla," p. 143. For other incubi stories in the same collection, see Herbert, *Catalogue of Romances*, 3:495 (nos. 206, 207, 208, 209, 212).

33. [Thomas of Cantimpré], *Bonum Universale*, p. 546 (cf. paras. 14, 15, 25, 33).

34. *Liber Commentarii in II sententiarum*, Dist. VIII. A. Art. V, in [Albertus Magnus], *Alberti Magni Opera Omnia*, ed. S. C. A. Borgnet, 38 vols. (Paris: Vivés, 1890–99), 27:174.

35. Hector Boece, *Scotorum historiae a prima gentis origine libri xvii* (Paris: Ascensius, 1527), f. 155a., lines 7–8 (bk. 8).

36. [Thomas of Cantimpré], *Bonum Universale*, p. 548; *Dives and Pauper*, ed. Barnum, 1, 2:118–19 (VI. xxi).

37. Carl Horstmann, "Die Evangelien-Geschichten des Homiliensammlung des Ms. Vernon," *Archiv für das Studium der neueren Spachen und Literaturen* 31 (1877):261.

38. A marginal gloss on 'fendis' [*demonia*] (Isa., 34:14) in the second version of the *Wycliffite Bible* reads, "that is, fendis incubi, other wodewosis, as doctours seien"; see [*Wycliffite Bible*], *The Holy Bible . . . by John Wycliffe and His Followers*, ed. Josiah Forshall and Frederic Madden, 4 vols. (Oxford: Oxford University Press, 1850), 3:284.

39. Siân Echard, "'Hic est Artur': Reading Latin and Reading Arthur," in *New Directions in Arthurian Studies*, ed. Alan Lupak (Cambridge: D. S. Brewer, 2002), pp. 49–67.

40. Geoffrey of Monmouth, *The Historia Regum Britannie of Geoffrey of Monmouth, 1: Bern, Burgerbibliothek, MS. 568*, ed. Neil Wright (Cambridge: D. S. Brewer, 1985), p. 72 [107]

(*In libris philosophorum nostrorum et in pluribus historiis repperi multos homines huiusmodi procreationem habuisse*).

41. [William of Auvergne], *De Universo*, II. iii, 25 (1674 ed., 1:1070aH). William cites a certain "Historia regnorum Occidentalium"; for an identification of this work with Jordanes's *Getica* [chap. 24], see Van der Lugt, *Le Ver, le démon, et la vierge*, p. 254n178.

42. [William of Auvergne], *De Universo*, II. iii, 25 (1674 ed., 1:1072aH).

43. [Caesarius of Heisterbach], *Dialogus Miraculorum*, ed. Strange, 1:124.

44. See Wade, *Fairies in Medieval Romance*, pp. 120–21.

45. Van der Lugt, *Le Ver, le démon, et la vierge*, pp. 219–20.

46. *Liber Commentarii in II Sententiarum*, Dist. VIII, A, Art. V, in [Albertus Magnus], *Alberti Magni Opera Omnia*, ed. Borgnet, 27:174–75.

47. Saint Thomas Aquinas, *Summa Theologiae, English and Latin*, Blackfriars, 60 vols. (London: Eyre & Spottiswoode; New York: McGraw-Hill, 1964–76), 9:43 [I^a q. 51 a. 3 ad 6]; [Saint Bonaventurae], *Doctoris seraphici S. Bonaventurae Opera omnia*, 10 vols. ([Rome]: Collegii S. Bonaventurae, 1882–1902), 2:220 (*In Secundum Librum Sententiaru*m, Dist. VIII, Pt.1, Art. 3, Qu. 1, Conclusio).

48. Stephens, *Demon Lovers*, pp. 63–69..

49. "Primo enim demones succumbunt viris in specie mulieris & ex eis semen pollutionis suscipiunt & quadam sagacitate nature ipsum semen in sua virtute custodiunt & postmodum deo permittente fiunt incubi & in vasa mulieris transfundunt ex qua transfusione homines generare possunt non tamen sic generati sunt filii demonum sed hominis. Hec ille: isto modo fertur generatum fuisse Merlinum"; see [Alphonse de Spina], *Alphonse dela Espina, Fortalitium Fidei in vniuersos christiane* (Lyon: Gueynard, 1525), f. ccclxii^v (bk. 5, Cons. 10, Diff. 3).

50. For the role of Merlin in this debate, see Van der Lugt, *Le Ver, le démon, et la vierge*, pp. 337–57.

51. Even Francis Dubost, who fully appreciates Merlin's double nature, takes Geoffrey's incubus-demon at face value; see "L'enfant sans père" in Dubost, *Aspects fantastiques*, 2:711–51 (chap. 21). One recent author who at least recognizes a fairy dimension to Merlin's begetting is Carol E. Harding in *Merlin and Legendary Romance* (New York: Garland, 1988). Many of my own readings here, however, were anticipated by MacCullough, *Medieval Faith and Fable*, pp. 53–56.

52. "Uiuit anima mea & uiuit anima tua, domine mi rex, quia neminem agnoui qui illum in me generauit. Unum autem scio quod, cum essem inter consocias meas in thalamis nostris apparebat mihi quidam in specie pucerrimi iuuenis et sepissime amplectens me strictis brachiis deosculabatur. Et cum aliquantulum mecum moram fecisset subito euanescebat ita ut nichil ex eo uiderem. Multotiens quoque me alloquebatur, dum secreto sederem, nec usquam comparebat. Cunque me in hunc modum frequentasset, coiuit mecum in specie hominis, <sep>ius atque grauidam in aluo deseruit. Sciat prudencia tua, domine mi, quod aliter uirum non agnoui qui iuuenem istum genuerit"; see Geoffrey of Monmouth. *Historia Regum, 1*, ed. Wright, p. 72 [107].

53. "In libris philosophorum nostrorum et in plurimis historiis reperi multos homines huiusmodi procreationem habuisse. Nam ut Apulegius de deo Socratis perhibet, inter lunam et terram habitant spiritus quos incubos demones appellamus. Hii partim habent naturam hominum, partim uero angelorum, et cum uolunt assumunt sibi humanas figuras et cum mulieribus coeunt. Forsitan unus ex eis huic mulieri apparuit et iuuenem istum ex ipsa generauit"; see Geoffrey of Monmouth, *Historia Regum,1*, ed. Wright, p. 72 [107].

54. One late twelfth-century MS of the *Historia* has copied the passage from Augustine, *City of God*, 15:23 at the bottom of the page on which the reference to Apuleius appears; see

J. Hammer, "Bref commentaire de la *Prophetia Merlini* du ms 3524 de la Bibliothèque de la Cathédrale d'Exeter," in *Hommages à Joseph Bidez et à Franz Cumont* (Brussels: Latomus, 1949), p. 112.

55. See Lewis, *Discarded Image*, pp. 40–44.

56. On the identity of the author, see David N. Dumville, "'Nennius and the *Historia Brittonum*," *Studia Celtica* 10 (1975):78–95.

57. Nennius, *British History and Welsh Annals*, ed. and trans. John Morris (London: Phillimore; Totowa, N.J.: Rowman and Littlefield, 1980), pp. 30, 71 (chap. 40). The Vatican recension is even more explicit: "uirum *in coitu* numquam cognoui" and "affirmauit quod filius eius patrem non haberet *carnalem*"; see *The Historia Brittonum*, vol. 3: *The 'Vatican' Recension*, ed. David N. Dumville (Cambridge: D. S. Brewer, 1985), p. 92.

58. London, British Library MS, Royal 7. D. I, f. 117a.

59. John Brugman's second life of Saint Lidwina, in *Acta Sanctorum Aprilis collecta, digesta, illustrata . . . Tomvs II. quo medii XI dies continentur* (Antwerp: Michael Cnobarus 1675), p. 326B (102).

60. *Roman de Brut*, ed. Arnold, 1:393–94 (lines 7414–34) and 394–95 (lines 7439–56).

61. Wace seems to have taken this from the so-called first variant version of the *Historia*; see Geoffrey of Monmouth, *The Historia Regum Britannie of Geoffrey of Monmouth, 2: The First Variant Version*, ed. Neil Wright (Cambridge: D. S. Brewer, 1988), p. 99 [106]. It is therefore all the more remarkable that he resists the first variant version's more critical attitude to Merlin's mother.

62. Robert Manning of Brunne, *The Story of England (1338)*, ed. Frederick J. Furnivall, 2 vols., Rolls Series (London: Longman, 1887), 1:283–84.

63. *Patrologia Latina*, 49:0713A.

64. Map, *De nugis curialium*, ed. James, pp. 320–21.

65. La3amon, *Brut*, ed. G. L. Brook and R. F. Leslie, 2 vols., EETS 250, 277 (London: Oxford University Press, 1963, 1978), 1:406 (lines 7938–48). Quotations are taken from the (fuller) B.L., MS Cotton Caligula, A. IX here, and punctuation has been modernized.

66. La3amon, *Brut*, p. 408 (lines 7872–80).

67. Geoffrey of Monmouth, *The Historia Regum Britannie of Geoffrey of Monmouth, 5: Gesta Regum Britannie*, ed. Neil Wright (Cambridge: D. S. Brewer, 1991), pp. 140–43 (5:457–69).

68. John Koch, "Anglonormannische Texte im Ms. Arundel 220 des Britischen Museums," *Zeitschrift für romanische Philologie* 54 (1934):38 (lines 165–77).

69. *Roman de Brut*, ed. Arnold, 1:394 (apparatus to line 7445).

70. *Roman de Brut*, ed. Arnold, 2:784 (lines [113–14]).

71. A thirteenth-century spell *Pur faies*, for instance, begins "Conjuro vos, elves"; see *Anglo-Norman Medicine II: Shorter Treatises*, ed. Tony Hunt (Cambridge: D. S. Brewer, 1997), pp. 224–25. Latham, *Elizabethan Fairies*, pp. 19–22, argues that a distinction between the two terms had arisen by the Elizabethan period.

72. Robert of Gloucester, *Metrical Chronicle*, ed. W. A. Wright, 2 vols., Rolls Series (London: Longman, 1887), 1:196.

73. O. S. Pickering, "*South English Legendary* Style in Robert of Gloucester's *Chronicle*," *Medium Ævum* 70 (2001):1–18.

74. *South English Legendary*, ed. D'Evelyn and Mill, 2:410.

75. Robert of Gloucester, "A Fifteenth-Century Prose Paraphrase of Robert of Gloucester's *Chronicle*," ed. Andrew D. Lipscomb, Ph.D. diss., University of North Carolina at Chapel Hill, 1990, p. 16.

76. Cologny, Switzerland, Martin Bodmer Foundation, MS 43, f. 29^r.

77. Geoffrey of Monmouth, *Historia Regum, 2,* ed. Wright, p. cxiv. An already sophisticated text was known to Wace in 1155, which suggests that this first variant version may well date to the 1140s.

78. William of Newburgh, *History of English Affairs,* ed. Walsh and Kennedy, p. 35 (*Proemium*).

79. *An Anglo-Norman Brut (Royal 13. A. XXI),* ed. Alexander Bell, ANTS, 21–22 (Oxford: Blackwell, 1969), pp. 137–38 (lines 5089, 5153).

80. *Castleford's Chronicle or the Boke of Brut,* ed. Caroline D. Eckhardt, 2 vols., EETS OS 305, 306 (London: Oxford University Press, 1996), 1:410 (lines 15232–33). *Monik* is not included in the *Middle English Dictionary* [MED]; it appears to be an aphetic form of *demoniak.*

81. *The Brut, or The Chronicles of England,* ed. Friedrich W. D. Brie, 2 vols., EETS OS 131, 136 (London: Kegan Paul, 1906, 1908), 1:57.

82. [Higden], *Polychronicon Ranulphi Higden,* ed. Babington, 5:278–79.

83. John Harding, *The Chronicle of John Hardyng,* ed. Henry Ellis (London: Rivington, 1812), pp. 114–15.

84. Robert de Boron, *Merlin, roman du XIIIe siècle,* ed. Alexandre Micha (Geneva: Droz, 1979).

85. Elspeth Kennedy, *Lancelot and the Grail: A Study of the Prose Lancelot* (Oxford: Clarendon Press, 1986), pp. 112–15; Elspeth M. Kennedy, "The Role of the Supernatural in the First Part of the Old French Prose *Lancelot*," in *Studies in Medieval Literature and Languages in Memory of Frederick Whitehead,* ed. W. Rothwell et al. (Manchester: Manchester University Press, 1973), pp. 173–84. See also Dubost, *Aspects fantastiques,* 2:719–20.

86. The late thirteenth-century Anglo-Norman version in B.L., MS Addit. 32,125; see A. Micha, "Les manuscrits du *Merlin* en Prose de Robert de Boron," *Romania* 79 (1958):88. See also Edward Donald Kennedy, "Visions of History: Robert de Boron and English Arthurian Chroniclers," in *The Fortunes of King Arthur,* ed. Norris J. Lacy (Cambridge: Brewer, 2005), pp. 29–46.

87. *Merlin, or the Early History of King Arthur,* ed. H. B. Wheatley, 4 vols., EETS OS 10, 21, 36, 112 (London: Kegan Paul, Trench, Trübner, 1865–99); Herry Lovelich, *Merlin, a Middle-English Metrical Version of a French Romance,* ed. Ernst A. Kock, 3 vols., EETS ES 93, 112 and OS 185 (London: Kegan Paul, Trench, Trübner, 1904–32).

88. Lister M. Matheson, "The Arthurian Stories of Lambeth Palace Library MS 84," *Arthurian Literature* 5 (1985):76–77.

89. [*Lucydarye*], *Late Middle English* Lucydarye, ed. Morrison, p. 55.

90. Henry Boguet, *Discours execrables des sorciers* (Rouen: Romain de Beauvais, 1606), pp. 61–61 (chap. 12), trans. by E. A. Ashwin as *An Examen of Witches,* ed. Montague Summers ([London]: Rodker, 1929), p. 33; Nicolas Rémy, *Demonolatreiae libri tres* (Frankfurt: Palthenius, 1597), p. 24 (chap. 6), trans. by E. A. Ashwin as *Demonolatry,* ed. Montague Summers (London: Rodker, 1930), p. 12.

91. Quotations from *Sir Gowther* in *Six Middle English Romances,* ed. Mills, pp. 148–68.

92. [Thomas Walsingham], *Thomæ Walsingham: Quondam Monachi S. Albani, Historia Anglicana,* ed. Henry Riley, 2 vols., Rolls Series (London: Longman, 1863, 1864), 1:199–200. See also a continuation of the *Chronicle of Walter of Guisborough* in Walter de Hemingford, *Chronicon Domini Walteri de Hemingburgh,* ed. Hans Claude Hamilton, 2 vols. (London: English Historical Society, 1848, 1849), 2:314–15. The *Historia Aurea* itself remains unedited; see V. H. Galbraith, "The *Historia Aurea* of John, Vicar of Tynemouth, and the Sources of the St Albans

Chronicle (1327–1377)," in *Essays in History Presented to Reginald Lane Poole*, ed. H. W. C. Davis (Oxford: Clarendon Press, 1927), pp. 379–98.

93. *Of Arthour and of Merlin*, ed. O. D. Macrae-Gibson, 2 vols., EETS 268, 279 (London: Early English Text Society, 1973, 1979), 1:51 (line 559).

94. Robert de Boron, *Merlin*, ed. Micha, p. 6 (cf. p. 22, lines 83–84).

95. [Gerald of Wales], *Giraldi Cambrensis Opera*, ed. Brewer, 6:133.

96. [Higden], *Polychronicon Ranulphi Higden*, ed. Babington, 1:418–21.

97. *Robert le diable*, ed. E. Löseth, Société des anciens textes français (Paris: Firmin Didot, 1903), pp. 5–6 (lines 58–72). Interestingly, when Étienne de Bourbon tells the story, he has no problem with the idea of demonic impregnation; see [Étienne de Bourbon], *Anecdotes historiques*, ed. Lecoy de la Marche, p. 145.

98. Robert of Gloucester, *Metrical Chronicle*, ed. Wright, 1:196.

99. [Higden], *Polychronicon Ranulphi Higden*, ed. Babington, 1:419.

100. See Van der Lugt, *Le Ver, le démon, et vierge*, p. 350.

101. Augustine, *City of God*, 3:548–49 (15:23); Le Goff, *Pour un autre moyen âge*, p. 228n17.

102. Gervase of Tilbury, *Otia Imperialia*, ed. Banks and Binns, pp. 96–97.

103. [Thomas of Cantimpré], *Bonum Universale*, p. 548. The meaning of *vt Dyanae* is not entirely clear; I have translated it as a dative singular, but it is possibly a nominative plural, *dianae* [followers of Diana], in apposition to *dusii*.

104. Daffyd Evans, "Wishfulfilment: The Social Function and Classification of Old French Romances," in *Court and Poet*, ed. Glyn S. Burgess (Liverpool: Cairns, 1981), pp. 129–34.

105. Purkiss, *At the Bottom of the Garden*, p. 53.

106. Cf. "the fairy mistresses of romance . . . are most widely known for using their supernatural powers to fulfill the desires of their chosen knights" (Wade, *Fairies in Medieval Romance*, p. 109) and "if there is a singe defining quality of the fairy monarch . . . it is not sexuality but power" (Cooper, *English Romance in Time*, p. 178).

107. *Historia septem sapientum 1*, ed. Alfons Hilka, Sammlung Mittellateinischer Texte, 4 (Heidelberg: Winter, 1912), pp. 13–14.

108. "Si tanto ardore libidinis insanirent, quomodo a sodomitica libidine immunes essent, ut vel in viros nostros, vel in masculos suos concupiscentia insanirent. Benedictus autem altissimus virilem speciem in hominibus a flagitiis eorum usque hodie sic servavit, ut nullus virorum ista nefaria libidine pollutus adhuc auditus sit" [Should they rage with such a fervor of lust, how might they be immune from homosexual lust, so that they might rage with desire either for our own men or amongst their own males? But the blessed supreme being has so preserved the virile character of men from their outrages to this day, that none of our men has been heard to have been polluted by this wicked lust up to now]; see [William of Auvergne], *De Universo*, II. iii, 25 (1674 ed., 1:1070bH–71aA.). The printed text reads, "autem altissimus, *qui* virilem speciem."

109. As, for example, in Thomas of Cantimpré's account of a fellow Dominican who saw a demon in the shape of a very beautiful woman entering his dormitory [*vidit demonem in specie pulcherrime mulieris in dormitorio venientem*] in the early hours of the morning; see [Thomas of Cantimpré], *Bonum universale*, p. 564.

110. [Burchard of Worms], *Bussordnungen*, ed. Wasserschleben, p. 658 (no. 140).

111. [William of Auvergne], *De Universo*, II. iii, 23 (1674 ed., 1:1065aB). I read *speciosissimam* where this edition has *speciosissi nam*.

112. *South English Legendary*, ed. D'Evelyn and Mill, 2:410.

113. See particularly Gingras, *Érotisme et merveilles* (2002).

114. Chestre, *Sir Launfal,* ed. Bliss, pp. 59–60.

115. *Lais féeriques,* ed. Micha, pp. 30–33, 88–91.

116. *Lais féeriques,* ed. Micha, pp. 114–15.

117. Anne Reynders, "Le Roman de Partonopeu de Blois est-il l'œuvre d'un précurseur de Chrétien de Troyes?," *Le Moyen Âge* 111 (2005):479–502.

118. *Partonopeu de Blois,* ed. Collet and Joris; [*Partonope of Blois*], *Middle English Versions of Partonope,* ed. Trampe Bödtker.

119. For analyses of this scene, see Dubost, *Aspects fantastiques,* 1:370–82; and Gingras, *Érotisme et merveilles,* pp. 392–94.

120. Kennedy, *Lancelot and the Grail,* p. 112.

121. Cf. Harf-Lancner, *Fées au Moyen Âge,* chap. 16: "Des fées aux enchanteressses" (pp. 411–31).

122. Chaucer, *Riverside Chaucer,* p. 183.

123. [Jean d'Outremeuse], *Myreur de hystors,* ed. Bormans and Borgnet, 4:54–55.

124. The whole passage runs to fifty-seven lines (10743–80); see [*Partonope of Blois*], *Middle English Versions of Partonope,* ed. Trampe Bödtker, pp. 436–37.

125. *Partonopeu,* ed. Collet and Joris, pp. 148, 160 (lines 1521, 1771).

126. Frank Klaassen, "Learning and Masculinity in Manuscripts of Ritual Magic of the Later Middle Ages and Renaissance," *Sixteenth Century Journal* 38 (2007):49–76. Cf. Michael Bailey, "The Feminization of Magic and the Emerging Idea of the Female Witch in the Late Middle Ages," *Essays in Medieval Studies* 19 (2002):120–34 ("Although never explicitly described in terms of gender, the practice of necromancy as clerical authorities conceived it seems to have been a decidedly masculine act" [p. 126]).

127. Bailey, "Feminization of Magic," p. 127.

128. Reginald Scot, *The Discouerie of Witchcraft* (London: by [Henry Denham for] William Brome, 1584), p. 377 (bk. 15, chap. 1) (*STC* [2nd ed.]:21864).

129. Scot, *Discouerie of Witchcraft* (1584), p. 405 (bk. 15, chap. 8).

130. Frank Klaassen and Katerina Bens, "Achieving Invisibility and Having Sex with Spirits: Six Operations from an English Magic Collection, ca. 1600," *Opuscula* 3 (2013):1–14. See also Briggs, "Some Seventeenth-Century Books of Magic," p. 460.

131. Frederika Bain, "The Binding of the Fairies: Four Spells," *Preternature* 1 (2012): 323–54.

132. Ginzburg, *Ecstacies,* p. 11.

133. See Eamon Duffy, *The Stripping of the Altars: Traditional Religion in England, c. 1400–c. 1580* (New Haven, Conn.: Yale University Press, 1992), pp. 266–98.

134. Lewis, *"De Audiendis Poetis,"* p. 17.

CHAPTER 4

1. C. F. Goodey and T. Stainton, "Intellectual Disability and the Myth of the Changeling Myth," *Journal of the History of Behavioral Science* 37.3 (2001):226–28.

2. A couple of particularly egregious errors: 1) William of Auvergne does *not* cite "'the Spaniards,' that is, . . . his contemporaries in the Dominican Order," for the view that changelings really exist (p. 227). The authors seem to have misunderstood *vulgaris illa Hispanorum nominatio, qua malignos spiritus . . . exercitum antiquuum nominant,* or "the common expression of the Spaniards, by which they term evil spirits . . . the 'ancient army.'" This is simply a

reference to a general Spanish term for the wild ride, as is made clear earlier in [William of Auvergne], *De Universo*, II. iii, 12 (1674 ed., 1:1037aB). 2) The changeling analogy in Jacques de Vitry's *Sermones Vulgares* is *not* one of three testimonies, "each of which provides evidence for the objective reality of the devil" (p. 228); the three witnesses are actually the law, the prophets, and the gospels, and those who hear them but do not follow them are like changelings who eat but do not put on weight.

3. MacCulloch, *Medieval Faith and Fable*, p. 35.

4. Gramsci, *Selections from Cultural Writings*, p. 195.

5. One of the exempla in B.L., MS Royal 7. D. I, for example, concerns a nun who prostitutes herself at a local fair, but while she is away from the cloister a demon provides a substitute so that no one notices her absence [*demon quidem interim idolum ipsius in equali forma optinuit itaque nunquam abisse mulier putabatur*] (f. 117^v); see Herbert, *Catalogue of Romances*, p. 495 (no. 209).

6. E.g., Briggs, *Fairies in English Tradition*, pp. 115–16.

7. Ralph of Coggeshall, *Chronicon Anglicanum*, ed. Joseph Stephenson, Rolls Series (London and Edinburgh: Longman, 1875), pp. 120–21. See, e.g., Katharine Briggs, *The Vanishing People: Fairy Lore and Legends* (New York: Pantheon, 1978), p. 100.

8. *A Middle English Treatise on the Ten Commandments*, ed. James Finch Royster (Chapel Hill: University of North Carolina Press, 1911), p. 4.

9. See Alaric Hall, "Calling the Shots: The Old English Remedy *Gif hors ofscoten sie* and Anglo-Saxon 'Elf-Shot,'" *Neuphilologische Mitteilungen* 106 (2005):195–209; and Alaric Hall, "Getting Shot of Elves: Healing, Witchcraft and Fairies in the Scottish Witchcraft Trials," *Folklore* 116 (2005):19–36. Curiously 'elf-shot' does not seem to be recorded in Middle English, despite occurring in both the Anglo-Saxon and in the early modern period; however, a possible Latin calque, a charm offering protection *a morsu alphorum*, appears in John Bromyard's *Summa Predicantium* (ed. 1586), 2:372b (S. XI. 12 [s.v. "sortilegium"]). Middle English does, however, use another term, 'elf-taken,' to describe a medical complaint, though this appears sometimes to be confused with descriptions of changelings. See OED and MED, s.v. "elf."

10. *Depositions and Other Ecclesiastical Proceedings from the Courts of Durham*, [ed. James Raine,] Surtees Society (London: Nichols, 1845), p. 100.

11. *Register of John Morton, III*, ed. Harper-Bill, p. 215 (no. 661).

12. Gui, *Manuel*, ed. and trans. Mollat, 2:20–21.

13. [Paris], *Chronica Maiora*, ed. Luard, 5:82.

14. Jean d'Arras, *Melusine*, ed. Donald, p. 105.

15. *Six Middle English Romances*, ed. Mills, p. 151.

16. Chaucer, *Riverside Chaucer*, p. 98.

17. Reidar Christiansen, "Some Notes on the Fairies and the Fairy Faith," *Béalodeas* 39–41 (1971–73):103.

18. Susan Schoon Eberly, "Fairies and the Folklore of Disability: Changelings, Hybrids and the Solitary Fairy," *Folklore* 99 (1988):58–77.

19. John Lindow, "Changelings, Changing, Re-exchanges: Thoughts on the Relationship Between Folk Belief and Legend," in *Legends and Landscape: Plenary Papers from the 5th Celtic-Nordic-Baltic Folklore Symposium*, ed. Terry Gunnell (Reykjavík: Háskólaútgáfan, 2008), pp. 215–34.

20. Cf. Jean-Michel Doulet, *Quand les démons enlevaient les enfants, Les changelins: Étude d'une figure mythique* (Paris: Sorbonne, 2003), p. 317.

21. [William of Auvergne], *De Universo*, II, iii, 25 (1674 ed., 1:1072bH–73aA).

22. Higden, *Speculum Curatorum*, ed. Crook and Jennings, pp. 132–33; Hansen, *Quellen und Untersuchungen*, p. 86; *Malleus Maleficarum*, ed. and trans. MacKay, 1:554 (182D–83A).

23. Jean-Claude Schmitt, *The Holy Greyhound: Guinefort, Healer of Children Since the Thirteenth Century*, trans. Martin Thom (Cambridge: Cambridge University Press, 1983), pp. 76–81. See also Baudouin Gaiffier, "Le Diable, voleur d'enfants," in *Études critiques d'hagiographie et d'iconologie* (Brussels: Société Bolandistes, 1967), pp. 169–93.

24. See Jenni Kuuliala, "Sons of Demons? Children's Impairments and the Beliefs in Changelings in Medieval Europe," in *The Dark Side of Childhood in Late Antiquity and the Middle Ages: Unwanted, Disabled, and Lost*, ed. Katariina Mustakallio and Christian Laes (Oxford: Oxbow Books, 2011), p. 79.

25. *Materials for the History of Thomas Becket*, ed. James Craigie Robertson and J. B. Sheppard, 7 vols., Rolls Series (London: Longman, 1875–85), 1:204.

26. Frederick C. Tubach, *Index Exemplorum*, Folklore Communications, 204 (Helsinki: Academia Scientiarum Fennica, 1981), no. 1695 (p. 139).

27. *Alphabet of Tales*, ed. Mary Macleod Banks, 2 vols., EETS OS 126/27 (London: Kegan Paul, 1905), 2:404 (no. 604). For its appearance in other exempla collections, see Tubach, *Index Exemplorum*, no. 49 (p. 12).

28. John Trevisa, *On the Properties of Things: John Trevisa's Translation of* Bartholomaeus Anglicus De Proprietatibus Rerum, ed. M. C. Seymour, 3 vols. (Oxford: Clarendon Press, 1975–88), 2:1136.

29. [*Golden Legend*], *Jacobi a Voragine Legenda aurea*, ed. Graesse, p. 381 (chap. 90) [Life of Saint Paul the Apostle]; Mandeville, *Mandeville's Travels*, ed. Seymour, p. 40 (chap. 8).

30. *Three Arthurian Romances: Poems from Medieval France*, trans. Ross G. Arthur (London: Everyman, 1996), pp. 46–70.

31. *The Romance of the Cheuelere Assigne*, ed. Henry H. Gibbs, EETS ES 6 (London: Trübner, 1868), p. 17 (line 331).

32. Étienne's word *matricide* here makes no literal sense; he presumably takes it to mean 'murderous mothers.'

33. For the Latin original, see *Anecdotes historiques*, ed. Lecoy de la Marche, pp. 326–27. The translation given here is based on Schmitt, *Holy Greyhound*, trans. Thom, pp. 4–6, but I have felt free to adapt it where necessary (Thom regularly translates *puer* as 'child' or 'baby,' for instance).

34. *Hertford County Records: Notes and Extracts from the Session Rolls, 1581–1698*, vol. 1, ed. W. J. Hardy (Hertford: Longmore, 1905), p. 3.

35. *Medieval Handbooks of Penance*, ed. McNeill and Gamer, pp. 198, 229, 246, 318, 350. See also Kuuliala, "Sons of Demons," p. 88.

36. *Councils and Ecclesiastical Documents Relating to Great Britain and Ireland*, ed. A. W. Haddan and W. Stubbs, 3 vols. (Oxford: Clarendon Press, 1869–78), 3:190.

37. Ranulph Higden speaks of "the passing of children through fire for the sake of insuring good health," in *Speculum Curatorum*, ed. Crook and Jennings, pp. 116–17. For a more fanciful explanation, see Filotas, *Pagan Survivals*, p. 122.

38. [Jacques de Vitry], *The Exempla or Illustrative Stories from the Sermones Vulgares of Jacques de Vitry*, ed. Thomas Frederick Crane (London: Folklore Society, 1890), p. 129.

39. P[aul] M[eyer], "*Chanjon*, enfant changé en nourice," *Romania* 32 (1903):452–53.

40. *Paris pendant la domination anglaise (1420–1436)*, ed. Auguste Longnon (Paris: Champion, 1878), pp. 245–47.

41. Anonimo Romano, *Cronica: Vita di Cola di Rienzo*, ed. Ettore Mazzali (Milan: Rizzoli, 1991), pp. 256–57; Mazzoli glosses *biscione* as 'figlio illegitimo' and *scagnato* as 'scambiato.'

42. *Les lais Villon et les poèmes variés*, ed. Jean Rychner and Albert Henry, 2 vols. (Geneva: Droz, 1977), 1:19.

43. François Villon, *Le Testament Villon*, ed. Jean Rychner and Albert Henry, 2 vols. (Geneva: Droz, 1974), 1:137.

44. The earliest citation in the OED is 1561, but Richard Huloet, *Abcedarium anglico latinum* (London: William Riddel, 1552 [*STC*:346:04]), has "chaungelyng chyldren *lamiae -rum pueri subdititii*" (C.iii^v); cf. William Horman, *Vulgaria* (London: Pynson, 1519 [*STC* (2nd ed.):13811]): "The fayre hath chaunged my childe," as a translation of *Strix vel lamia pro meo suum parvulum supposuit* (D.i).

45. For instance, the word appears five times in *Of Arthour and of Merlin* and in the *Chester Plays* (two and four citations respectively in the MED), and twice in both the *South English Legendary* and *King Alisaunder* (once each in the MED).

46. W. R. Childs, "'Welcome, My Brother': Edward II, John of Powderham and the Chronicles, 1318," in *Church and Chronicle in the Middle Ages*, ed. Ian Wood and G. A. Loud (London: Hambledon Press, 1991), pp. 149–63; Roy Martin Haines, *King Edward II: Edward of Caenarfon, His Life, His Reign, and Its Aftermath* (Montreal: McGill-Queens University Press, 2003), pp. 43–44.

47. *The Anonimalle Chronicle 1307–1334*, ed. W. R. Childs and J. Taylor (Leeds: Yorkshire Archaeological Society, 1991), p. 94.

48. Particularly interesting is a passage in Robert Holcot's *Super librum Sapientiae* (*Lectio* clxxxix); see Beryl Smalley, *English Friars and Antiquity in the Early Fourteenth Century* (Oxford: Blackwell, 1960), p. 325.

49. *Chronicon de Lanercost, MCCI–MCCCXLVI*, ed. Joseph Stevenson (Edinburgh: Bannatyne Club, 1839), p. 236.

50. *Vita Edwardi Secundi*, ed. Wendy R. Childs (Oxford: Clarendon Press, 2005), p. 148.

51. *Anonimalle Chronicle*, ed. Childs and Taylor, p. 94. It would also, of course, have served to quash rumors that Prince Edward had been switched for Powderham by his nurses, but since the reason given for their doing this was that their carelessness had led to the baby's mutilation (either by falling into a fire or being savaged by a pig!), Powderham's own appearance would have been sufficient refutation.

52. Robert Fabyan, *The New Chronicles of England and France*, ed. Henry Ellis (London: Rivington, 1811), p. 628.

53. Ronald Hutton, "The Making of Early Modern British Fairy Tradition," *Historical Journal* 57 (2014):1146.

54. *Ancrene Wisse*, ed. Bella Millett et al., 2 vols., EETS 325, 326 (London: Oxford University Press, 2005, 2006), 1:43.

55. *Of Arthour and of Merlin*, ed. Macrae-Gibson, 1:53 (line 680).

56. *Secular Lyrics of the XIVth and XVth Centuries*, ed. Rossell Hope Robbins (Oxford: Clarendon Press, 1952), no. 118, p. 106.

57. *The Early South-English Legendary, or Lives of Saints*, ed. Carl Horstmann, EETS OS 97 (London: Trübner, 1887), p. 421 (lines 321–22).

58. *Mum and the Sothsegger*, ed. Mabel Day and Robert Steele, EETS OS 199 (London: Oxford University Press, 1936), p. 14 (Passus 3, line 45).

59. *Of Arthour and of Merlin*, ed. Macrae-Gibson, 1:17 (line 205).

60. Bishop Richard Corbet, *Certain elegant poems, written by Dr. Corbet, Bishop of Norwich* (London: Andrew Crooke, 1647), p. 47 (*Wing* [2nd ed., 1994]:C6270) [punctuation modernized]; modern editions read, wrongly, *sprung* for *stolne*. Reginald Scot is less charitable: "with these fables is maintained an opinion, that men have beene begotten without carnall copulation (as [Andreas] Hyperius and others wate that Merlin was, An. 440) speciallie to excuse and mainteine the knaueries and lecheries of idle priests and bawdie monkes; and to cover the shame of their louers and concubines" (Scot, *Discouerie of Witchcraft* [1584], p. 85 [bk. 4, chap. 10]).

61. *Kyng Alisaunder*, ed. G. V. Smithers, 2 vols., EETS OS 227, 237 (London: Oxford University Press, 1952, 1957), p. 97 (B-text, lines 1708–18).

62. *Royal Historie*, ed. Furnivall, p. 42 (lines 1338–43).

63. *Early South-English Legendary*, ed. Horstmann, pp. 92–101.

64. *South English Legendary*, ed. D'Evelyn and Mill, 2:536 (line 97). Of the four MSS collated by D'Evelyn and Mill, one (B.L., MS Cotton Junius D. IX) is reported as reading *dame comon*, clearly a misreading of *conion*.

65. William Langland, *Piers Plowman: The A Version*, ed. George Kane (London: Athlone Press, 1960), p. 62 (lines 87–88).

66. *The Chester Mystery Cycle*, ed. R. M. Lumianski and David Mills, 2 vols., EETS SS 3, 9 (London: Oxford University Press, 1974, 1986), 1:170.

67. It is unclear why Lumianski and Mills should emend to *congeon* (as opposed to *congion* [cf. Play 8, line 328]), or even *conjion*, here. In both this and the previous instance the scribes seem to have had difficulty with the word; at Play 8, line 328 they give *coninge* Hm, *connyon* R, and *conge* B, and at Play 10, line 145, *commen* Hm, *connion* A, *conine* B, *conioyne* H.

68. Is this a confused recollection of the notoriously difficult passage in Gen. 6:2, "The sons of God seeing the daughters of men, that they were fair, took themselves wives of all which they chose" (Douay-Rheims)? Augustine seeks to explicate this passage immediately after his discussion of *incubi* and *dusii* in *City of God* (15:26).

69. *The York Plays: A Critical Edition of the York Corpus Christi Play as Recorded in British Library Additional MS 35290*, ed. Richard Beadle, 2 vols., EETS SS 23, 24 (London: Oxford University Press, 2009, 2013), 1:293.

70. *Six Middle English Romances*, ed. Mills, pp. 148, 166.

71. Alaric Hall, "The Evidence for Maran, the Anglo-Saxon 'Nightmares,'" *Neophilologus* 91 (2007):299–317. For various fifteenth-century folk remedies for the *quauquemare*, see *Évangilles des quenouilles*, ed. Jeay, pp. 141–42.

72. *English and Scottish Popular Ballads*, ed. Child, no. 121, st. 31.

73. Sharon L. Collingwood, *Market Pledge and Gender Bargain: Commercial Relations in French Farce, 1450–1550* (New York: Peter Lang, 1996), pp. 59–61.

74. See particularly "a good tract on the Decalogue," quoted in Owst, "Sortilegium," pp. 302–3.

75. *Fasciculus Morum*, ed. Wenzel, pp. 578–79.

76. Idley, *Instructions to His Son*, ed. D'Evelyn, p. 114 (lines 377–80).

77. Linda E. Marshall, "Sacral Parody in the *Secunda Pastorum*," *Speculum* 47 (1972):720–36.

78. Richard Kieckheffer, *Magic in the Middle Ages* (Cambridge: Cambridge University Press, 1990), pp. 7–8.

79. See MED, s.v. "forspeken" (c).

80. The MED gives the following examples: "Thys swerde woll I kepe but hit be takyn fro me with force" (Malory, *Works* [Win-C], 64/9); "and takynge with enmys of the shippes

wolle" (*Pet.Hen.VI* in *Archaeol.Ael.n.s.3.* 185); "As fysshes þat ar in the see By soden takyn with an hooke" (Idley, *Instructions to His Son*, 1,1430); "I wolde not for my hat Be takyn with sich a gyle" (*KEdw.& S.*[Cmb Ff.5.48], 228); "Dravale . . . was takyn with enemyis" (*Paston*, 2. 135).

81. *The Dictionary of syr Thomas Eliot knyght* (London: Berthelet, 1538 [*STC* (2nd ed.):7659]), s.v. "Lamiae."

82. *Promptorium parvulorum*, ed. Albert Way (London: Camden Society, 1865), p. 138 n1.

83. John Gardner, *The Construction of the Wakefield Cycle* (Carbondale: Southern Illinois University Press, 1974), p. 110.

84. *The Towneley Plays*, ed. Martin Stevens and A. C. Cawley, 2 vols., EETS SS 13, 14 (London: Oxford University Press, 1994), 1:254.

85. See David R. Cartlidge and J. Keith Elliott, *Art and the Christian Apocrypha* (London: Routledge, 2001), pp. 107–14.

86. *Ludus Coventriae or The Plaie called Corpus Christi*, ed. K. S. Block, EETS ES 120 (London: Oxford University Press, 1922), p. 284 (lines 381–84).

87. *Chester Mystery Cycle*, ed. Lumiansky and Mills, p. 484 (App. 1c).

88. William Langland, *Piers Plowman: The B Version*, ed. George Kane and E. Talbot Donaldson (London: Athlone Press, 1975), p. 609 (Passus 18, line 46).

89. Rosemary Woolf, "The Effect of Typology on the English Mediaeval Plays of Abraham and Isaac," *Speculum* 32 (1957):805–25.

90. V. A. Kolve, *The Play Called Corpus Christi* (Stanford, Calif.: Stanford University Press, 1966), pp. 57–100.

91. Arnold Williams, "Typology and the Cycle Plays: Some Criteria," *Speculum* 43 (1968):677–84.

92. D. W. Robertson, "The Question of Typology and the Wakefield *Mactacio Abel*," *American Benedictine Review* 25 (1974):158.

93. Siegfried Wenzel, "The Moor Maiden—A Contemporary View," *Speculum* 49 (1974):74.

94. *English Lyrics of the XIIIth Century*, ed. Carleton Brown (Oxford: Clarendon Press, 1932), pp. 32, 180.

95. O. S. Pickering, "A Third Text of 'Sey me viit in þe brom,'" *English Studies* 63 (1982): 20–22. As presented, the exchange is parodic, but some more primitive transaction seems to underlie it. For a clear demonization of this motif, see Barillari, *Protostoria*, pp. 160–63.

96. *Religious Lyrics of the XIVth Century*, ed. Carleton Brown, 2nd ed. (Oxford: Clarendon Press, 1924), pp. 229, 286.

97. This poem is discussed at length by Siegfried Wenzel, *Poets, Preachers and the Early English Lyric* (Princeton, N.J.: Princeton University Press, 1986), pp. 210–11, 230–32. Wenzel demonstrates its secular origins but does not explore its supernatural attributes. Both springs and hawthorns, however, are associated with fairies. In the prose *Merlin*, for instance, the hero is enchanted by Nimiane in "the foreste of brochelonde [under] a bussh that was feire and high of white hawthorne full of floures"; see *Merlin*, ed. Wheatley, 3:681.

98. See *REED: Cheshire, Including Chester*, ed. Elizabeth Baldwin, Lawrence M. Clopper, and David Mills, 2 vols. (Toronto: University of Toronto Press, 2007), 1:lxxi.

99. See *REED: Chester*, ed. Lawrence M. Clopper (Toronto: University of Toronto Press, 1979), pp. 170, 172–73, 175–76, 179, 183–84, and passim.

100. *REED: Chester*, ed. Clopper, p. 198; *REED: Cheshire, Including Chester*, ed. Baldwin, Clopper, and Mills, 1:345, annotation to line 14 ("capes & canes"); cf. *REED: Chester*, ed. Clopper, p. 354: "Christe in stringes".

101. *REED: Cheshire, Including Chester*, ed. Baldwin, Clopper, and Mills, 1:346.

102. James Simpson, *Reform and Cultural Revolution: 1350–1547*, vol. 2 of *The Oxford English Literary History* (Oxford: Oxford University Press, 2002), p. 509.

103. Woolf, "Effect of Typology," p. 825.

104. Thomas, *Religion and the Decline of Magic*, p. 88.

105. Bromyard, *Summa Predicantium*, Trinitas 4, 13, quoted in G. G. Coulton, *The Medieval Village* (Cambridge: Cambridge University Press, 1926), pp. 265–66.

106. From the *Workes* of Mr. William Premble (d. 1623), quoted in Thomas, *Religion and the Decline of Magic*, p. 194. In the Middle Ages an idea seems to have circulated that the soul resided in the bloodstream; see Walter L. Wakefield, "Some Unorthodox Popular Ideas of the Thirteenth Century," *Medievalia et Humanistica* 4 (1973):26, 30–31.

107. Robert Mannyng of Brunne, *Handlyng Synne*, ed. Idelle Sullens (Binghamton: State University of New York Press, 1983), p. 238.

108. Wakefield, "Some Unorthodox Popular Ideas," p. 30 and n20.

109. Cited in Arnold, *Belief and Unbelief*, p. 231. A similar stress on the dignity of labor is to be seen in a reported claim that "a newly built church [was] no holier than the implements that built it" (Wakefield, "Some Unorthodox Popular Ideas," p. 27).

110. See Kittredge, *Witchcraft in Old and New England*, pp. 23–72 (chap. 2: "English Witchcraft Before 1558").

111. R. H. Nicholson, "The Trial of Christ the Sorcerer in the York Cycle," *Journal of Medieval and Renaissance Studies* 16 (1986):125–69, has argued for a parallel with English fifteenth-century show trials that employed accusations of witchcraft for political purposes; the parallel is certainly close, but its relevance for civic theater is less obvious.

112. Boudet, "Condamnations," p. 149 (art. 7).

113. Idley, *Instructions to His Son*, ed. D'Evelyn, p. 114 (lines 381–83).

114. *Lower Ecclesiastical Jurisdiction in Late-Medieval England: The Courts of the Dean and Chapter of Lincoln, 1336–1349, and the Deanery of Wisbech, 1458–1484*, ed. L. R. Poos (Oxford: British Academy, 2001), p. xi n3.

115. *Depositions from the Courts of Durham*, ed. Raine, pp. 27, 29 (3), 33 (2).

116. *Lower Ecclesiastical Jurisdictions*, ed. Poos, p. 463.

117. *Register of John Morton, III*, ed. Harper-Bill, nos. 518, 661, 663, 803. For other cases, see Kathleen Kamerick, "Shaping Superstition in Late Medieval England," *Magic, Ritual & Witchcraft* 3 (2008):31–34.

118. *Register of John Stafford, Bishop of Bath and Wells, 1425–1443*, ed. Thomas Scott Holmes, 2 vols., Somerset Record Society 31, 32 (London: Harrison, 1915, 1916), 2:226. See also Rider, *Magic and Religion*, pp. 70ff.

119. *Lincoln Diocese Documents, 1450–1544*, ed. Andrew Clark, EETS OS 149 (London: Kegan Paul, 1914), p. 111.

120. Sometime between 1432 and 1443 a man called Henry Hoiges brought a suit in Chancery accusing a local priest of employing "the sotill craft of enchauntement wycchecraft and socerye" against him (*Calendars of the Proceedings in Chancery, in the Reign of Queen Elizabeth*, ed. John Bayley, 3 vols. [London: Record Commission, 1800–1832], 1:xxiv). Presumably he appealed to the chancellor because he assumed his case would stand little chance in an ecclesiastical court.

121. Philippe de Thaon, *Le Livre de Sibile*, ed. Hugh Shields, ANTS, 37 (London: Anglo Norman Text Society, 1979), p. 55 (lines 11–14).

122. [Higden], *Polychronicon Ranulphi Higden*, ed. Babington, 2:403.

123. Robert of Gloucester, *Metrical Chronicle,* ed. Wright, 1:371 (lines 5106–7).

124. "À l'instar de la fée médiévale, la Sibylle vit, par exemple, dans un monde en marge de l'univers des vivants . . . elle a le don de prophétie, et elle bénéficie, à défaut de l'immortalité, d'une longévité extraordinaire"; see Josiane Haffen, *Contribution à l'étude de la Sibylle médiévale* (Paris: Belles lettres, 1984), p. 49.

125. William L. Kinter and Joseph R. Keller, *The Sibyl: Prophetess of Antiquity and Medieval Fay* (Philadelphia: Dorrance, 1967), pp. 46–79.

126. *Évangiles des quenouilles,* ed. Jeay, p. 78 (line 55), and passim.

127. *REED: Cheshire, Including Chester,* ed. Baldwin, Clopper, and Mills, 1:147.

128. Though in the earliest English version, *Romance of the Cheuelere Assigne,* ed. Gibbs, he is called Enyas.

129. *Le Roman en prose de Tristan,* ed. E. Löseth (Paris: Bouillon, 1891), pp. 171–85; *The Vulgate Version of the Arthurian Romances,* ed. H. Oskar Sommer, 8 vols. (Washington, D.C.: Carnegie, 1908–16), 6:97; Malory, *Works,* ed. Vinaver, 2:639.

130. *Das Mittellateinische Gespräch Adrian und Epictitus: Nebst verwandten Texten (Joca Monachorum),* ed. Walther Suchier (Tübingen: Niemeyer, 1955), p. 32.

131. *REED: Cheshire, Including Chester,* ed. Baldwin, Clopper, and Mills, 1:147.

132. Cf. *The Wedding of Sir Gawain Dame Ragnelle,* ed. Thomas Hahn, in *Sir Gawain: Eleven Romances and Tales,* ed. Thomas Hahn (Kalamazoo: Medieval Institute Publications, 1995), pp. 41–80, or du Guesclin's fairy bride, Tiffany de Raguenel.

133. Richard K. Emmerson, "'Nowe ys common this daye': Enoch and Elias, Antichrist, and the Structure of the Chester Cycle," in *Homo, Memento Finis: The Iconography of Just Judgment in Medieval Art and Drama,* ed. David Bevington (Kalamazoo: Medieval Institute Publications, 1985), pp. 89–120.

134. For example, John C. Coldewey, "Watching the Watchers: Drama Spectatorship and Counter-Surveillance in Sixteenth-Century Chester," *Studia Anglica Posnaniensia* 38 (2002):131–46. The first to make this case in detail was Harold C. Gardiner, *Mysteries' End: An Investigation of the Last Days of the Medieval Religious Stage* (New Haven, Conn.: Yale University Press, 1946).

135. James J. Paxson, "Theorizing the Mysteries' End in England, the Artificial Demonic, and the Sixteenth-Century Witch-Craze," *Criticism* 39 (1997):481–502.

136. Richard K. Emmerson, "Contextualizing Performance: The Reception of the Chester Antichrist," *Journal of Medieval & Early Modern Studies* 29 (1999):89–119.

137. *REED: Cheshire, Including Chester,* ed. Baldwin, Clopper, and Mills, 1:148.

138. *REED: Cheshire, Including Chester,* ed. Baldwin, Clopper, and Mills, 1:147.

139. *Middle English Treatise,* ed. Royster, p. 4.

140. Gregory, *Rye Spirits,* pp. 189–92.

CHAPTER 5

1. Geoffrey of Monmouth, *Historia Regum, 1,* ed. Wright, p. 74. Geoffrey later mentions that Arthur was taken to Avalon to be healed of his wounds [*ad sananda uulnera sua in insulam Avallonis euectus*], but since he also describes these wounds as mortal [*letaliter uulneratus est*] and ends with a prayer for his soul [*anima eius in pace quiescat*], he endorses the idea that Arthur is truly dead (p. 132).

2. Geoffrey of Monmouth, *Life of Merlin / Vita Merlini,* ed. and trans. Basil Clarke (Cardiff: University of Wales Press, 1973), pp. 103–3 (lines 929–38).

3. Geoffrey of Monmouth, *Life of Merlin / Vita Merlini*, ed. and trans. Clarke, pp. 112–13 (lines 1122–24).
4. *Roman de Brut*, ed. Arnold, 2:693–94.
5. E. K. Chambers, *Arthur of Britain* (London: Sidgwick & Jackson, 1927), p. 250.
6. Chambers, *Arthur of Britain*, p. 249. See also J. S. P. Tatlock, "The English Journey of the Laon Canons," *Speculum* 8 (1933):454–65.
7. Chambers, *Arthur of Britain*, p. 265.
8. E.g., Paul Dalton, "The Topical Concerns of Geoffrey of Monmouth's *Historia Regum Britannie*: History, Prophecy, Peacemaking, and English Identity in the Twelfth Century," *Journal of British Studies* 44 (2005):688–712.
9. *Chronicles of the Reigns of Stephen, Henry II, and Richard I*, ed. Richard Howlett, 4 vols. (London: Longman, 1884–89), 2:703–8.
10. A twelfth-century commentary on the *Prophesies of Merlin* explains *exitus eius dubius erit* as "quia dubitatur an sit vivus an mortuus. Omnium scilicet haec est superstitio, Britonum, Guallorum et Cornubiencium" [because it is doubted whether he is living or dead; this is the particular superstition of all the Bretons, Welsh, and Cornish]; see Jacob Hammer, "A Commentary on the *Prophetia Merlini* (Geoffrey of Monmouth's *Historia Regum Britanniae*, Book VII)," *Speculum* 15 (1940):414–15.
11. *Patrologia Latina*, 207:958C (*Passio Reginaldi Principis*), and 112A, 154C (*Epistolae*).
12. Chambers, *Arthur of Britain*, p. 272.
13. Joseph of Exeter, *The Trojan War, I–III*, ed. and trans A. K. Bate (Warminster: Aris and Phillips, 1986), pp. 152–53.
14. Edmund G. Gardner, *Arthurian Legend in Italian Literature* (London: J. M. Dent, 1930), pp. 10–11.
15. *Patrologia Latina*, 204:847B (*Elegia de Diversitate Fortunae et Philosophiae Consolatione*, 1:157–58).
16. John Gillingham, *The English in the Twelfth Century: Imperialism, National Identity, and Political Values* (Woodbridge: Boydell Press, 2000), p. 30.
17. William of Newburgh, *History of English Affairs*, ed. Walsh and Kennedy, p. 33 (*Proemium*).
18. Françoise Le Saux makes a case for the *Vita Merlini*'s being Layamon's direct source here, but the parallels are not conclusive; see Le Saux, *Laȝamon's Brut: The Poem and Its Sources* (Woodbridge: D. S. Brewer, 1989), pp. 113–14.
19. Laȝamon, *Brut*, ed. Brook and Leslie, 2:750 (lines 14277–82) [punctuation modernized].
20. [Geoffrey of Monmouth], *Historia Regum*, 5, ed. Wright, pp. 246–49 (bk. 9, lines 296–317).
21. [Geoffrey of Monmouth], *Historia Regum*, 5, ed. Wright, pp. xli–xlii. See Lucy Allen Paton, *Studies in the Fairy Mythology of Arthurian Romance* (Boston: Ginn, 1903), pp. 45–47.
22. Cf. Ulrich von Zatzikhoven's description of the fairy castle in which Lancelot is brought up, in von Zatzikhoven, *Lanzelet, eine Erzählung*, ed. K. A. Hahn (Frankfurt: Broenner, 1845), p. 6 (lines 202–40).
23. *Oxford Book of Medieval Latin Verse*, ed. Raby, pp. 187–89 (no. 135).
24. [Geoffrey of Monmouth], *Historia Regum*, 5, ed. Wright, pp. 48–49 (bk. 9, lines 314–15). Wright translates this as "the court of the king of Avallon," but it is possible that Avallon is actually the king's name here: i.e., "the court of King Avallon." The *De Antiquitate Glastoniensis Ecclesiae* says that Avalon might have been named after a certain Avalloc who lived there with his daughters, and Gerald of Wales suggests a similar etymology: "after a certain Avallon, at one time ruler of that land" [*a [A]vallone quodam, territorii illius quondam dominatore*]; see Chambers, *Arthur of Britain*, pp. 266, 273.

25. *Chronicle of Lanercost*, ed. Stephenson, p. 23.

26. *Chronicles*, ed. Howlett, 2:707 (line 1281); I am grateful to Christopher Berard for this reference.

27. Peter Dronke, *The Medieval Poet and His World* (Rome: Storia e Letteratura, 1984), pp. 304–7.

28. [Gerald of Wales], *Giraldi Cambrensis Opera*, ed. Brewer, 6:75–78 (*Itinerarium Kambriae*, 1:8).

29. Chambers, *Arthur of Britain*, p. 269.

30. Chambers, *Arthur of Britain*, p. 272. The sentence is ambiguous since the subject of *decepti* could be either *Judaei* or *Britones*; rhetorically, however, one might expect Gerald to be suggesting that the Britons are worse than the Jews.

31. James P. Carley, *Glastonbury Abbey: The Holy House at the Head of the Moors Adventurous*, 2nd ed. (Glastonbury: Gothic Image, 1996), pp. 177–78.

32. Richard Barber, *King Arthur in Legend and History* (London: Cardinal, 1973), p. 64.

33. Map, *De nugis curialium*, ed. James, p. 155.

34. For the spread of news of this discovery, see *Haut Livre du Graal*, ed. Nitze and Jenkins, 1:59–72.

35. Giles Constable, "Forgery and Plagiarism in the Middle Ages," *Archiv für Diplomatik* 29 (1983):1–41.

36. Timothy Lewis and J. Douglas Bruce, "The Pretended Exhumation of Arthur and Guinevere," *Revue Celtique* 33 (1912):434.

37. Chaucer, *Riverside Chaucer*, p. 170.

38. [Jean d'Outremeuse], *Myreur des histors*, ed. Bormans and Borgnet, 4:56.

39. For further references to Ogier and Avalon, see Paton, *Studies in Fairy Mythology*, pp. 74–80; Paton was unaware of the Jean d'Outremeuse passage.

40. Roger Sherman Loomis, "The Legend of Arthur's Survival," in *Arthurian Literature in the Middle Ages*, ed. Roger Sherman Loomis (Oxford: Clarendon Press, 1959), pp. 67–69.

41. *Middle English Debate Poetry*, ed. Conlee, p. 186 (line 185).

42. John Lydgate, *Fall of Princes*, ed. Henry Bergen, 4 vols., EETS ES 121–24 (London: Oxford University Press, 1924–27), 3:909 (bk. 8, lines 3100–3101).

43. [Étienne de Bourbon], *Anecdotes historiques*, ed. Lecoy de la Marche, p. 321.

44. Gervase of Tilbury, *Otia Imperialia*, ed. Banks and Binns, pp. 336–37.

45. [William of Auvergne], *De Universo*, II, iii, 24 (1674 ed., 1:1067aC); *disgladiatos* is clearly a calque on French *desglaivés*, or 'put to the sword.'

46. *Criminal Trials in Scotland, I, ii*, ed. Robert Pitcairn (Edinburgh: Tait, 1833), p. 51.

47. *Fasciculus Morum*, ed. Wenzel, pp. 578–79.The antecedent of the phrase *que in nostro vulgari dicitur elves* is unclear; *dicitur* is presumably a slip for *dicuntur*, and I have accordingly adapted the word order of Wenzel's translation to clarify that "who in our native tongue are called *elves*" refers back to the '*reginas*' and '*puellas*' [queens and girls].

48. *Fasciculus Morum*, ed. Wenzel, p. 13.

49. See R. W. Chambers, *Widsith, a Study in Old English Heroic Legend* (Cambridge: Cambridge University Press, 1912), pp. 95–100.

50. Chaucer, *Riverside Chaucer*, p. 156.

51. Karl P. Wentersdorf, "Chaucer and the Lost Tale of Wade," *Journal of English and Germanic Philology* 65 (1966):274–286.

52. See Owst, "Sortilegium," p. 278n1.

53. This item appears in a *Libellus de Bruto et Britonibus secundum Bedam*, in an early fifteenth-century British Library MS, Cotton Vespasian D IV, f. 139b; see Chambers, *Widsith*, p. 254.

54. On the origins of the *Fasciculus Morum*, see Siegfried Wenzel, *Verses in Sermons* (Cambridge, Mass.: Medieval Academy of America, 1978), pp. 26–41.

55. Gervase of Canterbury, *Historical Works*, ed. William Stubbs, 2 vols., Rolls Series (London: Longman, 1879, 1880), 2:238.

56. A similarly incongruous blending of Christian and fairy beliefs is to be seen in an account of the founding of Evesham Abbey at a site where "three unearthly and beautiful women" had been observed singing in a forest; see Hutton, "Making of Early Modern British Fairy Tradition," p. 1140.

57. *Floriant et Florete*, ed. Harry F. Williams (Ann Arbor: University of Michigan Press, 1947), pp. 244–45 (lines 6237–48).

58. Chrétien de Troyes, *Le Chevalier de la Charrette (Lancelot)*, ed. Alfred Foulet and Karl de Utti (Paris: Garnier, 1989), pp. 108, 220.

59. *Romance of Guy of Warwick (Auchinleck and Caius MSS)*, 3:655.

60. Douglas Kelly, "Two Problems in Chrétien's *Charrette*: The Boundary of Gorre and the Use of *Novele*," *Neophilologus* 48 (1964):115–21.

61. See J. H. Mozley, "A Collection of Mediaeval Latin Verse in MS. Cotton Titus D. XXIV," *Medium Aevum* 11 (1942):10, 31–32 (no. 64).

62. *Reliquiae Antiquae*, ed. Wright and Halliwell, 1:105.

63. See *Romance of the Cheuelere Assigne*, ed. Gibbs.

64. Allen, "Orpheus and Orfeo," pp. 107–8.

65. Thomas of Cantimpré, *Bonum Universale*, pp. 548–53 (paras. 17–22).

66. "Qui hominum viventium corpora, ut Dianae, subito ex hominibus rapiebant, & cum ea, delusi homines, in alias regiones delata vidissent, quae apud se mortua astimabant, illa iam immortalia facta credebant, & in deorum numero computabant. Sic & et nos etiam temporibus modernorum frequenter audivimus, quasi in agone mortis positas mulieres subito rapi, et earum loco a daemonibus figmenta deponi, & ipsa figmenta simillima raptis corporibus, quasi mortua sepeliri; visas vero postea feminas, et inter homines conversatas"; see Thomas of Cantimpré, *Bonum Universale*, pp. 548–49.

67. *Sir Orfeo*, ed. Bliss, p. 18 (line 187).

68. See, e.g., Burchard of Worms's condemnation of the belief that women can kill and eat Christians at some sort of Sabbat, "and replace their hearts with straw or wood or something similar, and then bring them back to life and grant them a period of respite for living"; see [Burchard of Worms], *The Corrector*, in *Bussordnungen*, ed. Wasserschleben, pp. 160–61 (cap. 158); *Patrologia Latina*, 140:973D. In an eleventh-century apocryphal life of Saint Stephen, the devil steals the child from his cradle and leaves an *ydolum* in his place; see Baudouin Gaiffier, "Le Diable, voleur d'enfants," in *Études critiques d'hagiographie et d'iconologie* (Brussels: Société Bollandistes, 1967), p. 182.

69. *Amadas et Ydoine: Roman du XIIe siècle*, ed. John R. Reinhard (Paris: Champion, 1926), pp. 203–40 (lines 5299–6522, esp. lines 6400–6453).

70. On the general metamorphoses of fairy gatherings into satanic sabbats, see Ginzburg, *Esctacies*. For the scholarly debate over transvection, see Stuart Clark, *Thinking with Demons* (Oxford: Oxford University Press, 1997), pp. 191–92.

71. Cambridge University Library, MS KK IV 24, f. 241r.

72. This story, frequently repeated in the early modern period (e.g., *Malleus Maleficarum,* ed. Mackay, 101B & 133A-B; 1:404 and 460, and 2:245 and 310–11), seems to have been best known from the *Legenda Aurea* (31 July). Étienne de Bourbon's (earlier and much fuller) version is omitted from Lecoy de la Marche's *Anecdotes historiques,* and I have quoted it here from Paris: B.N. MS Latin 15970, f. 413a.

73. Bruce Mitchell, "The Faery World of Sir Orfeo," *Neophilologus* 48 (1964):156.

74. "Women are yet alive who tell they were taken away when in Child-bed to nurse Fairie Children, a lingering voracious Image of their [*these*] being left in their place, (like their Reflexion in a Mirrour,) which (as if it were some insatiable Spirit in ane assumed Bodie) made first semblance to devour the Meats that it cunningly carried by, and then left the Carcase as if it expired and departed thence by a naturall and common Death"; see Robert Kirk, *The Secret Commonwealth of Elves, Fauns, and Fairies, 1691,* ed. Andrew Lang (London: David Nutt, 1893), p. 12.

75. Jeff Rider, "Receiving Orpheus in the Middle Ages: Allegorization, Remythification and *Sir Orfeo,*" *Papers on Language & Literature* 24 (1988):345.

76. Fletcher, "*Sir Orfeo* and the Flight from the Enchanters," p. 162.

77. Neil Cartlidge, "Sir Orfeo in the Otherworld: Courting Chaos?" *Studies in the Age of Chaucer* 26 (2004):225.

78. I do not include here religious allusions *in potentia,* such as Orfeo's harp alluding to King David's harp (Rider, "Receiving Orpheus," p. 357), the *ympe tree* alluding to the Garden of Eden (D. M. Hill, "The Structure of Sir Orfeo" *Mediaeval Studies* 23 [1961]:136–41 [at 140]), or *underne* alluding to the noon-day demon (John Block Friedman, "Eurydice, Heurodis, and the Noon-Day Demon," *Speculum* 41 [1966]:22–29). But, as Morton W. Bloomfield ("Symbolism in Medieval Literature," *Modern Philology* 56 [1958]:73–81) wisely wrote, "with sixteen meanings for the peacock who is to decide between them?" (81).

79. This is apparently one of the elements that leads D. M. Hill to call this part of the poem "strangely and profoundly Christian" ("Structure of Sir Orfeo," p. 141).

80. Malory, *Works,* ed. Vinaver, 3:1240–41.

81. Map, *De nugis curialium,* ed. James, pp. 344–45.

82. "In Bauaria virum nobili familia natum, extincta vxore, tantum animi dolorem cepisse, vt nullam admitteret consolationem, ac vitam ageret in solitudine. Tandem vbi nullum finem lugendi faceret, vxorem eius comparuisse, excitatam a mortuis, ac dixisse, se quidem semel confecisse curriculum vitae a natura datum, atque a deo iussam vti eius adhuc consuetudine diutius, hac tamen condicione ac lege, ut matrimonium morte solutum denuo per Sacerdotem solenni ritu iungeretur, vtque deinceps ipse abstineret blasphemis convitiandi verbis, quibus vti consueuerat, se enim horum causa ei redemptam fuisse, atque iterum excessuram e vita , cum primum eiusmodi aliquod verbum edidisset. His actis, illam curasse rem domesticam, vt antea, & aliquot etiam peperit liberos, semper tamen fuisse tristem ac pallidam. Post multos vero annos maritum vesperi potum & ancillae iratum, edidisse verba quae non debebat; interea illam disparuisse e cubiculo, vnde marito allatura erat poma, ac reliquisse muliebrem vestem, sic corpore stantem, quasi phantasma, ad cistam, vbi poma seruabantur. Haec audiui, inquit Sabinus, ex multis viris fide dignis, qui affirmabant, Ducem Bauariae eadem retulisse Duci Saxoniae pro veris"; see Iohann Georg Godelman, *Tractatus de magis, veneficis et lamiis* (Frankfurt: Basse, 1601), p. 37, cited in Cameron, *Enchanted Europe,* p. 115.

83. "A romance's other world was a fictive world created to stand over and against the equally fictive world of its central aristocratic society"; see Rider, "Other Worlds of Romance," p. 115.

84. Claude Lecouteux, *Chasses fantastiques et cohortes de la nuit au moyen âge* (Paris: Imago, 1999).

85. Other recent authorities who have associated Hellequin with the dead include Ginzburg, *Ecstasies*, p. 191; and Jean-Claude Schmitt, *Ghosts in the Middle Ages: The Living and the Dead in Medieval Society*, trans. Teresa Lavender Fagan (Chicago: University of Chicago Press, 1998), pp. 93–121.

86. Orderic Vitalis, *The Ecclesiastical History of Orderic Vitalis*, ed. and trans. Marjorie Chibnall, 6 vols. (Oxford: Clarendon Press, 1969–80), 4:239.

87. Map, *De nugis curialium*, ed. James, pp. 26–31.

88. See, e.g., *Luque la maudite*, in Gaston Raynaud, "Trois dits tirés d'un nouvau manuscrit de fableaux," *Romania* 12 (1883):224–26.

89. [William of Auvergne], *De Universo*, II, iii, 24 (1674 ed., 1:1066aG).

90. Paul Meyer, "Notice du MS. Bibl. Nat. Fr. 25439," *Bulletin de la société des anciens textes Français* 25 (1899):61. *Luiton* is the reading of a fifteenth-century MS copy (MS Fr. 25439 reads *lou ui t?u*); Meyer suggests that *genes* is cognate with *jana* 'sorcière' (p. 62).

91. [*Lucydarye*], *Late Middle English* Lucydarye, ed. Morrison, p. 55 (line 879).

92. Raoul de Presles, *de Civitate Dei*, liv. 15, chap. 23 (from Paris, MS B.N., Français 173, ff. 94r, 95r).

93. *Mum and the Sothsegger*, ed. Day and Steele, p. 6 [Passus 1, line 90].

94. Adam le Bossu, *Le Jeu de la feuillée*, ed. Ernest Langlois, 2nd ed. (Paris: Champion, 1968), p. x.

95. In Huon de Méri's *Torneiment Anticrist*, when *Cointise* [Gallantry] enters the field on a horse with silk trappings decorated with little bells, the sound reminds the narrator of "la maisnie Helequin" (lines 686–87).

96. [Étienne de Bourbon], *Anecdotes historiques*, ed. Lecoy de la Marche, p. 321 (no. 365): "in similitudinem militum venancium vel ludencium, qui dicuntur de familia Allequini vulgariter vel Arturi."

97. [William of Auvergne], *De Universo*, II, iii, 24 (1674 ed., 1:1066aG).

98. *High Book of the Grail*, trans. Bryant, p. 144; *Haut Livre du Graal*, ed. Nitze and Jenkins, 1:222.

99. [Étienne de Bourbon], *Anecdotes historiques*, ed. Lecoy de la Marche, p. 321 (no. 365).

100. *Patrologia Latina*, 154:1051–52 (Ekkhard reports that a recently deceased count called Emicho was seen among them).

101. *Patrologia Latina*, 212:731C.

102. In fact a marginal note in one thirteenth-century manuscript reads *de familia hellequini* at this point (Thomas de Mayo, "William of Auvergne and Popular Demonology," *Quidditas* 28 [2007]:64). William had mentioned Hellequin earlier ([William of Auvergne], *De Universo*, II, iii, 12 [1674 ed., 1:1037aB]).

103. [William of Auvergne], *De Universo*, II, iii, 24 (1674 ed., 1:1065bB).

104. [William of Auvergne], *De Universo*, II, iii, 24 (1674 ed., 1:1067aC).

105. [William of Auvergne], *De Universo*, II, iii, 14 (1674 ed., 1:1044bG).

106. [William of Auvergne], *De Universo*, II, iii, 24 (1674 ed., 1:1066aF).

107. [William of Auvergne], *De Universo*, II, iii, 24 (1674 ed., 1:1067bB).

108. [William of Auvergne], *De Universo*, I, i, 60–62 (1674 ed., 1:676–79).

109. E.g., R. W. Southern, "Between Heaven and Hell: Review of Jacques le Goff, *La Naissance du Purgatoire*," *Times Literary Supplement*, 18 June 1982, pp. 652–53; Graham Robert Edwards, "Purgatory: 'Birth' or Evolution?," *Journal of Ecclesiastical History* 36 (1985):634–46; Robert

Easting, "Purgatory and the Earthly Paradise in the *Purgatorio Sancti Patricii*," *Citeaux: Commentarii Cistercienses* 37 (1986):23–48; Gurevich, *Medieval Popular Culture*, pp. 148–49; B. P. McGuire, "Purgatory, the Communion of Saints, and Medieval Change," *Viator* 20 (1989):61–84.

110. Jacques Le Goff, *La naissance du purgatoire* (Paris: Gallimard, 1981), pp. 149–52; Jacques Le Goff, *The Birth of Purgatory*, trans. Arthur Goldhammer (Chicago: University of Chicago Press, 1984), pp. 108–10. See also Le Goff, *L'imaginaire médiévale*, pp. 84–98.

111. Alan E. Bernstein, "Review of *La naissance du purgatoire* by Jacques Le Goff," *Speculum* 59 (1984):182.

112. "Artù nell'Etna," in Arturo Graf, *Miti, leggende e superstizioni del medio evo* (1892/3; Milan: Mondadori, 1985), pp. 321–38.

113. For the story itself, see Gervase of Tilbury, *Otia Imperialia*, ed. Banks and Binns, pp. 334–37; for the dates, ed. cit., pp. xxviii, xl.

114. [Caesarius of Heisterbach], *Dialogus Miraculorum*, ed. Strange, 2:324–25 (12:12). "Vulcano" appears to be a reference to the island in the Sicilian archipelago.

115. [Étienne de Bourbon], *Anecdotes historiques*, ed. Lecoy de la Marche, pp. 32–33.

116. Le Goff, *Naissance du purgatoire*, pp. 419–21; trans. Goldhammer, pp. 313–14.

117. *Thomas of Erceldoune*, ed. Nixon, 1:40 (Thornton MS, lines 185–88).

118. William of Newburgh, *History of English Affairs*, ed. Walsh and Kennedy, pp. 120–21 (bk. 1, chap 28).

119. *Lais féeriques*, ed. Micha, pp. 96–97 (lines 567–68).

120. Sir John Mandeville, *Mandeville's Travels*, ed. Seymour (1967), pp. 197–98 (chap. 30).

121. References to the Latin *Tractatus* are taken from Karl Warnke's edition of Marie de France's *Espurgatoire S. Patrice* (Halle: Niemeyer, 1938). Unless noted, the β text is cited.

122. Robert Easting, "The South English Legendary 'St Patrick' as Translation," *Leeds Studies in English* 21 (1990):120.

123. Le Goff, *La Naissance du purgatoire*, p. 54; trans. Goldhammer, p. 33.

124. *Visiones Georgii*, ed. L. L. Hammerich, in *Det Kgl. Danske Videnskabernes Selkab. Historisk-filologiske Meddelelser*, vol. 18, pt. 2 (Copenhagen: Bianco Lunos, 1930). Twenty MSS of the *Visiones Georgii* survive, and another four are known to have existed; see Bernd Weitemeier, *Visiones Georgii: Untersuchung mit synoptischer Edition der Übersetzung und Redaktion C* (Berlin: Erich Schmidt, 2006), pp. 111–19, 202–4.

125. There is a faint echo of this motif in the *Vision of William of Stranton*: "thow shalt fynd men . . . lich in shap and colour to men of thi owne contree þat ben levyng, but þei ben evel spirites"; see *St Patrick's Purgatory*, ed. Robert Easting, EETS 298 (Oxford: Oxford University Press, 1991), p. 80.

126. *Visio Ludovico de Francia*, ed. Max Voigt, in *Beiträge zur Geschichte der Visionenliteratur im Mittelalter I.II.* (Leipzig: Mayer & Müller, 1924), pp. 230–35.

127. Sonia Maura Barillari, "Le città delle dame: La sovranità ctonia declinata al femminile fra l'irlanda e i Monti Sibillini," *L'Immagine Riflessa*, n.s. 18 (2009):112.

128. Robert Easting, "Peter of Cornwall's Account of St. Patrick's Purgatory," *Analecta Bollandiana* 97 (1979):397–416; the story is on pp. 413–16.

129. Easting takes this to mean that his penis has been turned to wood, but *virga* can also denote the male member itsef (cf. MED, "yērd" (n. [2], 5[a]).

130. *Visio Ludovico de Francia*, ed. Voigt, in *Beiträge*, pp. 129–30.

131. *St Patrick's Purgatory*, ed. Easting, p. 24 (st. 139).

132. The *Visiones Georgii* make the torments of purgatory different in degree and duration, but not in kind, from those of hell (ed. Hammerich, pp. 201–4).

133. *South English Legendary,* ed. D'Evelyn and Mill, 1:96. The *Visiones Georgii* (ed. Hammerich) make the point that the punishments differ only in degree and duration, not in kind (pp. 201–4).

134. Easting, "Purgatory and the Earthly Paradise" (1986), pp. 40–41.

135. For the English versions, see Easting, "South English Legendary 'St Patrick,' " p. 119; for the French ones, Paul Meyer, "Notices sur quelques manuscrits français de la bibliothèque Phillipps à Cheltenham," *Notices et extraits des manuscrits de la Bibliothèque nationale et autres bibliothèques* 34 (1891):239.

136. *South English Legendary,* ed. D'Evelyn and Mill, 1:100; cf. lines 172, 199–214.

137. Marie de France, *Espurgatoire S. Patrice,* ed. Karl Warnke (Halle: Niemeyer, 1938), pp. 69, 75, 77, 89; cf. lines 845–72 (p. 61).

138. Thomas of Cantimpré, *Bonum universale,* pp. 553–54; *Middle English Debate Poetry,* ed. Conlee, pp. 178–91.

139. Easting, "Purgatory and the Earthly Paradise" (1986), pp. 29–31.

140. Easting, "Purgatory and the Earthly Paradise" (1986), pp. 42–46.

141. Ernst Robert Curtius, *European Literature and the Latin Middle Ages,* trans. Willard Trask (1948; New York: Harper, 1963), pp. 195–200.

142. Trevisa, *On the Properties of Things,* ed. Seymour, 2:791. The idea goes back to [Isidore of Seville], *Isidori Hispalensis episcopi Etymologiarum sive Originum,* ed. W. M. Lindsay, 2 vols. (Oxford: Clarendon Press, 1911), vol. 2, bk. 14, ch. 6, para. 8.

143. Howard Rollin Patch, *The Other World According to Descriptions in Medieval Literature* (Cambridge, Mass.: Harvard University Press, 1950).

144. See Georges Doutrepont, *Les mises en prose des épopées et des romans chevaleresques du XIVe au XVIe siècle* (Brussels: Palais des académies, 1939); Harf-Lancner, *Fées au moyen âge,* pp. 280–81. The *Prose Ogier* is cited here from *Ogier le Dannoys* [a facsimile edition of Verard's 1498 print], ed. Knud Togeby (Munksgaard, 1967).

145. Harf-Lancner, *Fées au moyen âge,* p. 284n54.

146. *South English Legendary,* ed. D'Evelyn and Mill, 2:408 (lines 207–8).

147. *Thomas of Erceldoune,* ed. Nixon, 1:38 (Thornton MS).

148. See *St Patrick's Purgatory,* ed. Easting, p. 238n128.

149. Marie de France, *Espurgatoire,* ed. Warnke, pp. 96–98.

150. C. M. Van der Zanden, *Étude sur le Purgatoire de saint Patrice* (Amsterdam: Paris, 1928), p. 119 (line 1116).

151. Sonia Maura Barillari, "Il Purgatorio di Ludovico di Sur: Un testo a cavallo fra Medioevo e Rinascimento," *Studi medievali,* 3rd ser., 49 (2008):803. For *talentum,* cf. Middle French, *taillant,* 'lame trenchante.'

152. *St Patrick's Purgatory,* ed. Easting, p. 108 (line 570).

153. Two earlier half analogues, one Germanic (in *De Gestis Langobardorum*), the other Celtic (in *Kulhwch and Olwen*), are both folkloric; see Laura Hibbard, "The Sword Bridge of Chretien de Troyes and Its Celtic Original," *Romanic Review* 4 (1913):189–90.

154. *Roman van Walewein (Dutch Romances, 1),* ed. and trans. David F. Johnson and Geert H. M. Classens (Woodbridge: Boydell and Brewer, 2000), pp. 172–77 (lines 3451–573).

155. *The Vision of Edmund Leversedge,* ed. W. F. Nijenhuis (Nijmegan: Katholieke Universiteit, 1991).

156. *Register of John Morton, III,* ed. Harper-Bill, p. 215 (no. 661).

157. As late as nineteenth-century France, this possibility was raised in the case of Saint Teresa of Lourdes; see Ruth Harris, *Lourdes: Body and Spirit in the Secular Ages* (New York and

London: Penguin, 1999), pp. 77–78. The medieval association of visions of Mary with hawthorns (see William A. Christian, *Apparitions in Late Medieval and Renaissance Spain* [Princeton, N.J.: Princeton University Press, 1981], pp. 35–36) may point in the same direction.

    158. See Gurevich, *Medieval Popular Culture*, pp. 135–36; [Caesarius of Heisterbach], *Dialogus Miraculorum*, ed. Strange, 1:58–61 (dist. 2, cap. 2), gives a particularly good example.

    159. Le Goff, *Naissance du purgatoire*, p. 395.

    160. Tubach, *Index Exemplorum*, no. 3378 (p. 263).

    161. Horstmann. "Die Evangelien-Geschichten," pp. 277–78 (no. 24); *The Northern Homily Cycle*, ed. Saara Nevanlinna, 3 vols. (Helsinki: Société Néophilologique, 1971–74), 2:203–6 (lines 12457–592).

    162. "De quodam valde religioso abbate legimus: Cum nouissima cogitaret et quid ei post hanc vitam futurum esset, inter alia cogitare cepit de gaudiis paradisi, et quomodo sancti absque tedio tam diu esse poterunt in loco vno. Et statim, dum esset in orto prope abbaciam, apparuit ei pucherrima auis; cum qua ludere cepit et valde delectabatur suauissimo cantu eius. Et reuersus ad se venit ad portam abbacie et omnia mutata reperit, nec ianitorem agnouit, nec ipse ab aliquo, quis esset, in monasterio cognosci potuit. Cumque diceret: 'Ego sum abbas talis monasterii qui statim ad meditandum in ortum exiui,' illi negantes et admirantes inspexerunt librum in quo scripta erant nomina preteritorum abbatum, et inuenerunt trecentos annos preteritos, ex quo ille prefectus fuerat monasterio memorato"; see [Jacques de Vitry], *Die Exempla*, ed. Joseph Greven (Heidelberg: Carl Winter, 1914), p. 18 (no. 10).

    163. E.g., in Paul Meyer, "Les Manuscrits des sermons français de Maurice de Sully," *Romania* 5 (1876):473–85.

    164. MacCulloch, *Medieval Faith and Fable*, p. 199; Patch, *Other World*, pp. 159–60.

    165. W. Howells, *Cambrian Superstitions, Ghosts, Omens, Witchcraft, Traditions, &c.* (Tipton: Danks, 1831), pp. 127–28; T. Gwynn Jones, *Welsh Folklore and Folk-Custom* (1930; Cambridge: Brewer, 1979), pp. 59–60.

POSTSCRIPT

    1. For Forman's text, see J. M. Nosworthy, "*Macbeth* at the Globe," *Library*, 5th ser., 2 (1947):115–16. Interestingly, Shakespeare's source for this scene, Holinshed's *Chronicles of Scotland*, reports the common opinion that "these women were either the weird sisters ... or else some nymphs or feiries" (William Shakespeare, *Macbeth*, ed. Kenneth Muir, in *The Arden Edition of the Works of William Shakespeare*, 9th ed. [London: Methuen, 1962], p. 178); while Peter Heylyn's description reads, "These two travelling together through a forrest were mette by three Fairies, or Witches (*Weirds* the *Scots* call them)" (*Mikrokosmos a little description of the great world* [Oxford: Lichfield & Turmer, 1625], p. 509 [*STC* (2nd ed.):13277]).

    2. Bishop Thomas Cooper, *Thesaurus linguae Romanae & Britannicae ... : Opera & industria Thomae Cooperi* (London: Berthelet, 1565): s.v. "Strix" (*STC* [2nd ed.]:5686); [John Baret], *An aluearie or triple dictionarie in Englishe, Latin, and French* (London: Denham, 1574): H. 343 (*STC* [2nd ed.]:1410).

    3. John Swan, *Speculum mundi or A glasse representing the face of the world* (Cambridge: T. Buck and R. Daniel, 1635), p. 403 (*STC* [2nd ed.]:23516).

    4. Adrianus Junius, *The nomenclator, or remembrancer of Adrianus Iunius physician ... now in English, by Iohn Higins* (London: Newberie and Denham, 1585), p. 427 (*STC* [2nd ed.]:14860).

5. John Florio, *A worlde of wordes, or Most copious, and exact dictionarie in Italian and English, collected by Iohn Florio* (London: Hatfield, 1598), s.vv. "Fata" and "Strega" (*STC* [2nd ed.]:11098). Richard Percival, *A dictionarie in Spanish and English, first published into the English tongue by Ric. Perciuale Gent* (London: Bollifant, 1599), p. 121 (*STC* [2nd ed.]:19620).

6. [William Barlow], *Three Christian sermons, made by Lodouike Lauatere, minister of Zuricke in Heluetia, of famine and dearth of victuals: and translated into English, as being verie fit for this time of our dearth*: by VV. Barlow Bachelar in Diuinitie (London: Thomas Creede, 1596), f. 22ʳ (*STC* [2nd ed.]:15322).

7. *Register of John Morton, III,* ed. Harper-Bill, p. 215 (no. 661).

8. *Early Modern Witches,* ed. Gibson, p. 29.

9. William Vaughan, *The arraignment of slander periury blasphemy, and other malicious sinne*s (London: Francis Constable, 1630), p. 202 (*STC* [2nd ed.]:24623).

10. See further, Latham, *Elizabethan Fairies,* pp. 163–70.

11. John Gaule, *Select cases of conscience touching witches and witchcrafts* (London: W. Wilson, 1646), pp. 48–50 (*Wing* [2nd ed.]:G379).

12. William Bullein, *Bulleins bulwarke of defence against all sicknesse, soarenesse, and woundes that doe dayly assaulte mankinde: by William Bullein, Doctor of Phisicke. 1562.* (London: Thomas Marshe, 1579), f. 56ᵛ (*STC* [2nd ed.]:4034). At least one case of "fairies" appears in the casebooks of the early seventeenth-century physician Richard Napier; see Ronald C. Sawyer, " 'Strangely Handled in All Her Lyms': Witchcraft and Healing in Jacobean England," *Journal of Social History* 22 (1989):475.

13. George Gifford, *A dialogue concerning witches and witchcraftes* (London: Tobie Cooke and Mihil Hart, 1593), f. Bᵛ (*STC* [2nd ed.]:11850).

14. See Richard Kieckhefer's foreword to the second edition of Elliot Rose, *A Razor for a Goat* (Toronto: University of Toronto Press, 1989), pp. vii–xiv.

15. Another influence comes from anthropology; cf. Rodney Needham's claim that it is an "almost universal premise subscribed to by anthropologists, that witches do not really exist"; *Primordial Characters* (Charlottesville: University Press of Virginia, 1978), p. 27.

16. For Scotland, see J. A. MacCulloch, "The Mingling of Fairy and Witch Beliefs in Sixteenth and Seventeenth Century Scotland," *Folklore* 32 (1921):229–44; and Diane Purkiss, "Sounds of Silence: Fairies and Incest in Scottish Witchcraft Stories," in *Languages of Witchcraft: Ideology and Meaning in Early Modern Culture,* ed. Stuart Clark (London: Palgrave, 2000), pp. 81–98. For Hungary, see Éva Pócs, *Between the Living and the Dead,* trans. Szilvia Rédey and Michael Webb (Budapest: Central European University Press, 1999), pp. 88–91. For Sicily, see Gustav Henningsen, " 'The Ladies from Outside': An Archaic Pattern in the Witches' Sabbath," in *Early Modern Witchcraft: Centres and Peripheries,* ed. Bengt Ankarloo and Gustav Henningsen (Oxford: Clarendon Press, 1990), pp. 191–215. For Spain, see F. A. Campagne, "Witch or Demon? Fairies, Vampires, and Nightmares in Early Modern Spain," *Acta Ethnographica Hungarica* 53 (2008):381–410.

17. See also Sonia Barillari, *Protostoria della Strega,* and Emma Wilby, *Cunning Folk and Familiar Spirits* (Eastbourne: Sussex Academic Press, 2005), esp. pp. 1–120.

18. Scot, *Discoverie of Witchcraft* (1584), pp. 109 (bk. 5, chap. 9), 42 (bk. 3, chap. 2), 66 (bk. 3, chap. 16), and 46 (bk. 3, chap. 5).

19. Boguet, *Discours execrables,* p. 107 (chap. 21); Boguet, *Examen of Witches,* ed. Summers, p. 57.

20. Cameron, *Enchanted Europe,* pp. 265–66.

21. Thomas Cooper, *The mystery of witch-craft Discouering, the truth, nature, occasions, growth and power thereof* (London: Nicholas Okes, 1617), p. 123 (*STC* [2nd ed.]:5701).

22. Brian Levack, *The Witch-Hunt in Early Modern Europe*, 2nd ed. (London: Longman, 1995), pp. 200–204.

23. Stephen Greenblatt, *Marvelous Possessions: The Wonder of the New World* (Chicago: University of Chicago Press, 1991).

24. This and subsequent references are to *The Riverside Chaucer*.

25. Richard Firth Green, "Changing Chaucer," *Studies in the Age of Chaucer* 25 (2003):27–52.

26. John A. Burrow, "Elvish Chaucer," in *The Endless Knot: Essays on Old and Middle English in Honor of Marie Borroff*, ed. M. Teresa Tavormina and R. F. Yeager (Cambridge: D. S. Brewer, 1995), pp. 105–11.

27. Francis Meres, *Palladis tamia Wits treasury being the second part of Wits common wealth* (London: P. Short, for Cuthbert Burbie, 1598), f. 279ʳ (*STC* [2nd ed.]:17834).

28. John A. Burrow, "*Sir Thopas* in the Sixteenth Century," in *Middle English Studies Presented to Norman Davis in Honour of His Seventieth Birthday*, ed. Douglas Gray and E. G. Stanley (Oxford: Clarendon Press, 1983), pp. 69–91.

29. "Mine owne John Poynz," lines 50–51, in Sir Thomas Wyatt, *Collected Poems*, ed. Kenneth Muir (London: Routledge and Kegan Paul, 1949), p. 186.

30. Burrow, "Sir Thopas," p. 78.

31. Matthew Woodcock, *Fairy in The Faerie Queene* (Aldershot: Ashworth, 2004), p. 93.

32. Frances A. Yates. "Elizabethan Chivalry: The Romance of the Accession Day Tilts," *Journal of the Warburg and Courtauld Institutes* 20 (1957):12.

33. Matthew Woodcock, "The Fairy Queen Figure in Elizabethan Entertainments," in *Elizabeth I: Always Her Own Free Woman*, ed. Carole Levin, Jo Eldridge Carney, and Debra Barrett-Graves (Aldershot: Ashgate, 2003), p. 108.

34. R. C. Strong, "The Popular Celebration of the Accession Day of Queen Elizabeth I," *Journal of the Warburg and Courtauld Institutes* 21 (1958):86–103.

35. Yates, "Elizabethan Chivalry," p. 15.

36. *The Progresses and Public Processions of Queen Elizabeth*, ed. John Nichols, 3 vols. (London: Nichols, 1823), 3:118–19.

37. *Progresses*, ed. Nichols, 2:186.

38. Thomas Holland, *Paneguris D. Elizabethae, Dei gratiâ Angliae, Franciae, & Hiberniae Reginae: A sermon preached at Pauls in London the 17. of November ann. Dom. 1599 . . . VVherevnto is adioyned an apologeticall discourse, whereby all such sclanderous accusations are fully and faithfully confuted, wherewith the honour of this realme hath beene vncharitably traduced by some of our adversaries . . .* (Oxford: Thomas Barnes, 1601), f. O[2]ᵛ (*STC* [2nd ed.]:13597).

39. James Sharpe, *The Bewitching of Anne Gunter* (New York: Routledge, 2001), pp. 91–94.

40. Samuel Harsnett, *A declaration of egregious popish impostures to with-draw the harts of her Maiesties subiects from their allegeance, and from the truth of Christian religion professed in England, vnder the pretence of casting out deuils . . .* (London: James Roberts, 1603), pp. 137–38 (*STC* [2nd ed.]:12880).

41. Scot, *Discouerie of Witchcraft* (1584), p. 88 (bk. 4, chap. 12).

42. E. Talbot Donaldson, *The Swan at the Well* (New Haven, Conn.: Yale University Press, 1985), pp. 43–49; Helen Cooper, *Shakespeare and the Medieval World* (London: Bloomsbury, 2013), pp. 218–19; Peter Brown, "Chaucer and Shakespeare: The *Merchant's Tale* Connection," *Chaucer Review* 48 (2013):222–37.

43. Donaldson, *Swan at the Well*, pp. 9–18; Cooper, *Shakespeare and the Medieval World*, pp. 213–14.

44. Dorothy Bethurum, "Shakespeare's Comment on Mediaeval Romance in Midsummer-Night's Dream," *Modern Language Notes* 60 (1945):90.

45. Thomas Campion, *The Works of Thomas Campion*, ed. Walter R. Davis (New York: Doubleday, 1967), p. 5. The editor claims that this song is based on the *Pervigilium Veneris*, but though Campion certainly adapts its refrain ("cras amet qui nunquam amavit quique amavit cras amet"), there are important differences: Proserpina is never mentioned; and not only does the *Pervigilium Veneris* (as its title implies) invoke Venus, but it is addressed to men, not women.

46. Michael Drayton, *The Poems of Michael Drayton*, ed. John Buxton, 2 vols. (London: Routledge, 1953), 1:179.

47. Drayton, *Poems*, 1:57–60.

48. Gregory, *Rye Spirits*, p. 192.

49. Gregory, *Rye Spirits*, p. 62.

50. C. J. Sisson, "A Topical Reference in *The Alchemist*," in *Joseph Quincy Adams: Memorial Studies*, ed. James G. McManaway, Giles E. Dawson, and Edwin E. Willoughby (Washington, D.C.: Folger Library, 1948), pp. 739–41.

51. Richard Levin, "Another 'Source' for *The Alchemist* and Another Look at Source Studies," *English Literary Renaissance* 28 (1998):213–18.

52. (London: T[homas] C[reede], 1595) (*STC* [2nd ed.]:19855).

53. (London: T. G., 1595) (*STC* [2nd ed.]:18758).

54. *The Acts of the High Commission Court Within the Diocese of Durham* [ed. W. H. D. Longstaffe], Surtees Society, 34 (Durham: Andrews, 1858), p. 116, cited in Thomas, *Religion and the Decline of Magic*, p. 202.

55. Lizanne Henderson and Edward J. Cowan, *Scottish Fairy Belief: A History* (East Linton: Tuckwell Press, 2001), pp. 127–38.

56. Robert Henryson, *The Poems of Robert Henryson*, ed. Denton Fox (Oxford: Clarendon Press, 1981), p. 136 (lines 118–19, 125–26).

57. Marion Stewart, "King Orphius," *Scottish Studies* 17 (1973):5 (lines 48–49). For the manuscript (Scottish Record Office, MS RH13/35), see Marion Stewart, "A Recently Discovered Manuscript: 'Ane tale of Sir Colling ye kny^t,'" *Scottish Studies* 16 (1972):23–24.

58. Gavin Douglas, *Virgil's Aeneid Translated into Scottish Verse by Gavin Douglas*, ed. David F. C. Coldwell, 4 vols., Scottish Text Society, 3rd ser.:25, 27, 28, 30 (Edinburgh: Blackwood, 1957–64), 3:1 (lines 17–19) and 3:228 (lines 153–55).

59. William Dunbar, *The Poems of William Dunbar*, ed. James Kinsley (Oxford: Clarendon Press, 1979), pp. 77 and 88 ("Flyting," lines 36 and 345), and p. 98 ("Norny," lines 4–6).

60. Brian Cummings, "Among the Fairies: Religion and the Anthropology of Ritual in Shakespeare," *in Humankinds: The Renaissance and its Anthropologies*, ed. Andreas Höfele and Stephan Laqué (Berlin: De Gruyter, 2011), pp. 71–89.

BIBLIOGRAPHY

MANUSCRIPTS CONSULTED

Cambridge, Mass., Harvard University, MS Riant 35.
Cambridge, University Library, MS KK IV 24.
Cologny, Switzerland, Martin Bodmer Foundation, MS 43.
London, B.L., MS Cotton Faustina A. VII.
London, B.L., MS Royal 14C. VII.
London, B.L., MS Royal 7D I.
London, Kew, National Archives, KB 27/755.
Paris, B.N., MS Français 173.
Paris, B.N., MS Latin 15970.

PRIMARY SOURCES

The Acts of the High Commission Court Within the Diocese of Durham. [Ed. W. H. D. Longstaffe.] Surtees Society, 34. Durham: Andrews, 1858.
Adam le Bossu. *Le Jeu de la feuillée.* Ed. Ernest Langlois. 2nd ed. Paris: Champion, 1968.
[Albertus Magnus]. *Alberti Magni Opera Omnia.* Ed. S. C. A. Borgnet. 38 vols. Paris: Vivés, 1890–99.
———. *De animalibus libri XXVI.* Ed. Hermann Stadler. 2 vols. Münster: Aschendorffsache, 1916, 1920.
Alphabet of Tales. Ed. Mary Macleod Banks. 2 vols. EETS OS 126, 127. London: Kegan Paul, 1905.
Amadas et Ydoine: Roman du XIIe siècle. Ed. John R. Reinhard. Paris: Champion, 1926.
Ancrene Wisse. Ed. Bella Millett et al. 2 vols. EETS 325, 326. London: Oxford University Press, 2005–6.
An Anglo-Norman Brut (Royal 13. A. XXI). Ed. Alexander Bell. ANTS, 21–22. Oxford: Blackwell, 1969.
Anglo-Norman Medicine II: Shorter Treatises. Ed. Tony Hunt. Cambridge: D. S. Brewer, 1997.
Anonimalle Chronicle 1307–1334. Ed. W. R. Childs and J. Taylor. Leeds: Yorkshire Archaeological Society, 1991.
Anonimo Romano. *Cronica: Vita di Cola di Rienzo.* Ed. Ettore Mazzali. Milan: Rizzoli, 1991.
Antoine de la Sale. *Le Paradis de la Reine Sibylle.* Ed. Fernand Desonay. Paris: Droz, 1930.
Aquinas, Saint Thomas. *Summa Theologiae, English and Latin.* Blackfriars. 60 vols. London: Eyre & Spottiswoode; New York: McGraw-Hill, 1964–76.

Aucassin et Nicolette, chantefable du XIIIe siècle. Ed. Mario Roques. Paris: Champion, 1929.
Augustine, Saint. *The City of God Against the Pagans.* Ed. and trans. William M. Greene et al. 7 vols. Cambridge, Mass.: Harvard University Press, 1957–72.
———. *On Christian Doctrine.* Trans. D. W. Robertson. New York: Bobbs-Merrill, 1958.
———. *Treatises of Marriage and Other Subjects.* Ed. Roy J. Deferrari. New York: Fathers of the Church, 1955.
Baret, John. *An aluearie or triple dictionarie in Englishe, Latin, and French.* London: Denham, 1574 (*STC* [2nd ed.]):1410).
[Barlow, William]. *Three Christian sermons, made by Lodouike Lauatere, minister of Zuricke in Heluetia, of famine and dearth of victuals: and translated into English, as being verie fit for this time of our dearth*: by VV. Barlow Bachelar in Diuinitie. London: Thomas Creede, 1596 (*STC* [2nd ed.]):15322).
[Bernard Silvestris]. *Bernardi Silvestris de Mundi Universitate.* Ed. Carl Sigmund Barach and Johann Wrobel. Frankfurt: Unveränderter Nachdruck, 1964.
Boece, Hector. *Scotorum historiae a prima gentis origine libri xvii.* Paris: Ascensius, 1527.
Boguet, Henry. *Discours execrables des sorciers.* Rouen: Romain de Beauvais, 1606.
———. *An Examen of Witches.* Ed. Montague Summers, trans. E. A. Ashwin. [London]: Rodker, 1929.
Boke of Duke Huon of Burdeux. Ed. S. L. Lee. 4 vols. EETS OS 40, 41, 43, 50. London: Trübner, 1882–87.
[Bonaventure, Saint]. *Doctoris seraphici S. Bonaventurae Opera omnia.* 10 vols. [Rome]: Collegii S. Bonaventurae, 1882–1902.
Borde, Andrew. *The Fyrst Boke of the Introduction of Knowledge.* Ed. F. J. Furnivall. EETS ES 10. London: Trübner, 1870.
Breton Lays in Middle English. Ed. Thomas C. Rumble. Detroit: Wayne State University Press, 1965.
The brideling, sadling and ryding, of a rich churle in Hampshire, by the subtill practise of one Iudeth Philips, a professed cunning woman. London: T[homas] C[reede], 1595 (*STC* [2nd ed.]:19855).
Bromyard, John. *Summa Predicantium.* 2 vols. Venice, 1586.
The Brut, or The Chronicles of England. Ed. Friedrich W. D. Brie. 2 vols. EETS OS 131, 136. London: Kegan Paul, 1906–8.
Bullein, William. *Bulleins bulwarke of defence against all sicknesse, soarenesse, and woundes that doe dayly assaulte mankinde: by William Bullein, Doctor of Phisicke. 1562.* London: Thomas Marshe, 1579 (*STC* [2nd ed.]:4034).
[Burchard of Worms]. *The Corrector. Die Bussordnungen der abendländischen Kirche.* Ed. F. W. H. Wasserschleben. Halle: Graeger, 1851:624–82.
[Caesarius of Heisterbach]. *Caesarii Heisterbacensis, Dialogus Miraculorum.* 2 vols. Ed. Joseph Strange. Cologne: Heberle, 1851, 1852.
Calendars of the Proceedings in Chancery, in the Reign of Queen Elizabeth. Ed. John Bayley. 3 vols. London: Record Commission, 1800–1832.
Campion, Thomas. *The Works of Thomas Campion.* Ed. Walter R. Davis. New York: Doubleday, 1967.
[Cantimpré, Thomas of]. *Thomae Cantipratani, Bonum Universale de Apibus.* Ed. George Colvener. Douai: Balthazar Beller, 1627.
Capgrave, John. *Abbreuiacion of Chonicles.* Ed. Peter J. Lucas. EETS 285. London: Oxford University Press, 1983.

———. *The Life of Saint Katherine*. Ed. Karen A. Winstead. Kalamazoo, Mich.: Medieval Institute Publications, 1999.
Cartulaire de l'Abbaye de Redon en Bretagne. Ed. Aurélien de Courson. Paris: Imprimerie impériale, 1863.
Castleford's Chronicle or the Boke of Brut. Ed. Caroline D. Eckhardt. 2 vols. EETS OS 305, 306. London: Oxford University Press, 1996.
La Chanson de Bertrand Du Guesclin de Cuvelier. Ed. Jean-Claude Faucon. 3 vols. Toulouse: Editions universitaires du Sud, ca. 1990.
Chaucer, Geoffrey. *The Riverside Chaucer*. Ed. Larry D. Benson et al. Boston: Houghton Mifflin, 1987.
Chaucerian and Other Pieces (A Supplement to the Complete Works of Geoffrey Chaucer). Ed. Walter W. Skeat. Oxford: Clarendon Press, 1897.
The Chester Mystery Cycle. Ed. R. M. Lumianski and David Mills. 2 vols. EETS SS 3, 9. London: Oxford University Press, 1974, 1986.
Chestre, Thomas. *Sir Launfal*. Ed. A. J. Bliss. London: Nelson, 1960.
Chrétien de Troyes. *Le Chevalier de la Charrette (Lancelot)*. Ed. Alfred Foulet and Karl de Utti. Paris: Garnier, 1989.
———. *Yvain (le Chevalier au lion)*. Ed. T. B. W. Reid. Manchester: Manchester University Press, 1942.
Chronicles of the Reigns of Stephen, Henry II, and Richard II. Ed. Richard Howlett. 4 vols. Rolls Series. London: Longman, 1884–89.
Chronicon de Lanercost, MCCI–MCCCXLVI. Ed. Joseph Stevenson. Edinburgh: Bannatyne Club, 1839.
Cooper, Bishop Thomas. *Thesaurus linguae Romanae & Britannicae... : Opera & industria*. London: Berthelet, 1565 (*STC* [2nd ed.]:5686).
Cooper, Thomas. *The mystery of witch-craft Discouering, the truth, nature, occasions, growth and power thereof.* London: Nicholas Okes, 1617 (*STC* [2nd ed.]:5701).
Corbet, Bishop Richard. *Certain elegant poems, written by Dr. Corbet, Bishop of Norwich*. London: Andrew Crooke, 1647 (*Wing* [2nd ed., 1994]:C6270).
[Coudrette]. *Le roman de Mélusine, ou histoire de Lusignan*. Ed. Eleanor Roach. Paris: Klincksieck, 1982.
———. *The Romans of Partenay, or of Lusignen, Otherwise Known as the Tale of Melusine*. Ed. Walter W. Skeat. EETS OS 22. London: Kegan Paul, 1866.
Councils and Ecclesiastical Documents Relating to Great Britain and Ireland. Ed. A. W. Haddan and W. Stubbs. 3 vols. Oxford: Clarendon Press, 1869–78.
Criminal Trials in Scotland, I, ii. Ed. Robert Pitcairn. Edinburgh: Tait, 1833.
Depositions and Other Ecclesiastical Proceedings from the Courts of Durham. [Ed. James Raine]. Surtees Society. London: Nichols, 1845.
The Dictionary of syr Thomas Eliot knyght. London: Berthelet, 1538 (*STC* [2nd ed.]:7659).
Dives and Pauper. Ed. Priscilla H. Barnum. 2 vols. (in 3 pts.). EETS 275, 280, 323. London: Oxford University Press, 1976–2004.
Douglas, Gavin. *Virgil's Aeneid Translated into Scottish Verse by Gavin Douglas*. Ed. David F. C. Coldwell. 4 vols. Scottish Text Society, 3rd ser.:25, 27, 28, 30. Edinburgh: Blackwood, 1957–64.
Drayton, Michael. *The Poems of Michael Drayton*. Ed. John Buxton. 2 vols. London: Routledge, 1953.

Dunbar, William. *The Poems of William Dunbar.* Ed. James Kinsley. Oxford: Clarendon Press, 1979.
Early Modern Witches: Witchcraft Cases in Contemporary Writing. Ed. Marion Gibson. London: Routledge, 2000.
The Early South-English Legendary, or Lives of Saints. Ed. Carl Horstmann. EETS OS 97. London: Trübner, 1887.
Elioxe. Ed. Emanuel J. Mickel, Jr. *The Old French Crusade Cycle I: La naissance du Chevalier au cygne.* [Tuscaloosa]: University of Alabama Press, 1977, pp. 1–129.
Elucidarium. Patrologia Latina, 172:1109A–1176D.
The Elucidation: A Prologue to the Conte del Graal. Ed. Albert Wilder Thompson. New York: Institute of French Studies, 1931.
[Engelhus, Dietrich]. *Chronicon Theodorici Engelhusii.* Ed. Gottfried Wilhelm Leibniz. *Scriptores Rerum Brunsvicensium.* Vol. 2. Hanover: Foerster, 1710.
English and Scottish Popular Ballads. Ed. Francis James Child. 5 vols., 2nd corr. ed., Mark F. Heiman and Laura Saxton Heiman. 1883–98; Northfield, Minn.: Loomis House Press, 2001–11.
The English Conquest of Ireland, A.D. 1166–1185, Mainly from the 'Expugnatio hibernica' of Giraldus Cambrensis. Ed. F. J. Furnivall. EETS OS 107. London: Kegan Paul, 1896.
English Lyrics of the XIIIth Century. Ed. Carleton Brown. Oxford: Clarendon Press, 1932.
English Register of Godstow Nunnery. Ed. Andrew Clark. EETS OS 142. London: Kegan Paul, 1911.
English Wycliffite Sermons, I. Ed. Anne Hudson. Oxford: Clarendon Press, 1983.
Esclarmonde, Clarisse et Florent, Yde et Olive: Drei Fortsetzungen der Chanson von Huon de Bordeaux. Ed. Max Schweigel. Marburg: Elwert, 1889.
[Étienne de Bourbon]. *Anecdotes historiques, légendes, et apologues tirés du recueil inédit d'Étienne de Bourbon.* Ed. A. Lecoy de la Marche. Société de l'histoire de France. Paris: Renouard, 1877.
Les Évangiles des quenouilles. Ed. Madeleine Jeay. Montreal: Presses de l'Université de Montréal, 1985.
Fabyan, Robert. *The New Chronicles of England and France.* Ed. Henry Ellis. London: Rivington, 1811.
Fasciculus Morum: A Fourteenth-Century Preacher's Handbook. Ed. and trans. Siegfried Wenzel. University Park: Pennsylvania State University Press, 1989.
Floriant et Florete. Ed. Harry F. Williams. Ann Arbor: University of Michigan Press, 1947.
Florio, John. *A worlde of wordes, or Most copious, and exact dictionarie in Italian and English.* London: Hatfield, 1598 (*STC* [2nd ed.]:11098).
Gaule, John. *Select cases of conscience touching witches and witchcraftes.* London: W. Wilson, 1646 (*Wing* [2nd ed.]:G379).
Geoffrey of Monmouth. *The Historia Regum Britannie of Geoffrey of Monmouth, 1: Bern, Burgerbibliothek, MS. 568.* Ed. Neil Wright. Cambridge: D. S. Brewer, 1985.
———. *The Historia Regum Britannie of Geoffrey of Monmouth, 2: The First Variant Version.* Ed. Neil Wright. Cambridge: D. S. Brewer, 1988.
[———]. *The Historia Regum Britannie of Geoffrey of Monmouth, 5: Gesta Regum Britannie.* Ed. Neil Wright. Cambridge: D. S. Brewer, 1991.
———. *Life of Merlin; Vita Merlini.* Ed. and trans. Basil Clarke. Cardiff: University of Wales Press, 1973.
[Gerald of Wales]. *Giraldi Cambrensis Opera.* 8 vols. Ed. J. S. Brewer, James F. Dimock, and George F. Warner. Rolls Series, 21. London: HMSO, 1861–91.

Gervase of Canterbury. *Historical Works*. Ed. William Stubbs. 2 vols. Rolls Series. London: Longman, 1879, 1880.
Gervase of Tilbury. *Otia imperialia: Recreation for an Emperor*. Ed. and trans. S. E. Banks and J. W. Binns. Oxford: Clarendon Press, 2002.
———. *Les Traductions Françaises des Otia Imperialia*. Ed. Cinzia Pignatelli and Dominique Gerner. Geneva: Droz, 2006.
Gifford, George. *A dialogue concerning witches and witchcraftes*. London: Tobie Cooke and Mihil Hart, 1593 (*STC* [2nd ed.]:11850).
Gobi, Jean. *Scala Coeli*. Ed. Marie-Anne Polo de Beaulieu. Paris: Centre de la Recherche Scientifique, 1991.
Godelman, Iohann Georg. *Tractatus de magis, veneficis et lamiis*. Frankfurt: Basse, 1601.
[*Golden Legend*]. *Jacobi a Voragine Legenda aurea*. Ed. Theodor Graesse. 2nd ed. Leipzig: Arnold, 1850.
Gower, John. *The Complete Works of John Gower: The French Works*. Ed. G. C. Macaulay. Oxford: Clarendon Press, 1899.
———. *The English Works*. Ed. G. C. Macaulay. 2 vols. EETS ES 81, 82. London: Oxford University Press, 1900–1901.
Grimm, Jacob, and Wilhelm Grimm, eds. *Deutsche Sagen*. 2 vols. in 1. 1816–18; Munich: Winkler, 1965.
[Gui, Bernard] Bernardus Gui. *Manuel de l'inquisiteur*. Ed. and trans. G. Mollat. 2 vols. Paris: Champion, 1926–27.
Guibert of Nogent. *Monodies* and *On the Relics of the Saints*. Trans. Joseph McAlhany and Jay Rubenstein. London: Penguin Books, 2011.
Guillaume de Palerne, roman du XIIIe siècle. Ed. Alexandre Micha. Geneva: Droz, 1990.
Hansen, Joseph, ed. *Quellen und Untersuchungen zur des Hexenwahns*. Hildesheim: Georg Olms, 1963.
Harding, John. *The Chronicle of John Hardyng*. Ed. Henry Ellis. London: Rivington, 1812.
Harsnett, Samuel. *A declaration of egregious popish impostures to with-draw the harts of her Maiesties subiects from their allegeance, and from the truth of Christian religion professed in England, vnder the pretence of casting out deuils. . . .* London: James Roberts, 1603 (*STC* [2nd ed.]:12880).
Le Haut Livre du Graal: Perlesvaus. Ed. William A. Nitze and T. Atkinson Jenkins. 2 vols. Chicago: University of Chicago Press, 1932.
Henryson, Robert. *The Poems of Robert Henryson*. Ed. Denton Fox. Oxford: Clarendon Press, 1981.
Hertford County Records: Notes and Extracts from the Session Rolls, 1581–1698. Vol. 1. Ed. W. J. Hardy. Hertford: Longmore, 1905.
Heylyn, Peter. *Mikrokosmos a little description of the great world*. Oxford: Lichfield & Turmer, 1625 (*STC* [2nd ed.]:13277).
[Higden, Ranulph]. *Polychronicon Ranulphi Higden monachi Cestrensis: Together with the English Translations of John Trevisa*. Ed. Churchill Babington et al. 9 vols. Rolls Series. London: Longman, 1865–86.
Higden, Ranulph. *Speculum Curatorum: A Mirror for Curates, Book I*. Dallas Medieval Texts and Translations, 13:1. Ed. and trans. Eugene Crook and Margaret Jennings. Leuven: Peeters, 2012.
High Book of the Grail. Trans. Nigel Bryant. Cambridge: D. S. Brewer, 1978.
The Historia Brittonum. Vol. 3: *The 'Vatican' Recension*. Ed. David N. Dumville. Cambridge: D. S. Brewer, 1985.

Historia septem sapientum 1. Ed. Alfons Hilka. Sammlung Mittellateinischer Texte, 4. Heidelberg: Winter, 1912.

Holland, Thomas. *Paneguris D. Elizabethae, Dei gratiâ Angliae, Franciae, & Hiberniae Reginae: A sermon preached at Pauls in London the 17. of November ann. Dom. 1599 . . . VVherevnto is adioyned an apologeticall discourse, whereby all such sclanderous accusations are fully and faithfully confuted, wherewith the honour of this realme hath beene vncharitably traduced by some of our adversaries. . . .* Oxford: Thomas Barnes, 1601 (*STC* [2nd ed.]:13597).

Horman, William. *Vulgaria.* London: Pynson, 1519 (*STC* [2nd ed.]:13811).

Horstmann, Carl, ed. "Die Evangelien-Geschichten des Homiliensammlung des Ms. Vernon." *Archiv für das Studium der neueren Spachen und Literaturen* 31 (1877):241–316.

Huloet, Richard. *Abcedarium anglico latinum.* London: William Riddel, 1552 (*STC*:346:04).

Huon de Bordeaux, chanson de geste du XIIIe siècle. Ed. William W. Kibler. Trans. François Suard. Paris: Champion, 2003.

Huon de Méri. *Le Torneiment Anticrist.* Ed. Margaret O. Bender. Romance Monographs, 7. Jackson: University of Mississippi Press, 1976.

Idley, Peter. *Peter Idley's Instructions to His Son.* Ed. Charlotte D'Evelyn. Boston: Modern Language Association of America, 1935.

[Isidore of Seville]. *Isidori Hispalensis episcopi Etymologiarum sive Originum.* Ed. W.M. Lindsay. 2 vols. Oxford: Clarendon Press, 1911.

[Jacques de Vitry]. *Die Exempla.* Ed. Joseph Greven. Heidelberg: Carl Winter, 1914.

———. *Exempla or Illustrative Stories from the Sermones Vulgares of Jacques de Vitry.* Ed. Thomas Frederick Crane. London: Folklore Society, 1890.

———. *Libri duo, quorum prior Orientalis, sive Hierosolymitanae: Alter, Occentalis Historiae nomine inscribitur.* Douai: Balthazar Beller, 1596.

James I, King of England. *Dæmonologie (1597); Newes from Scotland (1591).* Ed. G. B. Harrison. New York: E. P. Dutton, 1924.

[Jean d'Arras]. *Melusine.* Ed. A. K. Donald. EETS ES 68. London: Kegan Paul, 1895.

———. *Mélusine, ou la noble histoire de Lusignan.* Ed. Jean-Jacques Vicensini. Paris: Librairie générale Française, 2003.

[Jean d'Outremeuse]. *Ly Myreur des histors, chronique de Jean des Preis dit d'Outremeuse.* Ed. Stanislas Bormans and Adolfe Borgnet. 7 vols. Brussels: Académie royale de Belgique, 1877.

[John Gerson]. *Joannis Gersonii Opera omnia nova ordine digesta, & in V. tomos distributa.* Antwerp: Sumptibus societatis, 1706.

[John of Salisbury]. *Frivolities of Courtiers and Footprints of Philosophers: Being a Translation of the First, Second, and Third Books and Selections from the Seventh and Eighth Books of the* Policraticus *of John of Salisbury.* Trans. Joseph B. Pike. Minneapolis: University of Minnesota Press, 1938.

———. *Policraticus.* Ed. K. S. B. Keats-Rohan. Corpus christianorum, 118. Turnhout: Brepols, 1993.

John Trevisa. *On the Properties of Things: John Trevisa's Translation of* Bartholomaeus Anglicus De Proprietatibus Rerum,. Ed. M. C. Seymour. 3 vols. Oxford: Clarendon Press, 1975–88.

Joseph of Exeter. *The Trojan War, I–III.* Ed. and trans. A. K. Bate. Warminster: Aris and Phillips, 1986.

Junius, Adrianus. *The nomenclator, or remembrancer . . . now in English, by Iohn Higins.* London: Newberie and Denham, 1585 (*STC* [2nd ed.]:14860).

Kent Records: Documents Illustrative of Medieval Kentish Society. Ed. F. R. H. Du Boulay. Ashford: Kent Archaeological Society, 1964.
Kirk, Robert. *The Secret Commonwealth of Elves, Fauns, and Fairies, 1691*. Ed. Andrew Lang. London: David Nutt, 1893.
Kyng Alisaunder. Ed. G. V. Smithers. 2 vols. EETS OS 227, 237. London: Oxford University Press, 1947, 1952.
Laȝamon. *Brut*. Ed. G. L. Brook and R. F. Leslie. 2 vols. EETS 250, 277. London: Oxford University Press, 1963, 1978.
[*Lai du Cor*]. *The Anglo-Norman Text of 'Le Lai du Cor.'* Ed. C. T. Erickson. ANTS, 24. Oxford: Blackwell, 1973.
Lais féeriques des XIIe et XIIIe siècles. Ed. Alexandre Micha. Paris: Flammarion, 1992.
Lancelot do Lac: The Non-Cyclic Old French Prose Romance. Ed. Elspeth Kennedy. 2 vols. Oxford: Clarendon Press, 1980.
Langland, William. *Piers Plowman: The A Version*. Ed. George Kane. London: Athlone Press, 1960.
———. *Piers Plowman: The B Version*. Ed. George Kane and E. Talbot Donaldson. London: Athlone Press, 1975.
Langtoft, Peter. *The Chronicle*. Ed. Thomas Wright. 2 vols. Rolls Series. London: Longmans, Green, 1866, 1868.
Leechdoms, Wortcunning, and Starcraft of Early England. Ed. Thomas Oswald Cocayne. 2 vols. London: Longman, Green, 1864.
Liber exemplorum ad usum praedicantium saeculo XIII. Ed. A. G. Little. Aberdeen: Typis academicis, 1908.
Life and Miracles of St William of Norwich. Ed. Augustus Jessop and Montague Rhodes. Cambridge: Cambridge University Press, 1896.
The Life of St Hugh of Lincoln. Ed. Decima L. Douie and Hugh Farmer. 2 vols. London: Nelson, 1961, 1962.
Lincoln Diocese Documents, 1450–1544. Ed. Andrew Clark. EETS OS 149. London: Kegan Paul, 1914.
Lovelich, Herry. *Merlin, a Middle-English Metrical Version of a French Romance*. Ed. Ernst A. Kock. 3 vols. EETS ES 93, 112 and OS, 185. London: Kegan Paul, Trench, Trübner, 1904–32.
Lower Ecclesiastical Jurisdiction in Late-Medieval England: The Courts of the Dean and Chapter of Lincoln, 1336–1349, and the Deanery of Wisbech, 1458–1484. Ed. L. R. Poos. Oxford: British Academy, 2001.
[*Lucydarye*]. *The Late Middle English* Lucydarye. Ed. Stephen Morrison. Turnhout: Brepols, 2013.
Ludus Coventriae or The Plaie Called Corpus Christi. Ed. K. S. Block. EETS ES 120. London: Oxford University Press, 1922.
Luque la maudite. Gaston Raynaud, "Trois dits tirés d'un nouveau manuscrit de fableaux." *Romania* 12 (1883):209–29.
Lybeaus Desconus. Ed. M. Mills. EETS OS 261. London: Oxford University Press, 1969.
Lydgate, John. *Fall of Princes*. Ed. Henry Bergen. 4 vols. EETS ES 121–24. London: Oxford University Press, 1924–27.
———. *Troy Book*. Ed. Henry Bergen. 4 vols. EETS ES 97, 103, 106, 126. London: Kegan Paul, 1906–35.
Malleus maleficarum. Ed. and trans. Christopher S. Mackay. 2 vols. Cambridge: Cambridge University Press, 2006.

Malory, Sir Thomas. *Works*. Ed. Eugène Vinaver. 2nd ed. 3 vols. London: Oxford University Press, 1971.
Mandeville, Sir John. *Mandeville's Travels*. Ed. M. C. Seymour. Oxford: Clarendon Press, 1967.
Manning, Robert, of Brunne. *The Story of England (1338)*. Ed. Frederick J. Furnivall. 2 vols. Rolls Series. London: Longman, 1887.
Mannyng, Robert, of Brunne. *Handlyng Synne*. Ed. Idelle Sullens. Binghamton: State University of New York Press, 1983.
[*Le Manuel des péchés*]. *Robert of Brunne's 'Handlyng Synne' with . . . William of Waddington's 'Manuel de Pechiez.'* Ed. F. J. Furnivall. EETS OS 119. London: Early English Text Society, 1901.
Map, Walter. *De nugis curialium: Courtiers' Trifles*. Ed. and trans. M. R. James. Rev. C. N. L. Brooke and R. A. B. Mynors. Oxford: Clarendon Press, 1983.
Marie de France. *Espurgatoire S. Patrice*. Ed. Karl Warnke. Halle: Niemeyer, 1938.
――――. *Lais*. Ed. Alfred Ewart. Introd. Glyn S. Burgess. Bristol: Bristol Classical Press, 1995.
Martianus Capella. *De nuptiis Philologiae et Mercurii*. Ed. Adolfus Dick. Stuttgart: Teubner, 1969.
Materials for the History of Thomas Becket. Ed. James Craigie Robertson and J. B. Sheppard. 7 vols. Rolls Series. London: Longman, 1875–85.
Medieval English Romances. Ed. A. V. C. Schmidt and Nicolas Jacobs. 2 vols. London: Hodder and Stoughton, 1980.
Medieval Handbooks of Penance: A Translation of the Principal libri poenitentiales and Selections from Related Documents. Ed. and trans. John T. McNeill and Helena M. Gamer. New York: Columbia University Press, 1938.
Meres, Francis. *Palladis tamia Wits treasury being the second part of Wits common wealth*. London: P. Short, 1598 (*STC* [2nd ed.]:17834).
Merlin, or the Early History of King Arthur. Ed. Henry B. Wheatley. 4 vols. EETS OS 10, 21, 36, 112. London: Kegan, Paul, Trench, Trübner, 1865–99.
Middle English Debate Poetry. Ed. John W. Conlee. East Lansing, Mich.: Colleagues Press, 1991.
Middle English Religious Prose. Ed. Norman F. Blake. London: Edward Arnold, 1972.
Middle English Treatise on the Ten Commandments. Ed. James Finch Royster. Chapel Hill: University of North Carolina Press, 1911.
Das Mittellateinische Gespräch Adrian und Epictitus: Nebst verwandten Texten (Joca Monachorum). Ed. Walther Suchier. Tübingen: Niemeyer, 1955.
Mum and the Sothsegger. Ed. Mabel Day and Robert Steele. EETS OS 199. London: Oxford University Press, 1936.
Neckam, Alexander. *De Naturis rerum*. Ed. Thomas Wright. Rolls Series. London: Longman, 1863.
Nennius. *British History and Welsh Annals*. Ed. and trans. John Morris. London: Phillimore; Totowa, N.J.: Rowman and Littlefield, 1980.
[Nider, John]. *RPF Ioannis Nider Ordinis Praedicatorum Theologi Praeceptorium*. Douai: John Bogarde, 1611.
The Northern Homily Cycle. Ed. Saara Nevanlinna. 3 vols. Helsinki: Société Néophilologique, 1971–74.
[Oddur Einarsson, Bishop of Skálholt]. *Qualiscunque Descriptio Islandiae: Nach der Handschrift der Hamburger Staats- und Universitäts-Bibliothek*. Ed. Fritz Burg. Hamburg: Selbstverlag der Staats- und Universitäts- Bibliothek, 1928.

Of Arthour and of Merlin. Ed. O. D. Macrae-Gibson. 2 vols. EETS 268, 27. London: Oxford University Press, 1973, 1979.
Of Shrifte and Penance: The ME Prose Translation of Le Manuel des Péchés. Ed. Klaus Bitterling. Heidelberg: Winter, 1998.
Ogier le Dannoys [a facsimile edition of Verard's 1498 print]. Ed. Knud Togeby. Copenhagen: Munksgaard, 1967.
Orderic Vitalis. *The Ecclesiastical History of Orderic Vitalis.* Ed. and trans. Marjorie Chibnall. 6 vols. Oxford: Clarendon Press, 1969–80.
Oxford Book of Medieval Latin Verse. Ed. F. J. E. Raby. Oxford: Clarendon Press, 1959.
[Paris, Matthew]. *Matthæi Parisiensis, monachi Sancti Albani, Chronica Maiora.* Ed. Henry R. Luard. 7 vols. Rolls Series. London: HMSO, 1872–83.
Paris pendant la domination anglaise (1420–1436). Ed. Auguste Longnon. Paris: Champion, 1878.
[*Partonope of Blois*]. *The Middle English Versions of Partonope of Blois.* Ed. A. Trampe Bödtker. EETS ES 109. London: Kegan Paul, 1912.
Partonopeu de Blois. Ed. Olivier Collet and Pierre-Marie Joris. [Paris]: Livre de poche, 2005.
Paston Letters and Papers of the Fifteenth Century. Parts 1 and 2: Ed. Norman Davis. Oxford: Clarendon Press, 1971, 1976. Part 3: Ed. Richard Beadle and Colin Richmond. EETS SS 22. Oxford: Oxford University Press, 2005.
Percival, Richard. *A dictionarie in Spanish and English, first published into the English tongue.* London: Bollifant, 1599 (*STC* [2nd ed.]:19620).
Percy Folio of Old English Ballads and Romances. Ed. Frederick James Furnivall and John Wesley Hales. 4 vols. London: De la More, 1905–10.
Philippe de Thaon. *Le Livre de Sibile.* Ed. Hugh Shields. ANTS, 37. London: Anglo Norman Text Society, 1979.
Procès de Condamnation de Jeanne d'Arc. Ed. Pierre Tisset and Yvonne Lanhers. 3 vols. Paris: Société de l'histoire de France, 1960–71.
Le Procès de Guichard, évêque de Troyes (1308–1313). Ed. Abel Rigault. Paris: A. Picard, 1896.
Procès en nullité de la condamnation de Jeanne d'Arc. Ed. Pierre Duparc. 5 vols. Paris: Société de l'histoire de France, 1977–88.
The Progresses and Public Processions of Queen Elizabeth. Ed. John Nichols. 3 vols. London: Nichols, 1823.
Promptorium parvulorum. Ed. Albert Way. London: Camden Society, 1865.
A quest of enquirie, / by women to know, / whether the tripe-wife were trimmed / by Doll yea or no / Gathered by Oliuer Oat-meale. London: T. G., 1595 (*STC* [2nd ed.]:18758).
[Ralph of Coggeshall]. *Radulphi de Coggeshall Chronicon Anglicanum.* Ed. Joseph Stephenson. Rolls Series. London: Longman, 1875.
REED: Cheshire, Including Chester. Ed. Elizabeth Baldwin, Lawrence M. Clopper, and David Mills. 2 vols. Toronto: University of Toronto Press, 2007.
REED: Chester. Ed. Lawrence M. Clopper. Toronto: University of Toronto Press, 1979.
Register of John Morton, Archbishop of Canterbury, 1486–1500, III. Ed. Christopher Harper-Bill. Woodbridge: Boydell & Brewer, 2000.
Register of John Stafford, Bishop of Bath and Wells, 1425–1443. Ed. Thomas Scott Holmes. 2 vols. Somerset Record Society 31, 32. London: Harrison, 1915, 1916.
Religious Lyrics of the XIVth Century. Ed. Carleton Brown. 2nd ed. Oxford: Clarendon Press, 1924.
Reliquiae Antiquae. Ed. Thomas Wright and J. O. Halliwell. 2 vols. London: Pickering, 1841, 1843.
Renaut de Beaujeu. *Le Bel Inconnu.* Ed. G. Perrie Williams. Paris: Champion, 1929.

Rémy, Nicolas. *Demonolatreiae libri tres*. Frankfurt: Palthenius, 1597.

———. *Demonolatry*. Ed. Montague Summers. Trans. E. A. Ashwin. London: Rodker, 1930.

[*Richard the Lionheart*]. *Der mittelenglische Versroman über Richard Löwenherz*. Ed. Karl Brunner. Vienna and Leipzig: Wilhelm Braumüller, 1913.

Robert de Boron. *Merlin, roman du XIIIe siècle*. Ed. Alexandre Micha. Geneva: Droz, 1979.

Robert le diable. Ed. E. Löseth. Société des anciens textes français. Paris: Firmin Didot, 1903.

Robert of Gloucester. "A Fifteenth-Century Prose Paraphrase of Robert of Gloucester's *Chronicle*." Ed. Andrew D. Lipscomb. Ph.D. diss., University of North Carolina at Chapel Hill, 1990.

———. *Metrical Chronicle*. Ed. W. A. Wright. 2 vols. Rolls Series. London: Longman, 1887.

Le Roman de Brut. Ed. Ivor Arnold. 2 vols. Société des anciens textes français. Paris: Firmin Didot, 1938, 1940.

Le Roman de la rose. Ed. Daniel Poirion. Paris: Garnier-Flammarion, 1974.

Le Roman de Rou. Ed. A. J. Holden. 3 vols. Société des anciens textes français. Paris: Firmin Didot, 1970–73.

Le Roman de Tristan par Thomas. Ed. Joseph Bédier. 2 vols. Société des anciens textes français. Paris: Firmin Didot, 1902, 1905.

Le Roman de Troie. Ed. Léopold Constans. 6 vols. Société des anciens textes français. Paris: Firmin Didot, 1904–12.

Le Roman en prose de Tristan. Ed. E. Löseth. Paris: Bouillon, 1891.

Roman van Walewein (Dutch Romances, 1). Ed. and trans. David F. Johnson and Geert H. M. Classens. Woodbridge: Boydell and Brewer, 2000.

The Romance of Guy of Warwick (15th-Century Version). Ed. J. Zupitza. EETS ES 25, 26 (reprinted as one vol., 1966). London: Early English Text Society, 1875, 1876.

The Romance of Guy of Warwick (Auchinleck and Caius MSS.). Ed. Julius Zupitza. EETS ES 42, 49, 59 (reprinted as one vol., 1966). London: Kegan, Paul, 1883–91.

The Romance of the Cheuelere Assigne. Ed. Henry H. Gibbs. EETS ES 6. London: Trübner, 1868.

Li romans de Claris et Laris. Ed. Johann Alton. Tübingen: Litterarischer Verein in Stuttgart, 1884.

A Royal Historie of the Excellent Knight Generides. Ed. Frederick J. Furnivall. London: Roxburghe Club, 1865.

The Saga of Tristram and Ísönd. Trans. Paul Schach. Lincoln: University of Nebraska Press, 1973.

Scot, Reginald. *The Discouerie of Witchcraft*. London: by [Henry Denham for] William Brome, 1584 (*STC* [2nd ed.]:21864).

[*Second Lucidaire*]. Ed. Doris Ruhe. *Gelehrtes Wissen, "Aberglaube" und pastorale Praxis im französischen Spätmittelalter: Der Second Lucidaire und seine Rezeption, 14.–17. Jahrhundert*. Wissensliteratur im Mittelalter, 8. Wiesbaden: Reichert, 1993.

———. Ed. Monika Türk. *'Lucidaire de grant sapientie': Untersuchung und Edition der altfranzösischen Übersetzung 1 des 'Elucidarium' von Honorius Augustodunensis*. Tübingen: Niemeyer, 2000.

Secular Lyrics of the XIVth and XVth Centuries. Ed. Rossell Hope Robbins. Oxford: Clarendon Press, 1952.

The Seege or Batayle of Troye. Ed. Mary Elizabeth Barnicle. EETS OS 172. London: Oxford University Press, 1927.

Shakespeare, William. *Macbeth*. Ed. Kenneth Muir. *The Arden Edition of the Works of William Shakespeare*, 9th ed. London: Methuen, 1962.

Sidrak and Bokkus: A Parallel-Text Edition. Ed. T. L. Burton. EETS 311, 312. Oxford: Oxford University Press, 1998, 1999.
Sir Gawain: Eleven Romances and Tales. Ed. Thomas Hahn. Kalamazoo: Medieval Institute Publications, 1995.
Sir Orfeo. Ed. A. J. Bliss. 2nd ed. Oxford: Clarendon Press, 1966.
Sire Degarré. Ed. Gustav Schleich. Heidelberg: Carl Winter's Universitätsbuchhandlung, 1929.
Six Middle English Romances. Ed. Maldwyn Mills. London: J. M. Dent, 1973.
Six Town Chronicles of England. Ed. Ralph Flenley. Oxford: Clarendon Press, 1911.
The South English Legendary. Ed. Charlotte D'Evelyn and Anna J. Mill. 3 vols. EETS OS 335, 336, 344. London: Oxford University Press, 1956, 1959.
[Spina, Alphonse de]. *Alphonse dela Espina, Fortalitium Fidei in vniuersos christiane*. Lyon: Gueynard, 1525.
St Patrick's Purgatory. Ed. Robert Easting. EETS 298. Oxford: Oxford University Press, 1991.
Swan, John. *Speculum mundi or A glasse representing the face of the world*. Cambridge: T. Buck and R. Daniel, 1635 (*STC* [2nd ed.]:23516).
Thomas of Erceldoune. Ed. Ingeborge Nixon. 2 vols. Copenhagen: Akademisk Forlag, 1980, 1983.
Three Arthurian Romances: Poems from Medieval France. Trans. Ross G. Arthur. London: Everyman, 1996.
The Towneley Plays. Ed. Martin Stevens and A. C. Cawley. 2 vols. EETS SS 13, 14. London: Oxford University Press, 1994.
Trois sommes de pénitence de la première moitié du XIIIe siècle. Ed. Jean-Pierre Renard. Louvain-la-Neuve: Centre Cerfaux-Lefort, 1989.
Ulrich von Zatzikhoven. *Lanzelet, eine Erzählung*. Ed. K. A. Hahn. Frankfurt: Broenner, 1845.
Vaughan, William. *The arraignment of slander periury blasphemy, and other malicious sinnes*. London: Francis Constable, 1630 (*STC* [2nd ed.]:24623).
Villon, François. *Le Testament Villon*. Ed. Jean Rychner and Albert Henry. 2 vols. Geneva: Droz, 1974.
Visio Ludovico de Francia. Ed. Max Voigt. *Beiträge zur Geschichte der Visionenliteratur im Mittelalter I.II*. Leipzig: Mayer & Müller, 1924.
The Vision of Edmund Leversedge. Ed. W. F. Nijenhuis. Nijmegan: Katholieke Universiteit, 1991.
Visiones Georgii. Ed. L. L. Hammerich. *Det Kgl. Danske Videnskabernes Selkab. Historiskfilologiske Meddelelser*, vol. 18, pt. 2. Copenhagen: Bianco Lunos, 1930.
Vita Edwardi Secundi. Ed. Wendy R. Childs. Oxford: Clarendon Press, 2005.
The Vulgate Version of the Arthurian Romances. Ed. H. Oskar Sommer. 8 vols. Washington, D.C.: Carnegie, 1908–16.
[Walsingham, Thomas]. *Thomæ Walsingham: Quondam Monachi S. Albani, Historia Anglicana*. Ed. Henry Riley. 2 vols. Rolls Series. London: Longman, 1863, 1864.
Walter de Hemingford. *Chronicon Domini Walteri de Hemingburgh*. Ed. Hans Claude Hamilton. 2 vols. London: English Historical Society, 1848, 1849.
Waltharius and *Ruodlieb*. Ed. and trans. Dennis M. Katz. New York: Garland, 1984.
Waltharius. Ed. Karl Strecker. 1947; Hildesheim: Weidmannsche Verlagsbuchhandlung, 1987.
Wars of Alexander: An Alliterative Romance. Ed. Walter W. Skeat. EETS ES 47. London: Trübner, 1886.
[William of Auvergne]. *De Universo* in *Guillielmi Alverni Episcopi Parisiensis . . . Opera Omnia*. 2 vols. Paris: Andrew Pralard, 1674, 1:593–1074.
William of Newburgh. *The History of English Affairs, Bk I*. Ed. and trans. P. G. Walsh and M. J. Kennedy. Warminster: Aris & Phillips, 1988.

William of Palerne: An Electronic Edition. Ed. G. H. V. Bunt. Ann Arbor: University of Michigan Press, 2002.

Wright, Thomas, ed. *A Selection of Latin Stories, from Manuscripts of the Thirteenth and Fourteenth Centuries*. London: Percy Society, 1842.

Wyatt, Sir Thomas. *Collected Poems*. Ed. Kenneth Muir. London: Routledge and Kegan Paul, 1949.

[*Wycliffite Bible*]. *The Holy Bible . . . by John Wycliffe and His Followers*. Ed. Josiah Forshall and Frederic Madden. 4 vols. Oxford: Oxford University Press, 1850.

The York Plays: A Critical Edition of the York Corpus Christi Play as Recorded in British Library Additional MS 35290. Ed. Richard Beadle. 2 vols. EETS SS 23, 24. London: Oxford University Press, 2009, 2013.

SECONDARY SOURCES

Allen, Dorena. "Orpheus and Orfeo: The Dead and the Taken." *Medium Aevum* 33 (1964): 102–11.

Arnold, John H. *Belief and Unbelief in Medieval Europe*. 2005; London: Hodder, 2005.

Ashliman, D. L. *Fairy Lore: A Handbook*. Westport, Conn.: Greenwood Press, 2006.

Bailey, Michael D. *Fearful Spirits, Reasoned Follies: The Boundaries of Superstition in Late Medieval Europe*. Ithaca, N.Y.: Cornell University Press, 2013.

———. "The Feminization of Magic and the Emerging Idea of the Female Witch in the Late Middle Ages." *Essays in Medieval Studies* 19 (2002):120–34.

Bain, Frederika. "The Binding of the Fairies: Four Spells." *Preternature* 1 (2012):323–54.

Barber, Richard. *King Arthur in Legend and History*. London: Cardinal, 1973.

Barillari, Sonia Maura. "Le città delle dame: La sovranità ctonia declinata al femminile fra l'irlanda e i Monti Sibillini." *L'Immagine Riflessa*, n.s. 18 (2009):67–112.

———. *Protostoria della Strega. Le Fonti Medievali Latine e Romanze*. Aicurzio: Castel Negrino, 2014.

———. "Il Purgatorio di Ludovico di Sur: Un testo a cavallo fra Medioevo e Rinascimento." *Studi medievali*, 3rd ser., 49 (2008):759–808.

Bartlett, Robert. *England Under the Norman and Angevin Kings, 1075–1225*. Oxford: Clarendon Press, 2000.

———. *The Natural and the Supernatural in the Middle Ages*. Cambridge: Cambridge University Press, 2008.

Bennett, Gillian. *"Alas, Poor Ghost!": Traditions of Belief in Story and Discourse*. Logan: Utah State University Press, 1999.

Bennett, Michael J. "Henry VII and the Northern Rising of 1489." *English Historical Review* 105 (1990):34–59.

Bernstein, Alan E. "Review of *La naissance du purgatoire* by Jacques Le Goff." *Speculum* 59 (1984):179–83.

Bethurum, Dorothy. "Shakespeare's Comment on Mediaeval Romance in Midsummer-Night's Dream." *Modern Language Notes* 60 (1945):85–94.

Bloomfield, Morton W. "Symbolism in Medieval Literature." *Modern Philology* 56 (1958):73–81.

Bonney, Françoise. "Autour de Jean Gerson: Opinions de théologiens sur les superstitions et la sorcellerie au début du XVe siècle." *Moyen Âge* 77 (1971):85–98.

Boudet, Jean-Patrice. "Les Condamnation de la magie à Paris en 1398." *Revue Mabillon*, n.s. 12 (2000–2001):121–57.
Bourke, Angela. *The Burning of Bridget Cleary*. New York: Penguin, 2001.
Brewer, D. S. "The Interpretation of Fairy Tales." *A Companion to the Fairy Tale*, ed. Hilda Ellis Davidson and Anna Chaudhri. Woodbridge: D. S. Brewer, 2003, pp. 15–37.
Briggs, Katharine Mary. *The Fairies in English Tradition and Literature*. Chicago: University of Chicago Press, 1967.
———. "Some Seventeenth-Century Books of Magic." *Folklore* 64 (1953):445–62.
———. *The Vanishing People: Fairy Lore and Legends*. New York: Pantheon, 1978.
Brown, Arthur C. L. "The Grail and the English *Sir Perceval*." *Modern Philology* 16 (1918–19):553–68; 17 (1919–20):361–82; 18 (1920–21):201–28, 661–73; 22 (1924–25):79–98, 113–32.
———. "A Note on the *Nugae* of G. H. Gerould's 'King Arthur and Politics.'" *Speculum* 2 (1927):449–55.
Brown, Carleton. "The Vernon Disputisoun bytwene a Christenmon and a Jew." *Modern Language Notes* 25 (1910):141–44.
Brown, Peter. "Chaucer and Shakespeare: The *Merchant's Tale* Connection." *Chaucer Review* 48 (2013):222–37.
Burke, Peter. *Popular Culture in Early Modern Europe*. Rev. ed. Aldershot: Scolar Press, 1994.
Burrow, John A. "Elvish Chaucer." *The Endless Knot: Essays on Old and Middle English in Honor of Marie Borroff*, ed. M. Teresa Tavormina and R. F. Yeager. Cambridge: D. S. Brewer, 1995, pp. 105–11.
———. "*Sir Thopas* in the Sixteenth Century." *Middle English Studies Presented to Norman Davis in Honour of His Seventieth Birthday*, ed. Douglas Gray and E. G. Stanley. Oxford: Clarendon Press, 1983, pp. 69–91.
Byrne, Aisling. "Fairy Lovers: Sexuality, Order and Narrative in Medieval Romance." *Sexual Culture in the Literature of Medieval Britain*, ed. Amanda Hopkins, Robert Allen Rouse, and Cory James Rushton. Cambridge: D. S. Brewer, 2014, pp. 99–110.
Cameron, Euan. *Enchanted Europe: Superstition, Reason, and Religion, 1250–1750*. Oxford: Oxford University Press, 2010.
Campagne, F. A. "Witch or Demon? Fairies, Vampires, and Nightmares in Early Modern Spain." *Acta Ethnographica Hungarica* 53 (2008):381–410.
Carasso-Bulow, Lucienne. *The Merveilleux in Chrétien de Troyes' Romances*. Geneva: Droz, 1976.
Carley, James P. *Glastonbury Abbey: The Holy House at the Head of the Moors Adventurous*. 2nd ed. Glastonbury: Gothic Image, 1996.
Carlson, David R. *Chaucer's Jobs*. New York: Palgrave Macmillan, 2004.
Cartlidge, David R., and J. Keith Elliott. *Art and the Christian Apocrypha*. London: Routledge, 2001.
Cartlidge, Neil. "Sir Orfeo in the Otherworld: Courting Chaos?" *Studies in the Age of Chaucer* 26 (2004):195–226.
Chambers, E. K. *Arthur of Britain*. London: Sidgwick & Jackson, 1927.
Chambers, R. W. *Widsith, a Study in Old English Heroic Legend*. Cambridge: Cambridge University Press, 1912.
Childs, W. R. "'Welcome, My Brother': Edward II, John of Powderham and the Chronicles, 1318." *Church and Chronicle in the Middle Ages*, ed. Ian Wood and G. A. Loud. London: Hambledon Press, 1991), pp. 149–63.

Christian, William A. *Apparitions in Late Medieval and Renaissance Spain*. Princeton, N.J.: Princeton University Press, 1981.
Christiansen, Reidar. "Some Notes on the Fairies and the Fairy Faith." *Béalodeas* 39/41 (1971/73):95–111.
Cirese, Alberto. "Gramsci's Observations on Folklore." *Approaches to Gramsci*, ed. Anne Slowstack Sassoon. London: Writers and Readers, 1982, pp. 221–47.
Clancy, Susan A. *Abducted: How People Come to Believe They Were Kidnapped by Aliens*. Cambridge, Mass.: Harvard University Press, 2005.
Clark, Stuart. *Thinking with Demons*. Oxford: Oxford University Press, 1997.
Cohen, Jeffrey Jerome. *Hybridity, Identity, and Monstrosity in Medieval Britain*. New York: Palgrave Macmillan, 2006.
———. *Of Giants: Sex, Monsters, and the Middle Ages*. Minneapolis: University of Minnesota Press, 1999.
Coldewey, John C. "Watching the Watchers: Drama Spectatorship and Counter-Surveillance in Sixteenth-Century Chester." *Studia Anglica Posnaniensia* 38 (2002):131–46.
Collingwood, Robin G. *The Philosophy of Enchantment: Studies in Folktale, Cultural Criticism, and Anthropology*. Oxford: Clarendon Press, 2005.
Collingwood, Sharon L. *Market Pledge and Gender Bargain: Commercial Relations in French Farce, 1450–1550*. New York: Peter Lang, 1996.
Constable, Giles. "Forgery and Plagiarism in the Middle Ages." *Archiv für Diplomatik* 29 (1983):1–41.
Cooper, Helen. *The English Romance in Time: Transforming Motifs from Geoffrey of Monmouth to the Death of Shakespeare*. Oxford: Oxford University Press, 2004.
———. *Shakespeare and the Medieval World*. London: Bloomsbury, 2013.
Coulton, G. G. *The Medieval Village*. Cambridge: Cambridge University Press, 1926.
Crane, Susan. *The Performance of Self: Ritual, Clothing, and Identity During the Hundred Years War*. Philadelphia: University of Pennsylvania Press, 2002.
Crehan, Kate A. F. *Gramsci, Culture and Anthropology*. Berkeley: University of California Press, 2002.
Cross, Roseanna. "'Heterochronia' in Thomas of Erceldoune, Guingamor, 'The Tale of King Herla,' and the Story of Meriadoc, King of Cambria." *Neophilologus* 92 (2008):162–75.
Cummings, Brian. "Among the Fairies: Religion and the Anthropology of Ritual in Shakespeare." *Humankinds: The Renaissance and Its Anthropologies*, ed. Andreas Höfele and Stephan Laqué. Berlin, Boston: De Gruyter, 2011, pp. 71–89.
Curtius, Ernst Robert. *European Literature and the Latin Middle Ages*. Trans. Willard Trask. 1948; New York: Harper, 1963.
Dalton, Paul. "The Topical Concerns of Geoffrey of Monmouth's *Historia Regum Britannie*: History, Prophecy, Peacemaking, and English Identity in the Twelfth Century." *Journal of British Studies* 44 (2005):688–712.
Dando, M. "Les anges neutres." *Cahiers d'études Cathares* 27 (1976):3–28.
Davies, O. "The Nightmare Experience, Sleep Paralysis, and Witchcraft Accusations." *Folklore* 114 (2003):181–203.
De Mayo, Thomas. "William of Auvergne and Popular Demonology." *Quidditas* 28 (2007): 61–88.
Dégh, Linda. *Legend and Belief: Dialectics of a Folklore Genre*. Bloomington: Indiana University Press, 2001.
Delisle, Léopold. *Recherches sur la librairie de Charles V, Pt. II*. Paris: Champion, 1907.

Donaldson, E. Talbot. "The Miller's Tale, A 3483-86." *Modern Language Notes* 69 (1954): 310-13.

———. *The Swan at the Well*. New Haven, Conn.: Yale University Press, 1985.

Dorson, Richard M. *The British Folklorists: A History*. London: Routledge, 1968.

Doulet, Jean-Michel. *Quand les démons enlevaient les enfants, les changelins: Étude d'une figure mythique*. Paris: Sorbonne, 2003.

Doutrepont, Georges. *Les mises en prose des épopées et des romans chevaleresques du XIVe au XVIe siècle*. Brussels: Palais des académies, 1939.

Dronke, Peter. *The Medieval Poet and His World*. Rome: Storia e Letteratura, 1984.

Dubost, Francis. *Aspects fantastiques de la littérature narrative médiévale, XIIème–XIIIème siècles: L'autre, l'ailleurs, l'autrefois*. 2 vols. Geneva: Slatkine, 1991.

———. "Merveilleux et fantastique au moyen âge: Positions et propositions." *Revue des langues romanes* 100.2 (1996):1-35.

Duffy, Eamon. *The Stripping of the Altars: Traditional Religion in England, 1400–1580*. New Haven, Conn.: Yale University Press, 1992.

Dumville, David N. "Ekiurid's Celtic Lingua: An Ethnological Difficulty in Waltharius." *Cambridge Medieval Celtic Studies* 6 (1983):87-93.

———. "'Nennius' and the *Historia Brittonum*." *Studia Celtica* 10 (1975):78-95.

Easting, Robert. "Peter of Cornwall's Account of St. Patrick's Purgatory." *Analecta Bollandiana* 97 (1979):397-416.

———. "Purgatory and the Earthly Paradise in the *Purgatorio Sancti Patricii*." *Citeaux: Commentarii Cistercienses* 37 (1986):23-48.

———. "The South English Legendary 'St Patrick' as Translation." *Leeds Studies in English*, n.s. 2 (1990):119-40.

Eberly, Susan Schoon. "Fairies and the Folklore of Disability: Changelings, Hybrids and the Solitary Fairy." *Folklore* 99 (1988):58-77.

Echard, Siân. "'Hic est Artur': Reading Latin and Reading Arthur." *New Directions in Arthurian Studies*, ed. Alan Lupak. Cambridge: D. S. Brewer, 2002, pp. 49-67.

Edwards, Graham Robert. "Purgatory: 'Birth' or Evolution?" *Journal of Ecclesiastical History* 36 (1985):634-46.

Elliott, Dyan. *Fallen Bodies: Pollution, Sexuality, and Demonology in the Middle Ages*. Philadelphia: University of Pennsylvania Press, 1999.

Emmerson, Richard K. "'Nowe ys common this daye': Enoch and Elias, Antichrist, and the Structure of the Chester Cycle." *Homo, Memento Finis: The Iconography of Just Judgment in Medieval Art and Drama*, ed. David Bevington. Kalamazoo: Medieval Institute Publications, 1985, pp. 89-120.

———. "Contextualizing Performance: The Reception of the Chester Antichrist." *Journal of Medieval & Early Modern Studies* 29 (1999):89-119.

Evans, Daffyd. "Wishfulfilment: The Social Function and Classification of Old French Romances." *Court and Poet*, ed. Glyn S. Burgess. Liverpool: Cairns, 1981, pp. 129-34.

Evans-Wentz, W. Y. *The Fairy Faith in Celtic Countries*. London: Oxford University Press, 1911.

Ferlampin-Acher, Christine. *Fées, bestes et luitons: Croyances et merveilles dans les romans français en prose (XIIIe–XIVe siècles)*. Paris: Presses de l'université de Paris-Sorbonne, 2002.

Filotas, Bernadette. *Pagan Survivals, Superstitions and Popular Cultures in Early Medieval Pastoral Literature*. Toronto: Pontifical Institute of Mediaeval Studies, 2005.

Fletcher, Alan. "*Sir Orfeo* and the Flight from the Enchanters." *Studies in the Age of Chaucer* 22 (2000):141-78.

Flint, Valerie. "Heinricus of Augsberg and Honorius Augustodunensis: Are They the Same Person?" *Revue Bénédictine* 92 (1982):148–58.
Forte, Stephen L. "A Cambridge Dominican Collector of Exempla in the Thirteenth Century." *Archivum Fratrum Praedicatorum* 28 (1958):115–48.
Fowler, Kenneth. *Medieval Mercenaries.* Vol. 1: *The Great Companies.* Oxford: Blackwell, 2001– .
Freccero, John. "Dante and the Neutral Angels." *Romanic Review* 51 (1960):3–14.
Friedman, John Block. "Eurydice, Heurodis, and the Noon-Day Demon." *Speculum* 41 (1966):22–29.
Gaiffier, Baudouin. "Le Diable, voleur d'enfants." *Études critiques d'hagiographie et d'iconologie. publiées à l'occasion du 70me anniversaire de l'auteur.* Brussels: Société Bolandistes, 1967, pp. 169–93.
Galbraith, V. H. "The *Historia Aurea* of John, Vicar of Tynemouth, and the Sources of the St Albans Chronicle (1327–1377)." *Essays in History Presented to Reginald Lane Poole*, ed. H. W. C. Davis. Oxford: Clarendon Press, 1927, pp. 379–98.
Gardiner, Harold C. *Mysteries' End: An Investigation of the Last Days of the Medieval Religious Stage.* New Haven, Conn.: Yale University Press, 1946.
Gardner, Edmund G. *Arthurian Legend in Italian Literature.* London: J. M. Dent, 1930.
Gardner, John. *The Construction of the Wakefield Cycle.* Carbondale: Southern Illinois University Press, 1974.
Gencarella, Stephen O. "Gramsci, Good Sense, and Critical Folklore Studies." *Journal of Folklore Research* 47 (2010):221–52.
Gier, Albert, "Comment on devient fée: La féerie chrétienne d'*Esclamonde*." *Die Welt der Feen im Mittlealter / Le monde des fées dans la culture médiévale*, ed. Danielle Buschinger and Wolfgang Spiewok. Greifswalder Beiträge zum Mittelalter 32. Greifswald: Reineke-Verlag, 1994, pp. 59–66.
Gillingham, John. *The English in the Twelfth Century: Imperialism, National Identity, and Political Values.* Woodbridge: Boydell Press, 2000.
Gingras, Francis. *Erotisme et merveilles dans le récit français des XIIe et XIIIe siècles.* Paris: Champion, 2002.
Ginzburg, Carlo. *Ecstasies: Deciphering the Witches' Sabbath.* Trans. Raymond Rosenthal. New York: Pantheon Books, 1991.
———. *The Night Battles: Witchcraft and Agrarian Cults in the Sixteenth and Seventeenth Centuries.* Trans. John and Anne Tedeschi. Baltimore: Johns Hopkins University Press, 1992.
Goodey, C. F., and T. Stainton. "Intellectual Disability and the Myth of the Changeling Myth." *Journal of the History of Behavioral Science* 37.3 (2001):223–40.
Graf, Arturo. *Miti, leggende e superstizioni del medio evo.* 1892/93; Milan: Mondadori, 1985.
Gramsci, Antonio. *Selections from Cultural Writings.* Ed. David Forgacs and Geoffrey Nowell-Smith. Trans. William Boelhower. Cambridge, Mass.: Harvard University Press, 1985.
———. *Selections from the Prison Notebooks.* Ed. and trans. Quintin Hoare and Geoffrey Nowell Smith. New York: International Publishers, 1971.
Green, Richard Firth. "Changing Chaucer." *Studies in the Age of Chaucer* 25 (2003):27–52.
Greenblatt, Stephen. *Marvelous Possessions: The Wonder of the New World.* Chicago: University of Chicago Press, 1991.

Gregory, Annabel. *Rye Spirits: Faith, Faction, and Fairies in a Seventeenth-Century English Town*. London: Hedge Press, 2013.
Gurevich, Aron. *Medieval Popular Culture: Problems of Belief and Perception*. Trans. Janos M. Bak and Paul A. Hollingsworth. Cambridge: Cambridge University Press, 1988.
Haffen, Josiane. *Contribution à l'étude de la Sibylle médiévale*. Paris: Belles lettres, 1984.
Hafstein, Valdimar Th. "The Elves' Point of View: Cultural Identity in Contemporary Elf-Tradition." *Fabula* 41 (2000):87–104.
Haines, Roy Martin. *King Edward II: Edward of Caenarfon, His Life, His Reign, and Its Aftermath*. Montreal: McGill-Queens University Press, 2003.
Hall, Alaric. "Calling the Shots: The Old English Remedy *Gif hors ofscoten sie* and Anglo-Saxon 'Elf-Shot.'" *Neuphilologische Mitteilungen* 106 (2005):195–209.
———. *Elves in Anglo-Saxon England: Matters of Belief, Health, Gender and Identity*. Woodbridge: Boydell Press, 2007.
———. "The Evidence for Maran, the Anglo-Saxon 'Nightmares.'" *Neophilologus* 91 (2007): 299–317.
———. "Getting Shot of Elves: Healing, Witchcraft and Fairies in the Scottish Witchcraft Trials." *Folklore* 116 (2005):19–36.
Hammer, Jacob. "Bref commentaire de la *Prophetia Merlini* du ms 3524 de la Bibliothèque de la Cathédrale d'Exeter." *Hommages à Joseph Bidez et à Franz Cumont*. Brussels: Latomus, 1949, pp. 111–19.
———. "A Commentary on the *Prophetia Merlini* (Geoffrey of Monmouth's *Historia Regum Britanniae*, Book VII)." *Speculum* 15 (1940):409–31.
Harding, Carol E. *Merlin and Legendary Romance*. New York: Garland, 1988.
Harf-Lancner, Laurence. *Les fées au moyen âge: Morgane et Mélusine; la naissance des fées*. Geneva: Slatkine, 1984.
Harris, Ruth. *Lourdes: Body and Spirit in the Secular Ages*. New York and London: Penguin, 1999.
Heller, Sarah-Grace. "Obscure Lands and Obscured Hands: Fairy Embroidery and the Ambiguous Vocabulary of Medieval Textile Decoration." *Medieval Clothing and Textiles* 5 (2009):15–35.
Henderson, Lizanne, and Edward J. Cowan. *Scottish Fairy Belief: A History*. East Linton: Tuckwell Press, 2001.
Heng, Geraldine. *Empire of Magic: Medieval Romance and the Politics of Cultural Fantasy*. New York: Columbia University Press, 2003.
Henningsen, Gustav. "'The Ladies from Outside': An Archaic Pattern in the Witches' Sabbath." *Early Modern Witchcraft: Centres and Peripheries*, ed. Bengt Ankarloo and Gustav Henningsen. Oxford: Clarendon Press, 1990, pp. 191–215.
Herbert, J. A. *Catalogue of Romances in the Department of Manuscripts in the British Museum, Vol. 3*. London: Trustees of the British Museum, 1919.
Hibbard, Laura. "The Sword Bridge of Chretien de Troyes and Its Celtic Original." *Romanic Review* 4 (1913):166–90.
Hill, D. M. "The Structure of Sir Orfeo." *Mediaeval Studies* 23 (1961):136–41.
Howells, W. *Cambrian Superstitions, Ghosts, Omens, Witchcraft, Traditions, &c*. Tipton: Danks, 1831.
Hufford, David J. *The Terror That Comes in the Night: An Experience-Centered Study of Supernatural Assault Traditions*. Philadelphia: University of Pennsylvania Press, 1982.

Hutton, Ronald. "The Making of Early Modern British Fairy Tradition." *Historical Journal* 57 (2014):1135–56.

———. *The Rise and Fall of Merry England: The Ritual Year 1400–1700*. Oxford: Oxford University Press, 1994.

Ingham, Patricia Clare. *Sovereign Fantasies: Arthurian Romance and the Making of Britain*. Philadelphia: University of Pennsylvania Press, 2001.

Jameson, Fredric. "Magical Narratives: Romance as Genre." *New Literary History* 7 (1975): 135–63.

Jauss, Hans-Robert. "Theorie der Gattungen und Literatur des Mittelalters." *Grundriss der romanischen Literaturen des Mittelalters* 1 (Generalités) (1972):103–38 [trans. in *Modern Genre Theory*, ed. David Duff. London: Longman, 1999].

Jeay, Madeleine. "Clercs et paysans au XVe siècle: Une relecture de l'épisode de l'arbre au fées dans les procès de Jeanne d'Arc." *Normes et pouvoir à la fin du moyen âge*, ed. Marie-Claude Déprez-Masson. Montreal: Editions CERES, 1989, pp. 145–63.

Jones, T. Gwynn. *Welsh Folklore and Folk-Custom*. 1930; Cambridge: Brewer, 1979.

Jones, William R. "Political Uses of Sorcery in Medieval Europe." *Historian* 34 (1972):670–87.

Kamerick, Kathleen. "Shaping Superstition in Late Medieval England." *Magic, Ritual & Witchcraft* 3 (2008):29–53.

Kauffman, Alexander L. *The Historical Literature of the Jack Cade Rebellion*. Farnham: Ashgate, 2009.

Kelly, Douglas "Two Problems in Chrétien's *Charrette*: The Boundary of Gorre and the Use of *Novele*." *Neophilologus* 48 (1964):115–21.

Kennedy, Edward Donald, "Visions of History: Robert de Boron and English Arthurian Chroniclers." *The Fortunes of King Arthur*, ed. Norris J. Lacy. Cambridge: Brewer, 2005, pp. 29–46.

Kennedy, Elspeth. *Lancelot and the Grail: A Study of the Prose Lancelot*. Oxford: Clarendon Press, 1986.

———. "The Role of the Supernatural in the First Part of the Old French Prose *Lancelot*." *Studies in Medieval Literature and Languages in Memory of Frederick Whitehead*, ed. W. Rothwell et al. Manchester: Manchester University Press, 1973, pp. 173–84.

Ker, W. P. "The Craven Angels." *Modern Language Review* 6 (1911):85–87.

Kieckheffer, Richard. *Magic in the Middle Ages*. Cambridge: Cambridge University Press, 1990.

Kiessling, Nicholas. *The Incubus in English Literature: Provenance and Progeny*. Pullman: Washington State University Press, 1977.

Kinter, William L., and Joseph R. Keller. *The Sibyl: Prophetess of Antiquity and Medieval Fay*. Philadelphia: Dorrance, 1967.

Kittredge, George L. *Witchcraft in Old and New England*. Cambridge, Mass.: Harvard University Press, 1929.

Klaassen, Frank. "Learning and Masculinity in Manuscripts of Ritual Magic of the Later Middle Ages and Renaissance." *Sixteenth Century Journal* 38 (2007):49–76.

Klaassen, Frank, and Katerina Bens. "Achieving Invisibility and Having Sex with Spirits: Six Operations from an English Magic Collection, ca. 1600." *Opuscula* 3 (2013):1–14.

Koch, John. "Anglonormannische Texte im Ms. Arundel 220 des Britischen Museums." *Zeitschrift für romanische Philologie* 54 (1934):20–56.

Kolve, V. A. *The Play Called Corpus Christi*. Stanford, Calif.: Stanford University Press, 1966.

Kuuliala, Jenni. "Sons of Demons? Children's Impairments and the Beliefs in Changelings in Medieval Europe." *The Dark Side of Childhood in Late Antiquity and the Middle Ages:*

Unwanted, Disabled, and Lost, ed. Katariina Mustakallio and Christian Laes. Oxford: Oxbow Books, 2011, pp. 71–93.

Lambert, Malcolm. *The Cathars*. Oxford: Blackwell, 1998.

Larrington, Carolyne. "The Fairy Mistress in Medieval Literary Fantasy." *Writing and Fantasy*, ed. Ceri Sullivan and Barbara White. London: Longman, 1999, pp. 32–47.

Latham, M. W. *The Elizabethan Fairies*. New York: Columbia University Press, 1930.

Le Fèvre, Yves. *L'Elucidarium et les Lucidaires: Contribution, par l'histoire d'un texte, à l'histoire des croyances religieuses en France au moyen âge*. Paris: E. de Boccard, 1954.

Le Goff, Jacques. *The Birth of Purgatory*. Trans. Arthur Goldhammer. Chicago: University of Chicago Press, 1984.

———. *L'imaginaire médiéval: Essais*. Paris: Gallimard, 1985.

———. *The Medieval Imagination*. Trans. Arthur Goldhammer. Chicago: University of Chicago Press, 1988.

———. *La naissance du purgatoire*. Paris: Gallimard, 1981.

———. *Pour un autre moyen âge*. Paris: Gallimard, 1977.

———. *Time, Work, & Culture in the Middle Ages*. Trans. Arthur Goldhammer. Chicago: University of Chicago Press, 1980.

Le Goff, Jacques, and Emmanuel Le Roy Ladurie. "Mélusine maternelle et défricheuse." *Annales: Économies, Sociétés, Civilisations* 26 (1971):587–622.

Le Saux, Françoise. *La3amon's Brut: The Poem and Its Sources*. Woodbridge: D. S. Brewer, 1989.

Lecouteux, Claude. *Au-delà du merveilleux: Des croyances du moyen âge*. Paris: Presses de l'Université de Paris-Sorbonne, 1995.

———. *Chasses fantastiques et cohortes de la nuit au moyen âge*. Paris: Imago, 1999.

———. *Les Nains et les elfes*. Paris: Imago, 1988.

Lehoux, Françoise. *Jean de France, duc de Berri, sa vie, son action politique (1340–1416)*. 3 vols. Paris: A. et J. Picard, 1966–68.

Levack, Brian. *The Witch-Hunt in Early Modern Europe*. 2nd ed. London: Longman, 1995.

Levin, Richard. "Another 'Source' for *The Alchemist* and Another Look at Source Studies." *English Literary Renaissance* 28 (1998):210–30.

Lewis, C. S. "De Audiendis Poetis." *Studies in Medieval and Renaissance Literature*, collected by Walter Hooper. Cambridge: Cambridge University Press, 1966, pp. 1–17.

———. *The Discarded Image: An Introduction to Medieval and Renaissance Literature*. Cambridge: Cambridge University Press, 1964.

Lewis, Timothy, and J. Douglas Bruce. "The Pretended Exhumation of Arthur and Guinevere." *Revue Celtique* 33 (1912):432–51.

Lindahl, Carl. "Folklore." *Medieval Folklore: A Guide to Myths, Legends, Tales, Beliefs, and Customs*, ed. Carl Lindahl, John McNamara, and John Lindow. 2 vols. Oxford: Oxford University Press, 2002, 1:334.

Lindow, John. "Changelings, Changing, Re-exchanges: Thoughts on the Relationship Between Folk Belief and Legend." *Legends and Landscape: Plenary Papers from the 5th Celtic-Nordic-Baltic Folklore Symposium*, ed. Terry Gunnell. Reykjavík: Háskólaútgáfan, 2008, pp. 215–34.

Loomis, Roger Sherman. *Arthurian Tradition and Chrétien de Troyes*. New York: Columbia University Press, 1949.

———. "Breton Folklore and Arthurian Romance." *Comparative Literature* 2 (1950):289–306.

———. "The Legend of Arthur's Survival." *Arthurian Literature in the Middle Ages*, ed. Roger Sherman Loomis. Oxford: Clarendon Press, 1959, pp. 64–71.

Lyle, E. B. "*The Wee Wee Man* and *Als y yod on a Mounday.*" *Ballad Studies*, ed. E. B. Lyle. Cambridge: D. S. Brewer, 1976, pp. 21–28.

MacCulloch, J. A. *Medieval Faith and Fable*. London: Harrap, 1932.

———. "The Mingling of Fairy and Witch Beliefs in Sixteenth and Seventeenth Century Scotland." *Folklore* 32 (1921):229–44.

Marshall, Linda E. "Sacral Parody in the *Secunda Pastorum*." *Speculum* 47 (1972):720–36.

Matheson, Lister M. "The Arthurian Stories of Lambeth Palace Library MS 84." *Arthurian Literature* 5 (1985):70–91.

Mayhew, A. L. "The Etymology of 'Deuce': Interjectional and Imprecatory." *Academy*, 30 January 1892, pp. 111–12.

McGuire, B. P. "Purgatory, the Communion of Saints, and Medieval Change." *Viator* 20 (1989): 61–84.

Meyer, Paul. "*Chanjon*, enfant changé en nourice." *Romania* 32 (1903):452–53.

———. "Les Manuscrits des sermons français de Maurice de Sully." *Romania* 5 (1876):466–87.

———. "Notice du MS. Bibl. Nat. Fr. 25439." *Bulletin de la société des anciens textes français* 25 (1899):66–63.

———. "Notices sur quelques manuscrits français de la bibliothèque Phillipps à Cheltenham." *Notices et extraits des manuscrits de la Bibliothèque nationale et autres bibliothèques* 34 (1891):149–258.

Micha, A. "Les manuscrits du *Merlin* en Prose de Robert de Boron." *Romania* 79 (1958):78–94, 145–74.

Mitchell, Bruce. "The Faery World of Sir Orfeo." *Neophilologus* 48 (1964):155–59.

Moore, R. I. *The Formation of a Persecuting Society: Authority and Deviance in Western Europe, 950–1250*. 2nd ed. 1987; Oxford: Blackwell, 2007.

Morey, Adrian. *Bartholomew of Exeter: Bishop and Canonist*. Cambridge: Cambridge University Press, 1937.

Morgan, Gareth. "Walther the Woodsprite." *Medium Aevum* 41 (1972):16–19.

Mozley, J. H. "A Collection of Mediaeval Latin Verse in MS. Cotton Titus D. XXIV." *Medium Aevum* 11 (1942):1–45.

Mroczkowski, Przemyslaw. "Incubi and Friars." *Kwartalnik Neofilologiczny* 8 (1961):191–92.

Murer, Konrad. "Die Hölle auf Island." *Zeitschrift des Vereins für Volkskunde* 4 (1894):256–69.

Murray, Margaret Alice. *The God of the Witches*. London: Faber and Faber, 1931.

———. *The Witch-Cult in Western Europe: A Study in Anthropology*. Oxford: Clarendon Press, 1921.

Needham, Rodney. *Primordial Characters*. Charlottesville: University Press of Virginia, 1978.

Nicholson, R. H. "The Trial of Christ the Sorcerer in the York Cycle." *Journal of Medieval and Renaissance Studies* 16 (1986):125–69.

Nosworthy, J. M. "*Macbeth* at the Globe." *Library*, 5th ser., 2 (1947):108–18.

O'Daniel, Victor F. *The First Disciples of Saint Dominic*. New York: Pustet, 1928.

Oring, Elliott. *Folk Groups and Folklore Genres: An Introduction*. Logan: Utah State University Press, 1986.

Orme, Nicholas. "An English Grammar School ca. 1450: Latin Exercises from Exeter (Caius College MS 417/447, Folios 16v–24v)." *Traditio* 50 (1995):261–94.

Owst, G. R. "Sortilegium in English Homiletic Literature of the Fourteenth Century." *Studies Presented to Sir Hilary Jenkinson*, ed. J. Conway Davies. London: Oxford University Press, 1957, pp. 272–303.

Partner, Nancy. *Serious Entertainments: The Writing of History in Twelfth-Century England*. Chicago: University of Chicago Press, 1977.

Patch, Howard Rollin. *The Other World According to Descriptions in Medieval Literature*. Cambridge, Mass.: Harvard University Press, 1950.
Paton, Lucy Allen. *Studies in the Fairy Mythology of Arthurian Romance*. Boston: Ginn, 1903.
Paupert, Anne. *Les Fileuses et le clerc: Une étude des Evangiles des Quenouilles*. Paris: Champion, 1990.
Paxson, James J. "Theorizing the Mysteries' End in England, the Artificial Demonic, and the Sixteenth-Century Witch-Craze." *Criticism* 39 (1997):481–502.
Pellegrin, Elisabeth. "Membra disiecta Floriacensia." *Bibliothèque de l'École des chartes* 117 (1959):5–56.
Peters, Edward. *The Magician, the Witch, and the Law*. Philadelphia: University of Pennsylvania Press, 1978.
Pickering, O. S. "*South English Legendary* Style in Robert of Gloucester's *Chronicle*." *Medium Ævum* 70 (2001):1–18.
———. "A Third Text of 'Sey me viit in þe brom.'" *English Studies* 63 (1982):20–22.
Poirion, Daniel. *Le merveilleux dans la littérature française du moyen âge*. Paris: Presses universitaires de France, 1982.
Poull, Georges. *Le Château et les seigneurs de Bourlémont, 1149–1412*. Corbeil-Essonnes: Private ed., 1962.
Pócs, Éva. *Between the Living and the Dead*. Trans. Szilvia Rédey and Michael Webb. Budapest: Central European University Press, 1999.
Purkiss, Diane. *At the Bottom of the Garden: A Dark History of Fairies, Hobgoblins, and Other Troublesome Things*. New York: New York University Press, 2000.
———. "Sounds of Silence: Fairies and Incest in Scottish Witchcraft Stories." *Languages of Witchcraft: Ideology and Meaning in Early Modern Culture*, ed. Stuart Clark. London: Palgrave, 2000, pp. 81–98.
Reynders, Anne. "Le Roman de Partonopeu de Blois est-il l'œuvre d'un précurseur de Chrétien de Troyes?" *Moyen Âge* 111 (2005):479–502.
Rider, Catherine. *Magic and Religion in Medieval England*. London: Reaktion Books, 2012.
Rider, Jeff. "The Other Worlds of Romance." *The Cambridge Companion to Medieval Romance*, ed. Roberta L. Kruger. Cambridge: Cambridge University Press, 2000, pp. 115–31.
———. "Receiving Orpheus in the Middle Ages: Allegorization, Remythification and *Sir Orfeo*." *Papers on Language & Literature* 24 (1988):343–66.
Rieger, Angelica. "'Dame plus bele que fée': Une expression proverbiale et son histoire dans les littératures française et occitane du moyen âge." *Die Welt der Feen im Mittlealter / Le monde des fées dans la culture médiévale*, ed. Danielle Buschinger and Wolfgang Spiewok. Greifswalder Beiträge zum Mittelalter 32. Greifswald: Reineke-Verlag, 1994, pp. 143–61.
Rigg, A. G. "John of Bridlington's *Prophesy*: A New Look." *Speculum* 63 (1988):596–613.
Robbins, R. H. "Middle English Misunderstood: Mr Speirs and the Goblins." *Anglia* 85 (1967):270–81.
Robertson, D. W. "Why the Devil Wears Green." *Modern Language Notes* 69 (1954):470–72.
———. "The Question of Typology and the Wakefield *Mactacio Abel*." *American Benedictine Review* 25 (1974):157–73.
Rojcewicz, Peter M. "Between One Eye Blink and the Next: Fairies, UFOs and the Problems of Knowledge." *The Good People: New Folklore Essays*, ed. Peter Narváez. 1991. Lexington: University Press of Kentucky, 1997, pp. 479–514.
Rose, Elliot. *A Razor for a Goat*. Toronto: University of Toronto Press, 1989.

Ruhe, Ernstpeter. *Elucidarium und Lucidaires: Zur Rezeption des Werks von Honorius Augustodunensis in der Romania und in England.* Wiesbaden: L. Reichert, 1993.

Sahlins, Peter. *Forest Rites: The War of the Demoiselles in Nineteenth-Century France.* Cambridge, Mass.: Harvard University Press, 1994.

Saunders, Corinne. *Magic and the Supernatural in Medieval English Romance.* Woodbridge: D. S. Brewer, 2010.

Sawyer, Ronald C. "'Strangely Handled in All Her Lyms': Witchcraft and Healing in Jacobean England." *Journal of Social History* 22 (1989):461–85.

Schmitt, Jean-Claude. *Ghosts in the Middle Ages: The Living and the Dead in Medieval Society.* Trans. Teresa Lavender Fagan. Chicago: University of Chicago Press, 1998.

———. *The Holy Greyhound: Guinefort, Healer of Children Since the Thirteenth Century.* Trans. Martin Thom. Cambridge: Cambridge University Press, 1983.

———. "Religion, Folklore, and Society in the Medieval West." Trans. Lucia Carle. *Debating the Middle Ages: Issues and Reading*, ed. Lester K. Little and Barbara H. Rosenwein. Malden, Mass.: Blackwell, 1999, pp. 376–87.

———. *Religione, folklore e società nell'occidente medievale.* Bari: Laterza, 1988.

———. *Le saint Lévrier: Guinefort, guérisseur d'enfants depuis le XIIIe siècle.* Paris: Flammarion, 1979.

———. "Les 'Superstitions.'" *Histoire de la France religieuse, 1*, ed. Jacques Le Goff and René Rémond. Paris: Seuil, 1988, pp. 497–99.

Sharpe, James. *The Bewitching of Anne Gunter.* New York: Routledge, 2001.

Simpson, James. *Reform and Cultural Revolution: 1350–1547.* Vol. 2 of *The Oxford English Literary History.* Oxford: Oxford University Press, 2002.

Sisson, C. J. "A Topical Reference in *The Alchemist*." *Joseph Quincy Adams: Memorial Studies*, ed. James G. McManaway, Giles E. Dawson, and Edwin E. Willoughby. Washington, D.C.: Folger Library, 1948, pp. 739–41.

Smalley, Beryl. *English Friars and Antiquity in the Early Fourteenth Century.* Oxford: Blackwell, 1960.

Southern, R. W. "Between Heaven and Hell: Review of Jacques le Goff, *La Naissance du Purgatoire*." *Times Literary Supplement*, 18 June 1982, pp. 651–52.

Speirs, John. *Medieval English Poetry: The Non-Chaucerian Tradition.* London: Faber and Faber, 1957.

Stephens, Walter. *Demon Lovers: Witchcraft, Sex, and the Crisis of Belief.* Chicago: University of Chicago Press, 2002.

Stewart, Marion. "King Orphius." *Scottish Studies* 17 (1973):1–16.

———. "A Recently Discovered Manuscript: 'Ane tale of Sir Colling ye kny^t.'" *Scottish Studies* 16 (1972):23–39.

Strong, R. C. "The Popular Celebration of the Accession Day of Queen Elizabeth I." *Journal of the Warburg and Courtauld Institutes* 21 (1958):86–103.

Sturm, Sara. *The Lay of Guingamor: A Study.* Chapel Hill: University of North Carolina Press, 1968.

Sullivan, Karen. *The Interrogation of Joan of Arc.* Minneapolis: University of Minnesota Press, 1999.

Swann, Marjorie. "The Politics of Fairylore in Early Modern Literature." *Renaissance Quarterly* 53 (2000):449–73.

Sweeney, Michelle. *Magic in Medieval Romance from Chrétien de Troyes to Geoffrey Chaucer.* Dublin: Four Courts Press, 2000.

Tatlock, J. S. P. "The English Journey of the Laon Canons." *Speculum* 8 (1933):454–65.
Thomas, Keith. *Religion and the Decline of Magic: Studies in Popular Beliefs in Sixteenth and Seventeenth Century England*. London: Weidenfeld & Nicolson, 1971.
Thompson, E. P. *Customs in Common*. New York: New Press, 1991.
———. *Whigs and Hunters: The Origin of the Black Act*. New York: Pantheon Books, 1975.
Tubach, Frederick C. *Index Exemplorum*. Folklore Communications, 204. Helsinki: Academia Scientiarum Fennica, 1981.
Valette, Jean-René. *La poétique du merveilleux dans le Lancelot en prose*. Paris: Champion, 1998.
Van der Lugt, Maaike. *Le ver, le démon et la vierge: Les théories médiévales de la génération extraordinaire*. Paris: Les Belles Lettres, 2004.
Van der Zanden, C. M. *Étude sur le Purgatoire de saint Patrice*. Amsterdam: Paris, 1928.
Van Engen, John. "The Christian Middle Ages as an Historiographical Problem." *American Historical Review* 91 (1986):519–52.
Vaultier, Roger. *Le Folklore pendant la guerre de cent ans*. Paris: Guénégaud, 1965.
Veenstra, Jan R. *Magic and Divination at the Courts of Burgundy and France*. New York: Brill, 1997.
Wade, James. "Abduction, Surgery, Madness: An Account of a Little Red Man in Thomas Walsingham's *Chronica Maiora*." *Medium Aevum* 77 (2008):10–29.
———. *Fairies in Medieval Romance*. New York: Palgrave Macmillan, 2011.
Wakefield, Walter L. "Some Unorthodox Popular Ideas of the Thirteenth Century." *Medievalia et Humanistica* 4 (1973):25–33.
Watkins, Carl S. "Fascination and Anxiety in Medieval Wonder Stories." *The Unorthodox Imagination in Late Medieval Britain*, ed. Sophie Page. Manchester: Manchester University Press, 2010, pp. 45–64.
———. *History and the Supernatural in Medieval England*. Cambridge: Cambridge University Press, 2007.
Weitemeier, Bernd. *Visiones Georgii: Untersuchung mit synoptischer Edition der Übersetzung und Redaktion C*. Berlin: Erich Schmidt, 2006.
Wentersdorf, Karl P. "Chaucer and the Lost Tale of Wade." *Journal of English and Germanic Philology* 65 (1966):274–86.
Wenzel, Siegfried. *Latin Sermon Collections from Later Medieval England: Orthodox Preaching in the Age of Wyclif*. Cambridge: Cambridge University Press, 2005.
———. "The Moor Maiden—A Contemporary View." *Speculum* 49 (1974):69–74.
———. *Poets, Preachers and the Early English Lyric*. Princeton, N.J.: Princeton University Press, 1986.
———. *Verses in Sermons*. Cambridge, Mass.: Medieval Academy of America, 1978.
Wilby, Emma. *Cunning Folk and Familiar Spirits*. Eastbourne: Sussex Academic Press, 2005.
Williams, Arnold. "Typology and the Cycle Plays: Some Criteria." *Speculum* 43 (1968):677–84.
Wilson, Stephen. *The Magical Universe: Everyday Ritual and Magic in Pre-modern Europe*. London: Hambledon and London, 2000.
Woodcock, Matthew. *Fairy in* The Faerie Queene. Aldershot: Ashworth, 2004.
———. "The Fairy Queen Figure in Elizabethan Entertainments." *Elizabeth I: Always Her Own Free Woman*, ed. Carole Levin, Jo Eldridge Carney, and Debra Barrett-Graves. Aldershot: Ashgate, 2003, pp. 97–115.
Woolf, Rosemary. "The Effect of Typology on the English Mediaeval Plays of Abraham and Isaac." *Speculum* 32 (1957):805–25.

Wormald, C. P. "The Uses of Literacy in Anglo-Saxon England and Its Neighbour." *Transactions of the Royal Historical Society* 27 (1977):95–114.
Yates, Frances A. "Elizabethan Chivalry: The Romance of the Accession Day Tilts." *Journal of the Warburg and Courtauld Institutes* 20 (1957):4–25.
Young, Simon. "Against Taxonomy: Fairy Families in Cornwall." *Cornish Studies* 21 (2013): 223–37.
———. "Some Notes on Irish Fairy Changelings in Nineteenth-Century Newspapers." *Béascna* 8 (2013):34–47.
Ziolkowski, Jan M. *Fairy Tales from Before Fairy Tales: The Medieval Latin Past of Wonderful Lies.* Ann Arbor: University of Michigan Press, 2007.

INDEX

Adam de la Halle, *Jeu de la feuillée*, 67, 175
Adam of Eynsham, 82
Africa, 116, 162
Agnès de Bourgogne, Duchess de Bourbon, 46
Alan of Lille, 149
Albertus Magnus, 39, 70, 83, 86, 164–65, 210–11n13
alien abduction, 41, 77, 217n114
Allen, Dorena, 6, 163, 166
Alnoth, 58
Alphabet of Tales, 142
Alphonse de Spina, 86
Ancrene Wisse, 123
Anonimalle Chronicle, 211–22
Apennines, 40, 45
Apuleius, *De deo Socratis,* 78, 87–88, 91
Aquinas, Saint Thomas, 59, 86, 221n86
Arabia, 67
Ardennes, 6, 67, 162
Aristotle, 61
Arles, 79
Arras, 6, 175
Arthurian Vulgate Cycle, 94
Ashley, Sir Anthony, 203
Aubrey, John, 66, 110
Auchinleck Manuscript (National Library of Scotland, Adv. MS 19.2.1), 63, 124, 183, 188
Augustine, boy healed by Saint Thomas, 115–16
Augustine, Saint, 3, 228n29; *The City of God*, 16, 44, 78–79, 87, 99, 142, 163, 174, 229n54, 237n68; *The Divination of Demons*, 62; *On Christian Doctrine*, 223n107

Bailey, Michael, 107, 219n40, 233n126
Barber, Richard, 155
Barenton, spring of, 35–39

Baret, John, *Aluearie or triple dictionarie*, 195
Barillari, Sonia, 182, 213n32, 238n95, 249n17
Barlow, William, *Three Christian Sermons*, 195
Bartholomaeus Anglicus, 116, 185–86
Bartholomew of Exeter, 226n168
Bedford, 53
Bekker, Balthasar, *The World Bewitched*, 197
Bennett, Gillian, 72
Benoit de Saint-Maure, 79
Bernardus Silvestris, 59
Bernstein, Alan E., 178
Biggleswade, 53
Bliss, A. J., 168
Bodmin, 149
Boece, Hector, *Scotorum Historia*, 83
Boguet, Henri, *Discours des Sorciers*, 95, 197
Bonaventure, Saint, 86
Book of the Dun Cow, 6
Bourlément family, 45, 218n16
Boyman, Jonet, 204
Breton lais, 101, 105; *Désiré*, 67, 69, 103, 107; *Graelent*, 103, 107; *Guingamor*, 65, 67, 103, 107, 111, 174, 180, 192; *Lanval/Sir Launfal*, 23, 55, 102–4, 106–7, 161; *Sir Orfeo*, 18, 67, 111, 145, 161, 163–64, 166–69, 171–72, 183, 187, 191, 204, 244n79; *Tydorel*, 58, 65, 67–69, 96, 99, 112; *Tyolet*, 67, 107. See also Marie de France
Brewer, Derek S., 71
Brideling, sadling and ryding, of a rich churle, 203
Briggs, Katharine, 4, 228n29, 233n130, 234n7
Brittany, 32, 34, 37, 67–68, 89, 100–101, 149, 153–54, 158, 160, 241n9
Brocéliande, forest of, 7, 32–37, 39, 45, 238n97
Bromyard, John, 22, 73, 81, 138–39, 234n9

Brown, Arthur, 33
Brut, 92–93, 95
Buin, Michel, 29
Bullein, William, *Bulleins Bulwarke*, 196
Burchard of Worms, *The Corrector*, 15, 49, 100, 243n69
Burke, Peter, 42–43
Burrow, John, 198
Byrne, Aisling, 74
Byzantium (Constantinople), 67, 105

Cade, Jack, 22
Caesarius of Heisterbach, *Dialogus Miraculorum*, 23, 48–49, 55, 85, 179–80, 193, 248n159
Cambrai, 6
Cambridge, 44, 83
Cambridgeshire, 141
Camlann, Battle of, 147, 154
Campion, Thomas, 202
canon, *Episcopi*, 166
Canterbury, 20, 159, 191
Capgrave, John: *Chronicle*, 53; *Life of Saint Katherine*, 20, 135–36
Carmarthen, 86, 98
Carter, Angela, 50
Cartlidge, Neil, 168–69
Cassian, Saint John, 89
Castleford, Thomas, *Chronicle*, 93
Charles V, King of France, 30, 45
Charles VI, King of France, *bal des sauvages*, 43, 218n9
Chaucer, Geoffrey, 9, 73, 194, 198–201, 203; apocrypha, *The Plowman's Tale*, 201; apocrypha, *The Romaunt of the Rose*, 56; *The Canon's Yeoman's Tale*, 197; *The Canterbury Tales*, 197–98; *The Franklin's Tale*, 105; *The Friar's Tale*, 52; *The House of Fame*, 38; *The Knight's Tale*, 101, 106, 198, 201–2, 204; *The Man of Law's Tale*, 113, 197–98; *The Merchant's Tale*, 36, 67, 159, 198, 201–2; *The Miller's Tale*, 54; *The Monk's Tale*, 32; *The Nun's Priest's Tale*, 197; *The Pardoner's Tale*, 141; *The Reeve's Tale*, 200; *Second Nun's Tale*, 102; *The Squire's Tale*, 157, 197; *The Tale of Sir Thopas*, 67, 74, 103–4, 197–99, 201–2, 205; *The Wife of Bath's Tale*, 50–52, 67, 74, 100, 105, 197, 201
Chevalier qui fist parler les cons, 67, 103
Cheyne, Thomas, 22

Chrétien de Troyes, 105; *Chevalier de la charette*, 66, 161–62, 187, 189; *Yvain*, 35–37, 39, 66
Cistercians, 178–79, 181
Clancy, Susan, 77
Clark, Stuart, 196–97, 243n71
Cleary, Michael, 43
Clerk, Marion, 19, 112, 141, 191, 195
Clonfert, 52
Cohen, Jeffrey Jerome, 12
Colin, Jean, 54
Collingwood, R. G., 70–71
Comper, 39, 46
Conrad of Höxter, 16, 212n26
Conrad of Marburg, 16–18, 212n25, 213n33
Constable, Giles, 156
Cooper, Bishop Thomas, *Thesaurus linguae Romanae & Britannicae*, 194
Cooper, Helen, 12, 33, 64, 70–71
Cooper, Thomas, *The mystery of witch-craft*, 197
Corbet, Richard, bishop of Norwich, 125
Cornwall, 3, 149, 241n9
Coudrette, *Melusine*, 29, 31, 215n89
Court of Love, 65
Coutumier of Brocéliande, 39
Crane, T. F., 118
Crehan, Kate, 8
Cresswell, John, 31–32, 44–45
cunning men and women, 4, 20, 22, 80, 112, 117, 158, 195–96, 203
Cyprus, 32, 85

d'Albornoz, Gil, 119
Dante Alighieri: *Inferno*, 24, 182; *Purgatorio*, 182–83
d'Aulnoy, Countess, 50
David I, King of Scotland, 40
de Beaujeu, Renaut, 64
Dégh, Linda, 72–73
de la Sale, Antoine, 40, 45–46, 61, 143
Derbyshire, 22
Devon, 4
Disputation between a Christian and a Jew, 19, 157, 185
*Dives and Paupe*r, 80, 84
Dolopathos, 143. See also *Seven Sages of Rome*
Dominicans, 15–17, 37–38, 48, 52, 73, 83, 117, 174, 180, 185, 232n109
Domrémy, 29, 46, 54, 67, 220n62
Donaldson, E. Talbot, 54

Doomsday, 2, 23–24, 62, 89, 144, 158, 184
Douglas, Gavin, 204
d'Ourches, Sir Albert, 146
d'Outremeuse, Jean, 53, 105, 157, 159
Drayton, Michael: *Dowsabell*, 202; *Nymphidia*, 202
Draco Normannicus, 149, 154
Dubost, Francis, 12, 72, 209n2, 225n150, 229n51, 231n85, 233n119
du Guesclin, Bertrand, 45–46, 60, 107, 218n17, 240n132
Dunbar, William, 205
Dunlop, Bessie, 158, 204
Durham, 112, 141, 203

Eadric the Wild, 40, 50, 79, 99–100, 161
Easting, Robert, 183, 185, 246nn110, 130
Edinburgh, 194, 199, 204
Edward II, King of England, 121–22
Einarsson, Oddur, 13–15
Ekkard von Aura, 176–77
Elias. *See* Enoch
Eliodor, 155, 161
Elizabeth I, Queen of England, 194, 199, 201, 204
Elucidarium, 15, 61, 174; English version, 15, 61, 95; French version, 15, 61, 174, 222–23n105
Elucidation, 50, 66, 107
Elyot, Thomas, 133
Emmerson, Richard, 145
Engelhus, Dietrich, *Chronicle*, 80–81
Enoch and Elijah (Enok and Helias), 141, 143–45, 154, 170, 176, 186
Estellin, Beatrice, 54
Étienne de Bourbon, 15, 48–49, 66, 116–18, 158, 166, 175–76, 179–80, 219n34, 232n97, 244n73
Eudo, 25, 89
Évangiles des quenouilles, 6, 72, 143
Exeter Grammar School, 38

fairies: dancing, 1, 54, 92, 158, 172, 182, 197; beauty of, 56; Celtic origins of, 5–7, 66, 178; creating effigies (figmenta), 1, 164–67, 177, 191, 234n5; feasting, 6, 15, 20, 39, 60, 81, 100, 180; fecundity of, 56, 58, 85–86, 99, 103, 112–14; fine hair of, 59, 103, 221n85; foretelling the future, 8, 61–62, 92, 142, 173, 191; and hawthorns, 137, 238n97, 248n158; homosexuality of, 100; hunting, 104, 107, 167–68, 172, 175–76; invisibility, 13, 65, 69, 83, 87–88, 104–5, 111, 164; mortality of, 56, 59–60, 89, 143, 162, 169, 177; as neutral angels, 23–26, 187; power over health, 8, 112, 117–18, 133, 141, 151, 179, 186, 234n9, 235n37; power over nature, 8, 107; power over weather, 8, 34–38, 174, 195; rape of, 27, 50–51, 56–57, 103, 107; sexuality of, 56–58, 78, 82–84, 99–102, 104, 107–8, 182; shapeshifting, 4, 18, 30, 52, 56, 58, 68–69, 82, 86–87, 97, 108, 165, 232n109; sleeplessness of, 68, 113, 221n84; warfare and jousting, 53, 60, 158, 172, 175–77, 181, 202; wealth of, 8, 19, 33, 56, 65, 82–83, 89, 102, 104, 107, 121, 168, 182, 184–85, 228n30
fairies, terms for, 2–4; arzei, 66, 176; dusii, 3, 16, 99, 163, 208n11; elves, 4–5, 21, 51, 54, 92, 95, 112, 132–33, 138, 187, 189, 197–98, 230n71; fadae/fata, 29, 54, 60, 79, 99, 112, 195, 208n18, 222n99; fairy, 208n18; fair folk (pulcher populum), 22; fauni, 5, 15, 59–60, 78–79, 82, 89, 116–17, 198; goblins, 5, 30, 38, 60, 174, 198, 207n9; good things (bonae res), 15, 29–30, 166, 212n30; hobgoblins, 42, 195; hobs, 5, 22, 131, 175; incubi, 3–4, 16, 44, 52, 61–62, 78–89, 91–92, 98–99, 112, 114, 174; ladies (dominae), 46, 48, 220n71; longaevi, 59; luitons, 2, 30, 79, 91, 174; mares, 4, 77, 128, 130–31, 138, 143, 195; *maufées*, 169; neptuni, 3, 208n10; netons, 2–3, 59; nymphs, 42, 59, 148, 153, 198–99, 202, 248n1; pans, 16, 44, 59, 78–79, 99; pouks, 5, 198; sylvans (silvani), 15–16, 42, 44, 50, 59, 78–80, 99–100, 210–11n13; woodwoses, 5, 84, 228n38
fairy king, 22; Goldemar, 80–81; Oberon, 25–26, 59–60, 62, 67, 69, 157, 186, 201–2; Pluto, 36, 198, 201, 204
fairyland, 208,n18, 213n47; Avalon, 9, 147–48, 150–51, 153, 155, 157, 160, 176, 178, 181, 185–86, 193, 197, 241n25, 242n40; entrance to, 33, 40, 61, 173–74, 187–88; food in, 26, 60, 104, 111, 179–80, 186; Gorre, 66, 161–62, 187; on islands, 103, 147, 150–51, 157, 186; time in, 19, 162, 173–74, 186, 191–92; underground, 13–14, 16–17, 39–40, 61, 69, 82, 161, 173, 176, 188, 190, 222n90; under water, 14, 40, 156–57; in wilderness, 91, 100; in woods, 7, 14, 33–34, 52, 55, 64, 67, 69, 96, 100, 103, 117, 153, 161–62, 174, 211n13, 238n97, 243n57

fairy queen, 22; Argante, 151; Dame Abonde, 79, 107, 143, 174; Diana, 99, 164, 166, 232n103; Mab, 201–2; Morgan le Fay, 53, 147, 149, 143, 155, 157, 160, 175, 186; Proserpina, 36, 198, 201–2; Sybil, 40, 45, 61, 143; Titania, 53, 201
Fasciculus Morum, 2, 130, 158–59, 212n23
Fenwick, Catharine, 112
Ferlampin-Acher, Christine, 47, 210n9
Filotas, Bernadette, 48–49, 235n37
Flanders, 165
Fletcher, Alan, 168, 219n50
Florio, John, *Worlde of Wordes*, 195
folklore, 6–8, 43, 46–48, 71–74, 110–11, 146, 174, 176, 178, 182, 191, 217nn114, 7, 228n30
Forli, 119
Forman, Simon, 194
Foucault, Michel, 8
Fournier, Jaques, Pope Benedict XII, 139
Fourth Lateran Council, 48, 53
France, 6, 12, 15, 43, 45–46, 73, 79, 104, 119–21, 123, 129, 139, 187, 197
Franciscans, 52, 86, 158–59
Froissart, Jean, 183

Gardner, John, 133
Gareth, 66
Gaule, John, *Select cases of Conscience*, 195
Gawain, 64, 157, 187, 189, 197
Geoffrey of Monmouth, 40, 61; *Historia Regum*, 85–92, 94, 96, 125, 143, 147–50, 240n1; *Vita Merlini*, 147, 150, 240n2, 241n18
Gerald of Wales, 16, 48, 150, 156, 170, 214n71; *De Principis Instructione*, 155–57; *Expugnatio Hibernica*, 53; *Itinerium Cambriae*, 56, 85, 98,155, 161; *Speculum Ecclesiae*, 150, 155–57, 241n25, 242n31
Germany, 6, 16, 18, 37, 44, 80, 115, 132, 171, 176, 178–79, 185, 197
Gerndt, Helge, 72
Gerson, Jean, 49, 74–75
Gervase of Tilbury, *Otia Imperialia*, 16, 23, 30, 41, 44, 48–49, 72, 78–79, 99, 101, 158, 179–80
Gesta Regum Britannie, 89, 151–53
ghosts, 32, 40–41, 45, 72, 170–71
Gifford, George, *A Dialogue concerning Witches*, 196
Gillingham, John, 150

Gingras, Francis, 106, 232n113, 233n119
Ginzburg, Carlo, 2, 109, 196, 213n37, 222n99, 243n71, 245n86
Glastonbury, 155–57
Gödelmann, Johann Georg, 170
Godfrey of Bouillon, 5
Godstow Abbey, 21
Golden Legend, 116, 212n23, 244n73
Goodey, C. F. and T. Stainton, 110
Goodman, Christopher, 143–45
Gowdie, Isobel, 204
Gower, John: *Cinkante Balades*, 56; *Confessio Amantis*, 198, 220n72
Graf, Arturo, 178
Gramsci, Antonio, 2, 7–8, 73–74, 109–10, 146
Gratian, 159
Gravier, Sir Peter, 46, 218n16
Greenblatt, Stephen, 197
Grimm, Jacob, 71
Gui, Bernard, 29, 112, 212n30
Guibert of Nogent, 76–78
Guichard, Bishop of Troyes, 59
Guido della Colonna, 79
Guillaume de Lorris, 56
Guillaume Larchevêque, Lord of Parthenay, 29, 215n89
Gunter, Anne, 200
Gurevich, Aron, 42, 211n17, 246n110, 249n110
Gwestin Gwestiniog, 99, 156

Haffen, Josiane, 143
Hafstein, Valdimar, 7
Hampshire, 203
hansels, 130
Harding, John, *Metrical Chronicle*, 93
Hardware, Henry, the younger, 137
Harf-Lancner, Laurence, 26, 60, 214n69, 222n98, 225n145
Harsnett, Samuel, 146, 200–201
Helias. See Enoch
Helinand of Froidmont, 176–77
Heng, Geraldine, 12
Henry I, King of England, 40
Henry II, King of England, 40, 85
Henry VI, King of England, 122
Henry VIII, King of England, 198
Henry of Marsburg, 216n100
Henryson, Robert, *Orpheus and Eurydice*, 204

heresy: Cathar, 8, 18, 24, 36, 213n32; fairy belief as, 16–18, 20–21, 36, 41, 49, 112, 141, 144, 166, 181, 212n30, 213n32; Lollard, 20, 39–39, 140, 144
Heriger, Bishop of Mainz, 6, 20
Herlequin (Hellequin, King Herla, etc.), 2, 79, 158–59, 161, 172–77, 182–83, 192, 245nn86, 103
Hermann of Tournai, 149
Hertford, 141
Hertford shire, 117
Higden, Ranulph: *Polychronicon*, 93, 98, 115, 143; *Speculum Curatorum*, 220n57, 221n85, 235n37
Higgins, John, 195
Historiae romanae fragmenta, 119
Hobbes, Thomas, 177
Holland, Thomas, 200
Honorius of Autun, 15
Hugh of Lincoln, 82
Hull, Thomas, 141
Hungary, 181, 196
Huns, 85
Huon de Méri, *Le Tournoiement de l'Anticrist*, 18, 36–38, 245n96

Iceland, 5, 7, 13–14
Idley, Peter, 21, 130, 141
India, 126, 186, 189
Infancy Gospels, 134
Inglethorp, 81
Ireland, 5, 43, 52–53, 163, 180
Italy, 7, 61, 119, 121, 150

Jacques de Vitry: exempla, 73, 192; *Historia Orientalis*, 37; *Sermones Vulgares*, 118, 123, 234n2
James I, King of England (James VI of Scotland), 14, 77–78, 204
Jameson, Fredric, 12, 64
Jauss, Hans-Robert, 71
Jean d'Arras, *Mélusine*, 6, 24, 29–32, 43–46, 49, 56, 58, 60, 62, 65, 69–72, 113
Jean de France, Duc de Berri, 30–32, 43–46
Jeanette de Veau, 46
Jews, 8, 19, 139, 141, 150, 155, 242n30
Joan of Arc, 1, 29, 46, 54
John II, King of France, 45
John of Bridlington, 62
John of Calabria, 46

John of Powderham, 121–22, 236n51
John of Salisbury, 61
John of Tynemouth, 96
John of Wildeshausen, 38
Jonson, Ben, *The Alchemist*, 203
Jordanes, *History of the Goths*, 85
Joseph of Exeter, 150
Julius Caesar, 60, 67
Junius, Adrianus, *The Nomenclator*, 195

Kelly, Douglas, 187
Kennedy, Elspeth, 105
Kent, 22, 146
Kieckheffer, Richard, 132, 249n14
King Arthur, 5, 9, 19, 34–35, 40, 49, 64, 67, 96, 143–44, 147–51, 153–60, 163, 170, 175–76, 179, 186
Kirk, Robert, 204, 244n75
Kolve, V. A., 136
Kramer, Heinrich, 49

Lai du Cor, 56
Land of Cockayne, 151
Lanercost Chronicle, 121
Langland, William, *Piers Plowman*, 127, 136, 198
Langtoft's Chronicle, 61
Laon, 149
Latham, W. M., 13, 230n71, 249n11
Lavater, Ludwig, 195
Layamon, *The Brut*, 89, 150–51, 153, 170, 241n18
Lazzaretti, Davide, 8
Lecouteux, Claude, 4, 172, 174, 208n11
Lee, Sir Henry, 199
le Franc, Martin, *Champion des dames*, 119, 121–22
Le Goff, Jacques, 12, 28, 43, 47–50, 72, 78, 178, 180–81, 183, 185, 191, 198, 209n27, 215n82, 217n4
Les Évangiles des quenouilles, 72
Levack, Brian, 197
Levin, Richard, 203
Lévy-Bruhl, Lucien, 70
Lewes, Battle of, 159
Lewis, C. S., 11–12, 14, 109, 194, 199, 204
Lidwina, Saint, 88
Limbourg brothers, 43
Lindow, John, 113–14, 234n19
Linnaeus, Carl, 113
London, 22, 95, 195, 202

Loomis, Roger Sherman, 39, 66, 209n27, 224n129
Lough Derg, 180–82
Lourdes, 248n158
Lovelich, Henry, 95
Lusignan family, 29, 32, 70–71, 99
Lydgate, John: *Fall of Princes* 158; *Troy Book*, 79
Lynceus, 13
Lyon, 37, 116

Mabinogion, 6
MacCulloch, J. A., 110, 220n63
Mack, John Edward, 41
Malleus Maleficarum, 49, 115, 244n73
Malory, Sir Thomas, 66, 143, 170
Man, Andro, 204
Mandeville, Sir John, 28, 116, 180, 235n29
Mannyng, Robert: *Handlyng Synne*, 73, 139, 226n168; *Story of England*, 89
Map, Walter, *De Nugis Curialium*, 2, 16, 25, 40, 48–50, 58, 69, 79, 89, 99–100, 156, 158, 161, 170, 173, 175, 227n13
Marie Antoinette, 43
Marie de Bourbon, 46
Marie de France: *Guigamer*, 104; *L'espurgatoire*, 185, 188; *Lanval*, 23, 103–4, 106–7; *Yonec*, 56, 58–59, 69, 91, 99–100, 169
Marshall, Linda, 131, 136
Martianus Capella, 59
Merchtem, 165
Meres, Francis, 198
Meridiana, 25
Merlin, 9, 60–62, 68, 85–98, 100, 105, 107, 112–13, 123–26, 143, 147–49, 151, 221n84, 229nn50–51, 237n60
Mirk, John, *Festial*, 142
Mitchell, Bruce, 167
Mont de Chat, 158
Montfort, lords of, 39, 46
Mount Etna, 179–80
Moore, R. I., 8
Morel, Jean, 54
Murray, Margaret, 18, 196
Musnier, Simonin, 54
Mussolini, 7
mystery plays, 9, 110, 127, 142, 145; *Chester plays*, 127–28, 130, 133–37, 141–45; *N-Town plays*, 134, 141; *Towneley plays*, 128–29, 131, 133, 135, 139; *York plays*, 127–30, 134, 139–40
Mytilene, 116

Nennius, 87
Neveling de Hardenburg, 79
Nider, Johannes, 49, 210–11n13
Norfolk, 81, 199
Northampton, 121
Northern Homily Cycle, 84, 192
Norwich, 20, 81–82, 125
Nottingham, 130

Ogier the Dane, 157, 186, 192, 242n40
Onewyn, 155–89
O'Quinn, Thomas, 52
Ordelaffi, Francesco, 119–20
Orderic Vitalis, *Ecclesiastical History*, 172–77
Oresme, Nicholas, 183
Origen, 23
Oring, Elliott, 72
Osbern de Bradwell, 111
Osbert Fitz Hugh, 44
Ostrogotha, 159
Ourches-sur-Meuse, 46
Oxford, 121, 200

Pannonia, 79
Paris, Matthew, 59, 112–13
Paris, University of, 6, 19, 25, 74, 140, 164, 178
Paston Letters, 22
Patch, Howard, 186, 188
Paxton, James, 145
Pennyfather, Mary, 117
Percival, Richard, *Dictionarie in Spanish and English*, 195
Percy, Sir Thomas, 31
Pereson, Jenkyn, 112
Peter I of Cyprus, 32
Peter Damian, *Ad perennis vitae fontem*, 152–53
Peter des Roches, Bishop of Winchester, 153
Peter of Blois, 73, 149–50, 154, 175
Petitcriu, 4, 66
Phillips, Judith, 203
Pierre de Bourlément, 46
Pinkie Cleugh, Battle of, 158
Plantagenet, house of, 70, 85, 99
Pliny, 116
Poitou, 30–31, 45
Poos, Lawrence, 141
purgatory, 27–28, 159, 177–85, 188–91, 193; Marie de France, *L'espurgatoire*, 184–85; *Owayne Miles*, 182–85, 187–90, 193; Peter

of Cornwall, 182; *Tractatus de Purgatorio Sancti Patricii*, 156, 178, 180–83, 185, 187–88, 190; *Visio Ludovici*, 182, 184, 188; *Visio Pauli*, 156; *Vision of Edmund Leversedge*, 190–91; *Vision of Fursey*, 190; *Vision of Tundale*, 178, 190; *Vision of William Stranton*, 188, 189, 246n126; *Visiones Georgii*, 181–82, 184, 188, 246n133, 247n134. See also Lough Derg; Mount Etna
Purkiss, Diane, 8, 41, 99–100
Puttenham, George, 198

Quest of enquirie . . . by Oliuer Oatmeale, 203

Rabelais, François, 202
Ralph of Coggeshalle, *Chronicon Anglicanum*, 111, 161
Raoul de Presles, 79, 174
Red Book of Ossery, 137
Rémy, Nicholas, 95
Renaut de Beaujeu, *Le Bel inconnu*, 59, 64
René d'Anjou, Duke, 46
Rennes, 32
Richard I, King of England, 38
Richard II, King of England, 124, 175
Richards, I. A., 12
Richard the Redeles, 124, 175
Rider, Jeff, 33, 167, 239n118, 244n79
Robert de Boron, 67, 94–95, 97, 125, 131
Robert of Gloucester, *Metrical Chronicle*, 91–92, 98, 100
Robertson, D. W., 136, 138, 168, 219n49
Robin Goodfellow, 22, 76
Robin Hood, 130
Rogers, Thomas, 203
romances, Dutch, *Roman van Walewein*, 189–90
romances, English: *Cheuelere Assigne*, 116, 163, 240n128; *Degaré*, 99; *Generides*, 65–66, 124, 126–27; *Guy of Warwick*, 67, 162; *Kyng Alisaunder*, 124, 126, 128; *Lybeaus Desconus*, 64–65; *Of Arthour and of Merlin*, 95, 97, 123–25; *Reinbrun*, 6, 17, 67, 161–62, 187; *Richard the Lionheart*, 69–70; *Seege or Batayle of Troye*, 220n71; *Sir Degarré*, 63, 65; *Sir Gawain and the Green Knight*, 145, 187, 198; *Sir Gowther*, 68–69, 96–98, 113, 129, 165; *Sir Launfal*, 23, 55, 102–3, 106, 161; *Sir Orfeo*, 18, 67, 111, 145, 161, 163–64, 166–69, 172, 183, 187, 191, 204, 244n79; *Sir Percyvell of Gales*, 66; *Wars of Alexander*, 56; *William of Palerne*, 55, 107, 220n67. See also Breton lais
romances, French: *Amadas and Ydoine*, 166, 169–70; *Aucassin and Nicolette*, 55; *Claris and Laris*, 32–34; *Coment Merlyn fu nee*, 90; *Continuation of Chrétien's Percival*, 116; *Désiré*, 67, 69, 103, 107; *Esclarmonde*, 25–26, *Floriant and Florete*, 160; *Graelent*, 103, 107; *Guingamor*, 65, 67, 103, 107, 111, 174, 180, 192; *Huon of Bourdeaux*, 5, 25–26, 59–60, 62, 67, 69; *Naissance du Chevalier au Cygne*, 59, 143; non-cyclic prose *Lancelot*, 58, 60, 67, 94, 105, 107, 221n84; *Partonopeu de Blois*, 6, 50, 57, 64–65, 67, 69, 100–101, 104–7, 169; *Perlesvaus*, 66, 176; *Robert the Devil*, 67, 69, 96, 98; *Roman d'Ogier*, 186, 192; *Tydorel*, 58, 65, 67–69, 96, 133; *Tyolet*, 67, 107. See also Breton lais; Chrétien de Troyes; Jean d'Arras; Marie de France
romances, Scottish: *King Orphius*, 204; *Thomas of Erceldoune*, 17–18, 26, 50–51, 56, 61, 111, 161, 180, 187, 191, 221n75
Rossignol, Jean, 119
Ruhr, river, 15, 80
Rye, 146, 203
Rypon, Robert, 73

Sabinus, Georg, 171
Saint Catherine, 127, 135
Saint Germain, 15, 166, 196
Saint Guinefort, 49, 116–17
Saint John the Apostle, 124
Saint Marina, 84
Saint Stephen, 20, 115
Saunders, Corinne, 12
Savoie, 158
Scala Coeli, 52, 212n28
Schmitt, Jean-Claude, 12, 52, 115–16, 217n6, 218n8
Scot, Reginald, *Discouerie of Witchcraft*, 66, 107–9, 143, 146, 196, 201, 237n60
Scotland, 5, 18, 52, 40, 52, 96, 158, 204–5
Scottish Chaucerians, 204–5
Sermoise, Philippe, 120
sermons and preaching, 1–2, 16–17, 38, 52–53, 118, 137, 158, 166, 195, 200, 234n2
Seven Sages of Rome, 100, 116. See also *Dolopathos*

Shakespeare, William: *King Lear*, 201; *Macbeth*, 194; *The Merry Wives of Windsor*, 4, 201; *A Midsummer Night's Dream*, 53, 201, 203; *Romeo and Juliet*, 201; *The Tempest*, 131
sibyls, 40, 45, 107, 142–43, 218n21
Sicily, 5, 85, 116, 160, 179, 196, 246n115
Sidrak and Bokkus, 28
Simon de Montfort, Earl of Leicester, 159
Simpson, James, 138–40, 142
Sisson, C. J., 203
snakes, as a paternity test, 116–17
Somerset, 190
South English Legendary, 23, 58, 92, 101, 124, 127, 184–85, 187–88
Spain, 196, 218n16, 248n158
Speght, Thomas, 158–59
Spenser, Edmund, *The Faerie Queene*, 50, 194, 198–99, 201
Stapleton, William, 79
Station Island, Lough Derg, 180–82
Stephen, King of England, 149
Stephen Langton, Archbishop of Canterbury, 85–86
Suffolk, 19, 82, 111–12, 141, 195–96, 199
superstition, 1, 20, 44, 48–49, 74, 130, 145–46
Sussex, 20
Swan, John, *Speculum Mundi*, 195
Swann, Marjorie, 74
Swarte Smekyd Smethes, 124
Switzerland, 6, 197

Taylor, Anne, 146, 203
Temple, Sir William, 66
Þáttr Þiðranda ok Þórhalls, 7
Thomas, Keith, 12, 66, 138
Thomas à Becket, Saint, 20, 115, 159–60
Thomas of Cantilupe, Bishop of Hereford, 81
Thomas of Cantimpré, *Bonum Universale de Apibus*, 3–4, 6, 16, 18–20, 37–38, 83–84, 99, 163, 166, 185, 191, 213n35, 227n23, 232n109
Thomas of Monmouth, 82–83
Thompson, E. P., 73
Tiffany de Raguenel, 45, 107, 240n132
Tirant, William, 119
Tolkien, J. R. R., 5
Trevisa, John, 60, 93, 98
Tristram, 4, 66
Triunein, 40, 156, 158, 163

Tyre, 150
Tyrwhitt, Thomas, 201

Uther Pendragon, 68, 96

Van Engen, John, 43, 138, 217n6
Vaucouleurs, 46
Vaughan, William, *The Arraignment of Slander*, 195
Vernon Manuscript (Oxford, Bodleian Library, MS Eng. poet.a.1): *Disputation between a Christian and a Jew*, 18, 185; *Life of Adam and Eve*, 23; *Northern Homily Cycle*, 84, 192
Villon, François, *Lais*, 119–21
Vincent of Beauvais, 177
Virgil, 105, 205; *The Aeneid*, 142, 176, 204; *The Eclogues*, 142
Virgin Mary, 2, 20, 69, 76, 96, 190, 195; confused with fairy queen, 17–19, 26–27, 186, 191, 248n158
Vortigern, 85–87, 89, 91, 98, 125

Wace: *Roman de Brut*, 79, 88–89, 91, 148–49, 230n61, 231n77; *Roman de Rou*, 34–37
Wachelin, 173
Wade, 158–59, 221n76
Wade, James, 12, 50, 217n114
Wales, 5, 40, 59, 98, 112–13, 144, 149–51, 155–57, 173, 192, 241n9
Walker, Brian, 203
Walsh, John, 4, 195
Walsingham, Thomas, 4, 96
Walter of Aquitaine, 5
Waltharius, 5–6
Wandlebury Hill, 44
Wenzel, Siegfried, 137, 238n97
Weston, Jessie, 66
Widsith, 158–59
wild horde, 52, 158, 172–73, 175–77, 181, 218n16, 233–34n2
wild hunt, 158, 172, 177
William I, King of Scotland, 40
William of Auvergne, *De Universo*, 6, 14–15, 48, 51, 53, 58–60, 62, 79, 84–85, 92, 100–101, 107, 114, 116, 118, 158, 164, 174–75, 177, 211 n13, 218n16, 221n85, 233n2
William of Canterbury, 115–16
William of Malmesbury, 149, 155

William of Newburgh, *History of English Affairs*, 16, 39–40, 61, 82, 92, 150, 156, 161, 180, 223n121
William the Conqueror, King of England, 40
Wisbech, 141
witchcraft and sorcery (also nigromancy, sortilegium, etc.), 18, 21, 38, 53–54, 64, 105–9, 133–36, 140–41, 146, 194, 196–97, 200
witches, persecution of, 9, 18, 86, 95, 107–8, 133, 145, 166, 193–94, 196–97, 199, 203–4

Woodstock, 199
Woodcock, Matthew, 198
Woolf, Rosemary, 136, 138
Woolmer, forest of, 96
Woolpit, 4
Worms, 176
Wyatt, Sir Thomas, 198–99

Yates, Francis, 199
Yeats, W. B., 5
Yorkshire, 39, 82
Young, Simon, 3, 213n52, 218n11

ACKNOWLEDGMENTS

In the course of writing this book I incurred many scholarly debts. My colleagues Drew Jones and Leslie Lockett were ever ready to answer my queries about medieval Latin, and Sarah-Grace Heller was equally helpful with any medieval French problems. My understanding of all things numinous benefited greatly from my conversations with Sarah Iles Johnston and Fritz Graf, and my tentative forays into folklore were encouraged by Dorrie Noyes and Ray Cashman. Learning that I was working on fairies, many friends, colleagues, and students offered me fascinating tidbits: Christopher Berard, Nancy Bradbury, Mary Dzon, Alan Fletcher, Eric Johnson, Michael Johnston, Lisa Kiser, Frank Klaassen, Alastair Minnis, Christine Rose, and James Wade all come to mind, but others have inevitably escaped my memory and to them I apologize. John Slefinger contributed diligently to formatting the bibliography, and my early modern colleagues Richard Dutton and Hannibal Hamlin kindly advised me on the Postscript. Two friends, one old and the other new, deserve particular mention: John Block Friedman, whose knowledge of medieval arcana, both natural and supernatural, is unparalleled, was unfailingly supportive of this project, and Simon Young, whom I have met only on line, generously offered to read and comment on a draft of the whole book; its final version profited enormously from his remarkable expertise. Finally, my wife Sharon Collingwood also read the whole book in draft and offered the kind of sensible criticism I've come to rely on. It goes without saying that if this book has many flaws, I have no one to blame but myself.

www.ingramcontent.com/pod-product-compliance
Lightning Source LLC
Chambersburg PA
CBHW030525230426
43665CB00010B/776